HARRIS MITCHELL

You Wanted To Know

A Harris Mitchell Book

GREENFIELD PUBLISHING
Box 247
BINBROOK, ONTARIO
L0R 1C0

Canadian Cataloguing in Publication Data
Mitchell, Harris, 1916- Harris Mitchell's You wanted to know Previous ed. had title: 1200 household hints. Includes index. ISBN 088678-001-2 1. Repairing - Amateurs' manuals. 2. Dwellings - Maintenance and repair - Amateurs' manuals. I. Title. II. Title: 1200 household hints. III. Title: You wanted to know. TH4817.3.M57 1983   643'.7   C83-098089-X

Printed and bound in Canada

HARRIS MITCHELL

You Wanted To Know

"GREENFIELD"

CONTENTS

ABOUT THE AUTHOR

As a magazine editor and writer, Harris Mitchell has been dealing with home problems for more than 30 years. During this time he has written hundreds of feature articles covering almost every phase of house construction, maintenance and improvement, and has appeared frequently on radio and TV as an authority on household problems.

He began writing his question-and-answer column, "You Wanted to Know", while editor of *Western Homes & Living* magazine, and continued the popular column when he became editor of *Canadian Homes* magazine and later homes editor of *Today* magazine. Ten years ago he started writing a syndicated column that now appears weekly in newspapers across Canada and brings more than 3,000 questions a year -- all of which he answers personally

The present volume is an expanded, completely revised and updated edition of earlier books based on his column that became best-sellers. Harris Mitchell's other books include *Home Crafts, Easy Furniture Finishing, Plywood Projects* and *The Basement Book*. He has also written several publications for Canada Mortgage and Housing Corporation on home maintenance and remodelling, including *How to Hire a Contractor*, and has been a consultant for all the Time-Life books in the *Home Repair and Improvement* series.

REMOVING FLOOR TILE ADHESIVE

I recently laid vinyl-asbestos tiles in the concrete floor of our basement. I used the prescribed tile cement and the recommended metal spreader according to instructions. After a couple of days, however, black tile cement squeezed up between the joints. How can I remove this?

In spite of your careful work, you must have put down too much adhesive. Most of the black adhesives are cut-back asphalt, which can be disolved with petroleum solvent (mineral spirits). Scrape off as much adhesive as you can with a putty knife or similar tool, then wet a cloth with the solvent and rub it briskly on the remaining stain. If the cloth is blackened, the solvent is working and the treatment should be continued. Use a steel wool soap pad and water to remove any remaining discoloration from the tile.

If the solvent-soaked cloth is not blackened, then a rubber-based adhesive must have been used. Scrape off as much as you can, then use a steel wool soap pad and water to remove the rest.

REMOVING WALL TILE ADHESIVE

There is plastic tile on all four walls of my bathroom, and I would like to replace it with ceramic tile. I can remove the plastic tiles without any trouble, but I can't seem to get the adhesive off the walls. Can you tell me how to do this, and how to prepare the plaster wall for ceramic tile?

Heat will soften the adhesive so it can be scraped off with a putty knife. Use a hairdryer or an industrial hot air gun. Paint remover may also work. Another trick is to sand the adhesive off with a power sander. It doesn't have to be taken off entirely, however; it's only necessary to make it reasonably smooth. The new adhesive layer will allow for minor surface variations.

Bare plaster or gypsumboard should be sealed with a primer recommended by the adhesive manufacturer. This is usually a bituminous compound that will waterproof the plaster wall.

LOCATING AN AIR CONDITIONER

We want to take our air conditioner out of the window and build it into the wall permanently. My husband says it should be put down low, under the window, and I say it should be near the ceiling, where the hot air goes. Who's right? And is there any preference as to which wall we should put it in?

Cold air vents for air conditioning systems are placed in the ceiling or high on a wall (just the opposite of warm air heating ducts, by the way) so your suggestion sounds better than your husband's. It should be placed in the coldest wall, so that the condenser unit outside can cool off the coils as quickly as possible. A north wall would be the best choice.

COVERING AN AIR CONDITIONER

Would you kindly tell me if it is necessary to cover the outside of our window air conditioner for the winter.

The manufacturers I spoke to say it is better to leave it uncovered, if you can't take it out of the window. This lets it dry out naturally when it gets wet (which often happens in the summer, of course). Covering it, on the other hand, keeps moisture inside and can promote rusting.

The only reason for covering it would be to keep out possible drafts, but if the vents are properly closed this should not be a problem. And you need a little fresh air anyway, even in the winter.

AIR LEAKAGE UNDER WALL

We are getting a cold draft from the crack under the baseboard at the bottom of our outside walls. What causes this and what can we do about it?

Air leakage at the wall and floor joint is common in wood frame houses. You can seal this simply by removing the baseboard and applying a bead of caulking compound along the crack at the base of the wall.

Aluminum

ICE ON ALUMINUM DOORS

We have two sets of sliding aluminum patio doors fitted with double glass. In the winter ice forms on the inside of the frame and the doors can't be opened. When the ice melts it makes a mess of our rugs and floors. What can be done to prevent the ice from forming?

The glass is insulated, but the metal frame is not, and that is where moisture vapor from the house is condensing and freezing. The only remedy is to reduce the humidity below the level at which condensation occurs on the cold metal. I don't know of any practical way to insulate the metal frame.

CURING AN ALUMINUM GRIDDLE

I bake scones on an aluminum griddle. I cleaned it recently with a steel wool soap pad, and since then everything sticks to it. What can I do to stop this?

Cast aluminum and cast iron are both porous enough to absorb a certain amount of oil or fat, and this creates an excellent, non-stick surface for cooking. Soap and hot water and scouring pads remove this, however, leaving only the bare metal, which food sticks to. Professional cooks never use soap and water on their frying pans or griddles; they just wipe them clean.

You can restore the non-stick surface by first removing any burned-on food with steel wool, then covering the griddle with a layer of cooking oil and heating it until it smokes for about 10 minutes. Cool and wipe off with a paper towel.

Cooks sometimes heat a layer of salt in the griddle or frypan first, then empty this out and put in the oil. Perhaps this helps; I don't know.

CLEANING ALUMINUM

I have an aluminun pot that has become blackened inside. How can I clean it?

Fill it with a solution of 2 teaspoons of cream of tartar to 1 quart of water. Bring the water to a boil and let it simmer a few minutes. The aluminum will be cleaner than you've ever seen it.

CLEANING ALUMINUM SIDING

Our home is finished with green aluminum siding that has developed a greyish film over much of its surface. It seems to be where it was exposed to water from the lawn sprinklers. Some of it comes off with hard scrubbing, but the surface remains dull and grey. Can you tell me how to clean this off?

The gray film and faded color may just be due to the paint chalking. This can often be removed by scrubbing with a solution of one tablespoon of trisodium phosphate (TSP) to a quart of water. If this doesn't restore the color, it may be a calcium deposit from the water. Try cleaning a small patch with vinegar. If this works, buy some muriatic acid at your hardware store and make a solution of 1 part acid to 20 parts water. Use this to clean the rest of the siding ... it's a lot cheaper than vinegar.

SCRATCHED APPLIANCE

I have a shallow scratch on a copper-tone refrigerator. Any suggestions on how to cover it successfully?

Get a small bottle of automobile touch-up paint in a matching metallic color.

REMOVING ALUMINUM PAINT

I have been trying to remove the paint from our brick fireplace. The top layers of colored paint came off easily enough with paint remover, but the base coat of aluminum paint won't budge. How can I get this off?

I suspect that a layer of aluminum metal on the surface is keeping the paint remover away from the paint film underneath. Since aluminum is readily attacked by strong caustic solutions, and lye makes a good paint remover anyway, I suggest that you try using a solution of one can of lye to a quart of water. Put it on with a string mop, rinse and brush off the softened paint.

Wear rubber gloves and be very careful to keep the lye solution off your skin, clothes, painted surfaces, and anything else you value. Mix it in anything but an aluminum pot.

ASPHALT PAINT ON FOUNDATION WALL

Our bungalow was built in 1975, and for some reason the builder applied the black waterproofing paint to the foundation wall, as much as 2' above the ground in places. It looks terrible but I'm told that nothing will stick to it, so it can't be painted over. I think it would be impossible to remove it all. I hope you can give us another suggestion.

The asphalt-based foundation coating can be covered with ordinary aluminum paint, available at any hardware store. The wall can then be painted with any exterior latex paint, if desired.

ASPHALT ON CONCRETE CARPORT

Our carport is a concrete slab, and we paint it every year. But within about a month the paint wears and peels off and is a real eyesore. We are going to have our asphalt driveway widened, and I thought I would have a layer of asphalt applied over the concrete. The paving contractor says this would work, but my husband doesn't think it would bond, and that we should have the concrete taken up and the asphalt put on a gravel base. What is your advice?

The asphalt would stick to the concrete well enough (this is how most blacktop roads are built), but asphalt is not a good material to use in a carport because the inevitable oil drips will dissolve and soften the concrete. That's why service stations always have concrete paving where the cars stop beside the pumps.

Concrete is a much better material for a carport, but don't try to paint it. The surface should merely be sealed with a 50:50 solution of boiled linseed oil and paint thinner, or kerosene. Brush this on and let it sink in. In half an hour use a cloth to remove any wet spots that remain, then allow it to dry for 48 hours before driving a car on it.

You'll have to remove all the paint from the concrete before you do this, of course. That can be done with a strong lye solution—one 9½-oz. can to a quart of water. Apply with a string mop, then scrape and hose off the softened paint.

ATTIC VENT FAN

We have a split-level house with central air conditioning. Someone has told us that an attic fan will save energy in the running of the air conditioner. What type of fan should be used and where should it be placed?

If you want to save energy—for air conditioning as well as heating—just put more insulation in the attic. You should have at least 6 inches of insulation between the ceiling joists, and 12" is recommended.

The attic also needs to be ventilated, but an energy-consuming fan is not necessary. Just provide at least one square foot of screened vent for every 150 square feet of ceiling. Half of the vent space should be located along the lower edge of the roof, under the eaves; the other half should be near the peak, either in the gable ends or on the roof surface.

ATTIC TOO HOT

Last year we had mineral wool insulation put between the attic floor joists, but the air up there is stifling in warm weather. I called the insulation contractor to see if I needed a vent in the roof, but was told that we didn't need one because we have wood shingles on the roof. Is this correct?

It depends how the shingles are applied. If the shingles are fastened to nailing strips laid across the rafters, and you can see the shingles themselves from the attic, then you should have plenty of ventilation. Cedar shakes are commonly laid this way, but not ordinary wood shingles. These are usually applied to plywood or other tight sheathing, which provides no ventilation at all.

However, since the attic is stiflingly hot, you obviously don't have enough ventilation up there, and I suggest you call in another contractor for advice and a quotation.

ATTIC VENTILATION

Should the louver in the gable end of the attic on a one-storey house be closed in winter to keep the heat in?

No. The insulation is in your ceiling, so there's no point in trying to keep the attic warm above it. Attic ventilation is essential during the winter to prevent condensation and frost on the underside of the roof, a common problem when moist air from the house escapes into the attic.

FINISH FOR BARN BOARD PANELLING

I would like to use barn lumber to finish the walls in our games room. Is there a home-made or commercial finish that can be applied to the boards to seal the surface; one that doesn't change the weather-beaten effect?

Any finish you put on will change the appearance of the wood to some extent. No finish is needed.

BARNBOARDS

We can get some beautifully weathered boards from an old barn, and I want to use them to panel our basement rumpus room. My husband says they will be infested with all kinds of insects, and refuses to have them in the house. Is he right?

It is unlikely that dry, weathered barnboards contain any insects. But all you have to do to be sure is to spray them with a 2% solution of chlordane, available from any garden supply store. Let them stay outside for a few days to dry, then put them up with an easy mind. Old, weathered boards like this are in great demand, and widely used for panelling in stores, bars and restaurants. There's no reason at all why they should not be used in your rumpus room.

2%
Chlordane
Solution

BASEMENTS

ARE BASEMENTS HEALTHY?

We have a 2-bedroom, concrete block bungalow with a completely finished basement . . . bathroom, bedroom, and a large recreation room. The walls are insulated and panelled and the basement is completely dry—so dry, in fact, that we have to use a humidifier in the winter. Our children sleep upstairs and we use the basement bedroom, but our friends tell us that this is very unhealthy. Could you please comment on this?

I think this myth originated when houses had damp cellars, not dry basements. As long as your basement is dry, warm and well ventilated, as most of them are today, your bedroom is just as healthy as any other room in the house.

BASEMENT AIR RETURN

I have recently finished putting in a recreation room in my basement. We have warm air heating outlets in the ceiling, but someone has told me that I should have a cold air return to the furnace as well. Is this right?

It certainly is. You can't force warm air into a room if there's no place for the cool air to get out. A finished basement should always be provided with a separate cold air return duct to the furnace. It also helps to eliminate that layer of cold air on the floor that makes so many basement rooms feel uncomfortable.

CRACK IN BASEMENT WALL

There are two hairline cracks in my poured concrete foundation wall, extending from the top of the wall to the floor. When it is very wet outside, these cracks leak. Is there anything we can paint on inside that will seal these cracks?

No. They will have to be patched and sealed from the outside. Dig down to the bottom of the cracks. Cover the cracks with a generous layer of fibrated asphalt roofing cement or foundation coating, about 12" wide. Over this lay a 6" strip of fibreglass roofing tape, covering the crack. You can buy this tape from a roofing supply company; if you can't find any, use strips of fibreglass window screen. Imbed the tape in the asphalt compound, then cover it with another generous layer of asphalt. Let the patch harden for a couple of days, then refill the hole, being careful not to damage the asphalt membrane.

BASEMENT CLOSET DAMP

I'm thinking of building a cedar closet in my basement, which is damp during the summer. Can I keep this dampness out of the closet by insulating it and building it away from the wall?

I'm afraid the dampness in the basement will penetrate the closet no matter how it's constructed, and there's a good chance that the clothes will become mildewed. The basement can be made much drier, however, if you insulate the walls and cover them with vapor barrier and panelling. During humid summer weather use a dehumidifier in the basement, and keep the doors and windows closed.

BASEMENT DAMP IN SUMMER

Why is our basement cool and clammy during the summer months, and what can we do about it?

The basement is always cooler than upstairs because the floor and part of the walls are below ground level. And when air is cooled its relative humidity increases, often to the point where condensation begins to form on the concrete. The dampness also causes mildew to grow on organic materials like paper, leather and clothing, and this produces the musty basement smell.

Insulating the walls will help, but the most effective remedy is to put a dehumidifier in the basement during the humid months. This will only work in a confined space, however, so be sure to keep the basement door and windows closed.

DAMPPROOFING BASEMENT WALLS

I am building a playroom in my basement. To keep out moisture I am stapling polyethylene sheeting to wood strips fastened to the wall, then I intend to apply wood panelling on top of the polyethylene. Is this a good procedure, or should I use insulating material as well?

If moisture is coming through the wall, applying polyethylene sheet as you describe will do little to keep it out of the basement. The only way to do that is to keep the moisture from coming through the wall. If the condition is very mild, one of the concrete waterproofing paints may do the job, but in most cases the walls must be given a waterproof coating on the *outside*, which means digging right down to the footings and applying two or more coats of a fibrated asphalt foundation coating.

It is strongly recommended that you insulate the basement walls, both for comfort and for economy. Up to 25% of the heat loss in a house can be through uninsulated basement walls. This will also prevent condensation on the concrete walls during the humid summer months.

The best way to insulate the basement is to build a 2 x 4 stud frame wall in front of the concrete and insulate this with 3½″ batts

covered with polyethylene vapor barrier and the panelling of your choice.

DEEPENING A BASEMENT

My basement is five feet deep and has a rubble foundation. Can I lower the basement floor three feet so I can build a recreation room?

Digging your basement deeper should be left to an experienced contractor who knows how to underpin the foundation and who would be in a position to provide you with liability insurance.

Rubble foundations are particularly hard to underpin, and you would also have to relocate drains and columns. You might also run into soil and water problems.

PREVENTING BASEMENT FLOODING

During last year's rainstorms, the sewer lines backed up in our area and we ended up with 5″ of water over the finished basement floor. I would like to know what we can do to prevent this happening if the sewer backs up again. Would it be safe to plug the floor drain in the basement?

A basement floor drain is rarely used, and there's no reason why you can't seal it to prevent water backing up into the basement. Instead of sealing it up entirely, however, you can install a special one-way floor drain valve that permits the drain to be used normally. This is a brass and rubber plug that fits inside the standard 4″ drain. Screws on the top are tightened to expand a rubber compression ring that seals the plug in the pipe. A float valve inside rises to plug the drain opening if water backs up the drain line. You can install it yourself.

A more expensive device is a one-way backwater valve that is installed in the drain line somewhere between the house and the sewer. This requires a plumbing permit and should be installed by a licensed plumbing contractor.

Plugging the floor drain to prevent back-flooding has one serious drawback, however. If the flood water rises outside the basement more than a few inches above the floor level, the water pressure may be strong enough to lift and crack the floor slab. It has happened frequently. Allowing the water to rise inside the house may not be very pleasant, but it will equalize the pressure on the floor and reduce the possibility of serious structural damage.

Basements

BASEMENT FLOOR

I am about to finish my basement, and would like some advice on the best method of constructing the floor. I had planned to lay 15-pound roofing felt over the concrete, then lay 2x3 sleepers 16" on centres. Over this I would place polyethylene film, then plywood. I plan to carpet the floor.

Some friends advise placing plastic foamboard between the sleepers; others say this is unnecessary. What is your advice?

Insulation is unnecessary on the floor, there is very little heat loss there. As a matter of fact, I see no need for a built-up plywood subfloor, either. It costs a lot in time and money, and accomplishes nothing. You would be better off to put the money into a better carpet.

BASEMENT LEAK

My house is about 2 years old, and has a persistent leak in the basement along a 6' crack between the floor slab and the foundation wall whenever the weather is wet. The builder tried to patch it with cement, but it didn't work. Now he wants to dig up the front of our house and fix it from outside, but this is going to make quite a mess. Is there any way he can do the job from inside?

The builder is right. The best remedy for a leak like this is to dig down and correct the faulty drainage that is causing it. Simply plugging the leak from the inside will allow more water pressure to build up, and this could lift and crack your floor slab.

FRAMING A BASEMENT WALL

The concrete foundation wall in our basement is only 4' high. On top of that is an open but insulated 2 × 4 frame wall set back from the edge of the concrete. I want to build some bedrooms in the basement but don't know what to do about this concrete ledge. Do I have to panel the wall in two sections?

The foundation wall should be insulated too, down to 2' below ground level. The best way to do this is to build a complete 2 × 4 stud wall in front of the foundation, extending straight up to the ceiling. Insulate this with 3½", R12 friction-fit batts, then apply polyethylene vapor barrier and the panelling of your choice.

In effect, this will give you two insulated walls above ground level, but that's were most

of the heat is lost so the extra insulation will serve a good purpose.

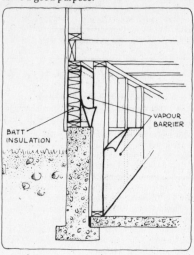

BATT INSULATION

VAPOUR BARRIER

LOWERING A BASEMENT

I want to lower my basement floor 12". The house is 45 years old and the basement walls are brick. I have broken the concrete floor and find that the wall footings are only 3" below the floor. How should I lower the floor?

I don't think you should do it. If you put the floor below the foundation footings there would be nothing to prevent water from seeping into the basement. And it would be a very tricky job to pour new footings under the present ones.

LOW-LYING BASEMENT

Our home is situated in a low-lying area. The cement floor in the basement is only two or three inches thick and it's damp much of the time. We want to put down indoor-outdoor carpeting and would like to know the name of the best sealer to use to waterproof the floor first.

I'm afraid there isn't one. Obviously your floor is below the water table much of the year, and there is no paint or sealer I know of that will hold back this kind of water pressure. The best cure is adequate drainage around the foundation footings, but from your description I rather think this is impossible in your location.

I suggest you install a sump pump under the basement floor. If this is able to keep your floor dry, you can paint it with any of the concrete floor paints, then lay the carpet.

RAISING THE BASEMENT

There is only 5'4" headroom between my basement floor and the ceiling beams. We can't go down because of the sewer level. Is there any way we can raise the ceiling?

It's possible to put steel beams under the house and raise it on jacks so that the foundation walls can be built up. But this is a fairly expensive operation because it takes a lot of time, requires disconnecting and extending all the water and sewer lines, and will almost certainly involve some repairs to the rest of the house. I think you'd find it cheaper to build an extension on the house.

WATERPROOFING BASEMENT FLOOR

I want to build a rec room in my basement, but the floor is rough and damp in a couple of places. I thought I would put on a new concrete topping with some kind of a waterproof layer between, but the ceiling is very low and I can only add about 1½". Do you have any suggestions?

To add a new concrete floor with a moisture-proof membrane underneath, you would need to add at least 3", preferably 4". A thin topping coat of latex-cement mixture can be applied directly to the present rough floor, however. You can buy a number of brands of latex-cement patching materials, or just the liquid latex which can be added to regular cement and sand to make a topping mixture that will adhere to the old concrete, even in very thin layers. These are available at all building supply stores.

Before you attempt to finish the floor, however, you'll have to eliminate the dampness where the problem originates . . . outside. Faulty or inadequate drainage is the cause. Check the earth around the foundation walls to make sure it is directing water *away* from the house. And see that the downspouts aren't emptying right beside the basement walls. If you find no remedy there, a sump pump may be the best solution.

WET BASEMENT — 1

Our basement walls seem to be constantly damp, and a white, fluffy powder forms on the walls and floor. What can we do to stop it?

The powdery efflorescence indicates that moisture is seeping through the concrete from outside. While concrete waterproofing paints will hold back small amounts of dampness, the best remedy is to correct the cause of the problem — inadequate or faulty drainage around the foundation.

Sometimes the trouble is due to the earth settling around the foundation walls, forming a depression that directs rainwater towards the house instead of away from it. This can be cured by building up the soil around the house.

Or it may be something as simple as a downspout discharging against the wall. A diversion pipe on the end of the downspout will correct this.

Generally, though, the problem is caused by inadequate drainage around the foundation footings. A drainage contractor should be called in to dig down and repair the drain tile. He should also apply a heavy coat of fibrated asphalt to the wall.

Where paving or other buildings prevent excavation outside the foundation, it may be possible to lay drainage tile inside by cutting a narrow trench through the concrete floor and connecting it to an existing floor drain or a sump pump.

WET BASEMENT — 2

We just bought a new house and after the first heavy rainfall water came into the basement. The next time it rained it took almost a week for the water in the basement to drain away. The builder tells us that the earth around the foundation has not settled yet, and that it will go away in a year or two. What can we do in the meantime?

Maybe the builder plans to go away in a year or two, but the problem won't. If the earth settles around your foundation you will have even more trouble with water in the basement, because the surface water will run towards your house instead of away from it.

The problem should be covered by your new home warranty, and your builder is responsible for correcting it. Write a letter to him, detailing the problem, and send a copy to the warranty office.

PAINTING BASEMENT WALLS

I bought a new house last year. It has a poured concrete foundation wall in the basement. I want to build a recreation room and would be glad if you would tell me what kind of paint

13

to use and how to apply it. I understand the walls must be treated with some kind of acid first.

A considerable amount of heat is lost through an uninsulated basement, and paint will do nothing to stop it. You should build a 2 × 4 frame wall against the concrete, put in 3½", R12 batts, then cover the wall with polyethylene vapor barrier and the panelling of your choice.

BASEMENT WALLS WET

We have a problem in our new house that has us completely baffled. During a cold winter, moisture forms on the top two feet of our basement walls, particularly in the corners. We even have moisture on the electric service panel. The basement is warm but unfinished. Last year I painted the outside of the foundation wall above the ground with a silicone waterproofing compound. Could this be causing the trouble?

No. You are simply getting condensation on the cold concrete and on the cold metal panel. I would guess that you are also troubled with condensation on your windows upstairs. If so, the humidity in your house is too high, due to insufficient ventilation during cold weather.

It will also help if you insulate the basement walls. This should be done anyway to reduce heat loss and lower fuel costs. You may be losing as much as 25% of your heat through the uninsulated basement walls. The best way to do this is to build a 2 × 4 frame wall in front of the foundation wall and put in 3½", R12, friction-fit batts, then cover them with polyethylene vapor barrier. Insulation should also be placed between the floor joists resting on the foundation. Panelling can be added later when you want to finish the basement.

NON-SKID FLOOR MAT

What can I put on the bottom of a bath mat to stop it from sliding on a highly polished ceramic tile floor?

Double-sided carpet tape works very well. Put a strip at each end of the mat.

BLACK STAINS ON BATHROOM WALLS

I'm having difficulty with black marks that keep appearing in the grout between the tiles around my bathtub and shower, and in the caulking around the tub. I've scrubbed this off several times with great difficulty, and replaced the tub caulk more than once, but the black stains keep coming back. Do you have any idea what causes these, and what can be done to eliminate them?

The black marks are a mold growth that is very common on bathroom tile grout and tub caulk, when these materials are kept constantly wet due to frequent hot baths and lack of ventilation. It's possible that the presence of soap in the water also encourages mold growth.

A strong solution of chlorine laundry bleach applied with a stiff brush, will remove the black stains, but they will keep coming back as long as the dampness continues, I suggest that you install a bathroom vent fan to reduce condensation — or train everyone in the family to wipe down the shower wall with a towel or face cloth after they have a bath.

BATHROOM VENT

We are going to install a ceiling vent in our bathroom to reduce humidity. Can we vent this into the attic?

No. This would cause serious condensation problems in the attic during cold weather. It must be vented directly outside, preferably through the bathroom wall, but it can also go straight up through the roof, or out through the gable wall. A suitable vent cap will be needed in either case. For maximum exhaust, the vent pipe should be as short and straight as possible. Smooth metal pipe is much better than the flexible, plastic, accordian-pleated pipe often sold for this purpose. Metal pipe should be wrapped with fibreglass insulation where it passes through the attic, to prevent condensation that would run back into the ceiling outlet.

BATHROOM TILE GROUT

We are going to have our bathroom remodelled, and would like to have ceramic tile on the walls and floor. Is there any way to avoid the common problem of black mold growth on the grout?

This is primarily due to the walls being left damp for extended periods, so one remedy is to wipe the tile walls down with a towel after a bath. Increased ventilation will also help to reduce condensation on the walls.

A contributing cause, however, is a porous cement grout that soaks up moisture and provides an excellent growing medium for mold. This is mainly due to poor workmanship. Properly applied, the standard white cement grout will have a hard, smooth, waterproof finish that almost looks glazed. This is achieved by filling the joints tightly, letting the grout set up properly before it is struck off, and keeping it moist long enough to let the cement harden completely. Ceramic tile work is a seemingly simple job that actually requires a lot of expertise. Unfortunately, not all the people who do this work have it.

CRUMBLING TILE AROUND TUB

A bathroom was put in our old farmhouse about 10 years ago by the previous owner. The ceramic tiles around the tub enclosure are bulging in places and the grout between them is falling out. The other walls in the bathroom are painted gypsumboard, and I think this has been used behind the tiles, too. Can you tell me how to correct this problem?

It sounds as if the walls have been panelled with standard gypsumboard instead of the special, waterproof grade that is made for use in bathrooms and other areas where excessive dampness can be expected. When gypsumboard gets wet it crumbles and must be replaced; there is no satisfactory way to repair it. You will have to remove the tiles, cut away the damaged gypsumboard and replace it with a solid panel of the waterproof grade. Tiles can then be applied with a mastic tile adhesive spread with a notched trowel, and the joints filled with white grout cement.

A much better solution, I think, would be to use one of the molded, sectional, plastic panel kits that are made to fit a variety of tub enclosures. To put one of these up you will only have to remove the loose tiles from the wall.

BATHROOM WALL TILES FALLING OFF

The north wall of our bathroom consists of ceramic tiles glued to gypsumboard. Behind this is a layer of polyethylene vapor barrier, stud framing filled with insulation batts, then exterior sheathing and siding. After we had

been in the house a couple of years some of the tiles began to fall off. The wall behind them was wet. After drying the wall I glued the tiles back, but a year or two later the same thing happened.

A builder told me that the vapor barrier was on the wrong side of the wall—on a north wall it should go on the outside, he said. I removed the exterior panelling and insulation and slashed the vapor barrier. I also drilled some holes in the bathroom wall to let the moisture out. (We take hot showers every day and the room is like a steam bath.) Now the tiles are coming loose again. Can you tell me what is causing the trouble and what I can do about it?

The builder gave you bad advice, I'm afraid. The vapor barrier was correctly placed and should not have been changed or cut. The main cause of your trouble is simply excessive humidity in the bathroom. The best remedy is to put in a vent fan and use it whenever you are having a bath. If the walls still get wet, wipe them down with a towel after every bath.

The other cause of your trouble is that the incorrect type of gypsumboard was apparently used behind the tiles. A special, waterproof type is made for this situation, but few builders bother to use it.

CHIPPED BATHTUB

We recently had our bathroom remodelled, including new fixtures. Now the edge of the colored bathtub has been chipped. I know I can get porcelain touch-up paint in white, but where can I get a color to match our fixtures?

Manufacturers of plumbing fixtures sell touch-up kits to match their color line. You can get one through your plumbing contractor. These paints don't go on as smooth as the original finish, of course, and they won't stand extensive exposure to water, but they look a lot better than a black chip.

You can also use automobile touch-up paint, available in many colors at all auto supply stores.

MOLD ON BATHTUB CAULKING

About six months after we moved into our new house we noticed black stains on the caulking between the bathtub and the wall tiles. How can we remove this and prevent it coming back?

The wrong type of caulking compound may have been used. The type made for use on

Bathtubs

bathtubs normally contains a fungicide to prevent this mold growth. Exterior caulking compounds don't need it.

Cut the caulking material away with a razor knife and treat the area with a strong solution of chlorine laundry bleach (two ounces to a cup of water). When dry, apply a caulking compound specifically labelled for use around bathtubs. Use the bleach solution to remove any black mildew stains from the tile grout, too. Apply with a stiff brush.

REFINISHING A BATHTUB

My husband used muriatic acid to remove rust stains from our bathtub and it made the porcelain rough. What can we do to restore it?

He should have used *oxalic* acid! The only way to restore the finish is to put on a new one. Use a 2-part epoxy paint, but roughen the entire tub with #120 silicon carbide paper first to provide a "tooth" for the new finish. Two coats should be applied. This finish will not be as smooth or even as the original finish, however, nor will it last as long. There are firms that do a better job with special spray equipment, but it's almost as expensive as a new tub.

REMOVING BATHTUB APPLIQUES

We put some of those decorative, non-skid plastic strips on the bottom of our bathtub a year or two ago. The kind with a peel-off, self-stick backing. Now I'd like to take them off, but nothing I use seems to have any effect on them. Do you have any suggestions?

These have a rubber-based adhesive that can't be removed with ordinary household cleaners or solvents. It can, however, be softened with contact cement thinner, available at any hardware store. A good trick is to heat the appliqué with a hair-dryer to soften the glue so it can be peeled up a bit, then brush the contact cement thinner underneath to finish the job. Use the thinner to remove any adhesive that remains on the tub.

ROUGH BATHTUB

The surface of our bathtub has developed a very rough and grainy texture that won't wash off. Is there anything I can do to remove it?

Roughness like this is sometimes caused by a buildup of lime deposit from hard water, and can be removed quite easily with vinegar. Just give it time to dissolve.

TILING A BATHTUB

Our old enamelled bathtub is badly worn, and I was thinking of re-surfacing it with those small ceramic tiles. What kind of cement and grout should I use?

Ceramic tile can be applied to the bathtub with waterproof tile adhesive, sold where you get the tile. This is applied with a notched spreader, and the tiles simply pressed in place. Standard white cement grout is used.

This isn't a very practical idea, however. The tile tends to be a bit lumpy, and it's difficult to lay in the curves and around the drains. Where the tile must be cut to fit, you may end up with some sharp edges.

REMOVING GROUT FROM BATHTUB

How do we remove the tile grout that dropped on our bathtub when we were applying the tile, and was allowed to harden?

Chip it off carefully. Unless it's an old, cast iron tub, you can probably use a dilute solution of muriatic acid, 1 part to 10 parts water, to remove any remaining cement grout from the porcelain enamel. Modern enamels are acid-resistant; the old porcelain finishes are not.

BATHTUB RING

We've just moved into an older home, and I'm having trouble trying to remove a dark ring around the bathtub. Can you tell me what to take this off with?

It may be a lime deposit from hard water, in which case vinegar will dissolve it. If not, try soaking it with a hot, strong solution of washing soda. This should soften it.

BATS

We have bats in our attic. Are they dangerous, and how do we get rid of them?

Bats aren't dangerous in the sense that they'll attack you, but they carry parasites that may bite humans and they are potential carriers of rabies. Their nesting areas also have an objectionable odor.

You may be able to get rid of them by scattering mothballs around the attic to drive them out, then covering all openings with ¼" wire screen mesh.

Another trick is to cut strips of aluminum foil about an inch wide and hang them in front of the bat entrances.

The only effective and reliable way to eliminate bats, however, is with 50% DDT in a wettable powder. This also gets rid of the parasites that might otherwise be left behind. Under present insecticide control laws you will have to pay a licensed exterminator to come and spray your attic with DDT.

RECHARGEABLE BATTERIES

I now have several tools and small appliances that operate on rechargeable batteries, but I can't find any information on how these should be maintained. Can they be damaged by being left on charge too long? Should they be stored charged or discharged? When fully charged, do they last as long as ordinary batteries?

These rechargeable nickel-cadmium, or nicad batteries are capable of being recharged hundreds of times over many years, but they do deteriorate with age and may die completely if overheated or overcharged consistently, or if internal short-circuits develop.

Most charging units supplied with nicad batteries are designed to recharge them fully in about 15 hours, and at this rate the batteries can be left on charge indefinitely without harm. Many manufacturers recommend that nicad batteries be stored this way.

But some nicad battery-operated tools and appliances come with a fast charger that will restore full voltage within two or three hours. The batteries should NOT be left on these charging units much beyond the time required to bring them to full voltage, otherwise they may be damaged by internal over-heating. For maximum battery life, nicads should be recharged before they are completely discharged.

Nicad batteries can be stored either charged or discharged, but they lose their charge during storage and should always be put on charge before being used if they have been stored for any length of time. Most manufacturers recommend charging nicad batteries fully before storage.

Rechargeable nicad batteries are now available as replacements for the conventional carbon-zinc batteries used in flashlights, toys, transistor radios, flash guns, and similar equipment. Many people don't realize that these are generally sold in a discharged condition, and must be put on charge before use. Special charging units for replacement batter-

ies are sold by each manufacturer. Actually, you should buy two sets of batteries and leave one set on charge when the other is being used.

A fully charged nicad battery only holds about one quarter as much power as an ordinary battery—but it can, of course, be recharged and reused a great many times.

It also produces somewhat less voltage than a conventional battery—1¼ volts per cell instead of 1½ volts. A 4-battery pack, for example, will only deliver 5 volts instead of 6. But unlike an ordinary battery, which gradually gets weaker as it is used, and may have to be thrown away when it still contains a fair amount of its power supply, a nicad battery keeps close to its full voltage until it is near the end of its charge, when it dies suddenly. So, in practice, the useful life of a charged nicad battery is not much less than a conventional battery.

ROTTING BEAMS

We bought an old farm house to use as a summer home, and I'm worried about the fact that there are rust-colored, mushroom-shaped fungi growing on the beams. Are they harmful, and what can we do to get rid of them?

The mushrooms themselves aren't harmful, but they indicate that decay organisms are growing inside of the beams, caused by continual dampness. You can check to see how far the decay has progressed by driving an ice pick or similar instrument into the beams, all along their length. If the beams are seriously decayed, you'll have to replace them to prevent serious damage. If the beams still seem solid, soak them with a wood preservative, then do everything you can to keep them dry, including keeping some heat on during the winter.

RUSTED BOLTS

The bolts holding my furniture together are rusty and hard to unscrew. How can I loosen them without damaging the furniture?

Penetrating oil, available at any hardware store, will do the job.

BRASS POLISH

I have obtained an old brass bed that is tarnished where the protective varnish has peeled off. What is the best way to polish it and refinish it?

First you will have to remove the protective coating. This is generally lacquer, which can be wiped off with a cloth soaked with lacquer thinner, available at any hardware store. Go over it two or three times with clean cloths to be sure to get it all off.

There are a number of excellent copper and brass cleaners on the market. If the brass is badly tarnished, I suggest applying the cleaner with fine steel wool, #0000 grade. An old-fashioned trick that still works is to use a cut lemon sprinkled with salt. A mixture of salt and vinegar will also remove the tarnish, but neither of these methods is as good as the new copper pot cleaners.

After you have polished the brass, and before you touch it with your fingers, apply a coat of clear lacquer by spray or brush. Such lacquers are available at all paint and hardware stores.

RESTORING BRASS

We have an old umbrella stand that has been sprayed with a copper-colored metallic paint several times. We sandpapered a small area to see what was underneath, and it appears to be either copper or brass, probably the latter. Can you tell us how to restore the original metal?

Any paint remover can be used to take off the present finish. Then use one of the brass or copper cleaners and #000 or #0000 steel wool to remove any surface discoloration and polish the metal. This can be protected with a thin coat of clear lacquer—either brushed or sprayed on.

BRASS AND BRONZE

What is the difference between bronze and brass, and how can I tell one from the other?

True bronze is a brownish alloy of copper and tin, but it is rare today because of the high cost of tin. It is almost indistinguishable, in any case, from the cheaper copper-zinc alloys used today for both bronze and brass. The only difference is color—brass is yellow, bronze is brown. The more zinc, the yellower the alloy but chemical treatments can also produce various shades of green. There is no definite dividing line between bronze and brass, however.

BRICK

RENOVATING BRICK BUNGALOW

I would appreciate your advice on renovating my 25-year-old brick bungalow. Many of the bricks are badly chipped and the mortar is falling out. Should I repoint and paint the bricks, apply stucco, or put on insulating aluminum siding?

Whichever you do, it is advisable to repoint the mortar joints first in order to strengthen the brick walls. Paint is certainly the cheapest new finish you can apply, but it rarely lasts more than a year or two before it has to be redone, so this just creates another big maintenance job. Neither paint nor stucco will provide any insulation, and this is now very important. Aluminum siding doesn't provide very much insulation, either. Even if it has an insulating backer-board it only has an insulation value of about R2; you need at least R10. The best way to get this is to apply 2 × 2 vertical strapping to the wall, put 1½" foamboard insulation between this, and then apply the siding. If you use polyurethane foamboard, this will give you close to R11. Blue Styrofoam will give an insulation value of R7.5, and the common white foamboard will be about R6. In each case you would add about R2 for the insulated siding.

CHALK ON BRICK

I would like to know if there is a way to get chalk marks off a brick wall. None of the cleaners I have tried work.

Muriatic acid will take them off. Mix 1 part acid to 10 parts water in a glass bowl or jar, and apply with a stiff brush. But wear rubber gloves and be careful to keep the solution off your skin, clothes, paint, metal, and anything else you value. It won't hurt the brick, though.

CLEANING BRICK

Can you tell me how to remove some black and yellow stains from off-white brick?

It depends on what kind of brick you have. If this is cement brick it can be cleaned with a solution of muriatic acid, . . . 1 part acid to 10 parts water (or the proportion given on the label). But if you have calcium silicate or sand-lime brick, you cannot use acid to clean it. You can only use a detergent or a solution of trisodium phosphate (a heaping tablespoon to a quart of water), and these may not remove the stains. Sand-lime brick is usually lighter in color and has a much finer texture than cement brick, which looks like . . . well, concrete.

BRICK COUNTERTOP

We're having a countertop stove unit built into an old brick counter. How should we treat the bricks so they'll be easy to clean and won't absorb grease splatters?

If you want a countertop surface that won't absorb grease and is easy to clean, don't use brick. At best you will only be able to arrive at a compromise treatment—such as several coats of urethane varnish—that has neither the rustic charm of natural brick not the practical value of plastic laminate or ceramic tile. You'd do better to save the bricks for the walls.

REPAIRING CRACKED BRICKS

Some zigzag cracks have developed in the brick wall of our house. The cracks are mainly in the mortar joints, but some of the bricks have cracked, too. How can I repair these?

The cracks can be filled with mortar mix or one of the concrete patching materials sold at all hardware and building supply stores. To patch the cracks in the bricks, color the mortar with a mineral pigment. This can be obtained at any ceramic tile or brick supplier and at some hobby stores, where it is sold for mosaic tile work. The colors are very strong, so you will need very little. Mix up a small batch to check the color.

CRUMBLING BRICK

The brick wall at the front of my house is crumbling along the bottom, just above the foundation. What causes this and what can I do about it?

Crumbling or "spalling" like this is generally caused by moisture getting into the brick and then freezing. Since this is happening along the bottom of the wall, I suspect that the weep holes between the bricks along the bottom row are plugged. These are supposed to let out any water that seeps through the wall and runs down behind the bricks.

Use a screwdriver or similar tool to clean out the weep holes, but be careful not to punch a hole through the flashing that runs down the wall behind the bricks and comes out over the foundation under the bottom course of bricks. You should also check the wall for cracks in the mortar joints. These should be filled with mortar mix.

EFFLORESCENCE ON SAND-LIME BRICK

My house is faced with a white sand-lime brick. In the last two or three years a white powder has appeared on the surface. What is this, and how can I eliminate it? Should I treat the bricks with a silicone water repellent?

The white power is efflorescence, a build-up of mineral salts leached out of the brick and left on the surface when the water evaporates. Ordinarily this is removed from masonry with a 1:10 solution of muriatic acid, but this may discolor sand-lime brick. Instead, just use water and a stiff brush.

Sand-lime or calcium silicate brick is more porous than either clay or cement brick, and this tends to cause the surface to flake or spall if it is treated with a water repellent, since it traps moisture and efflorescence salts inside instead of letting them come to the surface.

FLOOR OF OLD BRICK

We're using some old brick inside our house, and would like to know if we could use this on the entrance floor, as well. Where we live, there might be a lot of dirt tracked in.

Used bricks are likely to be too soft and powdery to be used for flooring. Brick dust and old mortar dust are liable to be tracked into the house.

And from what you say, it appears that you should have a floor that's easy to clean. Quarry tile would go nicely with brick, and it's very easy to clean.

GREEN STAINS ON BRICK

Patches of a green powder have formed on the red clay brick walls of my house. What causes

this discoloration and how can I remove it?

This is generally caused by the presence of certain mineral salts in the clay. It can be removed by brushing with a very strong solution of lye—one 9½-ounce can to a quart of water. Wear rubber gloves and glasses and be careful to keep the caustic solution off everything but the bricks. A white deposit will appear on the bricks, but this can be removed with water after a few days.

PAINT MARKS ON BRICK

The previous owner of our house apparently dripped white paint on the brick walls when he was painting the eavestroughs, then tried to wipe it off with a rag and turpentine. The result, of course, is a number of ugly white smears on the brick. Paint remover helped a bit, but it won't get the white stain out of the porous brick. Do you have any suggestions?

An artist friend of mine recently found the perfect answer to this problem. Starting with a bright red trim paint, he added some yellow ochre pigment and a touch of navy blue until he got a color that matched the brick. Then he thinned the paint with about 20% solvent and brushed it on the stained bricks. "It went on perfectly and the white patches have disappeared," he tells me. If you've got a good eye for mixing colors, you can do as well.

PAINT PEELING OFF BRICK

I have a solid brick house about 100 years old. The brick was painted 10 years ago and I repainted it last summer, scraping off all the loose paint and finishing with an exterior acrylic latex. During the winter this started to peel off again. The paint company claims that this is because the old brick has lost its hard surface and I am, in effect, trying to paint a pile of clay. Is there something I can spray or paint on to harden the surface again?

I doubt very much that the peeling paint is caused by soft brick. It is more likely due to moisture penetrating through the walls from inside the house and condensing behind the paint surface during cold weather. Water *vapor* passes through brick very easily, and modern houses have a vapor barrier on the inside wall to prevent this.

If you also have trouble with condensation on your windows during cold weather, or if the paint is peeling most noticeably outside of the bathroom and kitchen, where most household moisture originates, then excess humidity in

the house is certainly the cause of the trouble. The remedy is to reduce the humidity by increasing the ventilation, such as by putting an exhaust fan in the bathroom or kitchen. Painting the interior walls with an oil-based paint would also help. (See also Condensation.)

PAINTING BRICK

I'd like to paint a brick fireplace to match the walls of a room. Is any special preparation or type of paint needed?

Exterior latex paint is better, but you can safely use regular interior latex wall paint on fireplace brick. Remember though—once the brick is painted it will be very difficult to get off.

PAINT STAINS ON BRICK

We live in a 2-storey house with white aluminum siding on the upper half and red brick below. Our problem is that the brick is turning white below the siding. Can you tell us what causes this and what we can do about it?

Like most people who have aluminum siding on their houses, you probably never noticed that the warranty on this material requires you to wash the siding thoroughly *at least once a year*.

All exterior house paints develop a chalky surface that is washed off by the rain. It helps to keep the siding clean and also prevents a buildup of paint layers that eventually causes peeling and flaking. But it can cause problems when it washes down on brick or other dark surfaces, as it has done on your house.

The factory finishes on aluminum siding are not supposed to chalk this badly, but they sometimes do, and that's why you're supposed to wash them every year. The best way to remove the chalk stain from the brickwork is to clean it with a high-pressure water spray and a detergent cleaner. You can rent such equipment from most tool rental stores. Or you can use a scrubbing brush and a solution of ¼ cup of trisodium phosphate (TSP) to a gallon of water.

PATIO BRICK

We want to pave our patio with brick. Can we use ordinary brick for this? And how should we lay it?

It's better to use a special paving brick for this purpose. Your building supply dealer can advise you on the best type available in your area.

Just lay the brick directly on a bed of sand about two or three inches deep and carefully levelled. There is no need to mortar between the joints; all you have to do is brush in some fine sand.

PROBLEMS WITH A BRICK-SAND PATIO

My son made a patio out of old bricks laid on sand, with sand also used as "mortar" in the gaps between the bricks. This past winter most of the sand was washed out of the gaps and some of the bricks cracked. What should we use to prevent this happening again?

There are a couple of problems here. Old, reclaimed bricks are generally too soft to be used for paving. Being very porous, they are also easily cracked by frost. Special, high-fired paving bricks should be used for patios and paths. Secondly, although laying bricks on a bed of sand is a good way to make a patio, they should be laid tight together, and fine sand merely swept over the surface to fill the cracks. Loose sand will not stay in wide "mortar" gaps, but a mixture of 1 part cement to 3 parts sand can be used if it is dampened after it is placed in the gaps.

RECLAIMED BRICK

We have faced our house with reclaimed brick, and now a white powder has formed on some that were laid while it was raining. We have tried removing it with a wire brush, but this damages the soft brick. What can we use to take it off? Also, my husband wants to apply silicone waterproofing. Is this advisable?

Reclaimed brick is often too soft to be used as a facing brick, and this appears to be part of your problem. A solution of 1 part muriatic acid (any hardware store) to 10 parts water will remove the white efflorescence, but with soft, porous brick this is likely to be a continuing problem. The silicone water repellent treatment is no longer recommended for brick, but in this case I think it's the lesser of two evils.

RE-USING OLD BRICK

We bought an old farm, and on it there is a brick house that is beyond repair. We plan to build a new home, and are hoping that we can re-use the old bricks. Is this possible? What should be done to the bricks before they are used?

Old brick is very popular, and frequently sells for more than new brick. But only the original face brick can be used to face the new house. The soft "backing brick" used behind this will not stand up to the weather, so you must separate the old brick carefully. There's nothing special you need to do to it except knock off the old mortar. This won't be difficult if it's a plain sand-lime mortar, which was commonly used up to about 50 years ago, but if a portland cement mortar was used, you may damage the brick in getting this off.

REMOVING PAINT FROM BRICK

One wall of our kitchen is brick that has been painted with several coats of enamel over the years. I'd like to get the brick back to its natural state. What's the best way to do this?

It's a messy job, and a very difficult one, because the paint will have penetrated into the brick to some extent. Start by using a paint remover, anyway, and a stiff brush to scrape off the softened paint. It may take two or three applications to remove all the layers.

RESTORING OLD BRICK

I would like to know how to remove paint from brick. We have a lovely old brick house that a previous owner painted grey some years ago. The paint is looking rather shabby now and I would rather restore the brick than repaint it. Some people tell me that sandblasting is bad for it, but I see a lot of brick houses that have been restored this way. What is your advice?

Sandblasting is certainly the fastest and cheapest way to remove paint, but it also removes the hard, weatherproof surface of the brick and leaves a rough texture that absorbs water readily—the most common cause of spalling or flaking. It also erodes the soft mortar, which allows more water to penetrate the brick.

There are better ways to do the job. Oil-based paints can be burned off and the brick then cleaned with chemicals. Latex paints can be removed with special chemical strippers used by some cleaning firms. Neither of these methods harms the brick. The only disadvantage is higher cost. But if you are concerned about the quality and durability of "a lovely old brick house," I don't think you should sandblast it.

Brick

REPAIRING BRICK WALLS

The basement walls in our old home are made of brick. I'm planning to insulate and panel the walls, but wonder if I should do some work on them first. The mortar joints are flaking and crumbling in some places. Is this serious enough to require repair or will the new panelling protect the brick?

The deterioration of mortar is a very slow process, but since you won't be able to get at the basement walls again after they have been panelled, it would be a good idea to restore them first. Remove the soft mortar to a depth of at least ½", using a screwdriver, chisel or similar tool. Then refill the joints with a wet mortar mixture and a pointing tool, both of which you can buy at most hardware stores. If you have much pointing to do, it will pay you to buy or make a mason's hawk, which is simply a piece of sheet metal or plywood about 15" square with a handle in the centre. It is used to hold the mortar while you're working on the wall.

ROMAN BRICK

My fireplace is made of red Roman brick, and I have been told that I can't clean this with muriatic acid or anything else. Is this true?

No. Roman or Norman brick is just a special size—12" long, instead of 8" (approximately; actual sizes vary). Like any other clay brick, it can be cleaned with one part muriatic acid (from any hardware store) to 10 parts water. Wear rubber gloves and be careful to keep the solution off everything but the brick.

SANDBLASTING BRICK

I have an old brick house that seems quite sound but the brick has darkened in places where the ivy used to grow. I was thinking of having it sandblasted very lightly, just enough to clean it. Will this harm the face of the brick or weaken the mortar joints?

Sandblasting doesn't do the brick and mortar any good, certainly, and I wouldn't recommend it for such a light cleaning job. A high-pressure, hot-water spray cleaner would do a better job and cost a lot less. You can get one of these at a tool rental shop, along with special chemical cleaners that are added to the spray automatically.

SLIPPERY BRICKS

The shady side of our brick patio is covered with a slippery green growth that I can't seem to get off. Is there any way to get rid of it permanently?

Not permanently, I'm afraid. You can kill the algae growth with a strong solution of household laundry bleach (chlorine) and then scrub it off with a stiff brush, but it will just keep coming back because the conditions are right and the air is full of algae spores.

STEEL SIDING OVER BRICK

I would like to put steel siding over the solid brick walls of my house. Should strapping be applied first, or will this cause condensation problems? This is an old home and the brick has been painted twice, but is peeling again.

Vertical strapping must be applied before the siding can be attached. But since you don't have any insulation in the solid brick walls, it would be a good idea to apply 1½" foamboard to the wall between 2 × 2 strapping (which is only 1½" thick, of course). The strapping can be applied with concrete nails or a nailing gun. The foamboard can be held in place with panel adhesive.

BRICK VENEER FOR BASEMENT WALLS

I am thinking of finishing the concrete walls in my basement with thin brick that can be applied with adhesive. Do you think this would be a good idea?

No. The walls should be insulated, and the thin brick will provide no insulation whatever. Nor will it prevent condensation on the walls during warm humid weather. Both of these factors control the comfort and livability of a finished basement. I suggest that you insulate the walls and provide a vapor barrier over the insulation (even if it has a built-in vapor barrier), then put up plywood backing for the brick veneer—or use any other type of panelling you want.

BRICK VENEER OVER INSULBRICK

We have Insulbrick siding on our wood frame house right now, and we want to put on real brick veneer. Some people tell us we should remove the Insulbrick first; others say leave it on for its insulation value. What do you recommend?

Insulbrick was very popular many years ago but is rarely used today. It consists of a 1"-thick sheet of softboard insulation covered with asphalt and mineral granules applied in a simulated brick pattern. The softboard has an insulation value of about R2.4, which isn't considered much today, but was quite a step forward in its time. It wasn't realized at that time, however, that the asphalt surface acts as a vapor barrier, trapping condensation inside the wall during cold weather. This can cause many problems.

If your Insulbrick siding shows no signs of curling, then it might be safe to apply brick veneer on top of it, but I think it would be wiser to remove it. Insulation is very important today, however, and will be even more valuable in the future as fuel costs go up, so I recommend that you have cellulose fibre or other insulation blown into the walls from the outside before the brick is applied. It will be a lot more difficult and expensive to have this done later.

BRICK WALL LEAKING

Two years ago I bought a new house of brick veneer construction, and ever since I have had trouble with water leaking into the basement over the top of the foundation wall. I have cleared out the drain holes in the bottom row of bricks, but the water still leaks through into the basement during rainy weather. The builder came and put caulking along the top of the foundation wall from the basement side, but this didn't do any good. He says there was not enough water repellent in the bricks and mortar.

The lack of a water repellent is certainly not the cause of your trouble. That can only be due to damaged or non-existent flashing, the strip of waterproof material that extends from the lower part of the sheathing behind the brick out over the top of the foundation wall. This, combined with the weep holes in the bottom row of bricks, diverts any water that leaks through the brick wall, and prevents it from coming through into the basement.

Metal is the best flashing, but heavy roofing paper is often used today because it's cheaper. It is also very easily damaged by a careless bricklayer, and it only takes one hole to cause the trouble you are having. Unfortunately there is no way to repair the flashing without taking the brick wall down and rebuilding it. A better caulking job along the top of the founda-

tion wall inside should keep the water out, but the best thing to do is find the source of the leaks through the brick wall. Look for cracks in the mortar joints or around the window frames. The former can be filled with any concrete patching material, the latter with caulking compound. If the trouble is caused by the use of a low-quality, porous brick, then it might help to apply a silicone water repellent, although this is not generally recommended today because it can cause spalling or flaking.

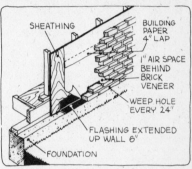

SHEATHING — BUILDING PAPER 4" LAP — 1" AIR SPACE BEHIND BRICK VENEER — WEEP HOLE EVERY 24" — FLASHING EXTENDED UP WALL 6" — FOUNDATION

'WEEP HOLES' IN BRICK WALL

When we moved into our brick veneer house I noticed that there were some vertical gaps in the mortar joints along the bottom row of bricks. I was afraid these would allow water to get through into the basement, so I filled them in. Now we DO get water coming through over the top of the basement wall when it rains very heavily, and I'm wondering if I did the right thing.

I'm afraid you made a mistake in filling the weep holes between the bottom course of bricks. They are there to let out any water that seeps through the brick wall. Flashing behind the bricks keeps this water from getting through into the basement, but if the holes are plugged the water will build up above the flashing and run down inside.

Use a ½" masonry drill to make holes in the vertical mortar joints along the bottom of the wall, but don't let the drill cut through the flashing just behind the air space at the back of the brick wall.

WHITE POWDER ON BRICK

We recently bought a 54-year-old brick house and have noticed that a white powder forms on one part of the wall. Should I seal all the brickwork with silicone, or just the part where the salt appears?

The white powder is called "efflorescence", and it's caused by water seeping through the brick, bringing with it dissolved salts that are left on the surface when the water evaporates. The water may be getting into the bricks through cracks in the mortar. Or it may even be coming from inside the house. This is probably the case if the efflorescence appears outside a bathroom or kitchen, where most household humidity originates.

A leaking eavestrough or downspout is another common cause of white efflorescence on brick walls.

The use of silicone water repellents is no longer recommended by brick authorities. It has been found to promote flaking or "spalling."

Check the wall carefully for cracks or gaps in the mortar. These can be filled very easily with premixed mortar (see Repointing). The efflorescence can be removed with a solution of 1 part muriatic acid (from any hardware store) to 10 parts water. Wear rubber gloves and protect your eyes with glasses.

CLEANING BRONZE

Can you tell me how to clean and polish the bronze plaque on a grave stone? It has turned almost totally black.

Although there are chemical treatments that will remove the tarnish, these will not restore the original appearance. The color of bronze varies according to the proportion of copper and tin used in the alloy and the type of patina applied in the final treatment of the metal. The tone can range from bright metal to dark brown and various shades of green, and art plays a bigger part than science in determining the result. Polishing a piece of bronze may take the whole process back to Step One again.

Most cemeteries will do this type of restoration work for a reasonable fee, but if you would like to do something about it yourself I suggest that you simply buff the plaque with fine steel wool (#0000) and lemon oil. Work on the raised areas first and leave some of the tarnish in the depressions to emphasize the lettering and decoration.

Bronze that is less badly tarnished can often be restored simply by rubbing with a soft cloth dipped in a mixture of lemon oil and rottenstone. To reduce further tarnishing, wipe the bronze with a cloth dampened with commercial boiled linseed oil, then buff with a soft cloth.

CLEANING BRONZE

I have been given a small bronze statue of a charging bull that I believe is fairly valuable. It is dark brown in color with hardly any shine at all, and I would like to restore the original polish. How can I remove the brown tarnish and reveal the bright metal?

The statue may be valuable now, but it won't be if you do that to it! Brown is the natural color of sculptural bronze, and much artistic skill is involved in achieving the right shading and color tone on a piece of work like this. Other than dusting it, and wiping occasionally with a damp cloth to remove fingerprints, if necessary, you should leave it alone.

REMOVING PAINTED BURLAP

How can I remove painted burlap from a plaster wall?

You are going to have a difficult time if it's been painted with anything but a water paint. Remove the paint near the top of the wall, using paint remover, then take off the burlap as you would wallpaper by wetting and stripping.

REMOVING BURLAP

A year ago we put burlap on our plaster wall with wallpaper paste. Now we want to take it off and restore the painted wall. How can we do this?

Soak the burlap with warm water to which regular wallpaper remover has been added. This should soften the adhesive enough to let you strip off the burlap. The wall will still be rather rough, however, and when it's dry you'll have to go over it with a sanding block to restore the surface for painting.

CANDLE-MAKING

The candles I make out of paraffin wax always seem to melt quickly at the edges and drip. How can I get them to stay firm and burn slowly like the ones you can buy?

The paraffin wax sold for household use has a very low melting point . . . around 120°. You should use special candle wax that has a melting point of 145° or more. You can buy this wax through hobby supply stores.

FROZEN CANNED GOODS

My husband and I have been having an argument about leaving canned foods in the cottage over the winter. He says they are perfectly safe to eat, but I doubt it. Some of the cans have been frozen and thawed several times.

As long as the seal is not broken, decay organisms cannot get into canned foods, and in that sense, they cannot "spoil". There is always the possibility of invisible hairline cracks developing, however, so your instincts are probably right; it is not worth the risk. There is another good reason for not eating canned foods that have been frozen; texture and flavor are both affected by freezing. While they may be perfectly safe to eat, they may not taste very good.

CARPETS

BASEMENT CARPET

We are building a recreation room in our basement and would like to put carpeting on the floor. Do you think this is advisable?

If a concrete floor is perfectly dry, any kind of carpeting can be laid on it. Often, however, a floor that seems to be dry may be slightly damp at some time of the year, either because of inadequate drainage during wet weather or because of condensation on the cool floor slab during hot, humid weather. Dampness can cause mildew to develop in the carpet fibres.

There is less chance of dampness if the floor is painted or tiled before the carpet is laid. In areas where there is high humidity during the hot summer months, a dehumidifier should be used in the basement and the doors and windows kept closed. It is better to use a separate underlay of waffle-back sponge rubber or porous urethane foam than to buy a carpet with a sponge rubber backing that has no ventilation underneath.

Wall-to-wall carpeting can be laid on concrete just as easily as on a wood floor. Smooth-edge, a narrow strip of wood with a slanting row of steel pins that grip the carpet backing, can be fastened to the floor around the perimeter of the room with special concrete nails or adhesive. The underlay fits inside the smooth-edge strip and the carpet is applied over them both. This job is best done by a professional.

BASEMENT CARPET MILDEWED

I cemented indoor-outdoor carpeting directly on the concrete floor of our basement rec room. Now, after two years, I notice two areas where there is mildew, and a number of places where the carpet has come away from the floor.

The mildew indicates that there is dampness in the concrete floor. This could either be caused by condensation during humid summer months (the remedy is to use a dehumidifier), or by ground water seeping through the concrete. Since the carpet adhesive is lifting away from the concrete, I suspect that inadequate drainage around and under the floor slab is the cause.

You may be able to cure the problem just by diverting a faulty downspout, or by building up the earth around the house so that surface water will run away from the foundation wall, instead of towards it. More likely, however, you'll have to have someone dig up and repair the drain tile system around the foundation footings...and that's a big job.

BATHROOM CARPET

We are remodelling our bathroom and would like to put down indoor-outdoor type carpeting. But, since we have small children who splash a lot of water around when they're having a bath, I'm not sure that this carpeting would be practical under these circumstances. What do you think?

Water does not harm these carpets, and as long as you use one with a waterproof backing, such as kitchen carpeting, the water won't damage the floor, either.

BATHROOM CARPET

We have just had our living room floor covered with polyester carpet with a jute backing and a foam rubber underlay. We have a piece left over that would fit our bathroom floor very nicely; it is now covered with ceramic tile. Would this be satisfactory? If so, how should the carpet be fastened down?

The polyester pile and the foam rubber underlay would be unaffected by the wet conditions to be expected in the bathroom, but the jute backing is liable to develop mildew. Carpeting made for use in bathrooms is all-synthetic, including the backing.

However, there's no reason why you shouldn't try it for a while. If the bathroom is not too damp it may last a long time. The easiest way to apply it is with a strip of double-sided adhesive tape around the edge. Apply this to the floor first, then strip off the protective paper and press the carpet in place. You'll find it easier to cut the carpet to size if you make a paper pattern first.

CARPETING BUCKLED

The wall-to-wall nylon carpeting in our house gets loose during the summer months. It tends to ripple when we walk on it. Is there anything we can do to prevent this happening?

The carpeting buckles because of the humidity—and because it wasn't laid properly. Jute backing expands as the humidity increases, and if the carpet has not been laid tightly enough this will make it buckle or ripple during damp weather, particularly if it was laid during the winter months when the humidity in the house is usually at its lowest. Have a professional carpet-layer come in to re-stretch it and trim off the excess. This isn't a do-it-yourself job, I'm afraid, because it requires special skills and equipment.

CHEWING GUM ON CARPET

Is there any way to remove gum from a rug without cutting it out?

Harden the gum with an ice cube then crush it with pliers and rub it out of the fabric. If any stain remains, sponge with cleaning fluid, and repeat if necessary.

CLEANING CARPET WITH DETERGENT

I tried to remove grease spots from my carpeting with dishwashing detergent, but the spots just got larger. Can you help me?

Dishwashing detergent should not be used on carpeting. It is too sudsy and leaves a film which itself attracts dirt. The combination of this and the remaining grease is probably what you have now. Use warm water to clean off the remaining detergent, blotting it up as you go. Then, if necessary, sponge the spot again with warm water plus a little ammonia. Dab, don't rub, and blot up as much as you can. The object is to remove the dirt, not spread it around.

COLOR POOLS ON CARPET

We had a light green, wall-to-wall carpet installed throughout our house over a year ago. Recently we noticed light and dark patches in certain areas. They don't come out with brushing, vacuuming or other cleaning, and I don't understand what has caused them. Can you help?

According to the Carpet Institute, this shading or "pooling" is not caused by fading or staining, but by light reflecting through the fibres in a different way. Traffic patterns sometimes cause the pile fibres to take a permanent set in one direction. Steaming and brushing will sometimes correct this.

LAYING CARPET ON CONCRETE

Would you please advise me if it is necessary to paint or seal a basement floor before putting down rubber- or sponge-backed carpet?

First check to see if there is any dampness in the floor. Lay a rubber mat down for a few days. If you see any sign of dampness under it when you lift it up, it's not advisable to lay any kind of flooring down until this is remedied, usually by correcting the drainage around the outside of the foundation. There's nothing you can paint on that will hold back any significant amount of moisture seeping through a concrete floor.

If the rubber mat test shows that the floor is dry, it is not necessary to paint it before laying carpet. This does keep the concrete from dusting, however, and will seal it against very small amounts of moisture that may sometimes be present.

CURLING CARPETS

We put down a new rug in our living room and have two large pieces left over that would make excellent scatter rugs, except that the corners keep curling up. Is there any way we can make them lie flat?

When tufted, rather than woven, carpets were introduced a few years ago, this was a common problem. Now nearly all tufted carpeting is made with an extra "skrim" backing of jute, which has eliminated the problem. Some inexpensive carpeting, however, is still made without a skrim back. There isn't much you can do about it, but strips of gummed carpet tape applied to the back may help.

DYEING A RUG

I have a large, light-colored rug that gets soiled very quickly. What can I use to dye it a darker color?

It is not practical to do this job at home, and it is rather expensive to have it done professionally. There is no guarantee on color or condition, and you should allow for up to 10% shrinkage. I think it would be better to stick with the color you have.

REMOVING FOAM-BACKED CARPET

When I wanted to replace our foam-backed carpeting, I found that the rubber had stuck to the floor. Can you tell me how to take it off?

Rubber-backed carpeting is generally glued to the floor. A special "release" adhesive is used today; this peels off easily and leaves nothing on the floor. It sounds as if your carpet was laid with the old, permanent adhesive. About all you can do is use a broad putty knife or similar tool to break the adhesive bond as you pull up the carpet, then sand and refinish the floor.

The other solution is to leave the carpet down as an underpad for a new carpet. A narrow strip can be cut off around the edge of the room, however, so that a tackless edging strip can be put down to hold the new carpet.

CARPETING FRONT STEPS

Our concrete porch and front steps have become pitted and discoloured. We are thinking of painting them or applying outdoor carpeting, but don't know what kind of materials to use or which is best. Do you have any suggestions?

The concrete should be cleaned and patched first, in either case, and when you have done this you may decide you don't need to paint it or carpet it. You can clean the concrete with a solution of muriatic acid, available at any hardware store. Mix it to proportions given on the label. Holes should be filled with one of the concrete patching materials.

There are a number of concrete porch paints on the market, but I really don't recommend using any of them. They begin to flake or wear off fairly quickly and must be repainted every year or two at best. Who needs another annual chore like this?

Outdoor carpeting is also a temporary treatment, although it will probably last several years under normal conditions. Use a latex-emulsion, water-based adhesive such as Ozite Ap400 or a solvent-based synthetic rubber adhesive such as Roberts No. 6033. The latter was developed for such carpet applications as swimming pool decks and is highly resistant to dampness.

GLUE ON CARPET

I dropped some contact cement on my wall-to-wall carpet, and nothing seems to take it off. Do you know of anything I can use?

You can buy contact cement solvent at most hardware stores. Used carefully, this should remove most of the spot. Better test it on a sample piece of the carpet first, however.

CARPETS AS INSULATION

We have 3" of fibreglass batt insulation in our ceiling and would like to increase it. I have a quantity of old carpeting, both wool and nylon, and was thinking of simply laying this on top of the joists in the attic. Do you think this is a good idea?

The average carpet probably has about as much insulation value as a fibreglass batt *of the same thickness*. But carpet is a great deal heavier. You need at least 3" more insulation, and if you put down that much carpet it might come through the ceiling.

NAIL POLISH ON CARPET

I spilled some nail polish on my gold nylon broadloom carpet. Is there any way this can be removed?

Acetone will dissolve nail polish, and can safely be used on nylon or wool—but not on some other carpet fibres. Apply it to the spot with a cotton pad, blotting immediately with a paper towel to soak up the dissolved polish, otherwise you'll just spread it over a larger area.

NON-SKID CARPETS

Is there a liquid latex compound that can be painted on the back of rugs to keep them from slipping?

It takes quite a bit of liquid rubber to coat a carpet, and this turns out to be a rather expensive way of doing it. It's much better to use one

Carpets

of the spray-on "release" adhesives made for laying certain types of indoor-outdoor carpeting.

NYLON CARPET MELTED

To dry a wet nylon carpet, my wife put newspaper on it and then applied a hot iron. The newspaper stuck to the rug in several places and we can't seem to get it off. Do you know anything we can do?

The iron has melted the nylon and fused it to the paper. All you can do is shave it off with scissors and hope that it won't show.

OUTDOOR CARPETING INDOORS

I want to put carpeting down on the concrete floor in our basement. Must I use an outdoor carpeting, or can I use any kind?

A lot of consumers, and not a few carpet salesmen, are confused about the uses of indoor-outdoor carpeting, and the industry is tending to phase out the term.

Many people assume that because a carpet is tough enough to stand up outdoors, it must also be the best carpet to use indoors. This is not necessarily true. To survive outdoor exposure, a carpet must be made of materials that will withstand sunlight as well as water and extreme temperatures. Nylon is the strongest carpet fibre, but it cannot stand up to ultra-violet light, so polypropylene is the fibre most commonly used for outdoor carpeting. The dyes that can be used outdoors are also limited, and generally not as bright as the colors that can be used on indoor carpeting.

If the floor is perfectly dry, any kind of carpet can be used, but a concrete floor is subject to possible dampness, and it is best not to use a carpet that contains any natural fibres such as wool or jute (commonly used in carpet backing) that might become mildewed. The carpet should be made entirely of synthetic materials. A nylon or acrylic carpet with a polypropylene backing would be perfectly satisfactory, and probably more attractive than a carpet made for outdoor use. Any "kitchen" carpeting can be used.

CARPET ON PLYWOOD DECK

We have a 700-square-foot plywood deck that is protected by the roof overhang, but does receive some sun and moisture. We are thinking of covering the deck with outdoor carpet. Is there a special paint or preservative that we should use first?

Moisture trapped under the carpeting will encourage wood decay in the plywood deck. There are a number of wood preservatives that can be used, but they will only slow the decay, not prevent it. The deck may last a few years, however, so you'll have to decide if it's worth it. I must admit that I know of no other surface treatment that would be any more successful than the carpeting.

RUST STAIN ON CARPET

We shampooed our living room rug recently, and when moving the furniture around we forgot about the metal glides on the bottom of the legs. Now we have several rust spots on our gold wool rug. Can you tell us any way to remove these spots?

Sponge the spots with a concentrated solution of oxalic acid crystals, which you can obtain at any drug store. (This may be packaged and labelled as Rust Remover.) Keep the stain wet until it has disappeared, then sponge the spot thoroughly with clean water and a little ammonia to remove the oxalic acid solution.

A 2% solution of hydrofluoric acid works even better, but this is difficult to obtain.

STATIC ELECTRICITY

I am concerned about the amount of static electricity shock I get every day. We have shag rugs throughout the house and I wear rubber-soled slippers to insulate me from the floor, but I get zapped every time I touch anything or anybody. My husband only gets shocked once in a while. What causes this and how can I avoid it?

Static electricity is produced whenever two different materials are rubbed together, such as the soles of your slippers and the fibres of the rug. When the air is damp the electricity dissipates very quickly, but when the air and your skin are dry the electricity builds up and you may get a shock of several thousand volts. It is harmless, however, because the current is extremely small. You probably get more shocks than your husband because your skin is drier.

One remedy is to increase the humidity in your house, but this is only a partial cure because you can only raise the humidity so far without causing condensation problems. Another remedy, believe it or not, is to put aluminum foil under the carpet. The kind sold at building supply stores is cheapest. This doesn't eliminate the static electricity entirely, but it reduces it considerably.

Spray-on anti-static chemicals are also available, but carpet manufacturers do not recommend them because they tend to attract dirt.

STORING CARPETS IN BASEMENT

I have three carpets that I would like to store in my basement. Can you tell me the best way to do this to prevent the formation of mildew?

If there is any dampness whatever in the basement, at any time of the year, I don't recommend storing your carpets there. There is no special wrapping or other treatment that will reliably prevent the formation of mildew. I suggest you have the carpets stored in a warehouse with controlled humidity and ventilation. See the Yellow Pages under Moving & Storage.

CARPETING OVER TILE FLOOR

The concrete floor in our basement is covered with tile, and during hot, humid weather, moisture condenses on the cold floor. I want to insulate the floor with carpeting, but can't seem to get consistent answers from the different salesmen I've talked to. Is it all right to carpet the floor? If so, what type of carpeting should I use and how should it be applied?

As long as the moisture on the floor is just condensation and not leakage through the slab, carpeting is perfectly practical. In addition to acting as insulation, the carpet must also serve as a vapor barrier to keep the humid air from reaching the cold slab, so you should use an indoor-outdoor carpet or kitchen carpet with a completely waterproof backing of sponge rubber.

Most carpet manufacturers are now recommending the use of a "release" adhesive to bond carpet to this type of floor. Two-sided tape can also be used, but it doesn't really prevent the carpet from buckling. With a release adhesive, the carpet can be peeled off at any time without damage to it or the floor.

VERANDAH CARPET

I have an enclosed but unheated verandah with a concrete floor. What kind of carpeting can I put down here, and should it have a rubber or a jute backing?

Any of the all-synthetic indoor-outdoor carpeting materials can be used in this situation . . . with or without foam backing. They can be glued directly to the concrete. A jute-backed carpet would not be suitable.

CARPETING A WALL

We have a smooth ceiling-high concrete wall in our basement, and I want to cover it with the same carpet we are going to use on the floor. Can you tell me how this is done?

First, make sure that no moisture is coming through the concrete from the earth outside. If the concrete is clean, dry and smooth, and not painted, carpet can be applied with an adhesive made specially for this purpose, such as Roberts #3810, which should be available through your carpet supplier.

A carpet with a plain jute backing is best, although a latex-backed carpet can be used. Vinyl-backed carpets are not recommended.

The adhesive can be applied with a lamb's wool paint roller or a notched trowel, and should cover about 25 square yards per gallon. The carpet must be applied to the tacky adhesive surface within 45 minutes.

This is a tricky job, however, and not really recommended as a do-it-yourself project. The weight of the carpet, the temperature of the wall, the humidity, and the thickness of the adhesive all influence the time that must be allowed before the carpet is applied to the adhesive, and you must be prepared to work quickly. A large piece of carpet is awkward enough to handle on the floor; you can imagine what it would be like on a wall!

WAX ON CARPET

Can you tell me how to remove candle wax from a rug? I was told to place a brown paper bag on the wax and then press it with an iron, but this just left some of the paper stuck to the rug. Now I have to get that off, too.

Hold an ice cube on the wax to harden it, then break or scrape off as much as you can. If you place a few layers of paper towel (not kraft paper!) over the spots and then apply a moderately hot iron, most of the remaining wax will be absorbed. What is left can be removed by

29

sponging with petroleum solvent (mineral spirits) or methyl hydrate.

CASTERS MARKING FLOOR

What can we do to stop the casters on our portable dishwasher from making marks on the kitchen floor?

The casters may be jammed with lint and thread from the floor. Tip the dishwasher back and examine them, remove any dirt, and apply a drop of oil to the swivel shaft and axle of each caster.

If this doesn't cure the trouble, you will have to replace the casters. The ball type are best, but the kind sold for wooden furniture will not fit on a sheet metal appliance. You need the kind with a nut and bolt attachment, and your hardware store may have to order these for you.

PROTECTING CAST IRON

I am restoring an old pot-bellied cast iron stove, and have had it sand-blasted to remove rust and dirt. It looks like new. Can you suggest any preparation that can be applied to keep it this way?

Cast iron doesn't rust very easily, and keeps well under ordinary household conditions. If you are going to use the stove, the best thing to clean it with is old-fashioned stove polish, if you can find a hardware store that still carries it. If you are not going to use it, apply a thin film of penetrating oil, kerosene or mineral oil.

RUST-PROOFING CAST IRON

I have a large cast iron Dutch oven. It is impossible to keep the inside free from rust, and this seems to taint the food. Is there something I can put on the inside to prevent it rusting?

Scouring it with table salt is one trick, but cast iron cooking utensils need to be cured to prevent rusting and food sticking. After it has been thoroughly cleaned, cover the bottom with cooking oil and put it on a high heat until the oil begins to smoke. Continue for about 10 minutes, then remove from heat and allow to cool. Wipe out excess oil.

To maintain the cured surface, do not scour the pot with soap or detergent after use; just wipe it clean with paper towels or a damp cloth.

THE TOMCAT PROBLEM

This may sound like a silly question, but we live in a basement apartment and are bothered by tomcats that spray our windows, and the smell is driving us to distraction. I've tried mothballs, but they don't work. Is there any remedy short of homicide?

It would be more a case of pesticide than homicide, I think! Other than that weak pun, I don't have much to offer. But ammonia sometimes works, I'm told. And so does cayenne pepper. And pet stores sell cat and dog repellents that sometimes work.

BLACK STAINS ON CEDAR

The cedar deck and siding on our cottage have turned black in areas where they have been wet. How can we remove this discoloration and how can we prevent it from coming back?

The black stain is a mold or mildew growth, and it can generally be removed by scrubbing it with a mixture of 1 cup of chlorine laundry bleach, ¼ cup of dishwasher detergent, and 1 quart of water. After this has dried, treat the wood with a pentachlorophenol wood preservative to prevent further mold growth.

NO CEDAR SMELL

The door to our cedar closet was removed for about two months while remodelling was under way. It no longer has a cedar smell. Has this destroyed its effectiveness? If so, what can we do?

The effectiveness of cedar in keeping moths away is questionable, at best. Only a certain kind of aromatic cedar from the southern U.S. is properly used in this way; the common Western red cedar has very little smell. Even assuming you have the expensive aromatic cedar, probably all you have lost is a pleasant smell, and you can buy scented sprays that will just about duplicate this.

CEDAR DECK TREATMENT

I have a 2-year-old cedar deck on the back of my house. It is in good shape but must have dried out quite a bit over 2 winters. Is there some kind of a treatment I should apply to restore the natural oils?

No. As long as the deck is properly drained and the wood is not in direct contact with the ground, where it would be kept damp, it will survive for a great many years without any special treatment. Oils, stains or other finishes are not recommended for a wood deck, since they cannot withstand traffic or exposure.

FINISH FOR A CEDAR DOOR

Some time ago you said that the best finish for cedar was no finish at all, but we have a new cedar front door that is only protected by a storm door in winter and a screen in summer, and I'm afraid it will get finger-marked.

My comment about no finish being required for cedar referred to cedar siding. As you note, a door must be protected from fingermarks and similar stains. The most durable finish is *four* coats of marine varnish.

FINISHING A CEDAR DOOR

Four years ago we put a Colonial-style cedar door on our house. On the advice of a paint salesman we applied a stain and two coats of high gloss urethane varnish on the outside, but left the inside with a stain only, "so the cedar can breathe." The dull finish inside must be cleaned constantly and the outside blisters so badly that we have to redo it every spring. This never happened to the enamelled door that we replaced. Would you please tell us the proper way to finish this door?

You were given some bad advice. A wood door should always be finished exactly the same on both sides, and on the four edges, too, to prevent warping due to uneven absorption of moisture. The lack of a varnish finish on the inside also permits moisture vapor to pass

through the wood and cause the outside finish to blister.

Strip off the old finish and apply *four coats* of any good exterior varnish, sometimes called "spar varnish." I don't recommend urethane for exterior use; it has a tendency to peel.

FINISHING CEDAR SIDING

I am going to use vertical cedar siding on the cottage I am building. I got conflicting advice on what finish I should use. Can you tell me what's best?

I have always maintained that the best finish for cedar is no finish at all. The second best is a pigmented, or semi-transparent stain. Cedar weathers naturally to a silvery driftwood grey that is very attractive, but stains are available that anticipate this coloring. They are sometimes called FPL or Madison Formula stains, after the Forest Products Laboratory in Madison, Wisconsin, where the formula was developed.

Pigmented stains are also available in a wide range of colors. Water-based "latex" stains have recently proved superior to some of the standard oil-based stains.

Although once widely used, linseed oil is not a very good exterior finish for cedar or any other wood, in my experience. Even "boiled" linseed oil is slow to dry, collects dust, and often remains sticky for years. And when this happens, there isn't anything you can do about it.

Nor are there yet any clear film finishes that can be recommended for exterior use on wood. They all crack or peel in time, and are very difficult to refinish. It's not the finish itself that fails, but the wood underneath. Ultraviolet inhibitors extend the life of the finish but don't eliminate the problem.

CEDAR FOR SAUNA

I want to build a sauna and have access to a supply of clean, #1 grade, used cedar lumber. Can I use this to panel the inside of the sauna, and what finish should I use on it?

Cedar is an excellent wood to use in a sauna, and should be given no finish at all. Just be sure to countersink all the nails inside the sauna so you don't sit on a hot nailhead!

CEDAR SHINGLES INDOORS

We are going to use cedar shingles on one wall of our kitchen, but have been told that they will discolor badly if we don't protect

them with something like varnish. What would you recommend?

I recommend that you leave the shingles alone. All wood darkens with exposure to light, but indoors this will be very slight. I have seen cedar shingles used in this way many times, and they look very attractive, but they have never needed any finish or other protection.

FINISHING A CEDAR SHOWER WALL

What finish should I use on a tongue-and-groove cedar wall around the tub-shower alcove in our bathroom? I was thinking of using satin urethane varnish, but I am concerned that water may get underneath it.

Cedar panelling is fine for a bathroom, but *not* for a shower stall...If the wood is left unfinished it will probably show water stains very quickly. And there is no finish that will seal the tongue-and-groove joints well enough to prevent water from soaking into the wood. If you don't intend to use the shower very often, a penetrating oil-resin sealer such as one of the Danish oil finishes might be satisfactory. Otherwise, I suggest that you cover the wood panelling with a waterproof material such as plastic laminate or a heavy-duty vinyl wallcovering.

OLD CEDAR SIDING

I have torn down an old house to rebuild a cottage and I want to know what to do to finish the cedar siding befor using it again.

You can use the lumber just the way it is, if it's sound, since it's probably better than new lumber. Cedar siding needs no finish whatever, unless you want to paint it.

CEILINGS

CLEANING A TEXTURED CEILING

The ceiling in the living area of our home has a rough-textured plaster finish. Smoke from our fireplace stained the ceiling and I would like to clean it before I paint it. What is the best way to remove this smoke stain?

Such ceilings usually consist of plaster mixed with a coarse aggregate that creates the tex-

ture. The plaster mixture is sprayed on and left unpainted. It cannot be washed because water will soften the plaster. All you can do is paint right over the smoke stains using a lambswool roller and latex paint.

CRACKED CEILING

We have a 12′ by 17′ dormer bedroom with a crack running the length of the room. I was thinking of finishing the ceiling with a rough-textured paint in order to cover the crack and some water stains. What should I use to fill the crack?

You don't say how long the crack has been there or if you have tried patching it before. Such cracks are usually caused by seasonal movement of the house as it expands and contracts with changes in humidity and temperature. If this is the case, I think you would be better off using a smooth paint that can be patched and repainted—you can't do this very easily with the textured paints. Seal the water stains with shellac before repainting, otherwise they will bleed through.

CEILING FAN TOO SLOW

My bathroom ceiling fan works well in warm weather, but when it gets cold outside the fan is slow to start. The colder it gets, the longer the delay. Do you have any suggestions?

The lubricant in the bearings is probably getting thicker as the temperature drops. Remove the fan (it should unplug from the ceiling vent), clean it with petroleum solvent (mineral spirits) and put a couple of drops of penetrating oil in the end bearings. This will soften the grease in the permanently packed bearings.

CEILING VENT FAN

I am thinking of installing a ventilating fan in the ceiling to pull air out of the house, into the attic, and then outside. I think this should cool the house during hot weather and remove moisture and cooking odors in the winter. Do you agree?

I'm afraid not. It would be better to spend the money on ceiling insulation. This will keep the house cooler in summer as well as save heat in winter, and it won't use any electricity. In any case, you couldn't use a ceiling fan in the winter because it would exhaust humid household air into the attic, creating condensation and frost under the cold roof.

CEILING GHOST MARKS

We have recently painted the inside of our house but lines on the ceiling have appeared just about where the joists would be. The lines look like dirt but won't wash off. We checked the insulation and it seems to be adequate. Would you know the cause?

Shadowing is also known as "pattern soiling" or "ghost marks." It is produced by uneven insulation: dust accumulates on cold surfaces more readily than on warm areas, so that plaster having wide differences in surface temperature will develop noticeable dirt shadows more quickly than surfaces where the temperature is uniform. More insulation in the ceiling will prevent this.

GYPSUMBOARD OVER CEILING TILES

The ceiling in our basement consists of 12" square acoustic tiles stapled to 1 x 3 strapping nailed at right angles to the ceiling joists. We want to put up a smooth gypsumboard ceiling instead. Can this be nailed directly over the tiles or do we have to remove these first?

The only place you could nail the gypsumboard to the joists is where they cross the strapping. Between the strapping there is no support for the softboard ceiling tiles and you would probably break the gypsumboard if you tried to drive a nail through it there. Instead, fasten the gypsumboard directly to the strapping with 1¾" flathead screws, spaced every 12".

Incidentally, the job will be easier if you use ³/₈" gypsumboard, which is 25% lighter than the customary ½" drywall panelling, but strong enough for this application.

CEILING INSULATION IS WET

About a year and a half ago we had cellulose fibre insulation blown in over the 2" layer of fibreglass batts in the ceiling. It cut down our heating bills as expected, but during the summer we noticed that the paint was beginning to peel off our bathroom ceiling. When I went up in the attic to investigate I found that the batt insulation was wet but the roof wasn't leaking. What has caused this and what can we do about it?

Humid air from the bathroom is passing through the ceiling and condensing within the batt insulation during cold weather. The added insulation has trapped this moisture and prevented it from being evaporated by the air cir-

culation in the attic, which is probably what happened before the new insulation was added.

An exhaust fan in the bathroom wall will remove much of the humidity, but you should also look for air leaks into the attic. A light fixture in the bathroom ceiling could be one source. The attic door or hatch could be another. A common source of air leakage is the space around the vent stack that extends from the basement to the roof. Household air can also leak into the attic through the gap around the chimney. These gaps should be plugged with fibreglass insulation. More ventilation in the attic will also help. You should have one square foot of open vent for every 300 square feet of attic.

CEILING LIFTS IN WINTER

Every winter large gaps appear between the ceiling and the inside walls of our 1-storey home. Over the kitchen cupboards there is sometimes a space of as much as 1½". As soon as the warmer weather comes the ceiling settles back in place again. Can you tell us what causes this and what we can do about it?

This is a relatively new problem that occurs only in houses with truss roofs, and it is not completely understood. Studies by the National Research Council indicate that it is caused by differences in the moisture content of the wood. During very cold weather the humidity is higher under the roof than it is just above the ceiling, and this causes the top "rafter" sections of the trusses to lengthen and lift the bottom "joists." (Actually, these parts of a truss are called "chords.") This doesn't seem to weaken the roof at all, but it certainly doesn't look very good.

Various construction changes are being considered to prevent this problem, but no one has any good remedies for houses that already have it. Reducing the insulation in the ceiling would reduce the amount of ceiling deflection, but that's not favored in these days of energy conservation. Increasing the ventilation in the attic crawlspace might help, but probably not much. There is yet no practical way to fasten the trusses down so they can't lift. Until more is known about this problem, it appears you'll just have to live with it.

LOWER CEILING TO SAVE HEAT

The ceiling in our one-storey house is ten feet high. Would it be worth while to lower the ceiling three feet or so to save money on our

Ceilings

heating bill?

Lowering the ceiling won't make any significant difference in your heating bill. However, adding more insulation to your present ceiling *will*. You should have at least 6" of insulation up there, preferably 12".

NEW CEILING OVER TILES

Our living room ceiling consists of perforated acoustic tiles glued to plasterboard. We'd like to change the ceiling without having to remove all the tiles and the cement. Do you have any suggestions?

You can apply a decorative, textured, plaster-like ceiling right over the ceiling tiles if you use a thick mixture of one of the plaster-based, textured paints available at all paint and hardware stores. This can be brushed on in swirls or other decorative patterns and will completely hide the acoustic tile.

PLASTER CEILING STAIN

Our dining room is an addition to our house, and quite a while ago the roof leaked and stained the unpainted plaster ceiling. A white powder has appeared in places, and there are a few fine cracks in the plaster. How should I paint the ceiling over this stain.

Brush off the white powder, fill the cracks with any plaster patching compound, and seal the stained area with a coat of shellac. Then paint as usual. It may take two coats to hide the stain, however.

REMOVING A CEILING

We plan to do some remodelling in our 1½-storey house, and I would like to remove the small ceiling in the upstairs room to create a "cathedral" effect, with the exposed rafters continuing right up to the peak of the roof. Can the present ceiling be safely removed? What would be the best way to insulate the sloping roof?

The ceiling is an important part of the roof structure, and should not be removed without consulting an experienced builder. The ceiling joists are known as collar braces, or collar ties, and they are there to reinforce the sloping roof rafters. (If you visualize the letter "A", you will see how the horizontal bar would keep the two sloping sides from collapsing under a load.)

It is also very difficult to insulate this kind of a roof adequately. The rafters are not thick enough to permit even minimum insulation, plus an air space for ventilation, and still leave enough of the rafters exposed for the effect you want. For this type of construction, the best place for the insulation is on top of the roof, under the shingles, but it's a bit late to do this now, unless you plan to re-shingle the roof.

RE-PAINTING CEILING

I made the mistake of painting our living room ceiling with a high-gloss plastic paint. I would like to re-paint it with a matt finish. Do I have to remove the glossy finish first, and what kind of paint should I use?

The next coat of paint won't stick properly unless you remove the glossy finish with sandpaper first. Any flat paint can then be used—oil-based, alkyd, latex.

UNEVEN CEILING

The ceilings in our new home—on both the main floor and upstairs—are not perfectly flat, but have shallow depressions in them about 6" wide running across the room about 4' apart. What causes this and what can be done about it?

This is the result of poor workmanship on the part of the drywall applicators. The 4' x 8' gypsumboard panels have bevelled or tapered edges that are supposed to be filled with joint compound in three stages to allow for shrinkage and produce an invisible joint. The workmen who did your house apparently rushed the job and did not fill the joints properly.

While this doesn't look very good, it produces no structural weakness in the ceiling and is not covered under your new home warranty. Any attempt to fill the joints after the ceiling has been painted would probably fail, in any case.

VARNISHED CEILING

We covered our cathedral ceiling with tongue-and-groove, clear cedar. We intended to leave this natural, but by mistake it was finished with varnish that was very sloppily applied. We hand-sanded a small area, but this seems to leave a white powder in the wood. Paint remover doesn't work very well, either. How can we take this finish off?

A scraper would be best, I think. Get one with a 3" replaceable blade, and a good supply of blades so that you can keep it sharp. A belt or vibrating sander could also be used (*not* the disc type) but would be very tiring. The white powder is just wood dust and can be removed with a damp cloth. I don't think paint removers are the answer in this situation.

No matter how you do it, this is going to be a tough job.

WATER SPOTS ON CEILING

Our split-level house is 3½ years old. When the weather warmed up after a severe cold spell a number of brownish water stains appeared about 4 inches in diameter on our bedroom ceiling. What can we do to prevent more serious trouble?

It sounds as if the spots are caused by frost melting under your roof and dripping on the ceiling. The frost forms for two reasons: Warm, moist household air is leaking into the attic through ceiling fixtures, a loose hatch cover, or inadequate vapor barrier in the ceiling. Secondly, there is not enough ventilation in the attic to remove the moist air before it can condense and freeze under the cold roof.

You need at least one square foot of screened vent for every 150 square feet of ceiling. Half of the vent area should be along the lower edge of the roof, the other half near the ridge.

Before you repaint the ceiling, seal the water stains with shellac.

REMOVING WAX FROM CEILING

How do I remove green wax that spattered on my kitchen ceiling when I was making candles last Christmas?

If the wax is chilled with an ice cube, it can probably be chipped off with a sharp knife. What remains can be washed off with petroleum solvent (mineral spirits) or paint thinner—this is inflammable, so be careful with it around the stove. If any stain remains on the ceiling, as well it might, all you can do is seal it with shellac and repaint the ceiling.

WET SPOT ON CEILING

We have a wet spot on the ceiling, close to the chimney. The roof flashing around the chimney has been checked, and a new roof put on, but the dampness persists. What could be the cause?

There could be several causes, but the chimney seems like the most likely place to look. If you have a gas furnace and an old, unlined chimney, condensation inside the flue could be the trouble. Again, if it's an old chimney, the mortar may be loose, allowing rainwater to seep in. Repointing the mortar is the answer.

On the other hand, it may not be the chimney at all. It could be frost under the roof in the attic. This melts next to the chimney and drops on the ceiling. Condensation of humid air in the attic is the cause, and ventilation is the cure.

CLEANING A CHARCOAL FILTER

Can you tell me how to clean the charcoal filter in my ductless range hood?

There is usually a separate grease and dust filter that can be cleaned very easily with soap and water. The activated charcoal filter is there to absorb odors. How well it does this is debatable, but the carbon can be reactivated to some extent by heating it in a 450° oven for about 30 minutes. This can only be done if the filter has a metal frame, of course. Replacement filters should be available where the range hoods are sold.

Chimneys

CHARCOAL AIR FILTERS

We have one of those ductless range hoods in our apartment kitchen, the kind that uses a charcoal filter to absorb smoke and cooking odors. The filters are very expensive, however, and I would just like to replace the charcoal but can't locate a source. Can you tell me what I can use instead? There must be a lot of other people who have this same problem.

Pet stores sell granulated charcoal for use in aquarium filters. You can also buy it at garden supply stores, which sell it for use in planters. These will work as well as the charcoal normally used in the filters. Or you can replace the charcoal filter with one made from a washable furnace filter, the fibre mat kind that can be cut to any size.

CHIMNEY BRICKS FLAKING

The bricks on our chimney are flaking badly. We had the mortar joints re-pointed a couple of years ago, but now they are crumbling again and the bricks are still flaking. What causes this and what can we do about it? Would a water repellent treatment help? We have a gas furnace, by the way, if that means anything.

This problem is generally caused by moisture getting into the bricks, then freezing, but the moisture usually comes from inside the chimney, not outside, so a silicone water repellent isn't going to help. Moisture can get in through open mortar joints, or through the space between the brickwork and the flue lining at the top of the chimney, if this isn't protected by a waterproof cap. The most common source of moisture, however, is the condensation of warm, moist furnace gases inside the chimney when they pass over the cold flue lining. This is a common problem with gas furnaces because they produce much more water vapor than oil ones, and the temperature of their flue gases is lower.

Normally, this condensation inside the chimney wouldn't cause any trouble, but very often the mortar joints in the flue lining are eaten away by acids in the flue gases, and this allows the moisture to leak through into the bricks. There isn't any way to repair the joints inside the chimney without taking it apart, so the best thing to do is have a double-walled metal flue installed inside it. A 6" metal vent requires a 7" space inside the present flue lining. If the lining is too small, a chimney expert can knock it out to make room for the metal flue lining.

The chimney will now only serve to hold up the metal vent, but the mortar joints should be filled to strengthen it and to prevent moisture from leaking through the face.

CLEANING METAL CHIMNEYS

We have an airtight wood stove with a double-walled metal chimney, and have decided to buy the equipment so we can clean it ourselves. The stores we have approached give us different advice on what kind of brushes to use. Some say to use a nylon brush because a steel brush will scratch the metal lining. Others say a plastic brush won't remove the creosote. Which should we use?

Even the experts disagree. Several of the chimney manufacturers state in their warranties that steel brushes should not be used, yet one of the largest sells a set of metal brushes to do the job. Company officials admit, however, that these *will* scratch the polished stainless steel lining but claim this does not affect its performance.

Chimney sweeps are also divided in their views on how to clean metal chimneys. Most use polypropylene or natural fibre brushes, but a sweep who has had 40 years' experience in Europe and Canada, and who is widely considered an authority on the subject, maintains that nothing but a steel brush will remove hardened creosote. This is more important, he points out, than preserving the polished finish of the stainless steel liner.

The best remedy, of course, is to prevent the buildup of creosote in the first place by using a stove that is not oversized and burning it correctly. (The use of an insulated *stovepipe* will also help.) If you do this, a brush with natural or plastic bristles may be all you need to keep the chimney clean.

DIRTY CHIMNEY

The concrete block chimney serving our oil furnace is badly soot-stained for about six feet down from the top. Can you tell me how to clean this off?

First I suggest you have the furnace adjusted. It must be burning very badly and wasting a lot of fuel if it's producing soot like this.

You can remove the smoke stains with a stiff brush and a solution of 1/3 cup of trisodium phosphate to a gallon of warm water. TSP is available at most hardware and paint stores.

FROST IN CHIMNEY

We have a fireplace in our living room, but during the winter months we have trouble with frost that builds up inside the chimney and drips down on the fire when we light it. The chimney is on an outside wall and the damper in the fireplace is kept closed when it's not in use. I would appreciate it if you could tell me what causes this problem and what we can do about it.

Humid household air is escaping up the chimney and condensing to form frost on the cold walls of the flue. The first thing to do is to get a tighter fitting damper in the chimney. The second thing to do is to check to see if the humidity in the house is too high. It is if you are also troubled with condensation on the windows during cold weather. The simple remedy for this is to increase the ventilation in the house.

METAL LINER FOR CHIMNEY

We have a gas furnace and there is some trouble with condensation inside the brick chimney. I have been told that I should put in a Type B metal liner. Is this just a galvanized pipe? Can I put it in myself?

No and yes. A Type B, or Class B, metal vent is a double-walled pipe (aluminum inside and galvanized outside) with an insulating air space between them. It is this insulation that prevents the condensation on the inside of the pipe. Type B vent pipe can be purchased from most heating and sheet metal firms. You will probably need a 6" (inside diameter) vent pipe but it is a good idea, and costs nothing, to ask your gas supplier to send an inspector around to advise you on the correct size and placement of the vent, particularly if you want to do the job yourself.

REQUIRED CHIMNEY HEIGHT

We have a 1-storey family room addition extending 12' out from the back of our 2-storey home. It has a low-pitched shed roof. My problem concerns the positioning of a fireplace and chimney in the family room. How tall must the chimney be if it comes up through the roof of the family room 10' from the 2-storey wall of the house? Or should it be father away?

The chimney must be at least 2' higher than any obstruction within 10' of it. Which means that if it is 10' from the 2-storey wall it must be at least 2' higher than the point where the shed roof of the addition meets the house wall. If possible, however, it would be better to move the chimney farther away from the house, perhaps by running it outside the family room wall, and to make it higher than the minimum requirement given above. You can't move the

fireplace chimney *closer* to the house without extending it above the 2-storey roof.

CARE OF CHOPPING BLOCK

What is the correct way to finish, clean and care for a maple chopping block?

No type of furniture finish should ever be applied to a wooden cutting board or chopping block—not varnish or urethane or Danish Oil or linseed oil or shellac or any of these "setting" finishes. Before it is used it should be brushed with cooking oil, and this can be repeated as needed to keep the wood from absorbing moisture and food odors. Wiping the board off with a damp cloth and baking soda will also help to keep it fresh and clean.

Eventually, however, the wood will get marked and stained, but it can be restored very easily by shaving the surface off with a scraper blade. Sandpaper can be used, but it doesn't do as good a job as a scraper, which you can buy at any hardware store. The kind with replaceable blades is best. After the block has been scraped clean, brush it with cooking oil again.

CLEANING

CLEANING ALUMINUM

Can you give me the name of the acid that is used to clean aluminum? I'd like to make my own cleaner.

Most commercial aluminum cleaners contain dilute solutions of hydrofluoric acid or phosphoric acid, or a combination of both, along with a little detergent, grease solvent, and thickeners. Hydrofluoric acid is extremely

Cleaning

dangerous to handle, and is not available to the general public, but phosphoric acid can be obtained at most drugstores. A 5% solution is quite safe to handle and will do a good job in cleaning aluminum. A few drops of detergent will help it spread evenly over the surface of the metal. Mop it on, let it foam for a minute or two, then wipe and rinse off thoroughly. Don't let it remain on the aluminum too long, or it will dull the surface. And never use it on anodized, colored aluminum.

Considering the cost, trouble, and the amount that will be used, however, you're probably better off to use one of the many aluminum cleaners that are available at hardware stores.

CLEANING ALUMINUM SIDING

Our house is faced with white aluminum siding. The two top strips under the eaves and the strip directly under the windows have become dirty, and ordinary cleaners don't seem to do any good. What should we use?

Use a stiff brush and my favorite, all-purpose cleaning solution—one tablespoon of trisodium phosphate (TSP, any paint or hardware store) to a quart of warm water, plus a squirt of detergent. Apply with a long-handled brush and rinse thoroughly.

CLEANING ASBESTOS SIDING

Do you know of any way I can remove dark stains from the asbestos shingle siding on my house? They are particularly noticeable under each window sill.

These stains are probably from dirt in the air, and you should be able to wash them off with a solution of trisodium phosphate (TSP, available at any hardware store)—one heaping teaspoon to a quart of water.

Asbestos shingles can be painted quite easily with any exterior latex paint.

CLEANING BATHROOM TILES

Without success, we've tried several household cleaners to remove a build-up of soap and minerals from the ceramic tile around our bathtub. What do you suggest?

The build-up is probably a deposit of lime from hard water, and this can be dissolved with vinegar.

CLEANING BURNED POTS

I have inherited a very nice set of heavyweight aluminum pots and pans. Some of them are badly caked with burned-on grease and I would like to know how to remove it.

Put the pots and pans in a plastic garbage bag along with a dish of straight ammonia. (Don't put the ammonia in the aluminum!) Tie the bag closed and leave it for two or three days. When the pans are removed you will find that the ammonia fumes have softened even the hardest burned-on grease. A little scraping and the use of a steel wool soap pad should complete the job.

CLEANING CAMEO BROOCH

How can I clean a cameo brooch?

Soak the brooch in a solution of household ammonia to loosen oil grit and film. Wash it in soap and water, rinse and dry. Don't use any harsh cleaners or sharp tools. Even a stiff brush can damage a delicate cameo.

CLEANING COPPER

I have an old copper pot that is practically black with tarnish. What chemical do I use to clean it?

There's an old trick that still works about as well as the modern "miracle" copper-cleaners. Just make a paste out of equal parts of flour and salt moistened with vinegar. Spread this on the tarnished copper. Wash off when the tarnish is removed and polish with any kitchen scouring powder.

CLEANING COPPER PLAQUE

We received a carved, copper wall plaque as a gift. It has a protective coating of some kind, but it's starting to tarnish in several places. How can I re-coat it?

Any of the clear spray lacquers sold at paint and hardware stores can be used for this purpose, but you'll probably have to strip off the present lacquer and clean the plaque first. The remaining coating can be removed with lacquer thinner (any paint or hardware store). There are many good copper cleaners on the market. When clean, wash and buff thoroughly and avoid getting your fingerprints on the copper, then spray with a coat of clear lacquer.

CLEANING COPPERTONE FIXTURES

I have three coppertone light fixtures above my kitchen sink which have turned dark in color. Should I replace them, or can they be restored?

If they are really copper and not just copper-colored paint, clean them with steel wool, then coat them with a clear lacquer spray.

If they are painted, clean them with any liquid household cleaner.

CLEANING CORAL

I brought a large piece of coral back from Florida, and now use it as a doorstop. I was wondering if you could tell me how to clean it and preserve it.

You can clean coral in lukewarm water with a few drops of hand-safe dishwashing detergent and a soft nailbrush. You don't need to do anything to preserve it, except stop using it as a doorstop!

CLEANING CORNING WARE

How do you clean, and keep clean, the inside of a Corning Ware coffee percolator? Nothing seems to take out the stain.

The stain is not in the Corning Ware itself, but in the lime deposit that builds up in hardwater areas if the percolator isn't cleaned thoroughly after use. The lime can be removed by filling the percolator above the stain level with one part vinegar and four parts water, then heating the solution just below the boiling point.

Another treatment that works well is to put about 1 tbsp. of dishwasher detergent in the pot, then fill it with hot water, stirring well. Let stand for an hour or so, then brush out and rinse.

If any stain remains on the surface, moisten a cloth or sponge with a solution of one part household bleach to four parts water, dip it in baking soda and scour out the percolator. Plain baking soda is an excellent material to use to clean out the percolator after each use; it prevents a build-up of discoloration.

CRAYON MARKS ON CONCRETE

My children have used the concrete hearth of our fireplace as a drawing board. How do I remove the crayon marks?

You can wash the crayon marks off with paint *thinner* (not remover), or petroleum solvent (mineral spirits). If a tinge of color still remains after several applications, apply a solution of one part muriatic acid (from any hardware store) to ten parts water. Wear rubber gloves and be careful to keep the solution off the floor, rugs, painted surfaces and, of course, yourself. Rinse thoroughly after the solution stops foaming on the concrete.

CLEANING CUT GLASS

Can you tell me how to remove a whitish film on the inside of a glass decanter I have inherited? I have no idea what the stain is or how long it has been there.

Sometimes a film like this is etched into the surface of the glass, and cannot be removed. You can test for this by scratching the film with the point of a knife; if this doesn't remove it, then it's etched on.

If it can be scratched, it can be removed. It may be a lime deposit from hard water. This can be dissolved with vinegar. If this doesn't work, put a few ounces of full-strength laundry bleach and a handful of sand in the vase and agitate vigorously.

CLEANING DISCOLORED CHINA

I have some valuable old china that has become discolored. Can I remove the yellow stains by soaking them in household bleach?

Such stains can often be removed with lemon juice and salt, or even with a damp cloth dipped in baking soda. If these don't work, try hydrogen peroxide.

CLEANING FIBERGLAS

Is it practical to wash sheer Fiberglas drapes in an automatic washing machine set for delicate fabrics? They can't be dry cleaned, and I find it a real chore to wash them by hand.

Fiberglas drapes can't be put in the washing machine because the tumbling action may damage the fibres—not because of the water temperature. They cannot be dry cleaned for the same reason. Most commercial laundries will wash Fiberglas for you, however.

CLEANING FLOOR POLISHER

How can I clean wax from my floor polisher brushes?

Cleaning

Wash the brushes first in mineral spirits (petroleum solvent) then in detergent and water.

CLEANING FUR COAT

I want to clean some pieces of an old Persian lamb fur coat. Can you tell me a safe way of cleaning it at home?

Cornmeal is an old-fashioned way to clean furs. Just sprinkle it on generously and brush it through. A modern dry shampoo is even better.

CLEANING GOLD BRAID

I would like to know how to clean a tarnished military crest made of gold and silver metallic thread. It is on a blue flannel mess jacket that has been dry cleaned.

You should never send gold braid or other decorations of this material to the dry cleaners. Once metallic thread has tarnished, there isn't much you can do to restore it, but an old naval trick is to rub the tarnished braid with a dry piece of bread.

Most gold and silver braid is now made with a metallized plastic foil that doesn't tarnish.

CLEANING HEARTH

When starting a fire in our fireplace one time, a piece of newspaper rolled out and burned on the fieldstone hearth, leaving a large yellow stain that we cannot remove. It looks awful. Can you help us?

Scrub it with a stiff brush and a solution of one heaping tablespoon of trisodium phosphate (TSP, available at any hardware store) to a quart of warm water.

CLEANING A LAMPSHADE

How can I clean a satin lampshade?

Providing the fabric is sewed on to the frame, not glued, you can safely dip it in warm water containing a little mild detergent. Rinse in plain water, then dry quickly with a fan or an electric hair dryer so the frame won't rust and stain the fabric.

CLEANING HUMIDIFIER PADS

We have a humidifier attached to our furnace, and over the winter the drum pads became encrusted with a hard deposit. They are quite expensive to replace and I understand that there is a solution that will clean them. Can you tell me what it is?

Vinegar will dissolve the lime deposit, but muriatic acid, available at any hardware store, is even cheaper. Soak the pads in a solution of 1 part muriatic acid to 20 parts water.

CLEANING KID GLOVES

Could you please tell me how to clean a pair of white kid leather gloves?

Wash them in mild soap and warm water, keeping the gloves on your hands. Rinse, pat dry on a towel, then remove the gloves, being careful not to stretch the leather. Blow into the gloves to puff them up, and hang them up to dry, away from sunlight and heat. When nearly dry, knead them gently, then put them on and rub them carefully to remove the wrinkles.

RESTORING LAUNDRY TUBS

Our concrete laundry tubs are badly stained on the inside, and I'd like to know how to clean them. I should add that we have a septic tank, and I wouldn't want to use anything that would harm it.

You may be able to remove the stains with a solution of one part muriatic acid (any hardware store) to 10 parts water. Apply this with a stiff brush and rinse thoroughly. The small amount of acid won't hurt the septic tank, in fact it may help neutralize the phosphates from detergents, but be careful to keep it off your skin and clothes.

And if this doesn't remove the stains, it will still put the concrete in perfect condition to be painted with a laundry tub paint.

STAINS ON LEATHER TABLETOP

I have been given an expensive coffee table with a leather top that has been marked by glass rings, spilled drinks, and food stains. How can I remove these, and how should I look after the leather?

Most leather that is used for this purpose is protected with a waterproof plastic finish, but this isn't impervious to all stains and it wears off in time, anyway. Unprotected leather is easily stained and rather difficult to clean. Unless you are very careful you are liable to alter the color of the leather or damage the finish.

A leather tabletop should be cleaned regularly. There are a number of proprietary leather cleaners and saddle soaps on the market, but for casual cleaning you can just use a soft cloth dampened with a solution of mild soap or detergent. The leather should then be patted dry with a clean cloth and given an application of any good, hard furniture wax.

The experts I talked to are reluctant to suggest stain removal treatments that are less than 100% safe, but they did offer the following suggestions.

Sponging with white vinegar will sometimes remove glass rings and water marks. Methyl hydrate or perchlorethylene or naptha, applied with a barely dampened cloth, will remove many oil-based stains. As with fabrics, sponge from the outside of the stain towards the centre. (These solvents can be found at most drug stores.)

It's important to understand, however, that there is a great variety of leather dyes and finishes, and that any of these stain removers may mark or discolor some leathers. The only safe way to use them is to test them first on some very small or inconspicuous area.

If the stains are bad, and won't come off, the easiest remedy is to remove the leather top and replace it. Leatherwork is a popular hobby, and many craft shops carry the materials. The use of a silicone water-repellent finish, as sold for shoes, will reduce the chance of staining.

LEATHER CLEANER

We have a chesterfield and three chairs made of leather, and they are getting very dirty. What should we use to clean them?

There are a number of very good commercial preparations on the market, but any pure, natural soap can be used to clean leather, if you're careful not to let it get too wet. Use a clean cloth, just dampened with the soap solution. Commercial "saddle soap" is better, however, because it contains oils and waxes to soften and preserve the leather. Here's a formula for one you can make yourself:

2 ounces soap powder
½ ounce neetsfoot oil or castor oil
½ ounce beeswax
8 ounces water

Dissolve the soap in the hot water. Heat the neetsfoot oil and wax together in a double boiler (not over an open flame) until the wax melts, then mix and pour into the hot soap solution. Stir until the mixture begins to thicken, then pour into cold cream jars or other containers. Apply with a damp cloth, then buff with a dry one. This should only be used on smooth leather, however, not on suede.

CLEANING DIRTY LUMBER

Our new cedar cottage has dirty footprints all over the inside walls and ceiling where the construction men walked on the lumber. What is the best way to remove it?

The best way is to get the builder to do it. It's his responsibility. The footprints must be sanded or scraped off, and it's a slow, hard job.

CLEANING MAHOGANY CUPBOARDS

Our kitchen cupboards are made of mahogany, and over the years they have become badly soiled where we keep touching them. Cleaners do not seem to remove this; what can we do about it?

The finish may be worn. Remove the finish, sandpaper the discolored areas, and refinish. Either that, or just paint the cupboards.

CLEANING OIL FROM BRICK

How can I clean red bricks and concrete blocks which were splashed with fuel oil?

Petroleum solvent or mineral spirits will remove the surface oil, but where it has penetrated the brick I doubt if you will be able to get it all off.

CLEANING OIL PAINTINGS

Can you tell me a simple, safe method to clean old oil paintings?

Art experts will tell you that it is not advisable for anyone but an expert to attempt to clean and restore a painting. However, if the painting is not valuable, and the surface is in good condition—that is, not cracked or flaking—you can clean off surface dirt with a clean, soft brush or pad of cotton moistened with cleaning fluid. Lay the painting flat on a table and rub it very gently. Do a small area at a time, and work slowly. If the surface appears dull, the gloss can be restored with a delicate application of cream furniture polish.

WASHING OILY CLOTHES

I use olive oil cream as a body rub, and have trouble getting it out of the towels and linen. No matter what laundry powder I use, an oily scum always forms and the linen never seems quite clean. Do you have any suggestions?

Soak the linen and towels overnight in a solution of one teaspoon of lye to three gallons of water to which the customary amount of your laundry powder has been added, then wash as usual.

CLEANING PARCHMENT

We have some parchment lampshades. How do I clean them?

This is an old-fashioned material, and I have some old-fashioned answers. An old recipe book says to rub the parchment with pieces of fresh white bread, or with a cloth dipped in milk.

POLISHING PEWTER

I have some very old pewter that has become dark grey, some pieces almost black, over the years. Can you tell me how to clean it?

You can buy a special pewter polish at most jewelry stores. If you prefer to make your own, for a dull finish (which most old pewter has) use a paste made of rottenstone and cooking oil. Apply with a soft cloth. For a brighter finish, use automobile rubbing compound. Rottenstone and automobile rubbing compound can be found at most hardware stores.

CLEANING PINE CHAIRS

I have some unpolished pine chairs that are dirty. I've been told to use sandpaper to clean them, but that seems an odd way to do it. Isn't there some commercial cleaner I can use?

We're not sure what you mean by "unpolished." If you mean they're unfinished, then sandpaper or steel wool is the best thing to use. If you mean they have a satin finish, they can be cleaned with any liquid household cleaner that is marked as safe for painted surfaces. Or you can use a solution of 2 teaspoons of trisodium phosphate (TSP) in 1 quart of water.

CLEANING SANDSTONE HEARTH

We just built a new house. It has a fireplace with a sandstone hearth that is marked by ashes. How can we remove these without harming the sandstone?

The best way to clean sandstone is with another piece of sandstone. Get a small, flat block, and use it like a scrubbing brush with a little water.

CLEANING A SHAG RUG

Our shag rug has become badly soiled and matted down in front of the chesterfield. How should I clean it?

A shag rug is much more difficult to clean than a short pile rug, but it can be done with several applications of any home rug cleaner if you will rake the pile in different directions for each application in order to clean all sides of the pile. You can buy a shag rake at almost any carpet store; use it to keep the pile from matting.

CLEANING SHEEPSKIN RUG

How can I clean a sheepskin rug?

The safest thing to do is to send it to a dry cleaning firm specializing in furs and leather. A good, old-fashioned remedy is to rub cornmeal into the fur, then brush it out. The cornmeal can be used several times.

You can also use one of the granular or powder rug cleaners.

CLEANING DIRTY SIDING

Our house is finished with knotty pine siding, which has developed black stains under the overlapping edges of the boards. I don't want to have to paint the siding. How can I remove the stains?

This is probably a mildew growth, and can be removed by scrubbing with a solution of 1 quart of chlorine laundry bleach, 1 cup of dishwasher detergent (that's *dishwasher*, not sink detergent), and 3 quarts of water.

CLEANING STARCH FROM IRON

How can I clean dried starch off my iron? I've tried scouring powders, vinegar, and nail polish remover, but none of them work.

Use a fine steel wool pad (#0000). This won't hurt the iron.

CLEANING STONE STEPS

My steps are flat-cut fieldstone. They are quite black and discolored. How do I clean them?

The black discoloration is probably caused by a mold or mildew growth on the stone. It can be removed by scrubbing with a solution of 1 cup of chlorine laundry bleach, 3 cups of water, and ¼ cup of dishwasher detergent. That's *dishwasher* detergent, not sink detergent.

CLEANING STUFFED TOYS

How can I clean stuffed toy animals?

They can be cleaned in a washing machine. If the white synthetic fur has turned yellow, use a powdered bleach, not a liquid bleach. Most stuffed toys are made with synthetic materials that should not be put in the dryer. Hang them up to dry. Stuffed toys can also be cleaned with rug cleaner.

CLEANING SUEDE

The collar of my suede coat gets soiled very quickly, and I'm getting tired of paying $15 or more to have it cleaned. Is there anything I can use to clean the oil stain off the collar myself?

I've been told that the dry powder hair "shampoos" do a very good job on suede. You just dust the powder on the soiled area, rub it in with your fingers, and then brush it off with a wire suede brush. Nuvola is one brand, but any of the dry shampoos will do, I'm sure, and there's no danger of any of them harming the suede.

CLEANING TERRAZZO

Someone made the mistake of mixing mortar on our terrazzo floor, and the lime has left a stain. Is there any way we can restore the original color?

Ordinarily, muriatic acid can be used to remove mortar stains from masonry surfaces, but terrazzo is made with marble chips, and these will be attacked by the acid. A tile or ma-

rble dealer may be able to supply a commercial cleaner that is safe for use on terrazzo, but I think the best thing to do is have it re-polished.

CLEANING A TRUNK

I'd like to know how to go about cleaning and restoring an old cloth-covered, wood-bound trunk.

Sponge it with soap and water, or any of the liquid household cleaners. Sand the woodwork and use steel wool on the metal parts. If the fabric is stained, apply a coat of enamel in the desired color, but thin it with about 10 per cent turpentine or paint thinner. Apply at least two coats of varnish to the woodwork, and protect the cleaned metal parts with a clear spray lacquer. The inside can be re-covered with self-adhesive vinyl.

CLEANING VELVET

The seat and arms of my velvet-covered swivel rocker are getting rather soiled. How can I clean it?

Velvet is a difficult material to clean, because the fibres tend to mat when they are wet. Cotton, acetate, and viscose velvet should be professionally dry cleaned, but nylon velvet can often be safely shampooed at home, then steamed to restore the pile. Any kind of velvet is much easier to clean if it has been given one of the soil-resistant treatments such as Scotch Gard or Zepel. And all upholstery should be cleaned before it gets seriously soiled—it's impossible to remove deeply ingrained dirt or oil discoloration from a piece of fabric while it is still on the furniture.

CLEANING VENETIAN BLINDS

We live in an apartment where venetian blinds are supplied. Although they are very serviceable, it is quite a job keeping them clean. Do you have any suggestions?

You can buy a special three-pronged brush in most hardware and department stores. Insert the prongs of the duster between the slats and you can clean three slats with one stroke. Some vacuum cleaners have special attachments for cleaning these, too.

Cleaning

CLEANING VINYL UPHOLSTERY

We have a white vinyl chesterfield that has picked up some colors from clothing in spots and has also turned slightly yellow. What treatment do you suggest?

Try a solution of chlorine laundry bleach, say one ounce to a cup of water. Apply this with a sponge or cloth, wearing rubber gloves.

CLEANING VENT HOODS

Can you tell me the best way to clean the screen that fits over the vent hood fan above my stove. The grease is gummy and won't wash off with ordinary household cleaners.

Hardware and auto supply stores carry special degreasing solvents that are brushed or sprayed on, then simply washed off.

CLEANING WALLS

Because our fireplace doesn't draw properly, a greasy film has been deposited on the walls and the ceiling and woodwork of our living room. What is the best way to remove this?

A solution of 1 tablespoon of trisodium phosphate (TSP, available at any hardware or paint store) to 2 quarts of water makes an excellent general household cleaner that will cut grease and is safe for painted surfaces. To avoid streaks, start at the bottom of the wall and work up. Clean all surfaces twice, using a fresh solution for the second cleaning, and then rinse with two or three changes of clean water and a new sponge.

CLEANING WHITE BUCKSKIN

We bought a good pair of white buck figure skates for our daughter, and now they've become scuffed and dirty. How can we clean them?

With sandpaper. Then apply a dusting of powdered chalk and brush off the excess.

CLEANING WHITE METAL

I have an 1898 communion set—two goblets, two plates and one tall decanter—that is made of "white metal." It is badly tarnished and I want to clean it to put it on display. Silver polish didn't do any good, but I hesitate to use any of the abrasive cleaners. What should I use?

White metal, also called Britannia metal, is really a high-grade pewter, harder and brighter than the usual alloy. It can be cleaned safely with household scouring powders or even very fine (#0000) steel wool. Silver polish will do for regular maintenance after the tarnish has been removed. Rinse thoroughly after cleaning.

CLEANING WICKER

What is the proper way to clean a wicker chair?

Clean it with a stiff-bristled brush and a warm salt solution to keep it from turning yellow.

CLEANING WOODEN BOWLS

I have some antique wooden dough bowls and a butter bowl and would like to know how to clean and preserve them. I have been told not to put them in water. Is this right?

You can wash them with hot water and a mild detergent, but don't *soak* them in water. A nylon scouring pad is very helpful. After the bowls are clean, wipe them with cooking oil.

CLEANING INTERIOR WOODWORK

The wood in my home is Douglas fir, or gumwood. It was cleaned a number of times with either boiled or raw linseed oil, and turpentine, I think. I've forgotten the formula. Can you tell me what to use?

Douglas fir is not the same as gumwood, so I'm not sure which you have. In any case, if the wood has been given several applications of boiled linseed oil and turpentine, I don't think you should apply any more. The wood will have absorbed enough to seal the surface, and any more is liable to get gummy and collect dirt.

If the wood is dirty, clean it with any of the liquid household cleaners marked as being safe for woodwork and painted surfaces (not all are). If it needs refinishing, I suggest you use a satin urethane varnish. It's a lot less work than rubbing with boiled linseed oil and turpentine and it makes a much tougher finish.

CLEANING YELLOWED FRIDGE

My white refrigerator has become very yellow. Nothing seems to clean it off. Is there anything we can do?

Several treatments can be used. Ordinary household bleach, used full strength, is often successful. Another is automobile rubbing compound, available at any auto supply store. This is a cream wax containing a mild abrasive, and it is used to rub down or smooth out auto body paint. It takes off a tiny film of paint from the surface, and it is presumably this action that removes the yellow discoloration. There is no magic chemical action here; *you* do the work, and on a large item it's a lot. It is an excellent treatment, however, if surface discoloration is the problem. For deeper stains, a bleach would probably work better.

YELLOWING WALLS

For years our house was heated by oil, and during this time I was constantly washing the walls, windows and curtains to remove a yellowish discoloration that quickly reappeared. But over a year ago we had a natural gas furnace put in, and the problem remains. It may even be getting worse. My neighbors don't seem to have this trouble. Can you tell us what is wrong with our house?

Although the furnace is usually blamed in cases like this, it is rarely the cause, as you have found out. It can't be local air pollution, either, or your neighbors would have the same trouble. I'm afraid you'll have to look at your own living habits for the cause. It could be your cooking . . . deep frying or open pan frying will soon coat the walls with an oily film that catches dirt. A good vent hood would be one solution.

But a much more likely cause is heavy smoking. If there are two or three people in the house who smoke heavily, tobacco tars will very quickly stain white walls and curtains and form a film on windows. We found that out when we stopped smoking in our house, and a number of other people have had the same experience.

DAMP CLOSETS

As soon as the cold weather comes, we have trouble with dampness on the outside wall of our bedroom closets. I used two coats of sealer before I painted, and I've tried taping plastic sheet to the outside wall, but still the dampness comes through. Do you have any suggestions?

The dampness isn't coming through the wall. It's caused by condensation due to two things: too much humidity in the house, and too little insulation in the wall. (I would guess that you have trouble with condensation on your windows, too, during cold weather.)

Increasing the ventilation in the house will reduce the humidity. Using louvered doors on the closets will also help. Leaving a light bulb burning in the closet will often warm it up enough to eliminate the condensation, but this is a rather uneconomical solution. The outside wall of the closet can be insulated with sheets of 1'' plastic foamboard, or beadboard, applied with adhesive.

DAMPNESS IN FRUIT CELLAR

We have a large cold storage room for fruits and vegetables opening off the basement of our new home. The ceiling of this room is actually the concrete slab of the front porch. The walls are also concrete. This past winter the temperature in the storage room was often below freezing, even with the one wall vent closed. The room was always damp, and there was frost on the ceiling and walls. Can you tell me how to correct these conditions so we can use the room as it was intended?

Dampness is needed in a cold storage room for fruits and vegetables, and so is ventilation, but the temperature should not be allowed to go below freezing. The recommended temperature range is from 2° to 7° Celsius (36° to 45° F.). To keep within this range you will have to insulate the storage room. The best way to do this is to glue 2'' foamboard directly to the concrete ceiling and to the outside walls down to 2' below ground level. Cut the foamboard into convenient panels, say 2' × 4', and use a caulking gun to run a bead of adhesive around the back edge of each panel. Press this firmly to the wall to make a tight seal and prevent condensation getting behind it.

Some heat will pass through the basement wall into the storage room, but ventilation can be used to control the temperature. Two vents are needed. Because the walls are partly below ground level, both of the vents will be located near the ceiling, but the intake vent should be ducted down to the floor level. The exhaust vent can be fitted with a fan controlled by a thermostat set at the required room temperature, and both vents should have weighted flaps that close automatically when the fan is not operating.

The ideal humidity for most fruits and vegetables is around 85%. This can best be achieved by keeping the floor wet most of the time. The produce should be kept on shelves or raised platforms. Weatherstrip the door as tightly as possible to keep the humidity in the storage room.

FRUIT CELLAR CHILLS BASEMENT

The cold air coming from the fruit cellar in my basement makes the adjoining recreation room very cold. Since I have no use for the fruit cellar, I have decided to insulate it. I can put fibreglass batts on the outside walls, but what should I use on the concrete ceiling, which is really the floor of our front porch?

If you have no plans to use the fruit cellar, why insulate all the walls and ceiling.? Just insulate the wall and seal the door between the cellar and your recreation room.

If you want to use the cellar for storage, however, you can insulate the ceiling with 2″ plastic foamboard applied directly to the concrete with panel adhesive.

CONCRETE

ALKALI vs CONCRETE

My basement walls are crumbling, apparently due to alkali in the soil—the house was built before alkali-resistant cement was available. Can anything be done to prevent further damage?

Various sulphates in the soil, commonly called alkalis, can indeed break down ordinary portland cement concrete. The only way to prevent

further damage is to dig down to the bottom of the foundation walls outside the house, and paint them with tar, asphalt, or other waterproofing membrane.

While you're down there, check the drain tile system around the footings to make sure it is working properly. Poor drainage may be contributing to the problem. The interior walls can then be resurfaced with a concrete patching compound.

REPAIRING CONCRETE BLOCK WALL

We have a solid brick house with a cement block foundation. Some of the blocks are beginning to flake off on the outside between the ground and the bricks. How can we repair this and prevent further trouble?

The concrete block wall should be "parged" or plastered with a cement stucco mix. Use one part cement to three parts sand, mixed with a latex solution instead of plain water. The latex provides a strong bond and permits the stucco to be trowelled on very thin. There are several brands of premixed stucco on the market. Dampen the wall before applying the stucco.

REPLACING A CONCRETE BLOCK

One of the 8″ x 8″x 16″ blocks in our masonry foundation wall has been shattered by a slight accident in our driveway. How can I replace it? The inside of the wall has been panelled as part of our recreation room.

Use a chisel to break the outside of the block into small pieces. Remove these and chisel the hollow core partitions back at least 4″ from the face. Fill the space with a half-block measuring 4″ x 8″ x 16″. Spread mortar on the bottom of the opening and on the sides and top of the block before it's pushed into place. Use a pointing trowel to fill the gaps with more mortar.

DRILLING CONCRETE

We had a new concrete floor put down over the old broken one in our unheated garage. In about three weeks it started to crack in all directions. Why?

Probably because it wasn't thick enough. Such a topping must be at least 3″ thick, and preferably 4″ or more. A special latex bonding solution should also be applied to the old surface before the new one is laid.

DRILLING CONCRETE

I want to drill a lot of holes in the concrete wall of my basement to put up special hangers. I tried using a carbide-tipped bit in my electric drill, but the bit gets dull after three or four holes and it would be expensive to keep buying new ones. Is there any better way to do this?

The easiest way to do this is with a hammer drill. It looks like a regular drill but with the turn of a switch it imparts a powerful hammer action to the bit. The combination of drilling and chipping makes the bit cut much faster and last much longer. You can rent a hammer drill at most tool rental shops.

You may find it more convenient to use a fastening gun that uses blank cartridges to drive special nails and other fasteners into the concrete. The low-velocity, piston-type unit is best for home use. It is safe and easy to use and makes no more noise than an ordinary hammer. These, too, can be rented.

LAYING A CONCRETE DRIVEWAY

I want to lay a concrete driveway and would like to know how thick it should be; how much gravel I need underneath it; and what kind of reinforcing I should put in the slab, wire screen or steel rods?

Contrary to popular opinion, a bed of gravel is not necessary under a concrete slab. It was once thought that this would prevent frost heave, but since water can collect in the gravel it is more likely to cause frost heave than prevent it. The best base for concrete is a reasonably level bed of firm, undisturbed earth.

Reinforcement serves no purpose in a slab on grade, either, according to the Portland Cement Association, although it was once believed to strengthen the slab and prevent cracking, and old ideas die hard. Slabs larger than 16 feet or so will crack anyway due to shrinkage of the concrete as it dries. The practice today is to put "control joints" in the concrete at least every 16 feet. These must extend one-quarter of the depth of the slab, and are either cut with a grooving tool and trowel while the concrete is soft, or with a power saw and a carbide blade after the concrete has set.

The recommended thickness for a driveway that will hold only passenger cars is 4 inches. If it must accommodate trucks, it should be 5 inches thick. You should use a 3,500-pound, air-entrained concrete mix.

EXTERIOR CONCRETE FINISH

After our new house was completed, the builder applied a thin cement wash to the concrete foundation walls above the ground. I would like to do some more of this. What does it consist of, and how do I put it on?

That would probably have been nothing more than a thin mixture of Portland cement powder and water. No surface preparation is necessary other than brushing it clean and wetting it down before applying the cement wash with a brush.

For a more decorative finish, you can use any exterior latex paint.

FROST DAMAGE TO FOUNDATION

We're planning to build a vacation cottage up north. Instead of just having a crawlspace under it, we would like to excavate and put in a full basement. Now we've been told that unless the cottage is heated all winter the concrete walls and floor may be cracked by the frost. Is this true?

According to the Portland Cement Association, there is no danger of this happening to poured concrete as long as there is good drainage around the foundation footings and under the floor slab.

First make sure that the basement floor will be above the winter water level of the soil in your area. (Your neighbors may be able to give you some information on this.)

Use an air-entrained concrete mix that will withstand freezing temperatures. Install drainage tile around the footings and connect this to a suitable runoff point. Instead of backfilling with the excavated soil, fill the trench to within a foot of the surface with gravel, then top with heavy clay soil built up around the foundation to direct surface water away from the house.

CONCRETE DRIVEWAY BREAKING UP

Last summer I put in a concrete driveway and power-trowelled the surface. It was a beautiful job. This spring when the snow melted large areas of the trowelled surface broke up and flaked off. I think this was caused by road salt. How can I repair it?

Concrete that is properly mixed, poured and finished will not be damaged by road salt. Just look at your city sidewalks; they're exposed to a lot more salt than your driveway but they don't break up like this. Improper finishing is the

Concrete

cause of your problem, and that beautiful trowelling work is the real villain.

Trowelling puts a smooth, dense skin on the concrete and is useful for industrial floors and similar applications where a very smooth finish is desired, but you don't want this on a driveway. There are two other reasons why trowelling is not recommended on outdoor paving. It breaks up the bubbles in air-entrained concrete that protect it from frost damage, and it can trap a layer of water under the surface, separating the trowelled finish from the concrete below. As a result, the surface layer delaminates and flakes off.

The proper procedure for finishing a driveway is to strike off and level the freshly-placed concrete with a straight 2 x 6, a foot or two longer than the width of the driveway, then immediately smooth it with a darby or float (a flat board with a handle) before any free water appears on the surface. After the surface water has evaporated and the concrete is stiff enough to sustain a footstep with only a slight indentation (no more than ¼") use a small wooden hand float about 12" long to produce a lightly textured surface. For a rougher finish, brush the surface with a broom. Keep the concrete damp for at least three days so it will harden completely.

To repair the damaged areas you will have to remove all the loose concrete, which can be located by tapping the surface with a hammer and listening for the hollow sound. Break up these areas with a 4- to 6-pound sledgehammer and remove all the pieces. Brush the surface clean and fill the depressions with one of the concrete patching materials available from your building supply dealer. You'll probably need a lot, so buy a brand that comes in large packages, such as 45-pound sacks.

A free folder on the construction of concrete driveways, sidewalks and patios is available from regional offices of the Portland Cement Association.

DRIVEWAY TOO SMOOTH

Last summer my husband poured a concrete driveway on the slope up to our garage. He worked long and hard trowelling it to get a smooth finish. The trouble is, he did too good a job. The surface is so smooth that even the slightest rain makes it slippery, and during snowy weather it was very difficult to get up the driveway. At this point we are prepared to break it up and start over, but I am writing to see if you have any other suggestions before we undertake this drastic remedy.

Some tool rental firms carry a gasoline-pow-

ered device called a concrete plane that can be used to cut grooves across the width of your driveway. The grooves are about ⅛" wide and should be spaced about ½" apart. The plane will cut 10 grooves at a time, and if it's sharp enough you should be able to do an average sized driveway in a day for a rental charge of about $35.

CONCRETE FLAGSTONES

I would like to make a walk from the house to the garden. A concrete walk would not suit the garden, and an authentic flagstone walk would be rather expensive. Is there an inexpensive type of walk I could make?

You can cast your own flagstone in concrete quite easily and most inexpensively. Basically, all you need is a shovel, a trowel, some 3" wide sheet metal strips, and cement. First, stake a garden hose into position to establish the desired curve of the walk. Remove the sod, and save some for filling in later. Form molds from the sheet metal strips by wiring the ends together, and bending the band of metal into irregular shapes to resemble flagstones. Fit these molds into the curved outline of the walk just like puzzle pieces, but spacing them approximately 2" apart. Push them into the soil about 1".

To prepare concrete: one measure of cement, two of sand and three of pea gravel is a good mix or, if you prefer, use ready-mixed concrete. In northern areas, air-entrained concrete should be used. Fill the molds with concrete, tamp and level (a little crown is desirable so the stones will shed water). Keep them damp for three days, then remove the molds by snipping the wired ends. You can re-use the molds and, in this way, build your walk in stages. (However, remove only enough sod to accommodate the actual number of stones to be laid at one time.)

Finally, scoop away some of the soil between the stones and replace with the sod you set aside, keeping it approximately ¾-inch below the top level of the stones. When you have finished, you will be amazed at the authentic appearance of your new "flagstone" walk.

CONCRETE FLOOR DAMP

I have a glassed-in side verandah with a concrete floor that seems to be damp and bothers my arthritis. How can I get rid of this dampness?

Mop fibrated asphalt foundation coating on the

concrete floor in two layers and lay staggered 2" x 3" wood sleepers in the second coat at 16" centers. Lay a ⅝" plywood sub-floor on top of the sleepers and nail securely. We suggest you use an indoor-outdoor carpet on top of this. (A sheet of 6-mil polyethylene film can be used in place of the asphalt coating.)

DUSTY CONCRETE FLOOR

The cement dust from our concrete floor is very bothersome. Is there something wrong with the floor?

Concrete that has been properly mixed, placed and cured will not powder like this, but unfortunately a lot of concrete floors do. Your building supply dealer can show you a number of concrete sealers, or you can use any of the new concrete floor paints. The cheapest treatment, however, is a solution of the ordinary waterglass that grandma used to preserve eggs. You can still get it at some hardware stores. Clean the concrete thoroughly to remove dirt and dust. Then brush on a solution of one part ordinary waterglass (sodium silicate) to four parts water. When this has *dried thoroughly*, scrub down with water, then apply a second coat of the waterglass solution. On very porous concrete, a third coat may be necessary.

You can't paint over waterglass, however. If you think you may want to paint or tile the floor later, you should use a magnesium fluosilicate sealer, available at your building supply dealer.

CONCRETE FLOOR COLOR

You recently recommended using a pigmented stain on a concrete patio. Would this be satisfactory on a basement floor?

A stain wouldn't be very good for a basement floor, because some of the pigment wears off and could be tracked through the house. A concrete floor paint would be much better. It gives a smooth finish that is easy to keep clean.

CRACKS IN FLOOR SLAB

We poured a concrete slab floor in our basement about a year ago. It measures 20′ × 45′ and is 5″ thick on 6″ of gravel. A good quality mix was used and the slab was kept damp for several days to cure properly. About three months later hairline cracks began to appear on the surface, and now they seem to be getting larger. We have an automatic sump pump that removes water from under the floor but

are afraid that it may still leak through the cracks. Can you tell us what caused the trouble and what we can do about it?

It is natural for concrete to shrink as it hardens, and a floor of that size requires at least three "control joints"—one every 15′. These are cuts extending one quarter the depth of the slab and filled with a flexible caulking compound. As the slab shrinks it will crack only at these joints instead of randomly across the face.

Obviously it's too late to do anything about this now, but I don't think you have much to worry about if there are only hairline cracks. Because builders seldom bother to put control joints in basement floor slabs, such cracks are common and, fortunately, they rarely cause any trouble.

If you want to paint the floor, the cracks can be filled by brushing them with a mixture of portland cement and water—about the consistency of heavy cream. Dampen the cracks first.

CONCRETE FLOOR CRUMBLING

I had a new concrete floor poured in our basement, but I don't think the contractor did a very good job. I'm continually sweeping up sand and cement. Is there something I can put on to harden it?

That's going to be an expensive repair job! Either the concrete mix contained too little cement, or it was incorrectly laid, with excessive trowelling and screeding before it had time to set. In any case, the faulty concrete will have to be broken up, removed and replaced with a new poured floor. If I were you I'd sue the contractor who did it!

POURING A GARAGE FLOOR

I am going to build a wood frame, 2-car garage next spring and would like to know if frost-deep footings are required under the concrete slab, and whether steel reinforcing mesh is needed. Any other information you can give me will be appreciated.

The concrete slab requires neither footings nor reinforcing. And contrary to popular belief it doesn't need a layer of gravel underneath it, either. Just dig out the soil to the depth required, leaving the bottom relatively smooth but undisturbed and naturally compacted. The slab should be 4″ thick, expanding to 6″ at the edges. To achieve this, simply slope the excavation around the perimeter of the slab, starting about 18″ in from the edge. Use a 3500 psi (25

Concrete

megapascals), 6% air-entrained concrete mix.

To prevent random cracking due to the natural shrinkage of concrete as it cures, slabs larger than 15′ should have control joints—grooves 1″ deep and about ⅛″ wide—cut in the partially set concrete with a grooving tool, or with a masonry saw after the concrete hardens. Since your slab will be about 24′ square, it should have two control joints crossing at right angles through the center point. A roof span of that size probably will also need a central beam with supporting posts, and these should rest on concrete pads at least 6″ thick and 12″ square.

CONCRETE FLOOR PAINT

Shortly after I painted our basement floor with (a well-known brand of concrete floor paint) I noticed that a white powder was forming in one area. When I brushed this off, the paint came with it, so I cleaned the area and repainted it. Now it's happened again. The floor had been down for about 13 years and seemed perfectly dry when I painted it. Would it be better to put floor tile down?

The white powder that's lifting the paint off is "efflorescence" and it's caused by moisture coming up through the floor and bringing dissolved salts with it, which are left on the surface when it evaporates. This moisture problem will interfere with anything you try to put down . . . tile, paint, or wood.

Concrete floor paints will hold back some moisture, but not always enough to prevent this problem. Try to find the source of water. It may just be a misdirected downspout, or ground that has settled around the house, directing water towards the foundation walls, instead of away from them.

At the worst, you'll have to dig down to the footings all around your house and repair the drainage system.

CONCRETE FLOOR SWEATING

Our house has a concrete floor covered with tile. For about a week during the hottest part of the summer the floor is damp. Will this do any harm to our rugs? How can we remedy the problem?

High humidity causes condensation on the cool floor slab, and the best remedy is to close the windows and use a dehumidifier or an air conditioner. If the floor is only damp for a few days I don't think it will damage the rugs, but if it lasts much longer than that mildew might develop in the jute backing. The use of a foam rubber underpad would prevent this, however.

CONCRETE FOOTINGS

How deep should concrete footings be dug in the ground?

All concrete footings must extend below the frost level which can range from a few inches to a few feet, depending on where you live. Check with your municipal building department.

FOUNDATION CRACKED

I purchased a new home about eight months ago. During a heavy rainfall after we moved in, a crack appeared in the basement wall, from floor to ceiling. The contractor came and patched it on the inside. Now another rainstorm has caused a second crack to appear on the opposite wall of the basement, and both cracks leak badly. Is this normal for a new house?

No. Dry, hairline cracks in the surface of a concrete foundation wall are not unusual, but cracks that extend through the wall and allow water to leak in are a sign of some construction fault, and may turn out to be very serious indeed.

At best, it may just be that the earth has settled a bit under the foundation, and now has stopped. If so, the crack should be repaired *from the outside* by chiselling it out about 1″ wide, and tapering in about 2″, then filling it with one of the concrete patching compounds. It should then be covered with a layer of fibrated asphalt roofing compound, a strip of fibreglass tape 6″ wide, and another layer of asphalt.

It is quite possible, however, that the earth was soft under the footings, or that it contains a lot of organic matter that will continue to decay and settle. In either case the cracks will get worse, the foundation will separate, and serious structural problems will develop in the rest of the house. Your 5-year warranty should cover all of this damage.

GREASE STAINS ON CONCRETE

Could you please tell me how I can remove barbecue grease stains from our concrete patio?

Make a paste of powdered chalk and petroleum solvent (mineral spirits) and spread it on the stains about ¼" thick. Cover this with a sheet of plastic food wrap taped down around the edges. Let this stand for a couple of hours, then remove the plastic and let the chalk mixture dry completely. Brush off. Repeat if necessary.

LEAKS IN CONCRETE WALL

I have trouble with water leaking through the holes in my basement wall where the wire form ties went through. How can I stop the leaking?

Such leaks can usually be stopped by chipping the holes out, breaking off the wire as deep as possible, and then filling the holes with a quick-setting hydraulic cement, such as Quick Plug, Water Plug, and Kwik Plug. These are simply mixed with water into a putty-like consistency, formed into a cone shape, and crammed firmly into the dampened hole and held there with the palm of the hand for 3 or 4 minutes until they set. The excess can then be sliced off with a putty knife and smoothed around the edge of the hole.

CONCRETE TOO LIGHT

I had a contractor redo a section of my concrete walkway about eight months ago. It looked a lot lighter than the old section when it was poured, but I was told it would darken as it dried. Instead of that it got lighter, and appears almost white now compared to the original section. It has also started to flake off. Altogether, it looks pretty bad. Do you have any suggestions?

It's natural for different concrete mixes to vary somewhat in color—portland cement itself varies in color from one manufacturer to another—but there shouldn't be as much difference as you describe. Too much water in the mix will lighten the color of concrete, however, and this could also be the reason for the flaking or "spalling". A new topping is the only remedy, but it will still be very difficult to get a good match with the old concrete.

OIL MARKS ON CARPORT

Oil dripping from the engine of our car has left a large dirty patch in the center of our carport, where the children like to play on a rainy day. How can I get this off the concrete?

Scrape off as much as you can, then spray or pour on one of the degreasing compounds sold by all auto supply dealers and most hardware stores. Brush this in thoroughly, allow to stand for 15 minutes or so, and then hose off. Repeat if necessary.

PAINTING CRACKED CONCRETE

There are a number of hairline cracks in my basement floor. Can I paint over these, or do I have to fill them first? If so, what should I use?

If a crack is visible, then it's too large to be covered by paint, and must be filled. Wet the cracks thoroughly, then brush on a thin mixture of straight Portland cement and water, working it into the cracks as much as possible. Alternatively, you could use one of the pre-mixed plaster patching compounds, applied with a putty knife. Sand smooth before painting.

CONCRETE PATIO PAINT

The top layer of our concrete patio was colored by the addition of pigments to the cement. In time this faded and began dusting, and I decided to use a concrete paint that was supposed to harden the surface and be very durable. I followed application instructions to the letter, but the finish was dangerously slippery when wet, and now it is flaking off and looks terrible. I don't want to have to paint the patio every year; what should I use?

I know of no really successful concrete patio paint. They all wear off, flake off with weathering, or fade. You are better advised to leave the concrete in its natural finish, or apply a pigmented shingle stain. Remove the remaining paint with commercial paint remover (washable type) or lye (1 can to 2 quarts of water).

PAINTING NEW CONCRETE

We are moving into a new home and want to paint the basement floor. We've been told to let the concrete cure for two months before we

paint it, but someone else has said we have to wait six months. What is the correct thing to do?

The waiting period—to let the concrete dry thoroughly before it's painted—lasts only three or four weeks after the house has been closed in and heated. You can test for dampness by laying a rubber mat on the floor for 24 hours or so. If you can see moisture underneath when you lift it up, the floor is not yet dry enough to paint.

Although not essential, it's a very good idea to etch the floor before painting. Wet the floor, then brush on a solution of one part muriatic acid to five parts water. Rinse thoroughly and allow to dry for at least 48 hours before painting. Be careful to keep the muriatic acid (a commercial grade of hydrochloric acid) away from your clothes, skin, metal, and painted surfaces.

REINFORCED CONCRETE

Some small cracks are beginning to appear in the poured concrete foundation walls and basement floor of our new house. We have learned that steel reinforcing rods were not used by the contractor. Do you think we should take him to court about this?

No. Steel reinforcing is rarely used in house foundations or floor slabs, and is not required by the building codes. Some engineers think it might be a good idea, but the cost would be far out of proportion to the limited, and questionable, benefit. Even concrete block foundation walls are not reinforced, and they're not nearly as strong as poured concrete, yet problems are very rare. Hairline cracks are caused by the natural shrinkage of concrete as it cures, and do not affect its strength. Larger cracks should be filled and sealed, however.

RESURFACING CONCRETE

The concrete floor of my garage is pitted and dusting badly in places. There are patches a foot or more in diameter and an inch deep, caused by salt dripping off the car. Is it possible for a home handyman to resurface a concrete floor like this? And if so, how should it be done?

To start with, this must have been a poor concrete job. Properly prepared and finished concrete would not do this. However, it is quite possible for you to patch and repair it yourself, although a complete new topping is a major undertaking.

First clean the surface thoroughly with water and a stiff brush to remove dirt and loose concrete. Oil spots should be sprinkled with trisodium phosphate (TSP) or one of the degreasing compounds sold at auto supply and hardware stores. These should be brushed in, then hosed off.

Etch the concrete with a solution of one part muriatic acid to 10 parts water (or a stronger solution if recommended on the label). Holes can now be filled with any of the latex-cement concrete patching materials. Mix and apply as directed, but keep the patches damp for at least two days to allow the cement to cure properly. This can best be done by covering the fresh patches with polyethylene film and, if necessary, sprinkling them with water occasionally.

To prevent further dusting of the concrete floor, it can be sealed with an application of 1 part boiled linseed oil to 1 part kerosene or petroleum solvent. Allow this to sink in for about an hour, then wipe off any surplus. An alternative treatment is a solution of sodium silicate, or waterglass, . . . which is excellent but difficult to find. Brush on a solution of 1 part waterglass to 4 parts water. Allow this to dry thoroughly, scrub down with water, then apply a second coat. Very porous concrete may require a third coat.

CONCRETE vs ROAD SALT

The concrete floor in my garage was badly pitted, presumably by road salt, and I had a new concrete floor put down. Now, just a year later, the new floor is also flaking and pitting badly. What can I do to protect the concrete from salt?

The problem is not caused by the salt but by a poor concrete job. Concrete that is properly mixed and applied will not be damaged in this way. You only have to look at downtown city sidewalks that have been exposed to heavy concentrations of road salt for five or ten years, say. You will see little evidence of pitting or spalling because they used a 3,500-pound, air-entrained concrete mix, did not trowel the surface until the concrete had begun to set, and kept it damp for at least three days to let it cure properly.

Brushing the concrete with a mixture of 1 part boiled linseed oil to 1 part kerosene or petroleum solvent will help to protect it from road salt, but it won't really compensate for a poor concrete job.

RUST STAIN ON CONCRETE

The iron railing around my front porch has made rust stains on the concrete steps. How can I remove the stains?

Wet the stains and sprinkle them with oxalic acid crystals, available from any drug store. Brush in, let stand until the stain is gone, then wash off.

For deeper or more stubborn rust stains you can use one part sodium citrate to six parts water. Ammonium citrate will work faster than sodium citrate, but may injure polished surfaces.

SEALING CONCRETE

We are moving into a new house and would like to know what to put on the garage floor to prevent oil and grease from staining it.

There are various brand name products that will seal and harden the surface of concrete, and these are available at building supply stores. An effective and inexpensive alternative, however, is simply boiled linseed oil and kerosene in equal quantities. Clean the concrete thoroughly first, allow to dry, then brush on a coat of the diluted linseed oil. After one hour, wipe off any wet patches with a dry cloth.

CONCRETE STEPS CRUMBLED

Late in the fall we poured our concrete steps and did not cover them against freezing. Later, we used salt to melt the ice on the steps. This spring, part of the steps have crumbled away. How can we repair them?

It sounds as though your concrete steps froze before they had a chance to harden. I don't think the salt was the cause of your trouble. Concrete should not be poured when the temperature is below 40°F.

You can repair your crumbled section by cleaning off all loose concrete and washing the part to be repaired with a stiff brush and water.

Buy a concrete patching compound and use as directed to build up your steps to the original condition. If much of the steps have crumbled away, you will have to use form boards to hold the new concrete to shape until it sets.

REPAIRING CONCRETE SLAB

Last fall we poured a concrete slab for a shed we plan to erect in our back yard. Unfortunately the temperature dropped below freezing before the concrete had hardened, and now the surface of the slab has started to flake off. Can you tell me how to put a new surface on this slab?

If you had used air-entrained cement for the concrete mix you probably wouldn't have had any trouble. Now you must remove all of the flaking surface. The best way to do this is with a 2- or 3-pound hammer. Go over the entire surface to loosen any areas that may appear to be sound but are really cracked. Brush and wash off all loose material, then apply a new topping, using one of the latex-cement patching materials that are sold at all building supply stores. You'll need quite a bit, so get one that comes in large packages. These materials can be spread very thin.

TILING A CONCRETE PATIO

We have a concrete patio about 10′ × 12′ just outside our dining room, and I would like to pave it with unglazed, red quarry tile. What should I use to stick the tile to the concrete and to fill the joints? Any other information you can give me will be appreciated.

If you live in a cold area you will need to use frost-proof tile. Most quarry tile is made for indoor use and can't withstand temperature extremes. Then you must see that the concrete deck is sloped so that water runs off. If there are any low areas, they should be filled with a concrete patching material before tiling.

A professional would probably use a special epoxy adhesive, but this is not recommended for the home handyman. One of the "thin-set" mortars would be best, preferably a dry, pre-mixed type that only needs water. But you can also do a good job with one of the concrete patching materials sold at hardware and building supply stores. It takes about ⅔-pound of dry mix for every square foot of patio, or about 80 pounds in your case, so choose one that comes in large packages.

For best results, etch the surface of the concrete with 1 part muriatic acid to 5 parts water before laying the tiles. To find out how many you will need and the spacing between them (between ¼″ and ½″), lay a dry run of tiles in both directions. Mark the spacing of the tiles on a layout stick made from a piece of 1 x 2 about 4′ long.

Apply the mortar to a few square feet of the patio at a time starting in a corner, using a ³/₈″ notched trowel. Lay the tiles in the mortar, checking the spacing with your layout stick, then press each tile in place firmly, tapping it with the handle of the trowel to level it. Use a string or carpenter's level to check the grade.

The joints should be filled with grey quarry tile grout, which is also available premixed. You will need from ½ to ¾ pound of dry grout mix for each square foot of patio. Mix according to directions, and use a rubber spatula or similar tool to force it into the joints and smooth it off level with the tile surface. Let this set for a few minutes, then sprinkle dry mix over the joints and rub in using a burlap pad. Sweep off the cement dust and wipe the surface of the tiles with wet burlap until it is clean.

Keep the patio covered with wet burlap for three days to let the mortar set properly. Wash any remaining cement dust from the surface. If necessary, brush with a solution of 1 part muriatic acid to 10 parts water and rinse thoroughly.

TILING ROUGH CONCRETE FLOOR

I wanted to lay self-stick asbestos tiles in the basement of our new house, but the floor is very rough and the tiles won't hold. What kind of adhesive can I use to make these tiles stick?

If the floor is too rough for the tiles to lay flat, adhesive isn't going to help. This sounds like a very poor concrete finishing job, and I suggest you try to get the builder to repair it. He can do this with an electric-powered grindstone, the kind used for polishing terrazzo.

BASEMENT WALLS FLAKING

My basement walls are of poured concrete construction, about 25 years old. They seem to be flaking off. A very thin layer of cement starts to whiten and bubble, then crumbles into dust when touched. Is there anything I can put on the concrete to preserve it?

I don't think the concrete is flaking. It sounds more like an efflorescence problem. This is a white powder that builds up on the surface of damp concrete. It may look as if the cement is crumbling but it actually consists of alkali salts that are leached out of the concrete and left on the surface when the moisture evaporates.

It's often the only sign of a moisture problem in a concrete wall, but it's unmistakable. If there's very little moisture coming through, one of the waterproofing paints may stop it, but from your description it appears unlikely that ANY paint would adhere to the concrete.

The only cure is really outside, where faulty or inadequate drainage is the cause. Check first to see if the earth has settled around the foundation wall, causing rainwater to run towards the house, instead of away from it. This can be cured by building up the earth. Make sure that downspouts are directed well away from the house, too. If none of these are the cause, you'll have to dig down to the foundation footings to check the drainage tile and

apply a waterproof coating to the outside of the basement wall.

CONCRETE OVER WOOD

My verandah floor is wood and is solid. Can I pour concrete over it?

It is not good practice to pour concrete on wood floors. Not only would the concrete crack, but the wood under it would rot in a very short time. If your wood is in good condition, it would be a better idea to repaint the floor.

CONDENSATION

CONDENSATION—CAUSES AND CURES

During the winter our windows drip so much we have to put towels on the sills to soak up the water...

A black mold growth forms in the upper corners of our bedroom walls during very cold weather...

The wardrobe closet on the outside wall of my bedroom is cold and musty, and mildew is getting into the clothes...

Frost forms on our aluminum window frames, then drips down the wall when it melts ....

All these troubles are caused by the same problem—condensation due to too much humidity in the house during cold weather.

Most people are confused about where the moisture comes from. Some think it's leaking in around the windows, because that's where they see it first. Many people find it hard to accept the fact that the moisture originates within the house, from such normal activities as washing, bathing, cooking—even breathing.

Unless this humidity is removed by ventilation, it soon builds up to the point where condensation will begin to form on any cool surface, the same way it forms on a cold bottle when you take it out of the fridge. Windows are usually the coldest surface in a house, but if the humidity in the house is high enough, and the outside temperature is low enough, condensation will form on walls and other surfaces as well. Another factor is air circulation, the lack of which causes increased condensation behind drapes and inside closets.

The amount of humidity you can have in your house depends on the outside temperature. When the outside temperature is -7° Celsius (20°F), condensation will begin to form on double-glazed windows if the humidity is as high as 40%. At 18° Celsius (0°F), the indoor humidity should be no higher than 30%.

If you have single-glazed windows, without storm panes, the humidity must be even lower—no more than 15% when the outside temperature is -18°C (0°F). Triple-glazed windows, on the other hand, will permit a higher humidity level than double-glazed or storm windows, but condensation will still form on them if the humidity in the house is high enough.

There's no need to measure the humidity level, however. All you have to do is watch your windows. When they begin to steam up, you've got all the humidity your house can stand. If you have a humidifier, turn it off. Chances are you won't need it at all.

The basic cause of excessive humidity is lack of ventilation. We're building our houses much tighter today than we used to. We're also using more electric heating, which doesn't provide the ventilation produced by a fuel-burning furnace. And because of increasing fuel costs, we're reluctant to open windows even when we know the house needs freshening.

Ventilation replaces humid household air with relatively dry outside air. In the average home the air needs to be changed completely about once every two hours to control humidity, eliminate odors and supply fresh air for the occupants and the furnace. Obviously this wastes heat, but there's no other way to lower the humidity unless you're prepared to change your living habits, such as reduce the number of baths the family takes. Very seldom does the excess humidity come from a source that can be corrected, such as an unvented clothes dryer or a stack of damp firewood in the basement.

Attic or roof vents are no help, incidentally; they don't ventilate the living areas of the house.

A dehumidifier won't do any good, either. It can only reduce the humidity to about 55%, and that's much too high to prevent condensation during cold weather.

The simplest way to ventilate a house, of course, is to open a window. Lighting a fire in the fireplace will also help. So will installing an exhaust fan in the kitchen or bathroom, where most of the household humidity originates. An exhaust fan won't work properly, however, unless the outside air can get into the house somewhere else, so you may still have to open a window.

To overcome the problem of cold drafts, those who have warm air heating systems can install an outside air duct into the cold air return plenum of the furnace, which then filters and heats the air before distributing it through the house. A manual damper in the duct will allow you to adjust the amount of fresh air that comes in.

You can install one of these yourself for about $10. Also available is a commercial model with a thermostatically-controlled damper that keeps the outside air duct closed when the furnace isn't on.

But however you do it, the important point is that increasing the ventilation of your house is the sure cure for condensation problems.

There's an interesting footnote to this explanation of condensation problems. Since household humidity is lowered by bringing in relatively dry outside air, it follows that excessively dry air in the house is caused by *too much* ventilation. And the best cure for that is not a humidifier, but weatherstripping and caulking to reduce air leakage. This will not only increase the humidity in your house but also reduce your heating costs.

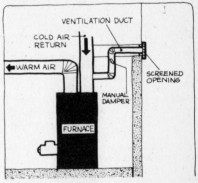

CONDENSATION IN THE ATTIC

Two years ago I put more insulation under our attic floor. I took up the rough floor boards, removed the loose fill insulation, and put down 4" fibreglass batts, then replaced the loose fill insulation. I covered the floor boards with heavy sheet vinyl, stapled in place.

Before, we used to get a lot of frost under the roof, but there is much less now. Instead, we are getting a great deal of condensation under the vinyl flooring, and it is causing the paint to peel off the bedroom ceiling below. Can you tell me what I did wrong?

The vinyl flooring is acting like a vapor barrier, trapping moist air from the house below the

Condensation

floor, where it condenses and drips through the insulation on to the ceiling.

You should remove the vinyl flooring so that the moist air can escape into the attic through the floor boards. Improved ventilation in the attic will prevent the formation of frost under the roof. You need at least one square foot of screened vent for every 150 square feet of ceiling.

CONDENSATION ON BASEMENT FLOOR

Our house is three years old and last year we finished the basement floor with three coats of paint. This year, for the first time, we have noticed condensation around the outer edges of the floor during hot, humid weather. We were planning on finishing the basement this winter, but now we're afraid the condensation on the floor will cause problems. What is your advice?

The concrete is cooler than the air during the hot summer months because it is below ground level, and this causes condensation to form on it. Before you painted the floor, the condensation was absorbed by the concrete; now it just sits on the surface. A simple remedy for this is to put a dehumidifier in the basement. There's no reason why you can't finish it as planned.

CONDENSATION ON BASEMENT WALL

When I finished my basement, I painted the concrete block walls with bituminous paint and then applied polyethylene sheet to prevent leakage. I then put a 2 x 4 stud wall from floor to ceiling and installed 3″ insulation batts. The walls were finished with wood panelling. The problem I am having is that condensation forms on the foundation wall behind the polyethylene and runs onto the floor, staining the bottom of the wood panelling.

You put the polyethylene vapor barrier in the wrong place. Its purpose is to prevent the moist air of the house from reaching the cold surface. It should have gone on the warm side of the insulation—on the room side, on top of the 2 x 4s. What you will have to do now is take off the wood panelling and apply an unbroken vapor barrier film on the stud wall. Use polyethylene tape to seal all seams in the vapor barrier. Then put the wood panelling back.

STORM WINDOW SWEATING

We live in a new home that is electrically heated. Since the cold weather has arrived we have experienced severe sweating on the inside of the outside storm pane of all our windows, although the bedroom windows seem the worst. I have been told that we need more ventilation between the panes, but I don't want to start drilling holes in the outside frame until I know if this is the right answer. What do you suggest?

The main problem seems to be leakage around the inside window, allowing warm, humid air to reach the cold outside pane. I don't know how your windows are constructed, but anything you can do to seal the inside window will help.

Some ventilation of the air space between the inside and outside pane is desirable, but not very much because this also cools the inside window and soon you would be getting condensation on that.

The third thing you can do to solve this problem is reduce the humidity in the house by increasing the ventilation. Electrically heated houses tend to get more humid than those heated with fuel-burning furnaces because they lack the ventilation provided by the chimney. Kitchen and bathroom vent fans are recommended.

CONDENSATION ON TOILET BOWL

I know the answer to condensation on a toilet tank is to insulate the tank or put a drip tray under it, but what can one do about condensation on the toilet bowl? If I need to put in a new toilet bowl, this will be an expensive problem.

I think the problem is caused by a water supply that is very cold, and a new toilet bowl wouldn't be the answer. One solution is to in-

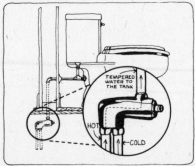

stall a thermostatic supply mixing valve and a hot-water connection. This mixes enough hot water with the supply to the toilet tank to bring it up to room temperature and thus prevent condensation. You will probably need a plumber to do this job.

CONDENSATION UNDER PORCH

I have a bungalow with a small porch (5' × 6') to the front door. In the basement below this there is a room of the same size. During cold weather there is a lot of condensation on the walls and ceiling of this room. Waterproof paint doesn't help. I now believe this is caused because there is no ventilation in this room, and I have been advised to drill some holes in the wall. The concrete is very thick and I would like your advice before I try this.

I don't think this would do much good, anyway. The best remedy is to insulate the concrete with 1'' or 2'' of plastic foamboard insulation applied directly to the walls and ceiling with a suitable panel adhesive. Apply a bead of adhesive around the back edge of each sheet of foamboard, then press it in place to seal it to the wall or ceiling.

WINDOWS ONLY STEAM AT NIGHT

Why do our bay windows steam up very badly at night, after we close the drapes and turn the thermostat down? They seldom steam up during the day.

There are three reasons why condensation occurs on windows more often at night than during the day. The lower thermostat setting increases the relative humidity of the air in the house. The lower outdoor temperature makes the windows colder. And the closed drapes cut off air circulation over the windows.

The best remedy is to reduce the humidity in the house by providing a little more ventilation. Opening the drapes will also help.

CONSTRUCTION—BUILDING PERMITS

I want to build a bedroom, a bathroom and a recreation room in my basement. Do I have to have a permit for this, and will it add to my taxes?

Yes to both questions. Actually, of course, a lot of do-it-yourself home improvement work is

done without bothering to take out building permits, but strictly speaking, this is illegal. If it involves any structural changes or electrical work, it's also dangerous. It's a simple matter to get permits to do your own work, including wiring and plumbing, and have it properly inspected. All such improvements are reported to the tax assessment department, however, and add to the value of your property for tax purposes.

CONSTRUCTION—CLOSETS ON OUTSIDE WALL

We need more wardrobe closets, and I want to build some on the outside wall of our bedroom. We live in a very cold area. Would there be any problem with this?

There is no reason why you shouldn't put wardrobe closets on an outside wall—as long as the wall is well insulated. If it isn't, there's a danger of condensation and dampness inside the closet, with resulting mildew problems. If you're not sure if the wall is adequately insulated, I suggest you build the closets on an inside wall.

CONSTRUCTION COSTS

We are planning to build a house and would like to know what type of construction is cheapest, including both materials and labor. And what is the most economical design, single-storey, 1½-storey, or 2-storey?

Standard wood frame is the least expensive form of house construction. And a 2-storey house is cheaper to build per square foot than a single- or 1½-storey house.

CROSS-BRACING

We purchased a new home about a year ago, and have now noticed some cracks in the plaster above the doorways and in the hall. A friend tells us this is because we don't have any cross-bracing between the floor joists, which we can see in the basement, just some narrow boards nailed along the bottom of the joists. He says the cross-bracing is necessary to strengthen the joists and distribute the weight evenly across them. If this is true, what should we do about it?

It isn't true. Cross-bracing, or bridging, is only there to keep the joists from warping or twisting out of position, and that can be done just as well with continuous strapping nailed along the bottom of the joists.

Your problem sounds like normal shrinkage, to me, caused by the use of "green" or wet framing lumber. The inevitable plaster cracks must be patched and repainted periodically until the house is thoroughly dried out.

CONSTRUCTION—FENCE POSTS

I built my picket fence 15 years ago, using 4 x 6 fir posts buried about three feet deep. I think they must be rotten by now. Should I have set the posts in concrete?

No. Wood should not be in direct contact with concrete; this keeps in the moisture and promotes rotting. It's best to keep the posts out of the ground entirely, and this can be done by bolting the wood posts to steel straps or bracket supports embedded in concrete piers.

CONSTRUCTION—FOOTINGS

I'm confused about how deep to dig the footings for a stone flower box in front of my house. It will be long and low, probably one foot high.

If you live in a low-temperature area the footings should extend below the frost line to prevent heaving and cracking during the winter. Your local building department can advise you how deep that is in your area.

CONSTRUCTION—FOUNDATION SETTLED

Windows and doors are jamming in my house because the foundation has settled. Is it possible for me to put in stronger footings without endangering the walls?

Yes, but this can be a risky job because of the danger of plaster and masonry cracking. I suggest you get a reliable, properly insured contractor to do this work. If you go ahead on your own, undermine the foundation walls in very short sections so that only a small portion of wall is left unsupported at a time. To avoid the danger of collapse or cracking, never dig under walls when the ground is wet. If the building and foundations are of masonry construction, undermine only two feet at any one time and never any closer than 6 to 8 feet apart. For a frame building resting on a concrete foundation, the wall can usually be undermined a length of about 4 feet at one time.

BUILDING A SAUNA

I want to build a sauna bath in our basement. Can I use ordinary cedar to line it with? And can I heat it with our gas furnace?

You can use unfinished cedar 2" tongue-and-groove planking, but don't expose any nail heads or other metal. It would not be practical to use your furnace, but you can buy special gas-fired sauna heaters.

SOLID TIMBER WALLS

I am planning to build a house with solid walls of 6 × 6 timbers. What do you think of this idea?

I think it's a very expensive way to build a house, and not a very good way either. The solid wood walls have an insulation value of R7 or R8, which is about half of what you need today. There is also the problem of running wires, pipes, vent stacks, etc., through the solid walls. It can be done, but it's more difficult than with conventional frame walls. And unless you have figured out some way of sealing the joints between all the timbers, air and water leakage will also be a problem.

ANTIQUING COPPER

I have a copper firehood that I would like to antique. How can I do it?

Dissolve half an ounce of Liver of Sulphur (sulphurated potash, or potassium sulphurata), available from a druggist or hobbycraft store, in half a glass of water. When this solution is wiped on, the copper will turn black. After it dries, rub the surface with steel wool to expose the bright metal in the highlights and leave it dark in the depressions.

NICKEL PLATING COPPER

Can I re-plate a nickel-plated copper tea kettle?

You can't do it yourself, but you can have it done by a jeweller or a commercial plating shop.

COOKING IN COPPER

I have a solid copper saucepan that no longer has a tin lining. Can I cook in it safely? How do I clean it? Is there any way I can get it re-lined?

Copper is an excellent metal for cooking utensils because it conducts heat quickly and evenly.

A tin or other metal lining is added to prevent the formation of "green rust," copper salts that not only affect the taste of food, but can be quite toxic.

You can use the copper pot as it is only if you keep it scrupulously clean. There are a number of very good copper cleaners on the market now or you can use the old-fashioned treatments: salt and vinegar, or salt and lemon juice.

It would be better, however, to get your copper saucepan tinned. Look in the Yellow Pages under "Tinning" and you may find a local firm that does this work.

COUNTERTOP BUBBLE

The plastic laminate on our kitchen countertop has bubbled up where a hot pan was put on it. Is there any way I can get this to stay down again?

What has happened is that the contact cement which holds the plastic laminate to the plywood countertop has been softened by the heat, allowing the laminate to pull away. The remedy is to reverse the process. Heat the area with an iron set at "rayon" or "synthetics" temperature to soften and re-activate the contact cement again, then immediately apply a heavy weight such as bricks or a bucket of water to hold the laminate down until it cools.

COUNTERTOPS—CERAMIC TILE

Can I place new ceramic tile on my kitchen counter without removing the existing tile?

Yes, but you may have trouble at the edges and around the sink. Clean your existing tile with detergent followed by a cleaning with mineral spirits, or petroleum solvent.

Apply adhesive, tile and grout as recommended by the manufacturer. You will have to remove and replace the sink, and probably the taps, as well. I think it would be much easier just to take off the existing tile.

HOLE IN COUNTERTOP

I burned a small hole through our plastic countertop with a hot pan. The hole is only about 1/4" square. Is there any way I can repair this?

Scrape or cut out the burned plastic and wood, then fill the hole with epoxy putty. This comes in two sticks; you cut an equal quantity of each and mix them thoroughly before application. The normal color is an off-white, but this can be tinted with universal paint pigments. Apply

the putty with a knife, then smooth and level the surface with a wet finger.

DULL COUNTERTOP

Is there any way to restore a plastic laminate countertop after it has been scuffed by rubbing too hard with a powdered cleaner?

One of the liquid acrylic floor polishes will restore the shine, but it won't wear as well as the laminate itself. It will have to be stripped off and re-applied periodically. There's no way to restore the shine permanently.

PAINTING A COUNTERTOP

The pattern is wearing off the plastic countertop in our kitchen. Also, I don't like the color. Can I paint it?

I wouldn't recommend painting it, although this can be done as long as you roughen up the surface first with medium-grit sandpaper or coarse steel wool. There is no paint as tough as the melamine plastic surface of these countertop laminates, though, and I think you'd be disappointed with the results. It would be much better to replace the countertop or apply a new panel on top of the present one.

REMOVING PLASTIC COUNTERTOP

How can I remove the old plastic laminate top from my kitchen counter so that I can put on a new one?

Although you can remove the laminate top by heating it with a propane torch to soften the contact cement, you may have a hard job getting rid of the old adhesive underneath, and this will show through the new countertop. It would be better to apply a new laminate on top of the old one, if it is firmly attached, or else replace the entire countertop, plywood and all.

VARNISH ON PLASTIC COUNTERTOP

I dropped some varnish on our plastic countertop while I was painting the kitchen cupboards. I've tried turpentine and gasoline without success, and don't want to scrape it off for fear of scratching the plastic. What can I use?

Any paint remover will do the job without harming the plastic.

PROTECTING PLASTIC COUNTERTOP

Is there any special polish I should use to protect my plastic laminate countertops?

No. A lot of people feel that they should put a magic, protective coating on things like enamel appliances, vinyl flooring, and plastic laminate, all of which are a good deal tougher than any polish. The melamine plastic surface of these countertop materials is harder than anything you can put on it.

RESTORING PLASTIC COUNTERTOP

Could you please tell me how to rejuvenate the surface of my plastic countertop. It is red, but the color has worn away in some places.

There is no way to restore the worn surface of plastic laminate. You will have to cover it with new laminate.

NEW PLASTIC COUNTERTOP

Can I put new plastic laminate directly on top of the existing formica counter in my kitchen, or do I have to remove the old countertop first?

If the present countertop is still cemented firmly in place, there is no reason why you can't apply a new one over it. But roughen the surface with coarse sandpaper before applying the contact cement.

REMOVING COUNTERTOP

I want to change the color of our kitchen counters. How can I remove the plastic laminate and put down a different color?

If the present countertop is firmly attached, you're better off just to apply new laminate on top of it, using contact cement. But roughen up the surface first with sandpaper, particularly around the edges.

If it's an old countertop with an aluminum moulding strip holding it down around the edge, you'll probably find that it can be peeled off quite easily once this edging strip has been removed. The adhesives they used in those days dried out after a few years. If the more recent contact cement was used, however, you can still peel the top off by squirting contact cement solvent under the edge as it's lifted up.

And finally, if the countertop was laid down with contact cement and you can't lift it to get solvent underneath, run a hot iron ("linen" setting) along the edge. This will soften the contact cement enough to let you peel the Arborite off. Before you apply the new countertop, use contact cement solvent to remove the adhesive that remains on the plywood base.

COUNTERTOP STAINS

There are some food stains on our plastic laminate countertop. How can I get these off without damaging the countertop?

Such food stains can usually be removed with full strength laundry bleach.

CORK DUST ON WALL TILES

We remodelled our front hall and have covered the walls 4' up with natural cork tiles. This looks very nice but we find that there is a lot of dust and small particles coming off the face of the cork. Is there some coating we should put on to prevent this?

Cork is wood, and a certain amount of sanding dust is to be expected on the surface of new tiles. This can be removed by vacuuming and wiping with a damp cloth. Any sealer that can be used will darken the cork.

RESTORING COWHIDE

I have a tanned cowhide rug that has become quite stiff. How should I treat it?

Leather gets stiff when the natural oils dry out. It can be softened by rubbing it with castor oil or neatsfoot oil. Neatsfoot oil, which is extracted from the feet of cattle, is considered the best oil for leather.

REPAIRING CRACKED VASE

We have a large cut glass vase with a hairline crack in it. This is almost invisible, but it leaks. How can I seal it?

Old-fashioned waterglass (sodium silicate), which grandmother once used to preserve eggs, will do the trick, but it isn't easy to find anymore. Some country grocery stores still carry it, however, and you can always order it from a drug store.

Dilute the syrupy liquid with an equal quantity of water. Paint it on the crack, wipe off any surplus and allow to dry thoroughly, then apply a second coat the same way.

COTTAGE ON DAMP GROUND

Our summer cottage is set on a foundation of concrete blocks, with an 18" crawlspace between the floor joists and the ground, which is always wet. I'm afraid this will rot the beams. Is there anything I can do to dry out the crawlspace?

Conditions certainly sound ideal for wood decay to develop. The only way to dry out the ground under the cottage is to dig a drainage ditch at the base of the footings all around it, and lead this ditch off to a runoff area at some lower spot. You then lay agricultural drainage tile or perforated plastic pipe in the ditch and cover it with gravel.

Other than that, all you can do is cover the damp earth under your cottage with overlapping sheets of polyethylene film weighted down with stones or gravel.

Finally, make sure that the crawlspace is well ventilated at all times through screened openings on opposite sides of the cottage.

CRAWLSPACE DAMPNESS

We have only half a basement. The other half is unexcavated, with the earth about two feet below the floor joists. Is it all right like this? If not, what should we do about it?

Open earth in the crawlspace can lead to dampness and condensation in the house. The best solution is to cover the earth with overlapping sheets of 6-mil polyethylene, held down with stones or a few shovelfuls of gravel.

EXCAVATING A CRAWLSPACE

We have a crawlspace under our house that we would like to have dug out for a family room. Would our present foundation be deep enough to do this, or do we need to pour another wall? How should this be done?

The foundation footings will have to extend below the new floor level, and it is doubtful if the present foundation goes that deep. This is a very tricky job, and one that should only be attempted by an experienced contractor. Call one in and discuss it with him. He may be able to suggest a better and cheaper way to add a family room.

REMOVING MELTED CRAYONS FROM UPHOLSTERY

A number of colored crayons were left on the couch in our camper and the sun melted them into the nylon slip-cover. How can I get this off without damaging the material? I took the cover to the dry cleaners and they told me they couldn't remove the crayon stain.

Ironing the fabric between several layers of paper towels will remove much of the wax. Replace the towels and iron again, as necessary. What remains can be dissolved with petroleum solvent (mineral spirits), but this works slowly, so be patient.

Actually, dry cleaning fluid will also dissolve the wax, but perhaps your cleaners didn't like the idea of all that colored wax getting into their cleaning solution.

SHINY SPOTS ON CUPBOARD DOORS

There are shiny spots on the matt finish of my mahogany kitchen cupboard doors, where my fingers touch them. They won't wash off. How can I remove them?

You can dull these spots down by rubbing them with #000 steel wool, in the direction of the grain.

Dehumidifiers

WOODGRAIN FINISH FOR CUPBOARDS

We would like to cover our painted kitchen cupboards with a real wood veneer or a plastic laminate with a good simulated woodgrain appearance. Can you tell me how to do this without rebuilding the cabinets?

There used to be a special, thin "cabinet laminate" made for just this purpose, but it's no longer available. The regular countertop laminate can be used, however, if you remove the paint from the cupboard. Cut the laminate to size and apply it with contact cement. It isn't practical to apply wood veneer, although you could re-face the doors with ¼" hardwood plywood applied with contact cement.

But I think the easiest, and certainly the cheapest material to use is a woodgrain vinyl with a self-stick backing, such as Contact or MacTac. These are sold at most hardware and building supply stores.

CUTTING BOARD GETS CUT

I have just had a maple chopping block put into a section of my kitchen counter. Now I find that my serrated bread knife makes cuts in the wood. I thought this type of cutting board wasn't supposed to show knife marks. How should I take care of it?

A real butcher's chopping block is made by laminating pieces of maple together so that their square-cut *ends* form the cutting surface. The result is much like a slice cut off a maple log; knife or cleaver cuts don't score the wood, they simply spread the end-grain apart temporarily. Ultimately the surface of the block does get worn and marked, however, and must be restored with a scraper blade.

You probably have a less expensive and more common maple cutting board, rather than a true chopping block. In this, strips of maple are laminated together lengthwise, like floor boards, with the grain running more or less parallel to the surface. The grain looks much more attractive this way, but it is also marked much more easily by knife cuts—particularly by a serrated knife, which is really a fine-toothed saw. But the wood is very hard, and if you use conventional, smooth-edged knives, the cuts will hardly be noticeable. And the surface can easily be restored, when necessary, simply by using a scraper, available at any hardware store.

PRESERVING A CUTTING BOARD

What should I use to preserve a cutting board counter top? It is made of birch.

Just wipe with vegetable cooking oil occasionally. When the cutting board gets stained or roughed up with cutting, you can renew the surface of the wood with a scraper blade, available at any hardware store. Oil the wood again before using.

USING DEHUMIDIFIER IN WINTER

Our windows drip with condensation during cold weather, and I am told this is because the humidity in our house is too high. I don't want to have to open the windows and bring in cold air, so I have been keeping a dehumidifier running. This worked all right in the summer, but it hardly collects any water at all now. What am I doing wrong?

A dehumidifier cannot work properly during the winter. It is only capable of reducing the humidity to about 60%, which is fine in the summer when the humidity is around 90%, but is much too high to prevent condensation problems during cold weather. Even with storm windows, condensation will form on the inside pane when the outside temperature is $-7°$Celsius ($20°$F.) if the humidity in the house reaches 40%.

The best way to reduce your humidity is to increase your ventilation. This gets rid of humid household air and replaces it with fresh and relatively dry outside air. Actually the outside air is just about as humid in the winter as in the summer, but the humidity drops drastically as the air is warmed to household temperature.

DEHUMIDIFIER

Our dehumidifier has an annoying hum and takes up floor space in our basement playroom. I propose setting it into the wall so that it will exhaust into the unused portion of the basement. Will this work?

If I understand you correctly, you intend to exhaust the *dehumidified* air into the unused part of the basement. That won't dry the air in the playroom, I'm afraid. Both the intake and output sides of a dehumidifier have to be in the same area.

DEHUMIDIFIER PRODUCES HEAT

Our basement was always the coolest spot in the house during the summer, but it was also clammy and tended to smell damp. Some weeks ago we bought a dehumidifier to put down there, and it has been working very well. I empty it two or three times a day and

the humidity has dropped about 10%. My problem is this. The basement now seems to be much warmer, and is not the cool refuge it used to be. I thought a lower humidity was supposed to make you feel cooler. Can you tell me what has happened?

It is not generally realized that a dehumidifier produces a substantial amount of heat just by changing water vapor back to a liquid. When water condenses it gives off as much heat as it would take to evaporate it . . . and you know how much heat it takes to boil away a gallon of water!

You will notice that the air coming out of a dehumidifier is warm. So, in effect a dehumidifier is actually a small heater. One with a rated capacity of 20 pints a day, for instance, will release 25,000 BTUs into the confined area of the basement. That's the amount of heat produced by the average home furnace burning steadily for 15 minutes. This could easily raise the air temperature in the basement by 10°F.

Actually, the increased room temperature helps to reduce the humidity, but it may not make the basement very comfortable. I suggest you compromise by setting the dehumidifier to a higher humidity level . . . or put in an air conditioner, which cools as well as dehumidifies.

DISHWASHER BUILDUP

We recently purchased a dishwasher, but our water supply is hard and we are getting a buildup of deposit on the inside. How can I get rid of this?

You can remove the deposit by putting three-quarters of a cup of liquid laundry bleach into the empty dishwasher and running it through the first wash. After this drains, add two cups of vinegar and run this through the rinse cycle, but not the drying cycle. Re-set the dishwasher for a full wash cycle using regular dishwasher detergent. You can wash a load of dishes at the same time, too, if you want to.

You can prevent the lime deposit buildup by adding half a cup of vinegar to the rinsing cycle about once a week.

DISINFECTING A HOUSE

We are renting a furnished house and I'm afraid the people who lived here before may have had diseases. What should I do to disinfect the house?

Contagious disease organisms cannot survive outside the body for very long, rarely more than a few hours, so there is no need to worry about catching anything from the house. Normal household cleanliness is all the attention that is required. Even clothing and bed linen is perfectly safe to use after it has been washed. Mattresses and books can be disinfected by exposure to fresh air and sunlight.

DISTILLED WATER FROM FRIDGE

Instead of buying distilled water for my steam iron—at close to $1 a gallon!—I was thinking of using the water I get when I defrost my fridge. If I remember my high school physics, this has to be distilled water. But now I see that some steam irons carry a warning that fridge defrost water should not be used. Why not?

You're perfectly right, the frost that builds up on a freezer is distilled water, and as long as it stays perfectly clean it can be used in a steam iron, or car battery, or anything else that requires distilled water. The trouble is that it doesn't stay clean. It usually runs out through the drip tray under the freezing compartment, or down the inside walls, and too often picks up particles of sugar or dried blood or other food that could ruin a steam iron very quickly. It isn't worth the risk. You can safely use the water from a dehumidifier, however.

DOOR FREEZING UP

During very cold weather our front door freezes tight, and is very difficult to open. A builder friend tells us that the only way to remedy this is to put in a solid cedar door. Do you have any other suggestions? I should add that our house is electrically heated and that we also have a problem with condensation on our windows.

Changing the door won't eliminate this problem, which is caused by the same thing that causes the condensation on your windows— too much humidity in the house. This is common with electric heating, since this lacks the ventilation provided by a conventional furnace and chimney. The cure is to increase the ventilation by opening windows or installing vent fans in the main sources of humidity, the kitchen and bathroom.

INSULATING DOOR

We need a new front door for our house, which faces north. Does a solid wood door or an insulated metal door have the best insulation value?

A 1½" thick solid cedar door has an insulation value of no more than R3. A metal door of the same thickness filled with polyurethane foam will have an insulation value of about R10. But make sure the door is well sealed with weather-stripping; this does more to conserve heat than the insulation value of the door itself.

REFINISHING A DOOR

The front door of our house has a clear finish in a medium walnut shade. It has been chipped in a few places and the wood shows white underneath. How can I patch up these spots and refinish the door?

The door was probably finished with a combination varnish-stain. It would be very difficult to stain the chipped areas to match the rest of the finish. The proper thing to do is remove all the old varnish, then refinish the door with a stain (if desired) and *four* coats of marine varnish.

SCRATCHED DOOR

We have a mahogany door, varnished, and our dog has scratched it outside. We want to cover the scratches without doing the whole door. What is the best solution?

This is a tough problem. You can't sand scratches out of thin veneer and fillers will show through varnish. The best solution is to get a new door. It is not expensive—mahogany doors are the cheapest you can buy. A bigger problem is how to cure the dog of scratching.

SLIDING DOOR STICKS

One of the lightweight sliding doors on the wardrobe closet in our bedroom keeps sticking. The others move very smoothly. Can you tell me how I can remedy this?

This is usually caused by the door panel riding a little too low, causing it to bind in the bottom track. It can be cured by adjusting the roller brackets at the top of the door. Turning the screw at the bottom of the bracket in a clockwise direction raises the door. Adjust both rollers until the door slides smoothly.

STICKING DOOR

We've just taken over an older house, and have found that several of the doors won't

close properly. That is, they won't quite close. Any pressure to close the door seems to spring the hinges slightly, yet I can't find anything that is keeping the door open. Do you have any suggestions?

I had the same problem myself recently, and tried several things until I discovered the cause, which was a buildup of many years of paint on the doorstop moulding on the hinge side of the door frame. A matching bead of paint along the edge of the door at this point adds to the problem.

Use a sharp chisel to remove the paint from the edge of the doorstop, and a sanding block to take the bead of paint off the edge of the door. I think you'll find it closes all right after that.

WARPED DOOR

Our front door has warped so badly there is a ¼" gap at the bottom through which wind and snow blows. The door faces the cold east winds and there is a hot-air vent blowing against the door inside the vestibule. I think this is what is causing the door to warp. I plan to put in a new door this spring. What kind would be best?

Hollow plywood doors are most likely to warp in a situation like this. A panelled door with solid stiles and rails (the vertical and horizontal members) would be better. Cedar is less likely to warp than most other woods, incidentally. A door with a solid, laminated wood core is also a better bet, but the safest buy of all is a steel door, which can never warp. Steel doors are available in all of the traditional panel styles and with better insulation against both heat and sound than a wooden door. Your building supply store can show you samples.

DOOR WON'T STAY OPEN

A friend of ours oiled the hinges on our bathroom door, and now it won't stay open. How can we correct this?

Don't blame your friend. The door is incorrectly hung, probably because the hinge-side of the jamb was warped out of position and is no longer plumb. If the door wants to close, it's because the lower hinge needs to be brought out a bit. Unscrew the hinge leaf from the jamb and cut a piece of thin cardboard to fit behind it, then replace the screws. If the door still closes by itself, insert another piece of cardboard. (If the door wanted to swing open, the solution would be to put a cardboard shim behind the *top* hinge leaf.)

CHANGING A DOOR LOCK

My front door has an old-fashioned mortice lock, the kind with a big escutcheon plate and a long-shafted key. Is there any way I can change this to a modern, pin-type cylinder lock without having to replace the door?

Conversion kits are available for replacing an old mortice lock with any modern lockset. These include special inside and outside escutcheon plates to cover the old keyhole, a special latch plate to cover the opening in the edge of the door, and a new strike plate. You simply have to drill one new hole in the door. Any hardware store should be able to sell you a lockset conversion kit.

LOCKS WITH MISSING KEYS

I recently purchased a 25-year-old house. Several of the door locks are the key-in-knob type, including two on the garage for which I have no keys. I would like to know how to take an impression of these locks so that I can have new keys cut.

I know of no way to take an impression of a pin-type cylinder lock like this. The best thing to do is replace the cylinder. This can be done by removing the lock handle and then finding the pin that releases the cylinder. (In some makes the lock cylinder is held in by a retaining ring that can be pried off after the handle is removed.)

If you take the cylinder lock to your hardware store you should be able to get a new one to fit your doorset . . . with keys, of course.

WORN DOORKNOBS

The finish seems to be wearing off our brass doorknobs, which look as if the plating is worn through. Can we get them replated?

What appears to be worn plating is probably the baked-on lacquer coating that protects the brass from tarnishing. Clean it off with lacquer thinner, then polish the knob with any mild brass cleaner. Buff with a dry cloth and then, without touching the knob, spray on a new clear lacquer coating to protect the finish. It won't be as tough as the original factory coating though, and may have to be re-done occasionally.

DOUBLE GLAZING

In a recent column you mentioned "double glazing". I've run into this term several times, but am not sure what it means. Would you please explain?

A double glazed window is simply one with two sheets of glass. This can be either an ordinary window plus a storm window, or, more commonly today, a sealed unit consisting of two sheets of glass spaced about ¼" apart. The purpose is the same . . . added insulation . . . partly to conserve heat, but mainly to eliminate or reduce condensation on the inside pane.

DRAFT THROUGH WALL OUTLETS

We have noticed a strong draft coming through the duplex outlets and switches on our outside walls. Is there any way we can seal these?

Most hardware stores now carry special foam plastic gaskets designed to fit under the face plate of duplex outlets and switches.

CLOSING THE DRAINS FOR WINTER

I will be away from my condominium apartment from November through March. The unit will be heated so I'm not concerned about frozen pipes, but I've been worrying about another problem. Isn't there a chance that the water in the traps in sinks and toilets will evaporate and allow sewer gases to enter the apartment? How can this be prevented?

That's an interesting possibility, but I've never heard of it happening. In any case, all you have to do to prevent it is close the sink drains and pour a little cooking oil in the toilet just before you leave.

DRIVEWAYS

ASPHALT PAVING

I want to get my driveway paved with black-top, and would like to make sure I get a good job. What is the best foundation, and how thick should the asphalt be?

First make sure that you get a signed contract that includes a complete description of the work to be done—the depth of the excavation (if any), thickness and type of base material, drainage requirements, thickness and grade of asphalt, total area to be covered, dates work to be started and finished, total cost. A deposit of 10% should be paid when the contract is signed by both parties. The balance is paid on completion of the work.

There should be a minimum of 4'' of crushed stone—preferably crushed limestone, which packs better than gravel. An HL3A asphalt mix is usually used for home driveways. It's smoother than the HL3 mix used for highways but not as strong. But if you have a steep driveway and need maximum traction, HL3 would be preferable.

The maximum thickness of compacted asphalt that can be applied in one layer is 2''. Any more than that and it will tend to be soft, unless it is applied in two layers. A home driveway doesn't usually require any more than one layer.

DO-IT-YOURSELF BLACKTOP

Can I pave my own driveway with blacktop? If so, how do I go about it?

It's not difficult if you can get three or four friends or neighbors to help you—on a week-day, because companies won't deliver hot asphalt on Saturday or Sunday.

First prepare the driveway. Dig it out, if necessary, and make sure it's sloped to drain away from the house. Put down a 6" layer of gravel and spread it to form a crown in the centre.

You'll have to buy the asphalt in bulk, then get the truck to back into your driveway and spread the loose asphalt in an even layer about 6" deep down its length. You and your friends will have previously armed yourselves with spreaders made by wiring 3' lengths of board to garden rakes. With these you spread the asphalt in an even layer at least 4" thick. Then

compact it with a large garden roller filled with water weighing about 250 pounds, its surface moistened with kerosene-soaked sacks to keep the asphalt from sticking.

Wear old boots and throw them away when you're finished.

FILLING HOLES IN DRIVEWAY

We were away from our home for several months and while we were gone a 40-gallon drum of stove oil on the side of the garage leaked onto the asphalt driveway. An area about 8' by 2' has turned soft and is crumbling. How can I repair this?

You will have to dig out the softened asphalt and replace it. Cold-set asphalt patching material is sold in sacks at most building supply stores, but this isn't very durable. Hot asphalt would be a better material to use but it may be difficult to get anyone to do such a small area.

The most practical solution is to fill the hole with concrete and then paint it with one of the driveway sealers.

GRASS IN BLACKTOP DRIVEWAY

The grass keeps growing through our black-top driveway, along the edge of the lawn. How can we prevent this?

If the grass is allowed to grow right up to the edge of the driveway, there's no way you're going to keep it from pushing through the asphalt. The grass should be kept at least 6" away from the driveway, preferably separated by a brick or concrete mowing strip.

MUSHROOMS GROWING THROUGH ASPHALT

We had our side drive asphalted two years ago...a very good job. Now we're getting mush-rooms pushing holes right through the drive-way. What can we do?

It may look like a good job, but if mushrooms are able to push through it, it isn't thick enough. It should be at least 2" thick.

Mushrooms grow from a network of mycel-lium threads that spread underground, and nothing you do to an individual mushroom will affect the growth underground. You would have to soak the entire area with a good garden fungicide, and that's not practical under a blacktop driveway.

REPAIRING A BLACKTOP DRIVEWAY

Our blacktop driveway has a number of cracks and a few holes, and the surface has become rough and grey. There isn't enough room to put another layer of asphalt on top, so I will have to patch and refinish this one. Can you tell me what I should use?

There are three types of blacktop sealer—asphalt-based, tar-based and acrylic. Asphalt-based sealer is the cheapest and gives a nice black finish, but it doesn't protect the blacktop from damage by oil or gasoline spills, as the coal tar and acrylic-based sealers do.

Before starting repairs, sweep and wash off the driveway. Very fine, hairline cracks can be filled with an application of one of the thick, tar-based sealers. Larger cracks, up to ⅜-in wide, should be filled with a butyl rubber caulking compound sold for this purpose, then coated with an asphalt-, tar-, or acrylic-based sealer.

Larger cracks and holes should be filled with one of the cold asphalt patching materials available at building supply stores. If the driveway has any soft patches caused by oil or gasoline spills, these should be dug out and filled with the cold asphalt patching material. The cold asphalt patches can be sealed immediately with an acrylic sealer, but not with a tar- or asphalt-based sealer. Before using these you must let the cold asphalt cure for at least 60 days.

DRIVEWAY RUST STAINS

My son washed out the battery compartment of his car on our asphalt driveway, and left rust stains a foot wide and 10 to 15 feet long. How can I remove them? I have tried detergent, gasoline, and kerosene.

Try mopping it with a solution of four ounces of oxalic acid in a quart of water. A stronger rust remover can be made of one part ammonium citrate or sodium citrate to six parts water. Citric acid and cream of tartar makes another rust-removing solution. One of these ought to work, and none should be harmful to the asphalt. Gasoline and kerosene, however, *are* harmful to asphalt.

DRIVEWAY SEALERS

Our asphalt driveway is about 10 years old, and we have sealed it with a coal tar emulsion every year. During this time the white vinyl floor in our kitchen has become quite brown in the traffic path from our back door. We would like to put down new flooring and don't want the same thing to happen to it. What kind of driveway sealer should we use?

Your trouble has been caused partly by too frequent use of the coal tar sealer, and probably by walking on it before it has had time to dry completely. An application once every 3 or 4 years should be enough. Next time, instead of the tar-based material, use one of the acrylic driveway sealers. These cost more than the coal tar emulsions, but they cover twice the area so the price works out about the same. And they are not as likely to stain the vinyl flooring.

DRIVEWAY STAINS

Our concrete driveway is stained with rust, oil, grease and undercoating. Can you tell me how to get these off without damaging the concrete?

Rust stains can be removed by wetting the spots and sprinkling them with oxalic acid crystals, available from any drugstore.

Auto-body undercoating can be removed with petroleum solvent (mineral spirits).

Grease and oil can be taken off with one of the grease removers sold at auto-supply stores, or with trisodium phosphate. Wet the spots and sprinkle generously with TSP, then brush in. Leave for 15 minutes or so, then brush again and hose off. Repeat if necessary.

GRASS AND WEED KILLER

Grass and weeds keep growing through the cracks in my concrete driveway. I've tried petroleum solvent and a number of commercial herbicides, but they either don't work or are too expensive for me (I'm an old-age pensioner). Can you suggest an inexpensive product that will do the job?

Yes, ordinary salt. Rock salt will do, but table salt dissolves faster. Sprinkle on generously, then hose in.

OIL STAINS ON CONCRETE DRIVEWAY

Our car leaked oil for a few months, and our concrete driveway is badly stained. The hardware store told us to use muriatic acid, but this hasn't done any good at all. I hate to have to replace the driveway just because of some ugly stains. Can you tell me what I can use to get rid of them?

Driveways

Three rounded tablespoons of lye to a gallon of water makes a very effective grease-cutting solution. You can also use trisodium phosphate, or TSP. Just wet the stains and then sprinkle them with TSP crystals. Brush in, let stand for 15 minutes or so, brush again, then hose off. Repeat if necessary.

RESURFACING A CONCRETE DRIVEWAY

We have a concrete driveway about 4" or 5" thick that is in good condition except that the surface has become rough and pitted. We would like to have it repaired with an asphalt topping. One company recommends breaking it up and putting in a new driveway, starting from scratch. They say the concrete would crack in cold weather if we put asphalt on top of it. Another firm says the present driveway will make a good foundation for asphalt paving. Who is right?

The second company. A solid, firmly established bed of concrete makes an ideal base for asphalt paving. That's the way our best roads are constructed. The only problem you might have is height, since you would be raising the driveway about 2". If that doesn't present any difficulty, there's nothing to worry about.

GRASS IN DRIVEWAY

Can you tell me how to get rid of grass growing in a gravel driveway? I paid $2.50 for a tin of pellets last summer that covered an area about 2' by 3', and it wasn't very successful even there. I want to have more gravel put down, but hesitate to do so until I can get rid of the grass.

Chemicals are only temporarily effective, and they're liable to damage adjoining lawns. The best solution is to remove all the gravel, level the ground underneath, and then cover it with a layer of 6-mil polyethylene sheet, which you can buy at any building supply store. Replace the gravel and add as much more as you want. The plastic film will keep grass and weeds from growing through.

"PAVING" A DRIVEWAY

Our cottage in the country has a gravel driveway that is hard to drive and walk on. Is there anything we can do with it other than have it blacktopped?

There are two things you can do. Crushed limestone, unlike gravel, will pack to make a firm surface. If this isn't available, you can sprinkle the gravel with asphalt emulsion, rake it in, tamp it down, sprinkle again, and cover with a thin coat of sand, then roll. Asphalt emulsion is sold by oil companies in 45-gallon drums, enough to do a large driveway. Sprinkle it on with an old watering can with the holes made much larger, while someone else wields the rake. Dark brown when it goes on, the asphalt emulsion turns black and hardens in a few hours. This system has been used for years to "pave" country roads, and it will work just as well on your driveway.

DRIVEWAY PAVING STONES

I was thinking of paving our driveway with concrete patio slabs either 12" or 18" square and about 2" thick, laid on a base of crushed gravel. Do you think these would be strong enough to support a large car?

No. The gravel base is not firm enough and the slabs are likely to shift, tip and be broken with the weight of the car. A better do-it-yourself paving material to use is the small, interlocking paving stones that are available in various colors and shapes. These are laid on sand, not gravel, and are firm enough to support a 20-ton tank.

DRY ROT

We're going to put up a ceiling in our basement, and want to know what we should do to prevent dry rot in the joists.

The term "dry rot" is very misleading. Actually all wood decay organisms require moisture, and dry wood will not rot. There would be some danger of decay in joists sitting over a damp crawl-space, but any wood that has been exposed to the dry air in a properly heated home for many months will certainly be too dry to rot.

In other words, you don't have to do anything but put up the ceiling the way you want it.

RECYCLING DRYER HEAT

We have a forced-air heating system with an electrostatic air filter and a fan that runs continuously. My clothes dryer is located near the furnace and I was thinking of installing an alternative vent for the dryer into the return air duct of the furnace, ahead of the filter. I figure this would recycle the heat and humidity normally lost through the outside dryer vent. At other times of the year the dryer would be switched to the outside vent, as usual. Do you think this is worthwhile?

It depends on the humidity of your house. If the air is very dry and you need extra humidity, it would certainly make sense to vent your dryer indoors. But if this causes the windows to steam up and drip, then it will just cause trouble.

There is a good chance, too, that the high humidity in the return air duct will interfere with the operation of the electrostatic air filter. In any case, it really isn't necessary to vent the dryer into the return air duct. Humidity soon equalizes itself throughout the house, so the dryer could just be vented into the room where it is located.

DUST FILTER

I suffer from an asthmatic condition and am bothered by dog and cat dust that somehow has got into our house. Is there any solution I can use to clear the air?

Only an electrostatic air filter will remove such fine particles. Such a filter can be installed quite easily in any warm air heating system and used 12 months of the year. Smaller room-sized units are also available.

DUST MOP TREATMENT

I seem to remember that my mother treated a string dust-mop with some solution to make it pick up the dust. Can you tell me what it was?

It was probably a dustcloth oil which used to be sold. It's easy enough to make yourself. Mix three parts light mineral oil and one part corn oil, and add a few drops of aromatic clove oil. Dip the mop or dust-cloth in this, wring it out, and store it in a plastic bag. After the mop has been used several times, wash it and re-treat.

An even simpler treatment is just to use an inexpensive lemon oil furniture polish, which is exactly the same thing, anyway. Sprinkle it on a clean mop and store it in a plastic bag until you're ready to use it. When the mop becomes dirty, wash it in warm water and detergent, wring it out, let dry, then reapply the oil.

ARE EAVESTROUGHS NECESSARY?

The roof of my bungalow is quite shallow and extends out about 20" at the front and back of the house. We have had a lot of trouble with ice dams in the eavestroughs causing water to back up under the shingles and leak down the inside walls. Someone recently suggested that eavestroughs are unnecessary, and that we should remove them to stop the ice dam problem. Is this so?

Eavestroughs are certainly not essential. If you have a serious ice dam problem it might be better to remove them, but this will increase the chance of basement drainage problems by allowing the roof runoff to drain down the outside of the foundation wall, and perhaps plug the drainage tile with silt. The winter roof runoff will also damage perennial plants and shrubs beneath the overhang.

The risk of a wet basement can be greatly reduced, however, if you run the lawn right up to the foundation walls and grade it so that the water runs *away* from the house. This will work best if the underlying soil is clay.

REPAIRING EAVESTROUGHS

The eavestrough on my house leaks at some of the joints. How can I stop the leaks?

Paint the joints on the inside with a generous coat of fibrated asphalt roofing cement. Allow the first coat to dry for 24 hours, then apply a second coat. If there are large gaps, apply the first coat of roofing cement, then cut a strip of fibreglass window screen as long as the joint and about two inches wider than the gap, press this into the cement, and cover with a second application of cement. When dry, apply a coat of aluminum paint.

ELECTRIC HEATER OVERHEATING

The cotton drapes along the window wall of our apartment have been singed by the electric baseboard heater—actually charred in one place. Is there any way we can adjust the temperature of these units?

An electric baseboard heater that will singe cotton does not meet safety standards, and you should report it immediately to your building superintendent. If he doesn't take prompt action, report it to your local electrical inspection authority. Meantime, either turn the faulty heater off or make sure that combustible materials are kept well away from it.

Baseboard heaters contain a safety device called a "linear cutout," which is a thin metal tube that runs the length of the heating element. It is set at the factory to turn the heater off if the temperature reaches 150° Celsius (300°F)—or less, in many cases—and this is well below the combustion point of cotton.

There have been a number of cases, however, where electricians have bypassed a faulty cutout instead of replacing it, and this can be very dangerous. To find out if the cutout is working, turn the room thermostat up to switch on the heater, then lean a piece of wood about 18″ long—a cutting board will do—against the baseboard to block the flow of air. The heater should turn off within five minutes without scorching the wood, and then keep cycling as it cools and reheats.

Cotton should not burn, either, but some of the synthetic fabrics might, so it is recommended that *any* combustible material be kept at least 3″ away from an electric baseboard heater.

ELECTRIC PLUG OVERHEATING

Why does the plug on our electric kettle get so hot? I have to use oven mitts to remove it. When our first kettle did that I figured there was something wrong with it, so I got a new one. After a few months it, too, started overheating. I've tried plugging it in different outlets, but it makes no difference. What could be wrong?

An electric kettle draws a very heavy current—about 13 amps—so a noticeable *warming* of the plug or wire is to be expected. But if it is uncomfortably hot to the touch, something is wrong. Most likely it is a poor connection inside the plug. Since the trouble started after you had been using the kettle for a few months, I suspect that you have damaged the connection inside the plug by pulling it out of the wall outlet by the cord instead of the plug—a common mistake.

The remedy is to cut off the plug and put on a new one, the kind with screw-on terminals. Those snap-on plugs with the pin-type contacts that puncture the cord cannot carry the heavy current drawn by an electric kettle. If you are careful to make good, tight connections on the plug, and not to pull it out by the cord any more, I don't think it will overheat again.

Another possibility is that the spring clips inside the outlet have become loose and are no longer holding the plug prongs tightly enough. The remedy is to replace the outlet.

ELECTRIC SHOCK

Sometimes I get an electric shock from my laundry tub. The tub is concrete but there is a metal edge around it, and I feel a shock if my hand is wet and I touch the tap. Our kitchen is directly above and I sometimes get a shock when I touch the tap there, too. What causes this?

This could be very dangerous. Get in touch with your local utility office right away. They will send someone to find the source of the trouble (probably a loose grounding wire on one of your appliances) and correct it.

ELECTRIC USAGE

Where can I get a chart that will tell me how much electricity is used by different appliances?

You can figure this out quite easily from the information marked on the appliance. Most of them show the wattage. A toaster, for instance, uses about 1,200 watts; an electric iron, 1,000 watts, which is one kilowatt. Electricity is charged by the kilowatt-hour, or KWH. If you pay 3¢ a kilowatt-hour, you can use an electric iron for one hour for 3¢. You can burn a 100-watt bulb for 10 hours for the same amount. A 60-watt bulb, on the other hand, takes nearly 17 hours to use up one kilowatt of electricity.

Some appliances, such as electric drills, vacuum cleaners and TV sets are marked with the amperage instead of the wattage. To find the approximate wattage, multiply the amperage by the voltage (120 volts). A black-and-white TV set uses about 2 amps, or 120 x 2 =240 watts, or about one-quarter of a kilowatt.

ELEPHANT'S EARS

I've been given a pair of elephant's ears. Unfortunately, they're very hard and dry, and have been creased badly in the packing. How can I

soften them up so they can be hung on the wall?

You're lucky you only got the ears! Our experience with this problem is limited, and we really don't know any experts to turn to. Someone here has suggested that you buy a 20-gallon drum of hand cream, then . . . .

Since the ears are leather, however, the usual treatment should apply. Rub neatsfoot or castor oil on them and work it in gently by hand to soften the leather. Eskimos chew hardened leather to soften it, but we don't really . . . .

BURNED ENAMEL POT

I burned some food on the bottom of an expensive enamel saucepan. What is the best way to get this off?

Put a strong salt solution in the pot and let it soak for a couple of hours. Cover the pot and bring it to a slow boil. This should remove the charred food.

EXHAUST VENT DRIPPING

I have noticed water dripping from around the exhaust fan in our bathroom ceiling during very cold weather. On checking in the attic I found a buildup of ice around the top of the vent pipe, just under the roof, inside the insulation that is wrapped around the pipe. When the vent fan is on for any length of time, this ice melts and runs down the outside of the pipe and drips through the fan grille. Would more insulation help?

For this to happen, two things must be wrong. First, you must have too much humidity in the attic; increasing the ventilation up there will reduce this. Second, there is apparently no vapor barrier over the insulation on the pipe. Wrap the insulation with polyethylene film and seal all joints with polyethylene tape. Be particularly careful about the part just under the roof; the plastic film should be spread out here and taped to the roof all around the pipe to prevent any moist air getting through and touching it.

It won't do any harm to increase the amount of insulation around the pipe while you're doing this, but that is not really the cause of the problem.

CHAIN LINK FENCE

We have a chain link fence around our property, but this year we plan to put in a swimming pool and would like to have more privacy. Do you have any suggestions?

You can make such a fence almost opaque by sliding venetian blind strips diagonally between the links.

FENCE LINE

The man who has the lot next to mine has built a fence right on the property line. Isn't there a law that says he has to build the fence back of it? My house is built so close to the line that I have trouble getting anything in or out, and I need every inch of space I have.

He can build a fence *up to* the property line, but not straddling it. All the fence must be on his side, in otherwords, unless you both agree to share it. You may need to hire a surveyor to find the exact location of the property line if you're going to start splitting inches this way. Is it worth it?

WHO OWNS THE FENCE?

For many years there has been a wire fence along one side of my property. It is fairly close to my house and quite a distance from my neighbor's. A week ago he removed most of this fence. I haven't spoken to him about it and I don't want to start an argument, but I would like the fence replaced. Can I make him put it back?

It depends on who owned the fence, and whose property it was on. If it was on his side of the property line he doesn't have to replace it if he doesn't want to. If it was on your side, he had no right to take it down and should put it back. You could charge him with trespassing if you wanted to, but that's hardly advisable.

If the fence was on the property line, then whoever put it up owns it. But common courtesy calls for some informal discussion before a step like this is taken. Since your neighbor didn't take the trouble to do this, I think you should bring the matter up now. At the worst, you can still put up another fence—on your side of the property line—although you may have to have a survey made to establish exactly where the line is.

FINISHING

REMOVING A HIGH-GLOSS FINISH

We have recently acquired a 30-year-old oak dining suite that is in find condition but has a very shiny finish that we don't like. How can we remove the high gloss?

Rub the surface down with #0000 steel wool, in the direction of the grain. Continue until the entire surface has an even, satin sheen. If this is still too shiny, switch to #000 steel wool.

REFINISHING
WOOD PANELLING

Several years ago I removed many coats of dark varnish from some oak panelling, and refinished it in a nice light tone. Gradually, however, it turned dark. Now I'm going to do another room with the same kind of panelling, and I want to know how to keep it from going dark.

You can't prevent oak, or any other wood, from turning dark when it's exposed to light. You can reduce the effect somewhat, however, by bleaching the oak after you've removed the present finish. Ordinary laundry bleach will work (neutralize with vinegar before refinishing) but you can buy good two-part wood bleaches at any paint store.

And a clean lacquer finish has less tendency to turn yellow than ordinary varnish or urethane.

FINISHING WOODEN
SALAD BOWLS

Would you please tell me the best way to refinish wooden salad bowls?

Rub them down to the bare wood with No.000 steel wool, wipe off all the sanding dust, then brush them with cooking oil. No other finish is needed.

REMOVING HIGH GLOSS
FROM VARNISH

The fine cedar panelling on the inside of my cottage was finished with high gloss, polyurethane varnish—I had wanted a satin finish. What is the best way to remove this varnish so that I can refinish the cedar?

There is no need to remove the varnish. All you have to do is rub it down with steel wool to take off the high gloss and give it an even satin finish. For a very soft, hand-rubbed furniture sheen, use #0000 steel wool. For a slightly flatter finish, use #000 steel wool. Always rub in the direction of the grain.

VARNISHING OVER WAX

Our 10-year-old house is panelled throughout in poplar, mahogany, and spruce. The only finish this has had is car wax. Now I'd like to put on a satin urethane varnish, but I don't know how to remove the wax.

You can dissolve the wax with petroleum solvent (mineral spirits), but this will just soak some of it into the wood. You can seal this in, however, with a generous application of shellac, and then apply a *regular* varnish. Urethane should not be applied over shellac.

FINISHING SLIDING DOORS

I have a clothes closet in my home with sliding fir plywood doors. I'm thinking of varnishing them. Is that a good idea, or what would you suggest?

Fir plywood has a "wild" grain that doesn't really look very good when it's varnished. The grain on different panels doesn't match, and there are usually patches in the face veneer that show up when you put on a clear finish. It would be much better to paint it with a good quality enamel. Use the recommended primer first, and be sure to do both sides of the door, even though one side may never be seen. This is necessary to prevent the wood from warping due to the uneven absorption of moisture.

FINISHING A ROSEWOOD PANEL

We have ordered rosewood panels to make into cupboards. Now, however, we have heard that this material is inclined to warp badly, so we are thinking of applying a sealer to prevent this. Then we want to use a urethane finish, and we may want to use a stain, too. What kind of sealer should we use under urethane?

If it's a good quality veneer panel, it will have the same kind of wood on both sides—show quality rosewood veneer on the face, and a poorer quality rosewood veneer on the back. This reduces the possibility of warping, but I don't think rosewood is any more likely to warp than any other wood.

If you want a urethane finish, there's no need for a sealer. And I don't think you'll want to use a stain, either, although it can be applied under the urethane if you want it.

But the most important thing to do to prevent the plywood from warping is to apply exactly the same finish to both sides of the panel—same finish, same number of coats.

This prevents the uneven absorption of moisture that causes plywood to warp.

REFINISHING A PIANO

We bought an old piano that has a very nice tone but a poor finish, with a number of scratches and cigarette burns. I want to take off the old finish and re-do it with polyurethane, but many people have told me this will ruin the tone. Do you think this is right?

No. It's conceivable that the rare tone of a valuable violin or a prized grand piano could be subtly altered by the type of finish applied, but somehow I don't think it could have any noticeable effect on an ordinary piano . . . unless you decided to cover it with padded chintz or line it with carpeting.

If you're going to worry about it, though, it's probably better not to try it. You'd always imagine you'd changed the tone, even if you hadn't. I'd do it . . . but the decision is up to you.

RESTORING OLD PINE

We have been removing the paint from old pine kitchen panels, doors, and window frames in an old farmhouse that we are trying to restore. Liquid paint remover wouldn't remove the many layers of paint as well as an electric scraper, but this has scorched the wood in places. How should we remove the burn marks? And what can we do about the white filler and putty that was placed in holes and cracks in the wood? These will show through the natural, clear finish that we planned to use.

The burn marks can just be sanded off. Although you could probably disguise the filler marks with a little wood stain applied with a small brush, it is customary in restorations like this just to apply a clear finish on top of them. They are authentic touches, after all.

It is worth noting, incidentally, that the wood was always intended to be painted, which is why it was filled. Our ancestors didn't like plain wood. So if you're really trying to restore it, you should repaint it!

RESTORING OAK TRIM

We recently purchased an old home and have discovered that the trim on our French doors and windows is oak. This has been painted with high-gloss enamel. How can we restore the oak?

Just strip off the old paint with paint remover. Sand, if necessary, to remove blemishes, and then apply at least two coats of satin urethane varnish.

LINSEED OIL FINISH STICKY

Last fall we bought a cedar storm door but the weather turned bad before we could install it. As a protection we applied a mixture of linseed oil and turpentine, but even though the door has been in a warm basement all winter it is still very tacky. How can this be corrected?

It sounds to me as if you applied the linseed oil mixture incorrectly. This is supposed to be brushed on, allowed to sink in for 15 minutes or so, and then wiped off with a dry cloth, leaving no wet oil film on the surface. You may have compounded the problem by using raw linseed oil instead of the so-called "boiled" type, which really just contains additives to make it dry faster.

The gummy film you have now should be removed with a scraper or paint remover before paint or varnish is applied.

LIGHTENING DARK STAIN

Our kitchen cupboards have a dark-stained wood grain finish. We would like to give them a lighter finish. How can we do this?

Paint remover will take off the varnish, and some of the stain, but you will probably have to sand to get down to the bare wood. Then use the stain you want and apply two or more coats of satin urethane.

EXTERIOR WOOD FINISH

I have just built a cottage with cedar siding on the outside. What kind of finish should I put on to protect the wood?

Cedar doesn't need any protection as long as it is used where it can dry out. Cedar weathers naturally to a lovely driftwood gray color, but if you don't want this you can give it a dark amber tone with one of the penetrating oil-resin sealers such as Danish oil. These are simply brushed on and allowed to sink in. Or you can color the cedar with a pigmented stain. It also takes paint very well, of course.

But there is no clear, glossy film finish for wood that will stand up to exterior exposure for more than a few years. The problem is not the finish itself but the deterioration of the surface of the wood. And when such finishes start to crack and peel, they are extremely difficult to redo; you must strip them back to the bare wood and start again. This goes for all varnishes, varnish-like "stains", polyurethane, epoxies, or any other plastic finish.

Linseed oil isn't recommended, either. At best it takes a long time to dry, and if it is applied too heavily it may stay sticky forever. And when several layers are built up, linseed oil has the same faults as other film finishes.

So forget about any kind of varnish. If you want to retain the natural appearance of the wood, give it an application of a water-repellent wood preservative, then leave it alone to weather naturally. Cedar contains natural preservatives and doesn't require additional treatment, but the repellent will reduce discoloration by mold.

If you don't like the look of weathered wood, then apply a pigmented stain in a cedar color. A stain lasts longer than a clear finish and is much easier to redo. Exterior wood stains are now available in a wide range of bright and subtle colors.

If you want to cover up the wood altogether, use one of the solid-color stains. These go on like a flat paint, but don't peel or blister.

Stains should not be used on decks, walks, balconies or verandahs because they aren't made to withstand traffic. These wood surfaces should *always* be left unfinished.

DARKER STAIN FOR KITCHEN CUPBOARDS

I want to have my kitchen cupboards restained to a darker tone, something like a deep walnut. Two different methods have been quoted by painters, and the price difference is about $300. One is to sand the cupboards down and re-stain them. The other is to strip them down with varnish remover and then re-stain. Which method do you recommend?

I see no need for any price difference at all. Sanding is a lot more work than using a varnish remover, but it doesn't do a better job so there's no point in paying extra for that. A certain amount of fine sanding is required anyway, to remove surface blemishes.

If the work is done by sanding alone, it means starting off with coarse sandpaper, and that can damage the edges of molding, etc., and is certainly not recommended if your cupboards have a thin wood veneer surface.

There's a third method that is even easier. Just clean the present finish, remove the surface gloss (if any) with steel wool, and then apply a coat of walnut varnish-stain. This is a

varnish that is already toned to the wood color required. A limited range of varnish-stains are available at paint stores, but you can make your own by adding paint pigments such as raw umber, Vandyke brown, and burnt sienna to ordinary varnish.

This method is not recommended, however, if the present finish is blotchy or uneven in color, because this would still show through the new finish to some extent.

FINISHING A CUTTING-BOARD

What is the proper way to finish a built-in wooden chopping block? I have been told to use turpentine and linseed oil, but this doesn't seem right to me.

Do not use turpentine and linseed oil or any of the other common wood finishes. Just wipe it occasionally with cooking oil.

FINISH FOR COTTAGE WALLS

We are building a cottage at the lake, and our inside walls are going to be panelled with V-joint white pine. We would like to finish them to keep the color as light as possible. Would you recommend shellac, varnish, urethane, or a semi-transparent stain?

Anything you put on the wood, even water, will change the color to some extent. I would suggest that you use a "natural", non-film finish that simply penetrates the wood and seals it, but otherwise leaves it looking as if nothing has been done to it. This is usually called a Danish Oil Finish, and any paint or hardware store is sure to have one of the two or three brands that are available.

The finish is simply wiped or brushed on, left for 15 minutes or so, and then wiped off. Nothing could be easier.

FINISHING—CHECKED VARNISH

Our varnished woodwork is dry and checked. How can we refinish it?

You will have to remove the old varnish with paint remover or by sanding. If the wood itself is checked, apply a wood filler in a matching tone, rubbing it across the grain with a coarse cloth. Sand, dust, and repaint with two coats of gloss or satin varnish, as desired. Sand lightly between coats.

FINISHING BARNBOARDS

I'm getting new kitchen cupboards, and would like to have them made from real barnboards. Could you please tell me how to treat the wood and what would make a good, serviceable finish?

Barnwood is generally left untreated, because anything you put on it will change its appearance. You would have to give the barnboards several coats of varnish to protect them against finger marks and other stains, and that's not going to look very rustic. For this reason I don't think barnwood is a very practical material to use for kitchen cabinets.

FIREPLACES

ACID BURNS ON FIREPLACE

I have done something wrong in cleaning my fireplace, and would appreciate your advice. The fireplace is grey stone with a raised hearth, and I cleaned it with a commercial grade of muriatic acid. It cleaned all right, but the hearth has turned a rusty color, and nothing I have tried will take it off. The brass firescreen has also been ruined by the acid.

You should have used *dilute* muriatic acid, one part to 10 parts water. These are acid burns, and they can generally be removed with a concentrated solution of oxalic acid crystals, available at any drug store (if they don't have it they can get it for you). Rinse thoroughly.

The brass firescreen can be cleaned with steel wool and any of the household brass and copper cleaners. When polished, spray the brass with a clear lacquer to protect it.

BASEMENT FIREPLACE DOESN'T DRAW

I have installed a Franklin fireplace in my basement recreation room. It looks good and works well except for one flaw. Most of the time when we light the fire we get a lot of smoke in the room before the chimney starts to draw, then it works fine. I think we need a stronger draft. Would it help if we installed one of those devices on top of the chimney that turns in the wind and keeps the open end pointed away from it?

Such a device does not look very good on a house, and I don't think it's necessary. All you need to do is open a nearby window a bit before you light the fireplace. This will provide the extra air that is needed until the chimney warms up.

One old trick is to warm the chimney before lighting the fire, by lighting a crumpled sheet of newspaper and stuffing it up the stove pipe.

But if the basement fireplace is having difficulty getting air, it's quite possible that your furnace won't be getting enough air either, when the fireplace is going. If you have a gas furnace, this could cause a back-draft that would suck flue gases back into the house; a potentially dangerous situation. I suggest you make sure that a window is open near the furnace, particularly when the fireplace is being used.

BURNING PAPER IN FIREPLACE

I have been told that paper should not be burned in a fireplace. Does this apply to rolled up newspaper logs and cardboard, too?

It isn't a very good idea to burn a lot of loose paper in a fireplace because it flares up quickly and can easily fall out onto the floor. But there is no reason at all why smaller amounts of paper shouldn't be burned in the fireplace. How else can you start a wood fire? There's nothing wrong with newspaper logs, either.

FIREPLACE DRAFT PROBLEM

We recently had some work done on the fireplace chimney, and were advised to add something called a "cathedral top" to keep out rain. The first time we lit the fire after this had been put on a puff of smoke would occasionally blow into the room as if there were a sudden down-draft. We used the fireplace regularly and this never happened before. Can you tell us what's causing it?

Apparently the cathedral top on the chimney is restricting the draft. Your chimney flue may be just barely large enough to serve the fireplace, and any reduction in the draft, even the small amount caused by the new rain-cap, could be enough to cause the fireplace to smoke. Check to see if opening a nearby window when the fire is lit does any good. If it does then this might be a simpler remedy than removing the rain-cap.

Fireplaces

CONNECTING FIREPLACE TO FURNACE CHIMNEY

We would like to install a Franklin fireplace in our basement recreation room. Are we allowed to connect this into the chimney presenting being used for our furnace? It will only be 2 or 3 feet away from the chimney.

If you call it a wood-burning Franklin *stove*, not a fireplace, you are allowed to connect it into the chimney below the furnace pipe, provided the flue is big enough to serve them both at the same time without interfering with the furnace draft. Unfortunately, this can only be determined by a furnace serviceman after the Franklin stove has been installed. A separate chimney would be much better.

CRAYON MARKS ON FIREPLACE

How can I remove crayon marks from the front of our sandstone fireplace?

Use an abrasive such as garnet paper or emery cloth. Do not use steel wool or other metallic abrasive; the metal that is rubbed off onto the sandstone will rust and discolor it.

FIREPLACE DOWN-DRAFT

We have a fireplace on the main floor and one in the basement. They use the same chimney, but separate flues, and both burn well. Yet when we use only the living room fireplace, smoke backs down into the basement. How can we stop the down-draft?

A tight-fitting damper in the basement fireplace would help. It might also help if you provided more air for the upstairs fireplace when it's burning. Your house may be so tightly sealed that the only place the air can get in to feed the fire is to come down the unused flue. Try opening a window when the upstairs fire is burning.

FIREPLACE PROBLEM

We have a fireplace in our basement recreation room, but it has never worked properly and is very difficult to light because the air wants to come DOWN the chimney, instead of go up. The fireplace opening is 25" by 38", and the chimney has the standard 8½" by 13" flue tile. Do you have any suggestions?

I think the flue is too small for the size of the fireplace. The area of the opening is 950 square inches, while the effective area of the flue is only about 80 square inches. It should be at least 1/10th the area of the fireplace opening— or 95 square inches, in this case. A 13" × 13" flue tile, or two 8½" × 8½" tiles, should have been used. You can't change them now, but you can reduce the size of the fireplace opening by adding a layer of firebrick on the bottom, or by putting in a 3" metal hood across the top.

I suspect, too, that you don't have enough ventilation in the basement to provide the extra air needed by the fireplace. Try opening a window near the fireplace next time you try to light it.

FIREPLACE BRINGS FURNACE FUMES

We had a double chimney and two fireplaces built in our home last year. The upstairs fireplace works fine, but when the basement fireplace is used it draws air down the furnace chimney and brings fumes into the house. The furnace room is about 5' × 6', but it isn't completely sealed off from the rest of the basement. Is there anything we can do to solve this problem?

That's a very dangerous situation, and it's caused by lack of ventilation in the furnace room. There is not enough fresh, outside air for the furnace, in other words. You should have a screened vent in the furnace room open at all times during the heating season. And when you want to use the basement fireplace, open a nearby window a little bit to provide the extra air needed for the chimney draft.

GLASS DOORS ON A FIREPLACE

How valid are the claims made for glass doors on fireplaces? I've been told that more heat will be radiated into the room if we install these, but they cost upwards of $100. Our fireplace draws quite well, but we have a tight house and have to leave a window open when the fire is on.

The problem with a conventional fireplace is that it draws more cold air into the house than it returns in heat. Glass doors with controllable air vents improve the efficiency because they reduce the amount of air required and also make the wood burn longer. But they don't increase the amount of heat radiated into the room; they reduce it. Glass doors do pass a fair amount of radiant heat, however, and since they cut down on air infiltration into the house (you probably won't have to open a window, for instance) you actually end up with more heat. They also let you enjoy the *look* of a fire, which is the only justification for having one in any case. Even the best fireplace is not an economical source of heat unless you have your own woodlot.

DOES A FIREPLACE REDUCE HEATING COSTS?

We are thinking of having a fireplace put in our basement family room. This is a fairly expensive project, however, and I am wondering if it will pay for itself in reduced heating costs. What is the most efficient type of fireplace to install?

To be perfectly frank about it, unless you have your own woodlot, I don't think any kind of fireplace will save money on heating. The main weakness of a fireplace is that it draws a lot of cold air into the rest of the house in order to keep the fire going in one room. That room will be warmed by the fireplace, but the rest of the house gets cold.

It is difficult to obtain reliable figures on fireplace efficiency, but most experts agree that even the best fireplace is far less efficient than a properly adjusted oil or gas furnace. The freestanding sheet-metal or cast-iron (Franklin-type) fireplaces are certainly more efficient than the conventional, built-in brick fireplace, however. And there are also built-in metal fireplaces that provide a circulation of warm air in addition to radiant heat. Adding glass doors to any fireplace that can take them will also increase its efficiency.

If you have to buy firewood or manufactured logs, I don't think you're going to save any money on heating, but there are other good reasons for having a fireplace, of course. After all, we don't expect a TV set or a new chesterfield to pay for itself; they're just supposed to give us some comfort and enjoyment. A fireplace is also a very satisfying addition to a home and well worth its modest cost, in my opinion.

The simple pleasure of sitting in front of your own cheery fire when a cold wind is howling outside is reason enough to have a fireplace. It won't save you money, but it's cheaper than a movie, and often a lot more interesting to watch.

INSTALLING A SECOND FIREPLACE

We have a new home with a fireplace on the main floor. The plans called for a second flue and a roughed-in fireplace in the basement, but these were changed. Can we install another fireplace in the basement and connect it into the upstairs fireplace chimney? If not, what would be the best way to do it?

It is against building regulations to connect two fireplaces to one chimney flue. But you can easily install a sheet metal fireplace in the basement—either free-standing or built-in—and use an insulated metal chimney that goes out through the basement wall and up the outside of the house. Such an installation will cost less than half the price of a brick fireplace and chimney. You can even do it yourself, if you want to save more money.

FIREPLACE LINED WITH COMMON BRICK

The fireplace in our basement recreation room was lined with ordinary rug brick instead of fire brick. It has never been used, and we have been told that it is not safe. Is this so?

Although fire brick is the proper material to use, ordinary brick will do reasonably well, particularly if it is coarse-grained "pressed" brick, rather than smooth, extruded brick, which will not last as long. There is no danger, in any case. It's just that the surface of common brick will flake off in time, with the drastic changes in temperature. For the amount of use you will be giving it, your fireplace should last for many years, then you can have it relined with fire brick if you want to.

LOOSE FIREPLACE MORTAR

I have had my fireplace redone twice and each time the fireclay bonding has become chalky and fallen out. What can I do to stop it?

Maybe your bricklayer or whoever did the job used the wrong mortar, for fireclay is not generally used for firebrick. Special high-temperature mortars should be used. The mortar joints should not be thicker than one-tenth of an inch, incidentally.

Fireplaces

PAINTING A BRICK FIREPLACE

The architect who designed our cement brick fireplace told us to paint it white and recommended spray application. The painter wants $100 to spray paint it. Can we paint it ourselves with a brush or roller? What kind of paint should we use? A paint store salesman told me to fill the mortar joints flush with the surface and then use a semi-gloss oil paint. Wouldn't this spoil the pattern of the bricks?

An oil-based paint should not be used on portland cement brick. Use an *exterior* latex paint. It doesn't have to be sprayed on; a brush works just as well, even in recessed mortar joints. There is no need to fill these.

FIREPLACE REPAIRS

Some of the bricks in our fireplace are cracked, and the mortar has come out in a few places. Is this dangerous, and how can we repair it?

It isn't likely to be dangerous at this stage, but holes, cracks, or open joints in the firebrick lining may cause the surface of the bricks to flake away and dangerous gaps to open up. Early maintenance will prevent serious damage.

It's fairly easy to repair fireplace brick, but you need special "refractory" mortar to withstand the high temperatures. Ordinary brick mortar can't be used. Pre-mixed refractory mortar is sold in tins at most building supply dealers. Brush out all the loose mortar and brick dust and then fill the crack or joint with the mortar, using a putty knife or a small trowel.

Small, hairline cracks can be filled by brushing on a thinned mixture of refractory mortar. Such a wash can also be used to cover up blackened brick and generally improve the appearance of an old fireplace.

FIREPLACE SMOKE STAINS

I have a stone fireplace and a brick fireplace in my house, and both of them are smoke-stained. Can you tell me how to clean them?

A solution of one heaping tablespoon of trisodium phosphate (TSP) to a quart of warm water makes a good fireplace cleaner. Wear rubber gloves and apply with a stiff brush, protecting the floor with newspapers. Rinse off thoroughly.

For more stubborn smoke stains, clay brick, cement brick, and concrete can be cleaned with a solution of one part muriatic acid (from any hardware store) to 10 parts water, but this solution should not be used on stone or on sand-lime (calcium silicate) brick. Wear rubber gloves and be careful to keep the solution off of everything except the fireplace.

Small smoke stains that resist the above treatments can sometimes be removed with one of the spray-on, powder-type spot removers such as K2r or Goddard's Dry Clean. Spray on, let dry, then brush off.

SMOKING FIREPLACE

We had a new fireplace and chimney built in our living room, but more smoke comes in the house than goes up the chimney. The contractor assures me that we have a proper vent and flue size, and the chimney is a foot higher than our house and the one next door. Both the contractor and myself are stumped. Any ideas?

The most likely answer is that your house is too tightly sealed and not enough air can get in to provide a draft up the chimney. Try opening a door or a window when you light the fire. If that helps, there's your answer.

One of the best solutions to this problem is to provide a separate fresh air intake at the back of the fireplace. Then you don't have to bring cold air into the house just to feed the fireplace. More fireplaces should be built like this, but there isn't much you can do about it once the fireplace is built.

An old trick that still works occasionally is to light a piece of newspaper and put it up the chimney before lighting the fireplace. This warms the chimney and gets the draft started.

The next possibility is that the flue *is* too small for the fireplace opening. The flue should be at least $1/12$th the area of the fireplace opening. Measure it and see; don't just take the contractor's word for it.

SMOKING FIREPLACE

We have a fireplace with two openings into adjoining rooms. It smokes badly. Is there anything we can do about it?

Your fireplace flue is probably too small to handle the double-sided opening. The area of the flue should be not less than $1/12$th the *combined* areas of the two fireplace openings. Since you can't increase the size of the flue, you must decrease the size of the openings. The best way to do this is by putting a sheet metal valance or hood across the top of each fireplace opening, sufficient to reduce it to the area required. You can also do it by putting another layer of firebrick on the bottom of the firebox.

UNUSED FIREPLACE SMOKES

We have two fireplaces, one in the living room, which we rarely use, and one in the basement recreation room, which we would like to use more often. The trouble is that whenever we use it we get a smokey smell in the living room, apparently coming from the unused fireplace. Can you explain what is happening and what we can do about it?

Your house is evidently very tightly sealed. When you light the basement fireplace it draws air into the house through any of the openings available, and one of them is the upstairs fireplace flue. Because the flue openings are close together at the top of the chimney, this actually sucks some of the smoke from the basement fireplace back into the house.

It would help to seal the upstairs fireplace damper more tightly, but the simplest remedy is to open a basement window when you are using the fireplace. This will also help it to burn better and smoke less.

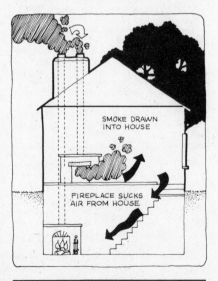

SMOKE DRAWN INTO HOUSE

FIREPLACE SUCKS AIR FROM HOUSE

FIREPLACE vs THERMOSTAT

We would like to put a Franklin heater or free-standing fireplace in our 11' × 21' living room, but the furnace thermostat is at the other end of the room and we are afraid the heater will interfere with its operation. We have a 2-storey house and the upper floor is rented.

The Franklin stove will certainly affect the thermostat and keep the rest of the house cold. You could overcome this by turning the thermostat UP a few degrees whenever the heater is on, but this is going to be a difficult procedure to regulate. It would be better to move the thermostat to a centre hallway or another room—or even to the suite upstairs.

ALGAE IN FISHPOND

Can you tell me how to keep algae from growing in the fishpond in my garden? I have to keep cleaning it and filling it all the time to keep the water clear.

Potassium permanganate, 1 grain to 8 gallons of water, will prevent the formation of algae in a fishpond. Dissolve the required amount in a few ounces of water, and add to the pool slowly. A grain is a very small amount. There are 438 grains to an ounce. An aspirin tablet weighs a bit more than 5 grains.

FLOORS

BLISTERING FLOOR WAX

I have been applying self-polishing wax to my kitchen linoleum for some time, always washing it thoroughly first. Now I find blisters forming in the areas where there isn't any traffic. The flooring itself seems to be in excellent condition, and I don't want to have to replace it. Can you tell me how to get rid of the blisters?

The blisters may be in the heavy coating of wax that has built up in the non-traffic areas. These "self-polishing" materials are very much like a thin varnish, and shouldn't be applied too often without removing the old layers with ammonia. Now it will take a great deal of hard scrub-

Floors

bing to get the build-up off, but that's what you'll have to do to get rid of the blisters. Use a solution of 8 ounces of household ammonia and 4 ounces of powdered floor cleaner to one quart of water.

DULL FLOOR

The gloss has worn off the linoleum floor in our kitchen, and paste wax doesn't bring it back. Is there something I can use to get the shine back?

When the gloss has worn off, there really isn't anything you can put on that will restore it. The self-polishing, liquid acrylic "waxes" are best, but they must be removed after two or three coats have been applied, and this is a lot of work. If I were you I'd stick to the paste wax and forget about the high gloss, or put down new sheet vinyl flooring.

NAILING FLOOR UNDERLAY

How can I nail plywood underlay so the nails won't work up and show through the floor tile?

Use special ringed or spiral flooring nails at least an inch longer than the thickness of your underlay and make sure they are hammered in firmly every 6" around the edges and every 12" across the face.

REMOVING FLOOR WAX

I have waxed our urethane-coated hardwood floors, but they seem to mark very easily. How can I take off the old wax?

Urethane is harder than the wax, so you don't really have to wax the floors unless you want to increase the shine (two or three times a year should be enough). There are several wax strippers on the market, but most of them are just petroleum solvent (NOT gasoline) which you can buy at any gas station. This is flammable and should be kept away from flames and used with plenty of ventilation.

ROTTED FLOOR IN BASEMENT

Some years ago we added two bedrooms in the basement, panelling the walls and putting in a built-up wood floor. We haven't used the rooms for the past few years and when I went into one recently my foot went right through the floor. Also I noticed mold growing above the baseboard along the outside wall. What has caused this to happen and what can I do about it?

You built the wood floor on damp concrete, and that has caused it to rot. Before you can put down a new floor you will have to eliminate the dampness, which is presumably caused by faulty or inadequate drainage around your foundation footings. I suggest you call in two or three drainage contractors for advice and estimates. There are several ways the drainage can be remedied, but none are cheap, I'm afraid.

Unless the concrete floor is very rough there's no need to go to the trouble and expense of a built-up wood floor. Tile or carpeting can be applied directly to the concrete.

ROTTING FLOOR JOISTS

Our house is about 22 years old, and there are signs of dry rot in a couple of the floor joists, which can be seen from the basement. Is this dangerous, and what can we do about it?

It just depends on how far the decay has gone. A small patch or two probably wouldn't cause any trouble, but should be treated with a wood preservative, anyway. If the joists are seriously weakened by decay, they will either have to be replaced or reinforced by nailing a length of joist lumber a few feet on either side of the weak point. Call in a builder for an expert opinion on the extent of the damage and an estimate on repairs.

The term "dry rot" is misleading, since any wood decay requires a fair amount of moisture. In other words, the basic cause of this problem is continued dampness in the basement. There are a number of possible sources—excessive humidity in the house due to inadequate ventilation, use of an unvented clothes dryer in the basement, damp foundation walls and floor caused by poor drainage. Unless there are corrected, more rot will develop.

BASEMENT FLOORING

Is it true that only vinyl-asbestos tiles can be laid on a concrete floor that is below ground level?

Any type of flooring can be laid on concrete as long as it is perfectly dry. But most basement floor slabs are damp at some time of the year, even when they appear to be dry. (A simple test for dampness is to lay a rubber mat on the floor for a few days; any dampness will be clearly visible when the mat is removed.)

Vinyl-asbestos tile and sheet vinyl with an asbestos backing will withstand a limited amount of dampness if applied with a latex adhesive. Foam-backed sheet vinyl and pure vinyl tile require special adhesives.

But if the concrete is very damp, I wouldn't recommend laying any of these materials until the condition has been remedied.

BUILT-UP BASEMENT FLOOR

Could you give me some advice on putting down a wooden subfloor in my basement? I plan to nail 1 × 2 strapping to the concrete, and put ½″ plastic foamboard insulation between this, then cover it with polyethylene vapor barrier before applying ½″ plywood. Finally, I'm going to lay down foam-backed carpeting. Is this the right way to do it?

There's nothing wrong with this except that it's a waste of time and money. If you're going to carpet the floor, why not lay it directly on the concrete? I know of no reason why you should put down a wood subfloor first. Certainly not for insulation. If you measured the temperature of your floor you would find it very close to the temperature of the room. The earth alone, at that depth, provides a lot more insulation than you would get from the built-up floor. The concrete floor would only be cold if it's damp, and in that case you shouldn't lay down a wood floor, anyway.

The money you would spend on the subfloor would be better spent on a good carpet and underpad.

DAMP FLOORS

The floor in our house is concrete covered with tile. It gives us no trouble for most of the year, but during the very humid weather in July and August there is a heavy condensation on the floor. How can we prevent this?

The only thing you can do is lower the humidity in the house by installing an air conditioner or a dehumidifier.

LEVELLING BASEMENT FLOOR

We want to finish our basement but have noticed that the concrete floor is not level. Is there a topping of some kind we can put on to level it before laying floor tiles, or do we have to put down a built-up wood floor?

The basement floor is normally sloped toward the floor drain for obvious reasons, but this is usually only about ¼″ to the foot. A slight grade like this is unnoticeable when you're walking on it, and floor tiles should be laid directly on the existing concrete.

But if your floor is very uneven it should be levelled before the tiles are laid. A new concrete topping is difficult to apply, and not always successful. It would be better to lay a wood subfloor. Dampproof the floor with asphalt foundation coating or 6-mil polyethylene film, then put down 2 x 4 "sleepers" on edge, spaced 16″ apart on centres. Nail 2 x 2 spacers 14½″ long between the sleepers about every 3', and use wood shims or other blocking to level the top of the sleepers. It isn't necessary to nail the floor frame to the concrete; weight will hold it firmly in place. Nail ⅝″ tongue-and-groove plywood subflooring to the sleepers with 1½″ ringed flooring nails spaced every 6″. Leave a space of ½″ between the plywood and the walls to ventilate the space under the subfloor. Insulation is unnecessary, by the way.

REMOVING PAINT FROM CONCRETE FLOOR

Can I take paint off our basement floor with ordinary paint remover?

The active ingredient in most paint removers is methylene chloride, a volatile chemical with toxic fumes. They should be used only in a well-ventilated place.

Considering the possible danger of using relatively large quantities of these materials in a place that is usually difficult to ventilate—as well as their rather high cost for such applications—it would be much better to do the job with ordinary household lye, one can to one quart of water, applied with a rag mop. When the paint is soft, in about five or ten minutes, clean it off with a stiff brush and lots of water. Then wash the floor with dilute muriatic acid, one part to ten parts water.

Lye is an excellent paint remover, but it must be used with care, too. Keep it (and the muriatic acid) away from your skin, clothes or other delicate surfaces. But there are no toxic fumes to worry about.

UNEVEN CONCRETE FLOOR

We want to paint or tile our cellar floor, but it is very uneven and the edges are flaking and pitted. How can we level it?

First check to see if the concrete is dry. If moisture is coming through at any time, no new surface will stand up very long. There are several ways of levelling the floor, but most of them mean raising the level to some extent. One method is to apply a coat of hot asphalt mastic at least ¾-inch thick. This must be done by properly trained men, and the necessary equipment is not available everywhere. A somewhat simpler method is a cold asphalt mastic levelling compound which is mixed with cement and sand. This topping mix can be applied from a thickness of about half an inch to 1½ inches; in other words, it will fill depressions up to one inch deep.

A new concrete topping will not adhere to the old floor unless it is at least two inches thick, or applied with special bonding compounds. Latex-cement mixtures and other plastic-based patching materials can be spread out very thin, however. There are several concrete patching compounds which can be put on in very thin layers. Your building supply dealer can show you what is available. Apply as directed.

CARE OF CORK TILE

Our rumpus room has a 15-year-old-cork tile floor that has had very little use. It looks dried out and dull in traffic areas, but is still shiny in others. There are also some grease stains I would like to remove. What is the proper way to clean and refinish a cork floor?

Cork is really a form of wood, and is generally treated and finished accordingly. Cork tiles come in three types: natural (unfinished), wax-impregnated, and factory-finished (usually with polyurethane). Either of the first two can be cleaned with sandpaper and petroleum solvent (mineral spirits). The latter needs only a damp mopping. Floor wax can be applied to all three types, if desired.

Your cork tiles evidently had a shiny factory finish. Where this has worn off, you can sand the tiles and apply two coats of urethane floor finish. Use fine sandpaper and a hand sanding block, or a lightweight, home workshop belt sander; don't use a heavy-duty floor sander or you're liable to go right through the tile.

If a large area of the floor is involved, however, you would be better off to sand and refinish the whole floor, rather than attempt to touch up just the worn areas. In this case, instead of applying a urethane floor varnish, you might prefer to apply several coats of paste wax. Professionals often melt the wax and brush it on. The advantage of a wax finish is that it doesn't wear through in traffic areas, as a varnish finish does.

STAINS ON CORK FLOOR

We recently bought an older home that has cork tile floors throughout. How can we remove stains and excess wax from these floors?

Without knowing what kind of cork tile you have, it is not possible to give accurate advice. Most cork tile, for instance, has a protective coating of vinyl or similar material. If yours has, you should be able to remove the built-up wax with any of the wax solvents sold in housewares departments. These should take the stains off, too, if they have not penetrated the surface of the tiles.

If the vinyl coating has worn off, the cork tile can be restored by sanding lightly with a power sander and #120 paper, then applying two coats of urethane.

BUCKLED FLOOR

A section of the hardwood floor in our living room has buckled and raised up. I think it got worse this last winter. What can we do about it?

The trouble is generally in the subfloor, not in the hardwood floor itself. Excess humidity sometimes causes the plywood subfloor to buckle, and some inferior grades have even been known to delaminate. Improper nailing will contribute to the problem.

If you've been having trouble with your windows steaming up in the winter, then humidity is your villain, and the remedy is to improve the ventilation of your house, to get rid of the moist air and bring in fresh, dry (yes, and *cold*) air.

Occasionally the trouble is caused by one or more of the floor joists buckling. The joists can be checked from the basement. If they're causing the trouble, call in a carpenter to cut, lower and brace the joists.

CARE OF HARDWOOD FLOORS

We have just bought a new house with gleaming hardwood floors, and I would like to have some advice on the proper way to maintain them. There are so many different floor care products on the market that I'm thoroughly confused. Can you help me?

The introduction of polyurethane finishes has made hardwood floors much more durable and easier to look after. They really require very little attention, and not nearly as much waxing and polishing as you might be led to believe by some of the TV commercials.

Heavy traffic areas should be swept or vacuumed every day to remove the abrasive dust that is responsible for most of the wear. The entire house should be done once a week for the same reason. Food spills should be wiped up immediately with a damp cloth or sponge.

In most homes it shouldn't be necessary to wax the floor more than twice a year. An occasional buffing, preferably with an electric polisher, will maintain the polish.

Only solvent-based, buffing polishes, either paste or liquid, should be used on wood floors. The self-polishing, water-based products that are widely used on vinyl and other resilient flooring are not recommended for use on wood. Solvent-based polishes are easily recognized by their gasoline-like smell.

Solvent-based polishes are self-cleaning; the old wax and dirt are removed by the solvent in the next application. For this reason it's important to change the applicator cloth or pad frequently while the polish is being applied, in order to get rid of the dirt and old wax.

Allow the wax to dry for about 30 minutes, then buff. If you are using an electric polisher, start with the brushes and finish with the lamb's wool pads. After use, wash out the pads and brushes thoroughly with soap and water and a little ammonia to prevent a buildup of hard wax.

Heel marks and most other spots can be removed by rubbing with #000 steel wool and a little floor polish, then buffing. Scratches and worn areas can sometimes be restored by applying a colored paste wax sold for this purpose. If the floor is badly worn, however, the only remedy is to have it sanded and refinished.

If improper application or insufficient polishing causes a sticky buildup of wax on the floor, this can be removed with a commercial cleaner or with a petroleum solvent (mineral spirits). These solutions are inflammable, so use with care.

CIGARETTE BURN ON FLOOR

I would like to know how to fix a cigarette burn on a hardwood floor.

Use a knife and/or sandpaper to remove the burned wood. If the depression is very shallow, just apply one or two coats of varnish, and the spot won't be noticeable. If it's deep, you'd have to fill it with a matching wood filler, sand, then varnish.

FLOOR FINISHES

We have an older house with oak floors that are badly in need of refinishing. We are going to have the work done by professionals, but before we get them in we must decide what we want. Some people say that urethane is best, but it seems too glossy for us. Is there a natural-wood finish that we can use on the floor? We also think that it might be nice to darken the wood. How can this be done? How many coats should be put on? Any other information you can give us about floor finishes will be appreciated.

Urethane varnish is the most durable floor finish available today, but it is not quite as miraculous as some manufacturers suggest. Like any other floor surface, it requires regular dusting and cleaning and occasional waxing to retain its high gloss, and eventually it will need refinishing.

Most people want a high-gloss floor these days, but semi-gloss or satin urethane varnishes are available.

The old floor should be sanded to bare wood, starting with #40 and finishing off with a fine, #120 paper. For an ultra-smooth finish, a paste filler can be applied next, but this is rarely used today. Remove all sanding dust with a vacuum cleaner. If you want to darken the wood, any of the semi-transparent stains can be applied. Oak takes stains beautifully, and a walnut tone is very attractive.

At least two coats of urethane varnish should be applied to the sanded floor. Some manufacturers recommend thinning the first coat about 10%; others don't. Many floor finishers speed the job by substituting a fast-drying shellac or lacquer sealer for the first coat of urethane varnish, but this is not recommended because these materials are not compatible with urethane.

It is also important that the first coat of urethane not be allowed to dry too hard before the next coat is applied. Twenty-four hours is generally considered the maximum time to allow between coats. If it dries much longer than that, it should be sanded lightly before the next coat is applied.

Lacquer floor finishes are also available. Their main advantage is their fast drying time—a second coat can often be applied within an hour. They can also be touched up in worn areas without doing the whole floor, because the new coat dissolves and blends with the old finish. Lacquers are not nearly as tough as the urethane varnishes, however.

If you're looking for a natural-looking, satin finish, use one of the penetrating sealers such as a Danish oil finish or plastic-in-oil. These are simply brushed on, allowed to sink in for 15 minutes or so, then wiped off. A second and third coat should be applied the same way. This type of finish can be touched up at any time simply by rubbing the worn or marked area lightly with steel wool and then wiping on another coat. Some of these penetrating sealers come with wood stains already in them, so the staining and finishing can be done with one material.

FINISHING A FLOOR

I refinished the hardwood floor in a small bedroom by hand, but it hasn't turned out too well. First I stripped off the old finish with varnish remover, then used steel wool and sandpaper. I applied a liberal coat of wood sealer according to the instructions on the label, but it took three days to dry, instead of eight hours, and came up blotchy. Finally I applied a clear gloss finish very sparingly with a 1″ brush, but this has dried very patchy and uneven. What did I do wrong?

I don't think there's anything seriously wrong. Since the floor had been sealed and finished before, you didn't need to put on a sealer again. This couldn't sink in to the wood the way it's supposed to, anyway, and that's probably why it took so long to dry.

It sounds as if you applied the clear finish *too* sparingly, particularly if you were only using a 1″ brush. A 3″ or 4″ brush is much better for floors. All you need to do, I think, is apply another coat of clear finish.

PAINT SPILLED ON WOOD FLOOR

While painting our baby's crib, my husband spilled paint on our hardwood floor, which has a plastic finish. How can we remove the paint without damaging the floor finish?

You can't. Anything that will take off the paint will also remove the floor finish. Do it anyway, then patch up the floor finish.

PARQUET ON CONCRETE

Our parquet floor, which was laid right on top of concrete, has gradually begun to turn black in places as if water is seeping in somewhere. We have taken up a few of the parquet squares and the floor underneath seems perfectly dry. What do you think is the trouble?

It is difficult to diagnose the problem at long range, but it does sound as if moisture is the culprit, even though the floor appears dry. A reliable test is to put about half a teaspoon of calcium chloride crystals on the concrete and cover with a square of polyethylene taped around the edges. If the concrete is damp, the crystals will absorb moisture and form droplets under the polyethylene within a day or two. If the crystals remain dry, then so is the floor.

An alternative is to lay down a rubber mat for a few days. Any moisture will show underneath when you lift the mat up.

If either test reveals moisture, check your drainage system around and under the concrete; repair or install a sump pump.

PARQUET ON PAINTED CONCRETE

I planned to finish my basement floor with prefinished parquet wood tiles. The trouble is that the floor has been painted. The tile manufacturer says not to lay his product on painted concrete, but the paint manufacturer says that floor tile can be laid over *his* product. I don't know which to believe. What should I do?

Paint and tile manufacturers have been in disagreement for years on this subject, but the evidence of my mail favors the opinion of the tile manufacturers. In other words, I would NOT attempt to glue parquet tile, or any other tile, to painted concrete. In fact I don't recommend laying wood tiles on *unpainted* concrete below ground level, where a certain amount of dampness is almost inevitable. The best tile to use on painted concrete is a self-adhesive vinyl-asbestos tile . . . the kind with a peel-off backing.

PEELING FLOOR FINISH

We had our hardwood floors sanded and given a polyurethane finish, then we applied a paste wax. In a few weeks the polyurethane began to peel off. When we complained about this we were told that we should not have used wax. What are we supposed to use on this kind of floor finish?

There's absolutely no reason why wax should

not be applied to polyurethane. It usually isn't necessary, mind you, but it certainly can't do any harm. And it couldn't possibly be responsible for the peeling. I suspect this was caused by the use of a lacquer sealer under the urethane, which is not recommended by any urethane manufacturer, but is still often used by floor finishers because it's faster and cheaper than just using urethane.

POOR POLYURETHANE FLOOR

About two months ago, I had a floor man come in and sand, stain, seal, and apply two coats of polyurethane finish to a large living-dining area. Now the finish has worn very dull and has a lot of scratches, although only two people and a kitten have been walking on it. I thought polyurethane was supposed to be a very hard, durable finish. Was I wrong?

It sounds as if your floor man used a poor grade of polyurethane varnish. Unfortunately, even one containing only a small percentage of urethane can be called a urethane finish on the label—there are no regulations requiring the percentage to be shown. The only thing you can do is add one or two coats of a high quality urethane varnish now, but you'll have to sand the surface lightly to provide a "tooth" for the new finish. Price and brand name are about the only guides you have to quality, and they are not infallible.

FINISHING A PINE FLOOR

We have lovely pine floors in our house that have been finished with a tung oil varnish once a year. We have been unable to get this this year and would appreciate your advice on what we should use. Will the floors have to be sanded before anything else is put on?

Tung oil varnish is harder than linseed oil varnish, but neither of them provides as tough a finish for floors as polyurethane varnish. Sand the present finish lightly before applying this, unless the floor is badly worn. In this case you should sand it down to bare wood and start again with two coats of polyurethane floor finish.

GAPS IN PINE FLOOR

We recently purchased a 100-year-old farmhouse with floors of 2" pine planking about 7" wide. Some of the planks have separated, leaving gaps up to ½" wide in places. What kind of filler should we use?

There isn't any putty-like material that will fill such large gaps satisfactorily. The proper thing to do, of course, is take up the planks and re-lay them. The next best thing is to cut some pine plank strips of various widths and glue them into the cracks. A matching wood filler could then be used to fill the small gaps left. After sanding, the floor can be finished with a penetrating sealer or two coats of satin urethane varnish.

HARDENING SOFTWOOD

We're restoring an old house and would like to retain the existing pine floors. Is there any material we can apply that will make them harder?

There's nothing that you can put on to harden the wood, but the toughest, hardest-wearing floor finish is urethane (or *poly*urethane) varnish, and this works just as well on softwood as it does on hardwood.

POUR-ON FLOORING

Several years ago we installed a pour-on, seamless flooring over asphalt tile. This consisted of a base coat followed by a plastic finish, colored flakes, and then more clear plastic. The floor is now showing signs of wear, but this material is no longer on the market. If I want to install new flooring of vinyl or ceramic tile, do I have to remove the old flooring first? And, if so, how do I get it off?

It would be a very difficult job to remove the old flooring. I think the best thing to do is to cover it with a new subfloor of ¼" plywood. Fasten this down with 1½-inch ringed flooring nails spaced every 6 inches around the edge of the panels and every 12 inches across the face. Then apply the new flooring to this.

RAISING SAGGING FLOOR

The floors in our 65-year-old house sag towards the centre. Previous owners have installed jack-posts under the main beam in the basement, and I am wondering if I should raise them to try and make the floor completely level. Or will this just create more problems? I can see where some cracks in the walls that have already been filled are starting to open again.

A sagging floor creates many problems, and I think you should try to correct it. The jack-posts should be raised very gradually, however, no more than $\frac{1}{16}''$ a day—just a fraction of a turn. Check the ends of the beam to make sure it is not being lifted instead of straightened. If so, stop moving the jack for a few days and wet the beam with a sponge or spray to make it more flexible, then resume jacking.

Levelling the floor may cause some new cracks, particularly where gaps had been filled, and you may decide not to level the floor completely (indeed, it may have had a slight sag ever since it was built). But it is better to repair these than to have tilted floors and doors that don't hang properly.

TOUCHING UP WORN HARDWOOD FLOORS

We have beautiful hardwood floors that I hate to see buried under carpets. In some traffic areas, however, the floor finish shows signs of wear. Is there any way we can spot finish these areas without having to refinish the whole floor?

If you're careful and patient, this can be done quite successfully. First you'll have to remove any wax with petroleum solvent (mineral spirits). Then roughen the surface of the areas to be refinished with fine sandpaper or medium grade steel wool (#00 or #000). Vacuum off the sanding dust thoroughly, then apply a coat of urethane floor varnish, thinned down with about 5% thinner by volume, being careful to keep the varnish to the areas that were sanded.

If the refinished areas look too glossy, you can dull them down by rubbing them in the direction of the grain with very fine steel wool (#0000). If they're a little too dull, apply paste wax and buff.

BURN IN VINYL TILE FLOOR

How can we repair a cigarette burn in permanently installed cushioned sheet vinyl flooring?

Cut out the burn carefully and insert a patch of the same material as your flooring. Use the adhesive recommended by the manufacturer of the flooring.

DULL FLOOR TILES

We've just bought an older house that is in good shape but I can't seem to get the kitchen tiles to shine. I've tried a number of different waxes and floor polishes, but the best they do is give a dull sheen. Is there anything we can paint on to restore the original finish?

It's quite possible that they never had a very high finish. Vinyl asbestos tiles, for instance are not as shiny as the more expensive pure vinyl tiles, and it's impossible to bring them up to a really high gloss with any wax or polish. The vinyl asbestos surface is simply not smooth enough.

Don't try to change this with a varnish or plastic finish. It may look nice for a little while, but when it begins to wear down in traffic areas you're in trouble, because there's no way to remove the old finish without ruining the floor.

GAPS IN FLOORING

The vinyl floor in our kitchen has cracked along the seam of the plywood underneath.

The most common cause of this problem is improper preparation of the subfloor. A lot of green lumber is used in building houses these days, and when this dries out the plywood underlay opens up. Sheet vinyl flooring gaps at the seams; vinyl-asbestos tile may crack. Proper preparation will prevent this trouble. A good grade of sanded plywood should be used—not sheathing grade—and it should be nailed or stapled every 6" around the edges and every 12" across the face with special flooring nails. The plywood should be laid with staggered seams, so there will be no continuous joint across a floor in either direction. Mistakes or shortcuts in laying the floor also contribute to the problem. The proper job calls for vacuuming the plywood thoroughly, applying a layer of special flooring felt, allowing the adhesive to dry overnight, laying the tile or sheet flooring with the proper adhesive, and sandbagging the sheet flooring seams. All the laying operations should be carried out in a constant temperature of more than 60°. One or more of these steps is often eliminated, or inadequately done, to cut costs. When trouble comes, there are no easy solutions. Sheet vinyl (but not linoleum) can be stretched and welded with the application of heat to close a seam gap of not more than $\frac{1}{8}''$. Individual tiles can be taken up, the open seam underneath filled, and new tiles laid. Chances are, however, that the subfloor will continue to move and cause more gaps and broken tiles in the future. There really isn't any cure for a poor flooring job except to rip it up and start over.

HEEL MARKS ON FLOOR

In our new house we already have a problem with black heel marks on our vinyl tile floors.

My mother tells me to use steel wool or an abrasive cleaner, but I'm afraid this might damage the floor. What should I do?

In this case, mother doesn't know best. Steel wool or abrasive cleaners will dull the glossy surface of the tile. Rubber heel marks can be removed quite easily with a rag moistened with petroleum solvent or paint thinner.

INDENTATIONS IN VINYL FLOOR

Which flooring will show indentations more—homogenous vinyl or vinyl asbestos?

Because it is more resilient, pure, homogenous vinyl flooring will show initial indentations more readily than vinyl asbestos, but pure vinyl flooring recovers faster.

INLAID FLOORS

Can you tell me what the term "inlaid" refers to in regard to floor coverings?

There are three different ways to put a pattern on resilient flooring materials like vinyl and linoleum. The cheapest way is to print it on the surface; this is how the old lino rugs were made. The second way is a combination of embossing and painting, where the paint is applied to a pattern that has been impressed into the surface. Most of the cushioned sheet vinyl flooring is made this way.

The third and most expensive method is inlaying. Die cut patterns or chips of various colors are deeply imbedded in the background plastic, and may actually extend right through to the backing. This is the meaning of the term "inlaid."

LAYING FLOOR TILE

I want to lay tile on the cement floor in our basement, but I've never done anything like this and I don't know how to go about it. Can you tell me?

First make sure the floor is dry. Don't trust appearances. Lay a rubber mat on the floor for two or three days, and then lift it up. If you see any sign of dampness underneath, it means you have a drainage problem. Fix this before you lay the tile. The floor must also be clean. Use a damp mop to remove dirt and dust.

The recommended tile for concrete below ground level is vinyl asbestos. Peel-off, self-stick tiles are the easiest to apply, but they're more expensive than the kind that are laid with adhesive. Most tiles are now 12" square,

but there are still a few 9" tiles around. Measure the floor and calculate how many tiles you need. Get a few extra; most dealers will give you a refund on any you don't use, but they may come in handy for repairs later.

Use the adhesive recommended by the tile manufacturer. A latex emulsion adhesive is the most popular type used today; it is light in color and can be cleaned up with water before it sets.

You often see application instructions that tell you to divide the floor into quarters with two chalk lines, and then start laying tile in the centre of the floor and work out to the walls. I've never seen a professional do it this way. The obvious and easiest place to start is in a corner, and then work out along the two walls.

You might end up with a very narrow tile along the opposite wall, but I really don't think that makes any difference on a basement floor. The alternative is to move the whole row of tiles over to equal the space at both ends, and then cut two complete rows of tiles to fit. This is wasteful as well as tedious.

Where a tile does have to be cut, this can be done simply by scoring it with a sharp knife and then bending.

If you're using self-adhesive tiles, just proceed to peel and stick. If you're using adhesive, apply this according to the instructions. Some are just brushed on, but most are applied with a notched spreader. Apply the adhesive to a small area at a time, enough for about a dozen tiles. The most common mistake is to use too much adhesive; the notches on the trowel must be the exact size recommended.

Lay each tile in place by butting the edge of it against the last tile and then dropping it down. Don't slide it into position. Most tiles have a distinct grain pattern, and it's generally best to alternate the direction of the pattern in each tile as you go, but you may prefer to lay them all in the same direction. Decide which you want, and then do it that way; don't lay them in a random pattern the way you happen to pick them up.

Press the tiles down firmly with your feet. There shouldn't be any excess adhesive, but if any squeezed up, remove it quickly.

And that's about all there is to it.

LIFTING TILES

Before we finished a recreation room in our basement, we had it professionally waterproofed, and new drain tile laid under the floor and around the foundation. The floor was always dry after this, then we had vinyl asbestos floor tile laid and within a few months it started to lift.

The floor man says it's due to dampness, and the waterproofer blames the floor layer.

If dampness is causing the tiles to lift, you would see evidence of this in the form of a mold-like white power, or efflorescence, under the raised tiles. If there is no sign of this, it probably means that the tile wasn't laid properly. In which case, you should have the raised tiles re-cemented and weighted down until the adhesive sets.

FLOOR TILES LIFTING

I have a problem with my basement floor tiles. The concrete seemed very dry, so I put down a coat of asphalt primer and let this dry. Then I laid vinyl-asbestos tile with a white latex adhesive put out by the tile manufacturer. Now the tiles are beginning to curl up. What did I do wrong, and how can I right it?

The trouble could be caused by dampness in the concrete, but I think it's because you used the wrong kind of adhesive on top of the asphalt primer. You should have used a black asphalt-latex adhesive that is compatible with the primer.

Actually, you didn't need to use the asphalt primer. These were used in the days of asphalt tile, which was applied with an asphalt adhesive (this black goo used to keep squeezing up between the tiles, you'll remember). Since the introduction of vinyl-asbestos tile and white latex adhesive, asphalt primers have not been required.

The best thing you can do now, I think, is remove the curling tiles—or all of the tiles— and re-lay them with a black asphalt-latex adhesive that will be compatible with the primer.

LIFTING TILES

A few years ago we painted our basement floor with a concrete floor paint, which claimed that tiles could be laid on top of it. About a year ago we bought top quality floor tiles and laid them with the recommended adhesive. Now they have started to curl up at the edges. Is there anything we can do about it?

Regardless of what the paint manufacturers say, tile manufacturers do not recommend the application of tiles on a painted surface. It may work 9 times out of 10, or 99 times out of 100, but sometimes the paint doesn't hold, and then you're in a lot of trouble.

I know of no solution other than removing all the tiles, stripping off the paint, then starting over again.

FLOOR TILES LIFTING

I laid an asphalt tile floor in my basement several years ago, and am now having trouble with a white fungus that is growing under the tiles and lifting them out of position. I have removed several of the tiles, scraped off all the fungus, and re-glued them, but they get pushed off again. Can you tell me why this happens and what I can do about it?

That's not a fungus. It's efflorescence, an inorganic white powder left behind when the water that is seeping through the concrete evaporates. Moisture is lifting the tiles, and the cause is faulty or inadequate drainage around the base of your foundation walls.

There are three possible solutions: 1) Have the drainage around the outside of the house checked and repaired. 2) Have drain tile laid under the edge of the floor *inside* the house and connected to the drain. 3) Put in a sump pump.

LINOLEUM BUCKLING

What can be done to a linoleum floor that buckles when it gets wet?

The best thing to do is take up the linoleum, scrape or sand the subfloor to remove the old adhesive, and then re-lay it with waterproof cement. If the water has rotted the fibre backing of the linoleum, however, you'd be better off to throw it away and put down one of the new vinyl flooring materials.

NAIL POLISH ON TILED FLOOR

I have spilled a bottle of colored nail polish on a vinyl asbestos tile floor. Neither nail polish remover nor acetone seems to touch it; they only roughen the surrounding tile area. How can I remove the polish without wrecking the floor?

All you can do is replace the damaged tile. Heat it with an iron or propane torch to soften the adhesive, then pull up. Apply a new tile with fresh adhesive.

PLASTIC FLOOR FINISH

I am trying to locate a liquid plastic that can be put on tile or linoleum floors. I read somewhere about one that was crystal clear, waterproof, and had a permanent shine, but I can't remember the name. Can you tell me what it is?

No varnish, lacquer, or other film finish should ever be used on tile or linoleum. They may look all right for a little while, but when they become worn in spots, as they all do, there is no way to strip off the old finish and re-do them. Anything that will remove the finish will damage the tile. And regardless of what you hear, there is no magic finish that stays glossy forever.

TILING OVER PAINT

I'm building a rec room in my basement and was planning on laying self-stick tiles on the floor. However, the floor has been painted with a very glossy paint that flakes off when anything heavy is dragged over it. Do I have to remove this before the tiles can be applied? If so, how?

Self-stick tile puts little strain on the floor surface, and it's quite possible that the paint is strong enough to hold the tile. But if you don't want to take a chance, the paint can be removed with a very strong solution of lye—one 9½-ounce can to a quart of water. Apply with a string mop, then scrape and wash off the softened paint. Wear rubber gloves and be careful to keep the lye solution off your skin and clothes.

RAISED SEAMS IN FLOORING

We laid some sheet vinyl flooring in our kitchen, with one seam down the centre. Now, three months later, it is buckling up at this join, forming a ridge about a quarter of an inch high. How can we correct this?

This generally indicates that the flooring has been forced together too tightly at the seam, or that the uneven factory edge was not trimmed off before the sheets were joined. The remedy is to cut out a strip of flooring about 5″ on either side of the seam, and replace this with a matching strip of flooring about 12″ wide. Cut and remove one strip, using a long metal straight-edge and linoleum knife, then lay the oversized patch strip in position against this cut edge. The new strip will overlap the other edge about 2″. With knife and straight-edge, cut through both the patch strip and the flooring underneath about 1″ in from the edge. Remove the waste strips from the patch and the flooring. Test to make sure the new patch now fits correctly, then apply with the recommended adhesive. Use a roller to press the two new seams.

REMOVING BASEMENT FLOOR TILES

I want to replace the vinyl-asbestos floor tiles in my basement. Can you tell me how to remove them?

Use a propane torch to heat the tiles. This will soften the adhesive and curl the tiles so they can be lifted off. The remaining adhesive will probably leave a rough floor surface, however, and this will have to be removed before you lay new tile.

If the present tile is firmly attached to the concrete, and tightly fitted, there is really no need to remove it. Just clean off any wax and dirt, fill any holes with a plaster patching compound, and lay the new tiles with an emulsion adhesive.

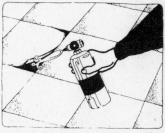

REPAIRING A VINYL FLOOR

Can you tell me how to repair a spot on the vinyl floor of our kitchen where I dropped a hot stove lid?

If it's a tile floor, the best thing to do is replace the damaged tile. If you can't just pry it up and peel it off, heat the tile carefully with a propane torch to soften the adhesive.

If it's sheet vinyl flooring, you can patch the spot, but you'll need a piece of the same flooring material a few inches larger than the damaged area. Lay this over the spot, adjust its position to match the pattern of the floor, if necessary, and then tape it in place. With a linoleum knife and a steel ruler, cut a rectangular patch large enough to cover the damaged area, cutting through *both the patch material and the original flooring*. Remove the taped piece of flooring and use the cut-out patch to replace the damaged section of the floor, which can now be lifted out where it has been cut. The patch should fit exactly. Glue it in place with the appropriate flooring cement.

REPLACING FLOOR TILES

The hallway in our basement is tiled with about 85 square feet of 9-inch asphalt tile, put down about 8 years ago. Some of the tiles are curling at the edges. I've tried gluing them down, but now I want to replace them with a new tile floor. Would you recommend using the peel-and-stick kind, or should I use adhesive?

The old tiles can be removed with heat, applied with an iron or a propane torch to soften the adhesive. Then you'll have to remove the old adhesive, or scrape it down until the floor is perfectly smooth. If it's the black, asphalt adhesive that was originally used with this type of tile, you'll find that a little petroleum solvent (mineral spirits) will help to remove it. But this is moderately flammable, so make sure the basement is well ventilated and that the furnace is turned off...the pilot light, too, if you have a gas furnace.

The preferred tile for a basement floor is vinyl-asbestos. (Asphalt tile is no longer made.) The peel-and-stick type is easiest to put down, but a little more expensive. For other types, follow the manufacturer's instructions about the correct adhesive to use.

Dampness in the concrete may be causing the asphalt tiles to curl. This should be cured by correcting the drainage around the foundation footings before any new tile is laid. To check for dampness, lay a rubber mat on the bare concrete for two or three days. If you see any sign of dampness when you lift it, you've got trouble.

REPLACING A FLOOR TILE

One of the floor tiles in our kitchen has been damaged and must be replaced. Unfortunately it is a very old pattern that isn't manufactured any longer, I am told. Do you have any idea where I might find a replacement tile?

Sure, just slide out the refrigerator and remove one of the tiles underneath it.

RE-TILING KITCHEN

I want to re-tile our kitchen floor. The present flooring is 9" × 9" tile, probably vinyl-asbestos, and it's in excellent condition, but we want to change the color and the pattern. Would it be satisfactory just to lay the new tile on top of the present tile. What kind of tile requires the least care?

It's possible to lay new 12" x 12" tiles on top of the old tiles as long as you strip off all the wax or other polish and roughen the surface slightly with sandpaper. I don't recommend it, however, because the joint marks of the old tiles will eventually show through. The best way to change the tiles is to put down ¼" ply-

wood underlayment, using 1½" ringed flooring nails every 6" around the edges and every 12" across the face. Apply the new tiles to this with the recommended adhesive. Use metal molding strips to cover the edge of the raised floor. The best kind of tile to use is a solid vinyl but this is much more expensive than vinyl-asbestos.

It would be easier, and probably better, to cover the old tiles with a cushion-backed, sheet vinyl flooring.

SHEET VINYL OVER TILE

The white vinyl tiles on our kitchen floor are still firmly in place, but their lustre is gone and every little dirt mark shows on the light color. I would like to lay sheet vinyl flooring on top of it. Can I do this myself? Do the tiles have to be removed first? Is a special underlayment required?

Yes to the first question and No to the others. All sheet vinyl flooring used to be stiff and hard to handle, requiring professional application, and some of it still is and does. But a new family of soft, flexible, cushioned flooring that is much easier to handle has come on the market in the last few years. It is easy to trim, comes in either 6' or 12' widths that eliminate seams in most rooms, and can be loose-laid or stapled. The cushion backing allows it to be laid directly over a tile floor that is not loose or curled. Any flooring dealer can show you samples.

SELF-STICK TILES ON CONCRETE

Our basement floor was painted a few years ago, and part of it has worn off. Now we would like to lay down self-stick vinyl tiles. Can this be done without removing the paint?

Yes. The self-stick tiles will adhere to paint or to bare, clean concrete, as long as the surface is dry.

SHELLAC ON TILE FLOOR

Somebody told me to paint our vinyl tile floor with shellac so that it would keep its shine. Now it is worn in spots and looks terrible. How can I get it off? I'm afraid to use paint remover.

If it was varnish, you'd be in real trouble, but shellac can be taken off quite easily and safely with methyl hydrate, available at any paint or hardware store. It's very inflammable, though, so provide plenty of ventilation and don't have any open flames around while you're doing the job.

ROUGHENED FLOOR TILE

Our recreation room floor consists of vinyl-asbestos tile laid directly on the concrete. The trouble I am having is that after I wax it the shine only lasts for a few days, then dull patches begin to appear and the surface becomes rough and grainy. Now the floor is no longer attractive and I am thinking of covering it with wall-to-wall carpeting. Will what is happening to the tiles also damage the carpet?

It sounds to me as if you have been using a solvent-based wax that is dissolving the surface of the tiles. Although some tiles are resistant to petroleum solvents, most manufacturers recommend using only water-based polishes, either wax emulsions or clear acrylics.

As long as the floor is dry, there's no reason why you shouldn't lay broadloom on it.

RUG STAINS ON FLOOR TILE

I have two small area rugs that have left stains on the vinyl-asbestos tile. The one in the kitchen has a binding around the edge that has left a yellow line on the floor. In the front hall I have a foam-backed rug that has left a dark stain over the entire area. Now I have to leave the rugs in place to hide the stains. Do you know of anything that will remove these?

Because such stains usually penetrate the surface of the tile, they are very difficult to remove. A strong solution of chlorine laundry bleach may work, however. If not, try #0000 steel wool. This may dull the surface slightly, but wax will restore it.

APPLYING NEW VINYL OVER CUSHIONED FLOORING

Our kitchen floor is presently covered with a cushioned vinyl flooring. We would like to put down one of the new, wet look, no-wax flooring materials. Can this be installed on top of the cushioned vinyl?

Yes, if you use the type that is simply stapled around the edge and is not applied with adhesive. Most of the sheet vinyls must be applied with adhesive, however, and for these it is necessary to remove the cushioned flooring first. This can be done by cutting the flooring

into 24"-wide strips and peeling off the vinyl layer. Then use a broad putty knife or similar tool to scrape the remaining felt off the floor. The new flooring can then be applied with the regular adhesive.

Handling, cutting and seaming the 6'-wide rolls of vinyl flooring is not an easy do-it-yourself project, however, particularly if you plan to use a thick, inlaid material.

VINEGAR STAIN ON FLOOR TILE

I spilled some vinegar on our kitchen floor, which is a blue vinyl tile, and didn't notice it for several hours. After I wiped it up and the floor had dried I discovered that the vinegar had taken the color out of the tile, leaving large white spots that won't wash off. Is there anything I can do to get rid of these marks?

Fortunately, they're just on the surface and can be removed with a fine abrasive. Automobile rubbing compound—an abrasive polish used on automobile finishes—will do the job, and so will #0000 grade steel wool. To restore the gloss, apply polish.

A HIGH-GLOSS FINISH FOR VINYL-ASBESTOS TILE

We have light-colored vinyl-asbestos tiles on our kitchen floor, and I have tried everything to give them a good polish, but they're still quite dull. There is the same kind of tile in the office where I work, and it has been brought up to a beautiful shine. Can you tell me what kind of floor polish or treatment I should use to get a high gloss like this?

It has always been difficult to get a good shine on vinyl-asbestos tiles, but professional maintenance men do it with "spray buffing," a technique that will also work for the homemaker, although it requires a little special care and one product that you won't find in your local grocery store.

You need an electric floor polisher (the heavier the better), a spray bottle, a wax-emulsion floor polish, and a buff-colored, 3M nylon polishing pad. Be sure to get a buff-colored nylon pad or a white polyester pad; other colors are too abrasive.

Begin by stripping the present polish from the floor and rinsing with a very dilute vinegar-and-water solution. Then apply three thin coats of wax-emulsion floor polish, the second coat within about 40 minutes of the first, the third an hour later. Buff between coats with the nylon pad. The following day apply a fourth coat.

Floors

In a week or two, damp-mop the floor and fill a spray bottle with one part floor polish to one part water. Apply a light *mist spray* to a small area of the floor and immediately start buffing it with the nylon polishing pads. Mist spray another area just ahead of the polisher and buff it before it dries.

Repeat this treatment once a week, keeping the spray to the main traffic areas and away from the walls. After a few such treatments you'll find you have the best shine you've ever seen on a vinyl-asbestos tile floor. And you will be adding such a thin layer of polish each time that it will be months before you will have to remove it. Experts can gauge the amount of the spray so well that it just replaces the amount that is removed by buffing, and they can go for years without having to strip back to the tile.

REMOVING TILE ADHESIVE

The adhesive is squeezing up between the joints of our floor tile. How can I remove it without damaging the tile?

First you have to find out what kind of adhesive it is. If it's black, it can be either an emulsion or a solvent type. Wrap a piece of cloth around your finger, moisten it with petroleum solvent (mineral spirits), and then rub it on the adhesive; if it shows signs of dissolving, it's a solvent-based adhesive. First scrape off as much as you can with a putty knife, then gently rub off the rest with solvent applied with a cloth. Wet the cloth with water and wring it out almost dry before using it to apply a few drops of solvent at a time. Just enough to soften and remove the adhesive.

If it's an emulsion type black adhesive, or one of the more common white latex adhesives, don't use a solvent. Scrape off as much as you can with a knife, and then use soap and water and either fine steel wool or a nylon scouring pad to rub off the rest. The adhesive should roll up into granules and brush off.

REMOVING VINYL FLOORING

The pattern has worn off the sheet vinyl flooring in our kitchen and we would like to replace it. It is firmly glued to the subfloor, however. How can we take it off?

It is very difficult to remove this type of flooring, and rarely necessary. Flooring materials that do not require full adhesive application, and need only be stapled or glued around the edges, can be applied right over the existing flooring. But if this has an embossed pattern or is badly damaged, or if you want to cover it with a material that must be laid with adhesive, the best thing to do is cover the existing floor with ¼" plywood or other underlayment material applied with 1" ringed flooring nails spaced every 6" around the edges and every 12" across the face. Stagger the sheets of underlayment to avoid a continuous seam.

If you *must* remove the present flooring, do it by cutting the vinyl wear layer in strips about 12" wide with a razor knife (it isn't necessary to cut right through to the floor). Peel the strips of vinyl off by pulling or by rolling them around a bottle. The felt backing that remains on the floor should be scraped off with a broad putty knife or similar tool. This usually contains asbestos fibres and SHOULD NOT BE SANDED. It is advisable to wear a dust mask.

REPAIRING SHEET VINYL FLOOR

Our dishwasher leaked and went unnoticed for an hour or so, and the strong detergent and hot water opened a seam in our recently laid cushion-backed sheet-vinyl floor. A strip about a foot long has curled up. Is there any kind of glue we can squeeze into the crack to restore the seam?

A special welding iron and solvents must be used to form an invisible watertight seam in this type of flooring. It's not a do-it-yourself job, I'm afraid. Contact the firm that laid the flooring, explain the problem, and ask them to send a repairman.

WATER MARKS ON VINYL FLOOR

Would you know how to prevent white water marks on a vinyl bathroom floor? The floor has been polished with a hard wax, but these stains only appeared recently when the floor was splashed with water.

Vinyl itself can't be marked by water, so it must be the wax that is discolored. I suggest you strip this off with wax remover, then switch to one of the self-polishing acrylics. Paste wax should not be used on vinyl.

PASTE WAX ON
NO-WAX FLOORING

I used a paste wax on my new, expensive, no-wax flooring. It is streaky and sticky and has no shine at all. How can I correct my mistake and restore the original shine?

There are three reasons why wax should not be used on no-wax flooring. First, it isn't necessary; the flooring already has a good shine. Second, wax doesn't adhere properly to the no-wax surface; it just smears around, as you've discovered. And third, paste wax contains solvents that can damage the flooring. You should be able to remove the wax with one of the liquid floor strippers or a solution of 1 cup of liquid ammonia and ¼ cup of a powdered floor cleaner to 1 gallon of water. If these water-based removers don't do the job, use a number of clean cloths dampened (not soaked) with petroleum solvent (mineral spirits). Don't leave the solvent on the floor any longer than you have to; buff it quickly with a dry cloth.

YELLOW VINYL

The white vinyl tiles on our kitchen floor have gone very yellow although I clean them regularly and use a self-polishing liquid wax. I've tried all kinds of cleaners to get rid of the yellow stain, but nothing works. Do you have any suggestions?

It could be a build-up of the floor polish. These clear, acrylic solutions are much like a very thin varnish, and they can build up to a tough, dirty film if too many layers are applied. Unless you're spray buffing (see previous item) no more than three or four applications should be made without stripping off the old polish with ammonia or other recommended remover. After this it becomes a very tough job.

If the yellow is not in the polish build-up, but the vinyl tiles themselves, try a strong solution of chlorine laundry bleach. This sometimes removes the discoloration. More likely, however, the color has developed in the vinyl, and cannot be removed. Manufacturers claim to have licked this problem in the newer vinyls, but it was common a few years ago.

GREASE ON SLATE FLOOR

Some potato chips were trodden into the slate floor in our entrance hall and left a dark, greasy patch. How can I remove it, and what kind of a finish should I put on to protect the slate?

Mix powdered chalk, or "whiting" with petroleum solvent (mineral spirits) to make a paste. Spread this on the stain about ¼" thick. When it is thoroughly dry, brush off, and the stain should go with it. Repeat if necessary.

Clear acrylic floor polish—the kind used on resilient flooring—makes a good finish for slate. Do not use varnish or urethane.

POLISHING SLATE FLOOR

I'm having difficulty maintaining a nice finish on the slate floor in our entry hall. I've used special slate sealers and waxes, but they take a lot of time and aren't very durable. Taking off the old finish and redoing it is a hard job. Can I use polyurethane varnish or some other material to give it a shine that's easy to maintain?

Slate is slate, and you should accept it and use it for what it is—harder and more durable than anything you could put on it. It is also, like any stone, dull or matt surfaced, and you should accept that, too. Varnish or plastic "sealers", as you've discovered, wear off very quickly, leaving an unsightly, patchy finish.

The simple truth is that slate requires no treatment at all. Just dust it regularly and damp-mop when required. A light waxing once in a while gives a slight gloss, and makes washing a little easier, but once or twice a year is enough. Clear acrylic floor polish can also be used.

If you want a high-shine floor, you should put down vinyl or hardwood, not slate.

SPRINGY FLOORS

The floor in our living room is very springy and I don't like it. How can this be remedied?

It depends on what's underneath. It may be that you just need another supporting post under the main beam that holds up the floor joists. But if the living room floor is completely open underneath, then you might be able to put a small beam and a supporting post under the joists in the centre of the floor. Or, if such a post would be in the way down there, you can double up on some of the floor joists . . . just nail a second joist to the one that's there. It doesn't even have to be the same length; a 6' or 8' piece of 2 × 8 nailed to 3 or 4 of the centre joists will probably strengthen them enough to hold the floor firm.

SQUEAKY SUBFLOOR

Last fall I bought and moved into a new, 2-storey house with a forced air furnace and a power humidifier that maintained a comfortable humidity level throughout the winter. Now we have started to get a lot of squeaks in the floors, which are ⅝" plywood covered with broadloom. The plywood is noticeably loose in some places. Our builder has driven 4" finishing nails into the floor through the carpet in some places, but this hasn't helped very much. Surely there must be a better way.

Inadequate nailing of the plywood subfloor is the cause of the trouble and the builder should fix it. To do this properly the carpet must be removed. Ringed, 1¾" flooring nails should be spaced every 6" along the plywood over every joist—and along the blocking under the end joints, too, unless tongue-and-groove plywood has been used.

DIMMING FLUORESCENT LIGHTS

We have a recessed ceiling in our living room, with fluorescent lights concealed behind the soffit. Is there any kind of a dimmer we can use to adjust the light level?

Fluorescent lights won't work on the dimmers that are now widely sold for use with incandescent bulbs, because they will not operate on a reduced voltage. A special ballast costing about $40 is required for each 4' tube, and you also need a special dimmer control.

A much less expensive solution is to put alternate fixtures on separate switches so that half the lights can be turned off.

FONDUE FUEL

Can you give me the formula for making my own fondue and chaffing dish fuel?

Fondue fuel is just methyl hydrate, which you can buy for half the price at any paint or hardware store.

COTTAGE FOUNDATION

We have an insulated summer cottage that we use about two weekends a month during the winter. We keep having trouble with doors that don't fit properly due to the shifting of the cement pads the building is presently sitting on. We are thinking of raising the cottage and putting it on a concrete block foundation wall about four blocks high, which will also give us space for a furnace. Do you think this will solve our present problem?

No. The frost will still heave the foundation if it's sitting on the ground, no matter how high it is. The only way to prevent frost heave is to put the foundation footings below the frost level in the cottage area. The footings should be poured concrete, but the foundation wall can be concrete block.

DAMAGE TO COTTAGE FOUNDATION

Our 2-year-old holiday home has a concrete block basement with an outside door at one end. Each winter the wall has shifted, the door has jammed and the cement coating on the outside has flaked off. We have no furnace in the basement, just a space heater upstairs, so the basement is not heated during the winter. Would it help if we lined the basement walls with plastic foamboard insulation and put an electric heater down there?

If one end of your basement is above the ground, the problem may be due to shallow footings under the foundation there. They must be below the frost level. Insulating the basement would not prevent frost heave; it would, in fact, promote it. Heating the basement *without* insulating it might prevent the earth outside the walls from freezing but this is an expensive solution.

Recent studies by the National Research Council have shown that frost heave is primarily due to poor soil drainage, so the remedy would be to dig down to the footings and put in drain tile running away to some lower point. Cover the tile with coarse gravel almost up to the ground level around the cottage. Adequate drainage should prevent further frost damage to your foundation walls.

FOUNDATION DRAINAGE

We are building a cottage on the shore of a lake and the water table is very high. What is the best way to keep this out of our basement? We are thinking of putting 4" plastic drain tile around the outside of the foundation, and running this through the gravel under the floor slab to a sump pump. Will this do the job?

If the basement floor is below the water table, the sump pump will have to drain the lake to keep it dry!

There's no practical way to keep water out of a basement that is below the water table. Theoretically it's possible to enclose the entire basement in a waterproof membrane, but even if this could be done successfully (which is unlikely) the water pressure under the floor slab would crack it. This could be laced with reinforcing steel, of course, but by this time the basement would cost more than you were going to pay for the cottage.

The foundation *footings* can be below the water table, but not the basement floor.

HEATING A COTTAGE

Two years ago we added an extension with a basement to our holiday cottage. The basement has a poured concrete floor and block walls, and we have left the electric heat on at 50°F. setting every winter to prevent frost damage to the foundation. This is quite expensive, however, since we don't use the cottage during the winter, and I would like to know if we should continue doing this now that the foundation has settled properly.

There is no clear answer to this question. It depends on the nature of the soil and the condition of the drainage around your foundation footings. If the soil is porous and the drainage is good, you don't need to keep the heat on. But if water builds up outside the walls and under the floor, frost heave could cause severe damage. Since you probably don't know how well the foundation is drained during the winter, you have a difficult choice to make. Perhaps the experience of similarly constructed cottages in the area will help you decide.

MOVING A FREEZER

When we moved our household effects across the city recently, one of the men told me not to plug the freezer in for three hours after it was delivered. This meant that some of the food was out of the freezer long enough to begin to thaw, even if it was well wrapped. Fortunately none of it spoiled, but I would like to know if it was really necessary to leave the freezer off that long.

It would only be necessary if the freezer was kept in an unusual position for more than a few minutes. If a large upright freezer is laid on its back in the moving van for instance, this can cause oil to leak into the compressor. After the freezer has been standing upright again for two or three hours the oil will seep back where it belongs and the power can be turned on. If this is done too soon the compressor will cycle repeatedly and no cooling will take place.

But this problem only occurs if the freezer was stored in the wrong position for any length of time, which can really only happen to an upright freezer. Tipping a freezer while it's carried up the stairs or onto the moving van won't cause any problems. Only in rare cases, then, is it necessary to leave a freezer turned off for a few hours after a move, but some movers give this advice just to be on the safe side.

FRESH AIR

I think we should have our bedroom window open a bit, even in cold weather, but my wife says that our warm air heating system provides all the fresh air we need. Is that true?

Unless you have a special outside air duct, which is not customary, the air in the heating system simply circulates through the house; there is no provision for fresh air in such a system.

Your wife is partly right, however, because a furnace does draw air into the house through cracks and holes in the construction. If it didn't do this, there wouldn't be any air to feed the combustion and go up the chimney. This air is more likely to come from the basement and the lower floor of the house than the upstairs bedrooms, however, particularly if the bedroom doors are closed. I'm sure you'd both be better off if you slept with the window open a bit.

ARE FRONT STEPS AN IMPROVEMENT?

When we bought our home, the front steps hadn't been built. Would the addition of these steps now add to our taxes?

Taxes are based on the assessed value of the house. A house is usually assessed as "habitable" at the time of occupancy, and technically any later additions that increase its value would bring an increase in the assessed value. But since steps to an existing front door are a normal part of any house, it's very unlikely yours would be considered an "improvement" in the usual sense. All such decisions, however, are up to the local assessment department, and each case must be considered separately.

FROST ON BASEMENT WALL

When I finished my basement I put up 2 × 4 stud framing and then used 2½" fibreglass batts plus a polyethylene vapor barrier before I put on the panelling. During the last two winters there was a buildup of frost on the wall behind the insulation. Then, when the warmer weather came, the frost melted and ran down onto the floor. What did I do wrong and how can I remedy it?

Frost

Theoretically the vapor barrier prevents warm, moist household air from passing through the frame wall and condensing or freezing on the cold concrete. But it doesn't work that well in practice, because there are lots of places where air can get behind the wall through gaps at the bottom, the top, or the ends. And since you have about a 1" space between the insulation and the foundation wall, convection currents will keep the humid air circulating over the cold concrete.

That's why it's better if there is no air space behind the insulation. In your case you should have used 3½" batts.

Another cause of this condensation is excess humidity in the house. I would guess that you have trouble with dripping or freezing windows during cold weather, too. Increasing the ventilation of your house will lower the humidity and reduce the condensation on your windows and your foundation wall.

FROST CRACKS CONCRETE BLOCK FOUNDATION

We have had trouble with the frost cracking our concrete block foundation wall for many winters, but the low temperatures we experienced this year caused more trouble than usual. A horizontal crack extends about 20' around two walls, just below ground level. It opened more than ³⁄₈" in places and we had trouble closing some of the doors in the house. I have patched these cracks several times, but would like to know if there is some way to stop them forming.

This problem is caused by something called "adfreezing." The wet earth around the foundation wall freezes to the concrete. When the ground heaves due to frost action, it lifts the house and the top of the foundation wall with it. The crack gets larger every year because soil particles fall into it and stop it from closing when the earth settles.

Adfreezing and frost heave only occur if the earth is wet, so good drainage is the best remedy. The earth against the foundation wall should be dug out to a depth of about 3'. Patch the cracks with any of the concrete patching materials and paint the wall below ground level with a coat of fibrated asphalt roofing compound. While this is wet, press into it a 3'-wide strip of 6-mil polyethylene film. Fill the excavation with 2½' of gravel and top with 6" of tamped soil built up against the foundation wall and sloping away from it to carry off surface water.

FROST ON STORM WINDOWS

We get frost on the storm windows of our upstairs rooms, and when the sun comes out this melts and runs down through the windowsill into the plaster below. We don't use these rooms, and keep the doors closed. Can you suggest a solution?

Yes, three. One, apply weatherstripping tape around the windows on the room side to prevent moist air from the house getting into the space between the windows. Two, drill a few small holes in the storm window frame, top and bottom, to ventilate the space between the windows. Three, lower the humidity in your house by providing more ventilation.

FROST ON ALUMINUM WINDOWS

A thick layer of frost builds up on the inside of our aluminum windows and sliding doors during very cold weather. How can we prevent this?

Aluminum door and window frames are available with an insulation barrier between the outside and inside metal surfaces to prevent this problem, but they are more expensive than solid metal frames and are rarely used in residential construction. The second reason for the frost build-up is excess humidity in the house. You can reduce this by increasing the ventilation to replace humid house air with dry outside air. Most of us are reluctant to do this during the heating season, but fresh air is just as necessary in the winter as it is in the summer.

FROST IN THE ATTIC

I had an addition built on my house and am having trouble with condensation and frost forming in the attic under the roof during very cold weather. On warm days this melts and drips on the ceiling, which consists of 12"-square tiles stapled to 1 x 3 furring strips. I had some insulation blown up there but now this gets wet. Nobody can tell me what causes this.

The main cause of your trouble is improper construction of the ceiling. The system you have is all right for a basement, but not under an attic. Warm, humid household air can pass easily through this type of ceiling into the attic, where it condenses on the cold roof.

The best way to remedy this now is to cover the existing ceiling with polyethylene film, stapled just enough to hold it in place, then apply gypsumboard panelling with screws driven through the ceiling tiles into the strapping. (You'll have to mark the position of the strapping on the tiles first with a chalk line.) Tape and fill all the joints, with special attention to the joint between the ceiling and the walls.

FROST HEAVE

Our cottage is set on concrete posts that don't go deep enough, and the result is that the cottage keeps shifting every winter. Is there anything we can do to prevent this?

The footings should extend below the frost level, of course, but if you're not able to do that now, here's a trick that may work.

Dig away some of the earth around the top of the posts, and then pour some old crankcase oil around them. Do this a couple of times in the late fall, before the ground freezes.

FROST LIFTS FLAGSTONES

Frost has lifted the flagstones in my patio and cracked the mortar joints. How do I reset these and prevent further damage?

Frost will not lift the flagstones if the ground below them is firm, sloped away from the house for drainage, and covered with a 3" layer of coarse sand under the paving stones. It would be best to remove all the flagstones and re-lay them. Pack the joints between the stones with a dry mixture of one part Portland cement to three parts sand. Tamp this in firmly, then dampen it with a fine spray from your garden hose and cover with a sheet of polyethylene film for three days to let the mortar harden completely.

FROST PENETRATION

When frost leaves the ground does it go down farther, or does it draw to the top? I have a water pipe 3½' below the ground and it only freezes at the end of winter when the spring thaws are just beginning. What causes this?

As long as the air temperature remains below freezing, the earth continues to freeze deeper. The colder the weather, the quicker and deeper the frost penetrates. Your pipe is evidently located at about the frost line, the maximum depth the frost normally reaches in your area. When the weather warms up, the ground begins to thaw—from the top down, naturally—but even when the surface is thawing for a short time during the day, night temperatures may be low enough to continue freezing the ground deeper, and that's when your pipe may get frozen.

The fact that frost doesn't reach its maximum depth until the very end of winter has given rise to the myth that it is the spring thaw that sends it there.

FRUIT CELLAR LEAKING

There is a fruit cellar under our concrete front porch, but during a heavy rain or after a snowfall water leaks into it. I have painted the porch floor several times with waterproofing paints, but they don't last very long. How can I waterproof the slab?

The concrete slab itself shouldn't leak like this, so I would think that the water is leaking around it, probably where it joins the house. Use a caulking gun to seal this.

FUEL OIL LEAK

Some time ago, while finishing our basement playroom, the carpenter put a nail through the oil pipe that runs under the new floor. This was not noticed until a considerable amount of oil had seeped under the floor for the full length of the room. We can't get rid of the smell of the fuel oil, and the vinyl tiles we laid on the wood sub-floor have bulged out of shape and won't stick down. Can you give us any advice?

I can give you my sympathy, and that's about all. The only possible solution I can think of is to tear up the floor, wash the concrete with petroleum solvent, and then lay a whole new floor, tiles and all. Since the carpenter is responsible, maybe he will donate at least the work if you buy the materials. Check to see if he has liability insurance coverage for this sort of thing. It may even pay you to take him to court.

FURNACES

CHIMNEY DAMPER OPEN

We recently had a new oil furnace installed and have noticed that the damper in the furnace pipe is always wide open, even when the furnace is off. Is this causing unnecessary heat loss up the chimney?

Yes. And even more important, it's probably reducing the air supply to the burner. This will lower its efficiency and cause a buildup of soot on the heat exchanger, which will further reduce the heat output of the furnace.

The barometric damper, as it is called, may simply be stuck, but perhaps it wasn't adjusted properly when it was installed. There's a knob at the top of the damper that is turned to adjust its balance. Normally this will leave the damper closed when the furnace is off and allow it to open slightly when the furnace comes on. But it should swing open and shut as the wind pressure over the chimney varies. This maintains a constant draft to the burner in spite of changes in outside air pressure.

Ask the furnace installer to come back and adjust the barometric damper so that it works properly. To do this he will have to check the draft pressures at the front and back of the furnace several times. There should be no charge for this.

DIRTY WALLS CAUSED BY FURNACE?

I have had an oil furnace in the house for 23 years and I can't seem to keep the walls clean even over one heating season. I have heard that gas is much cleaner, and I wonder if it would pay me to make the switch. I do my own painting and am tired of having to do it so often.

There is no question that gas burns cleaner than oil. But that only refers to the gases that go up the chimney. It should have no effect whatever on the air in your house unless there is something drastically wrong with your furnace, in which case you would certainly smell it.

If your walls are getting dirty very quickly, it must be due to air conditions outside or inside your house. If your neighbors have the same problem, it probably means that there is a lot of industrial air pollution in your area. If they don't, then I would look for causes inside, such as an unusual amount of fry cooking, or a lot of smoking. After many years of puzzling about this problem, I recently discovered that cigarette smoking is the most common cause of yellowing walls, curtains, and other household surfaces.

FURNACE DRAFT REGULATOR

We had a new oil furnace installed in our house last year, and it works fine. The only thing that bothers me is that there is no draft regulator on the pipe between the furnace and the chimney, as I have seen on all other new furnaces. I called the contractor about it but he says it isn't necessary.

A barometric control damper on the chimney IS necessary. It keeps the draft through the furnace at a steady pressure in spite of wind and weather changes outside. This conserves heat and reduces fuel consumption.

FURNACE FAN DOESN'T COME ON

My oil furnace doesn't work properly and no one seems to know why. When the burner comes on it runs for a few minutes, then shuts off. Only occasionally does the fan start while the burner is going. I'm sure most of the heat is going up the chimney because we can't get the temperature of the house above 64°F, although the thermostat is set for 70°. The oil company serviceman put in a new fan motor but that hasn't helped. I'm tired of burning oil and not getting any heat. Can you tell me what the trouble might be?

It sounds as if the temperature settings on the furnace fan control are incorrect. Either the safety cut-off is set at too low a temperature or the fan "on" control is set too high—or both. This is a very simple adjustment to make and any competent serviceman can do it in less than five minutes. Ask him to set the "on" temperature at 110°F and the "off" at 85°.

HOUSE COLD WITH NEW FURNACE

I live in an old, 1½-storey house that was comfortably heated, until last winter, by the original gravity hot-air, oil-fired furnace. Last winter I made the mistake of having a new, forced-air furnace installed, and have been cold ever since. I have no doubt that if I turned up the heat without regard to cost I could be very warm, but of course this is out of the question. Do you think it would help if I had the house insulated?

It certainly would, but if your new furnace is not keeping the house as warm as the old one, I think you should call the heating company that installed it and ask them to fix it. There must be something seriously wrong.

I am puzzled, however, by your comment that the house would be warm if you turned the heat up. Presumably you set the thermostat at the temperature you want. If your house isn't getting to that temperature, turning the thermostat up higher isn't going to help. But if you mean that you have set the thermostat low to reduce heating costs, then you can't blame the low temperature on the furnace.

NOISY FURNACE FAN

Our warm air furnace is so noisy it sometimes wakes me up when it comes on at night. The furnace has been regularly maintained and I keep the fan motor oiled and the filter clean, but the roar of the air through the ducts is very annoying. Can anything be done to reduce it?

It sounds as if your fan is running too fast. It is easy to fix and you can probably do it yourself. The fan belt pulley on the motor is adjustable. Turn off the furnace, lift the motor to reduce the tension on the belt, then undo the setscrew that holds the outside half of the pulley to the motor shaft (you'll need an Allen or hex wrench for this). Unscrew the outer half of the pulley counterclockwise to widen the gap and let the belt ride farther down. In effect, this reduces the diameter of the pulley and slows down the rotation of the fan. Tighten the setscrew against the flat spot on the side of the motor shaft, then start the motor. Readjust if necessary.

You may find it even more relaxing if you turn the fan on with the "manual" switch at the beginning of the heating season and let it run constantly. A low, steady noise can be less disturbing than a sudden start from total silence, particularly in the middle of the night. Running the fan constantly is recommended by many heating experts because it keeps the air in constant circulation and maintains an even temperature from floor to ceiling throughout the house.

TWO-SPEED FURNACE FAN

When I had central air conditioning added to my furnace, they installed a two-speed fan motor. Later in the year I had to have a lot of work done on the furnace by my oil supplier, and when it was finished I noticed that the two-speed motor had been replaced by a single-speed motor. I get conflicting advice on which is best. Do you think I should call the oil company and have them replace the two-speed motor?

Definitely. Not only is this required for the efficient operation of the air conditioner, it also permits constant air circulation during the heating season—low speed when the furnace is off, high speed when it is on. This helps to keep an even air temperature throughout the house, from room to room and floor to ceiling. As a result, the thermostat can be lowered 1° or 2°F without any loss of comfort, and you will save money, in spite of the additional time the motor is running.

FURNACE FUMES IN HOUSE

Can you tell me what would be the cause of oil fumes coming up through the heating ducts from the furnace in the basement?

If it is just the smell of fuel oil—which is pretty easy to recognize—then there's probably an oil spill or leak somewhere in the furnace room, and the fumes are being drawn into the cold-air return duct in the basement and circulated through the house. The remedy is to stop the leak or clean up the spill. One of the degreasing compounds sold at automobile supply stores can be used to remove oil from the concrete floor.

But if you are getting the acrid smell of burning oil, and perhaps some smoke, then there must be a leak in the combustion chamber of the furnace. This can be very dangerous and should be checked by a furnace serviceman right away. A smoke candle can be used to find leaks in the upper part of the combustion chamber, but very often this is rusted out around the bottom of the furnace, which should be checked visually after the burner is removed.

LEAKING OIL PIPE

Is there any product that will stop a leak in the oil pipe connection to the burner of my furnace?

You should be able to fix it just by tightening the nut behind the joint. If not, ask your fuel oil dealer to send a serviceman to make a new connection.

NOISY FURNACE

Not long ago we purchased a new house with a gas furnace and a forced warm air system. Our problem is with the furnace, which does not run smoothly. It vibrates so much that the dishes rattle in the kitchen cupboards when it is on. When you're close to the furnace you can hear a sort of rumble. Upstairs you can hear a whine in the ductwork. The builder and heating subcontractor tell us that noises like this are normal in a new home, and pretty soon we won't notice them at all.

Such noises are certainly not normal, and the heating contractor should correct them under the terms of your warranty. The vibration can only come from the fan or the fan motor. The fan could be out of balance, but a rumbling sound often indicates that the motor bearings are faulty. A whining sound in the ductwork,

Furnaces

on the other hand, could be caused by the ducts being too small or having too many sharp bends. Whatever the cause, it can be corrected. Some fan and duct noise must be expected, of course, but not the aberrant sounds you describe.

NOISY FURNACE

My furnace makes a booming noise when it comes on, and we can smell soot and oil. How can we remedy this?

Your problem could be caused by faulty ignition or dirty electrodes, but most likely it is due to insufficient burner draft. If you prop open the little viewing port in the front of the furnace, this may cure the trouble. If not, call in a serviceman.

FURNACE NOISE

Our warm air furnace makes a funny noise, like an airplane motor, for about 10 seconds before the fan comes on. The gas maintenance man couldn't find out what it was; do you have any ideas?

It sounds to me as if you have a loose fan belt. This should be slack enough to slip a little when the motor starts, to avoid putting too much of a load on the motor, but if it's too loose the motor will race for a time before the fan begins to turn.

You can check this quite easily yourself by removing the panel in front of the fan and watching until the furnace starts up. The solution is simple: just tighten the fan belt with the appropriate adjustments provided on the motor mount. The belt should flex about ¼" when you press it with your finger.

FURNACE NOZZLE: REPLACEMENT vs CLEANING

When the service man came to check my oil furnace he put a new nozzle in the burner and charged me for it. I think he could have cleaned the old one; it looks all right to me.

A new nozzle only costs about $3.25, and it's well worth it. The tiny hole in a burner nozzle is very accurately calibrated to pass a specified quantity of oil. In one year about 800 gallons of fuel oil will pass through this tiny nozzle. If the hole is worn just a thousandth of an inch larger, it may throw your furnace out of balance. Cleaning the nozzle isn't going to help; a new one should be put in every year, when the furnace is serviced for the season.

REDUCING FURNACE OUTPUT

My neighbor says he has reduced his fuel oil consumption by having a smaller nozzle put in the burner. Doesn't this just mean that the burner will be on for longer periods, and will still use the same amount of oil to heat the house?

That sounds reasonable, but it isn't quite as simple as that. A furnace takes about 10 minutes to warm up and reach peak efficiency. If it cycles too often it may never reach its maximum performance level and during the off cycles a lot of heat will be lost up the chimney.

The longer the furnace is on, and the shorter the off periods, the less heat will be wasted. The only way to adjust the heat output of an oil furnace is to change the size of the nozzle. Putting in a nozzle one or two sizes smaller will make the furnace run longer while burning the same amount of oil. And the off cycles will be shorter, of course. Ideally, the nozzle should be sized so that the furnace will run almost constantly during the coldest weather.

Time the on and off cycles of your furnace during very cold weather. If it stays off as long as it is on (or longer), then it is probably overfired and is wasting heat that could be saved simply by putting in a smaller nozzle. Your furnace serviceman can do this for you in a few minutes, and should also perform a combustion efficiency test and readjust the burner at the same time to ensure maximum performance.

FURNACE SIZE

I have bought a 1,700-square-foot, 2-storey house that is being built in a local subdivision. Two contractors are putting in the heating systems. One recommends a 55,000-BTU gas furnace; the other would put in a 75,000-BTU model. Is there any disadvantage in having a furnace that is larger than necessary?

The correct size for a furnace can only be determined by making careful heat loss calculations from the house plans, but my guess is that the smaller furnace would be your best buy.

There has long been a tendency for heating firms to over-estimate the size of furnaces—partly, of course, because bigger furnaces cost more. Heating engineers estimate that most home furnaces are anywhere from 25% to 50% oversized. This means they will be off much of the time, even in the coldest weather, which will result in a substantial loss of heat up the chimney.   The most efficient size for a furnace is the one that is just large enough to keep the house comfortable at the lowest temperature expected in the area. In other words, the furnace should run almost constantly in cold weather.

FURNACE SERVICING

My oil bills seem very high and I'm not sure that my furnace is properly adjusted. The serviceman cleans and adjusts it every year, but it never takes more than half an hour. Is there any way I can find out if my furnace is operating at maximum efficiency?

Although there has been some improvement in recent years, oil furnace servicemen still are not taking the time to tune furnaces properly. To measure and adjust combustion efficiency, the serviceman must do a complete flue gas analysis, checking the carbon dioxide level, the flue temperature, and the smoke number. And to take such measurements, he must make a ¼" hole in the smoke pipe near the back of the furnace. If there is no such hole, then no one has ever checked the combustion efficiency of your furnace, *or adjusted it correctly.* A proper cleaning and servicing takes at least 1½ hours.

STORING FURNACE OIL

Does fuel oil used for home heating deteriorate if it's kept in storage for a long time?

No, it keeps indefinitely without any change in quality.

FURNITURE CARE

ALLIGATORED FINISH

The finish on my coffee table has broken up into a crazy-quilt pattern of fine cracks that resemble an alligator skin. What causes this and is there anything I can do about it?

This is caused by exposure to heat or sunlight, and it happens more commonly to lacquer finishes than any others. If yours IS a lacquer finish, the cure is quite simple. First clean off all the wax with petroleum solvent (mineral spirits) and then brush on a generous application of lacquer thinner. Let it stand for a minute or two to soften the finish, then brush it out again just as if you were applying a new finish, which, in effect, you are. Allow it to dry for a couple of hours before rubbing it down with very fine steel wool (#0000).

Test the lacquer thinner first on some hidden part of the finish to see if it softens it. If not, you don't have a lacquer finish and will have to strip off and refinish the tabletop in order to remove the alligatoring.

ANTIQUE SIDEBOARD CRACKED

We have an antique English walnut sideboard that has developed two large cracks in the top. Is there anything we can use to fill these?

Plastic wood doughs toned to match different kinds of wood are available at most hardware stores, but getting them to match the color and grain pattern exactly requires considerable skill. The top would have to be completely refinished.

You're better off to leave the wood the way it is. Any attempt to patch it will reduce its value as an antique, no matter how well it's done.

DULL MARK ON TABLETOP

I recently bought a walnut table with a highly polished finish. The other evening I was serving tea and put my kettle on the table, but placed a dish towel under it. Half an hour later I found that the kettle had left a dull spot on the table. Polish won't take it out and I hate to sand it down and refinish it. Is there something else I can do?

Rub the dull spot in the direction of the grain with a pad of No.0000 steel wool and a few drops of lemon oil. This should bring it up to a satin sheen. If a higher gloss is needed to match the rest of the finish, apply a little paste wax and then buff.

DUST ON PLASTIC FURNITURE

I am having great difficulty removing dust from some clear plastic cube tables that I have. The dust seems to stick to the plastic like a magnet. Dusting with a damp cloth helps, but the dust is soon attracted again. It seems to be worse during cold weather. Is there anything I can do to keep the plastic from attracting dust?

When you rub a cloth over the plastic you create a static electricity charge that attracts the oppositely charged dust particles. Apply to the cloth a few drops of one of the anti-static liquids sold for cleaning phonograph records. Or you can make your own anti-static solution very cheaply with one part ethylene glycol (automobile anti-freeze) to four parts water.

GOUGES IN TABLETOP

There are some long gouges, about $\frac{1}{32}''$ deep, in our old oak kitchen table. What is the best way to remove these?

The best way is to strip off the finish, then sand down the gouges and refinish. Alternatively, you can remove the finish and then fill the gouges with an oak-toned wood filler sold for this purpose. Sand the filler smooth, then refinish.

HEAT FILM ON FURNITURE

My walnut dining room table has been left next to the hot air register, and the leaf hanging down beside it is covered with a grey film that furniture polish will not remove.

Fortunately, blemishes like this are usually just on the surface, and can be removed with a gentle abrasive such as automobile rubbing compound, #0000 steel wool, or rottenstone and light mineral oil. Rub in the direction of the grain, checking the surface frequently to make sure the entire area of the piece is covered evenly. If the finish is slightly dulled by this treatment, apply a light coat of paste wax and buff to restore the gloss.

LINSEED OIL POLISH?

I understand that there is a formula for linseed oil and turpentine that can be used to clean furniture. Can you tell me what it is?

I was told to clean our mahogany kitchen cupboards with a mixture of linseed oil, turpentine, and vinegar. The kitchen smells of turpentine and the cupboards are sticky. What can I do?

A mixture of boiled linseed oil, turpentine, and vinegar, in roughly equal proportions is an old-fashioned cleaner-polish that was used on shellac and varnish finishes. It never was a very good polish, however, and it will do more harm than good to modern furniture finishes. A little mineral spirits (petroleum solvent) on a cloth makes an excellent cleaner to remove grease and wax build-up.

MINERAL TURPENTINE

We have a teak table that has been marked with glass rings and food stains. A folder that came with the table said to clean it with Mineral Turpentine, but neither the store we

bought the table or anyone else seems to know what this is.

Mineral turpentine is the same thing as petroleum solvent or mineral spirits. But the best way to remove the marks you speak of is to rub the table down with very fine steel wool (#0000) in the direction of the grain. Don't worry, this will *improve* the finish! Follow with an application of teak oil, then buff with a soft, dry cloth.

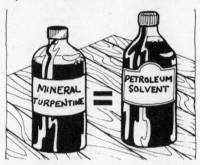

CARE OF PECAN FURNITURE

We have a dining room suite made from pecan wood and wonder what kind of oil or polish to use on it.

Pecan is a dense, heavy hardwood related to hickory. Any of the common paste, liquid, or spray furniture polishes can be used, but sparingly, as with any good furniture. A paste wax is generally considered best, used about twice a year. The rest of the time just wipe with a damp cloth.

PERFUME DAMAGE TO FURNITURE

I spilled a few drops of perfume on the dresser of my new, expensive, solid mahogany bedroom suite. I wiped it off quickly, but it has dulled the glossy finish. How can I restore it?

This shouldn't have happened. Perfume is alcohol, and all of the gloss finishes used on good furniture today are supposed to be unaffected by it. Check the furniture tags to see what they say about the finish. If it is claimed to be resistant to alcohol, then go back to your furniture store and ask them either to repair the finish to your satisfaction, or replace the suite.

FURNITURE MARKED BY PLASTIC CLOTH

My dining room table top has been marked by the design of a plastic table cloth. How can I remove it?

Rub it with automobile "rubbing compound," a mild abrasive polish used on automobile finishes and sold in all automobile supply stores. Or use #0000 grade steel wool and a little lemon oil. Always rub in the direction of the grain, never across it.

PROBLEMS WITH FURNITURE FINISH

We had three burled myrtle tables custom-made just over a year ago. The hand-rubbed finish began to crack and lift after a few months, we took the tables back and had a new semi-gloss finish applied. Now, after about a month, I notice that the top of one table is cracking and lifting again along what appears to be a centre seam. I should mention that we have a humidifier on all the time in our apartment and I also keep the drapes drawn to avoid direct sunlight on the furniture. I would appreciate any help you can give us with this problem.

From your description, it appears that these are veneer-topped tables, and that the veneer is lifting where it is joined in the centre of the table. This would be a manufacturing fault; the veneer is not properly bonded to the surface. I'd take them back to the cabinetmaker again.

"PROTECTING" AN OLD FURNITURE FINISH

I have recently purchased an antique mahogany table that I plan to use in the kitchen. The finish is in very good condition and I would like to protect it with a coat of urethane varnish. How should this be applied?

Applying a coat of urethane varnish is hardly the way to protect the old finish. That will simply cover the fine antique finish with something quite different, and probably not as good. If you must use the table in the kitchen, protect it with a pad and tablecloth.

PROTECTING ENAMEL

I painted a table with Chinese Red enamel, but it seems rather soft and I think it needs something to keep it from being scratched by dishes, etc. What should I use?

Enamel may take several weeks to harden completely, then it is usually tough enough to withstand normal use. If you still find you need additional protection, you can apply a coat of urethane varnish if you sand the surface lightly first to remove the gloss and provide a "tooth" for the urethane finish. The amber tone of the urethane varnish may alter the color of the enamel, however.

The best protection, of course, would be to cover the tabletop with a sheet of glass supported on tiny pads of red felt. Use ¼" glass and have the edges polished.

REGLUING CHAIR LEGS

I have tried several times to reglue a loose leg into the seat of an old rocking chair, but after a few months it comes loose again. I've squirted several different kinds of glue into the hole and none of them work. Do you have any suggestions?

Adding new glue on top of old glue is like trying to paint on sand. You'll have to scrape the dried glue off both parts of the joint before refitting, and you'll need to remove the rocker and one or two legs to do this. If any of the other parts are loose you might as well take the whole chair apart while you're at it. Hot vinegar will soften most old glues, and a rubber mallet will separate the joints without marking the wood.

Sand or scrape all the old glue off both parts of every joint, then check the fit. There are several ways to tighten loose joints, but the common trick of pushing toothpicks into the gaps isn't one of them. To make a tight glue joint, the wood must fit snugly all around. One method is to make a saw cut in the loose-fitting end of the leg and drive in a small wooden wedge to expand it enough to fit the hole. Another remedy is to brush glue around the end and then wrap it with a single layer of thread. When dry, check the fit; apply a second layer of thread the same way if necessary.

One of the pale yellow cream glues (usually identified as "carpenter's glue") is best for this job. The refitted joints should be held together tightly while the glue is drying. An improvised clamp can be made by wrapping several turns of rope around the parts and then twisting them together with a screwdriver or similar tool.

REMOVING CANDLE WAX

Candle wax dripped onto my mahogany table. How can I remove it without damaging the surface?

Harden it with an ice cube and it will just lift

103

off. Clean the surface with a cloth moistened with petroleum solvent (mineral spirits) or paint thinner.

REMOVING DECALS FROM FURNITURE

I have some furniture that has been "decorated" with decalcomanias—or transfers, as we used to call them—on top of semigloss, oil-based paint. How can I remove them without damaging the paint?

They can be removed the same way they were applied, by soaking them with warm water and sliding or rubbing them off. The best way to do this is to cover them with wet blotting paper or a folded paper towel. It may take 15 minutes or more to soak through the decal to the adhesive base. Another method is to rub the decal gently with a cloth moistened with lacquer thinner. But check first to make sure this won't damage the finish.

REMOVING HIGH GLOSS FINISH

I recently had two mahogany chairs reupholstered, and when they came back I was dismayed to find that the wood had been finished with a clear, high-gloss lacquer. Is there any way I can remove this without ruining the upholstery?

It isn't practical to remove the lacquer finish without taking off the upholstery, but I don't think you have to. You can remove the high gloss and take it down to a soft, satin, hand-rubbed sheen with #0000 steel wool, rubbed in the direction of the grain.

REMOVING SCRATCHES FROM CLEAR PLASTIC

The clear plastic dustcover on my hi-fi record player was marred by some rubbing marks made when it was sent in for repair work. I made it worse when I tried to remove the marks with household cleaning powder. The manufacturer tells me that this model is no longer made, so I am desperate. Can you tell me how I can restore it?

One simple trick is to apply a clear acrylic floor polish to the scratches, using a toothpick or a fine brush. For a much better job, remove the fine scratches by sanding the spots with wet silicon carbide paper, starting with #320 grit and working gradually up to #600. This should leave no more than a slightly dull, satin finish

with no visible scratches. A glass-like finish can be achieved by rubbing with some metal polish and a soft cloth.

RESIN BUBBLING THROUGH FINISH

We recently purchased a pine gate-leg table, which we placed beside the window in our apartment. Unfortunately the heat of the sun caused the resin in the wood to bubble on the surface of the finish. How can I remove the bubbles of resin without injuring the finish?

If the resin has lifted the finish, it will have to be removed entirely. The surface of the wood should then be washed down with petroleum solvent (mineral spirits) and sealed with shellac before it is refinished. Don't use urethane varnish over the shellac; use a regular varnish.

CARE OF ROSEWOOD

I have acquired some Scandinavian rosewood furniture and would like to know the best way to look after it. Should I use teak oil or lemon oil or some other polish?

Rosewood is much harder than teak, is naturally oily, and generally has an impervious lacquer finish. For these reasons, the use of teak oil (which is just a thinned linseed oil) is not recommended, because it cannot penetrate the surface of the wood and is liable to form a gummy film. Scandinavian furniture stores usually sell a special rosewood oil, but a lightweight mineral oil such as lemon oil or baby oil works just as well. Apply the oil once or twice a year using a pad of #0000 steel wool.

REFINISHING ROSEWOOD

We have a dining room table made from a rosewood grand piano. Over the years there has been a buildup of wax that I have tried to take off with varnish and wax remover, but it's still sticky. Is there something better I could use?

If you really mean you've used *varnish* remover, that could be the cause of the sticky surface you have now. In this case the only cure is to finish the job by taking off ALL the old finish with varnish remover, then sanding and refinishing with a penetrating oil-resin sealer such as Danish oil finish (there are several brands).

All you need to use to remove wax is petroleum solvent (mineral spirits) and some clean rags.

VARNISHING ROSEWOOD

I have a new rosewood coffee table, but it's not shiny enough, and I was thinking of putting on a coat of varnish. Is this a good idea?

No! If you want a higher polish, just apply a good paste wax, using a pad of very fine steel wool (#0000), rubbing only in the direction of the grain.

RUBBER MARKS ON FURNITURE

We placed a radio with four rubber feet on top of our pecan table, and this has left four dark rings on the finish. Is there any way to remove these?

Not without refinishing the table, I'm afraid. The stain is caused by the migration of anti-oxydents and other chemicals from the rubber to the furniture finish. It develops *inside* the finish, so it can't be removed with surface abrasives, as many other stains can. And I've been unable to find a chemical that will bleach it out.

Rubber chemists tell me that non-staining rubber is available and should be used in this application, but apparently the people who make the rubber feet don't know about it, or don't know there's a problem.

FURNITURE SCRATCH

We have just acquired the first scratch on our French Provincial dining suite. The scratch is about 2" long and 1/16" deep in a very noticeable place: I know if I oil it the scratch will just turn dark. What can I put on to make it blend into the polished fruitwood finish?

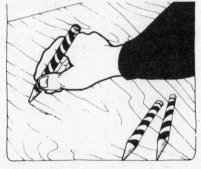

Most hardware stores carry a line of wax sticks in colors to match various wood finishes. You just rub the stick across the scratch, then buff with a soft cloth. A child's crayon will work just

as well, if you can find the right color.

If the scratch happens to be more or less parallel with the grain of the wood, this treatment should hide it very effectively. But if it runs across the grain use different colored crayons to match the grain tones.

SPRAY POLISH HAZE

I refinished our coffee table with several coats of varnish rubbed down with rottenstone and oil, and have kept it beautifully polished with an application of paste wax about twice a year. Recently, while I was away, my daughter used one of the new spray waxes on it, and now it has acquired a haze or bloom which I can't seem to remove.

This is probably caused by the combination of a silicone spray with the existing wax coating. You will have to remove both completely, then repolish with paste wax. Rub down the surface with a clean, soft cloth soaked with petroleum solvent or paint thinner. Repeat several times, *using a clean cloth every time* to avoid redistributing the film.

When the surface is thoroughly clean and dry, the paste wax treatment that was originally used should restore the table's fine finish.

STICKY CEDAR CHEST

My daughter has a cedar-lined chest which she isn't able to use because a sticky substance comes from the wood and ruins everything she stores in it. Is there anything we can do to stop this?

This sticky substance is probably pitch, which you can remove with turpentine or paint thinner. After that, seal the pitch spot with two or three coats of shellac. If all of the wood is sticky and has to be covered with shellac, you will, of course, no longer have an aromatic cedar chest; it will be just another wooden chest.

CLEANING STICKY FURNITURE

We bought an old dining room suite that needs cleaning. It feels sticky and I can scrape some of the dirt off with my fingernail, but it won't wash off. There is also some tar that was spilled in one of the buffet cupboards. Can this be removed, too, without harming the finish underneath?

Petroleum solvent (mineral spirits) or paint thinner (not *remover*) will take off the built-up wax and dirt, and also the tar, without harming the finish. Use several clean cloths, and end with a dry one to buff the surface. If there are

105

surface blemishes on the finish, such as heat marks or water rings, rub the entire surface with #0000 steel wool, working always in the direction of the grain. If you want a higher gloss, apply a light coat of paste wax.

TEAK CRACKING

We have some carved teak furniture that we bought when we lived in the Orient. It was fine while we were there, but since we moved back here it has started to crack. What can we put on it to prevent this happening?

It's our dry winter air that causes the trouble. The humidity in many homes goes below 10% at times, which is less than you'd find in the Sahara Desert. Our furniture is made from wood that has been kiln dried to a moisture content of 6-8%, so it can stand the dry winter air in our homes. (The *absorption* of moisture during the humid months can be a problem, however.) Furniture made in tropical countries has a much higher moisture content. This is fine for their climate, but the furniture explodes when it's exposed to our desert-dry air.

Finishes will slow the drying to some extent, but not enough to keep the wood from cracking and checking. Nothing you can paint on the wood will do any good. The only remedy is to raise the humidity in your home during the normally dry winter months.

LINSEED OIL ON TEAK

When we bought a new teak bedroom suite the salesman told me to treat it with a mixture of one part boiled linseed oil and two parts petroleum solvent. I left this dressing on too long before polishing it, and the linseed oil set up and got tacky.

I tried putting a second coat on, but this didn't do any good, and I've tried to remove the sticky film with the solvent as well as other cleaners, but nothing works. What should I do?

I'm afraid I have bad news for you. Once the linseed oil sets, it's impossible to remove it without taking off at least some of the original finish. The best you can do, I think, is scrub it down with #000 steel wool and petroleum solvent (mineral spirits), rubbing in the direction of the grain. If the furniture has a matt, natural wood finish, as I suspect it does, this won't hurt it. After you've taken all the gummy oil off the surface this way, you can restore the finish by wiping on the same solution you used before, but this time only leave it on for 15 minutes or

so, and then buff it off thoroughly with a soft, dry cloth. Never leave a wet film of linseed oil or teak oil on the surface.

RESTORING TEAK TABLE

I have some water marks, a slight cigarette burn, and other blemishes on my teak coffee table. How can I clean these off and restore the finish?

Rub the entire table down with #000 or #0000 steel wool, paying particular attention to the stained and burned areas. Then wipe on a coat of teak oil, or Danish oil finish available in any hardware store, or a solution of one part boiled linseed oil and one part turpentine. Let this soak in for 15 minutes or so, and then wipe off any surplus with a clean cloth. Don't leave any oil on the surface, or you'll end up with a sticky finish.

RESTORING TEAK FINISH

I had a scratch on the top of my teak table and followed your instructions on removing it, using very fine sandpaper and teak oil. The scratch came out all right, but the finish is quite dull where I sanded it. How can I get this to match the rest of the finish?

You have probably oiled the tabletop many times over the years, gradually building up a smooth and glossy linseed oil finish. One coat of teak oil will not match this, but several coats will. Allow at least a week between coats.

A faster way to do it is to use one of the penetrating oil-resin finishes, such as Danish oil, that are available at paint and hardware stores. These are applied the same way as the teak oil—brush on, allow to sink in for 15 minutes or so, then wipe off—but only 24 hours is needed between coats. They also contain resins that provide a harder finish.

VENEER PROBLEM

We had a beautiful walnut buffet cabinet made for us 15 years ago by a European craftsman. Eventually it became scratched and faded, so I repaired, stripped, sanded, and refinished it. It turned out beautifully.

Now the problem: After it was made, my husband painted the four small sliding doors "To get a contrast". Later he changed his mind and decided to apply wood veneer. He tried to glue this on, but the glue didn't stick to the paint and the veneer came out all bubbly. Also he had used rosewood, because he said he liked the grain better than walnut.

Is there anything I can do to get the reddish color out of the wood? Will the veneer continue to bubble? It looks ghastly. Is there any way I can get if off? What should I do?

Remove the sliding doors and have someone make four more out of ¼" walnut plywood. Any cabinetmaker or woodworking shop that makes store display cases will have some of this wood lying around and shouldn't charge very much for cutting it to size. (Don't throw the old doors away; give them to the cabinetmaker for size—and to get his sympathy.)

WARPED BOARDS

I recently bought an old dining room table which proved to be black cherry under many layers of varnish. I want to refinish it, but the boards are slightly warped. What can I do to correct this?

Warping is caused by uneven drying of the wood, usually because only one side is sealed, and it can be cured by reversing this process. Strip the finish off both sides of the boards, then take them outside and pour very hot water on the *concave sides*, soaking them well. Turn the wet sides down on the grass and leave them in the sun. After a few hours (or perhaps a few days) you will find that the warp has flattened out. In some cases it may be necessary to put some heavy rocks on the boards. Bring the boards inside and let them dry out slowly in the house to see if the change is permanent, then seal both sides with shellac or a thin coat of urethane varnish.

WATER STAINS ON MAHOGANY

I have a mahogany buffet with a large greyish stain caused by leaving a damp rag on it for a couple of days. Is there any way to restore the finish?

Water stains like this are usually just on the surface, and can be removed with any gentle abrasive, such as automobile rubbing compound (a paste used for smoothing auto body finishes), powdered cleaners, even toothpaste. If the surface of the wood has been roughened by the water, apply the cleaner with #0000 steel wool.

WAX BUILD-UP

I have a dining room suite which is about 10 years old. It has accumulated a wax build-up from the spray wax and lemon oil I have been using, and now the surface seems a little sticky. How can I take it off without damaging the finish?

Use a cloth moistened with petroleum solvent (mineral spirits) or turpentine.

WHITE RINGS ON FURNITURE

How can I remove a white ring made on an oak dining table by a hot dish?

Such heat and water marks are usually not as bad as they look. They can often be removed by rubbing with a cloth pad moistened with methyl hydrate. If this doesn't do the job, the heat marks can be rubbed off with a mild abrasive, then repolished—use a dab of automobile rubbing compound on a soft cloth folded over your finger. While normally used to rub down and polish an automobile finish, it's ideal for your job because it removes the white marks and restores the polish at the same time. You can buy it at any automobile supply store.

YELLOWED FURNITURE FINISH

I have an off-white bedroom suite that's gradually turning yellow. Is there anything I can use to restore it?

It may simply be a buildup of old wax. Try cleaning it with petroleum solvent (mineral spirits) or paint thinner. If this doesn't work, try bleaching the discoloration with ordinary laundry bleach, starting with a tablespoon in a cup of water, and increasing the strength as required. If this doesn't work, you may be able to remove the discolored surface of the finish with automobile rubbing compound, a mild abrasive cream that's used to smooth and polish automobile finishes. And if *that* doesn't work, I've run out of suggestions.

FURNITURE FINISHING

RE-DOING AN ANTIQUE FINISH

A few years ago I finished my kitchen cupboards and breakfast nook with an antique kit consisting of a base color and a dark graining medium that was simply wiped on. Now the finish is beginning to chip off down to the old paint. I have asked several paint dealers how to patch this up or refinish it, but they can't give me an answer. Can you help me?

The easiest thing to do is sand the edges of the chipped areas, feathering them back far enough so they won't show, then repaint, either with a good enamel or another antiquing kit. It isn't practical just to patch up the chipped areas.

FINISHING CANE BAMBOO

I have some verandah furniture of cane bamboo that is weatherbeaten and needs refinishing. How do I go about it?

Sand it with paper or steel wool to remove all the old finish and weather marks, then spray on a coat or two of clear lacquer.

BEESWAX FINISH

I have stripped a piece of furniture and am ready to refinish it. After I put on an oil stain I want to apply beeswax. I am told that after I do this I never have to polish it again. Can you tell me how this should be done? Does the wax have to be melted?

Wax of any kind is not a good finish for raw wood. It doesn't seal the wood properly, and it prevents any other finish from ever being applied. It should only be used as a polish over a sealer finish such as varnish, lacquer, urethane, or a penetrating oil-resin finish such as Danish oil. But beeswax is too soft and sticky to make a very good polish. Paraffin and carnuba waxes are much superior.

BLACK FINISH

I have a birch dining suite with a blond finish. I would like to refinish it in a flat black to match the rest of the decor. Should I take off the present finish, and what type of stain or paint do I use to get the effect I want?

It isn't necessary to remove the present finish, but it should be sanded to roughen the surface and provide a "tooth" for the new finish. You can then apply a straight flat black enamel. Best results are obtained with two coats.

FINISHING BOOKSHELVES

We bought a set of unfinished bookshelves that are put together with spindle-like dividers or legs. They are probably softwood. We wanted a light walnut color, so I applied a mixture of boiled linseed oil and turpentine, then a coat of varnish stain. Luckily I only did one shelf, because the grain came up rough and the color is very uneven. Can you tell me the correct way to do this?

You'll have to strip the varnish off the one shelf and sand it down to the bare wood again in order to have it match the rest of the shelves. Next, wipe all the wood with a wet rag and let it dry. This will raise the grain "nap," which you can then remove by sanding with very fine paper (#220 garnet) or #0000 steel wool.

Choose an oil- or water-based stain in a color tone that is a bit lighter than you want (softwood usually stains darker) and test on the underside of the lower shelf to find out how much to put on. Wipe it on, let it sink in a bit, then wipe it off. If it's too light, repeat. If it's too dark, wipe it off quicker. Stain the rest of the unit, allow to dry at least 24 hours, then apply two coats of satin urethane varnish, sanding lightly between coats.

BUBBLES ON NEW FURNITURE FINISH

I removed the old finish from a table, then applied stain and a coat of urethane varnish. A lot of tiny bubbles and craters formed on the surface, so I sanded it lightly again and applied another smooth, even coat of urethane, but now the same trouble has appeared. Can you tell me what I'm doing wrong?

If the bubbles weren't in the finish when you brushed it on, there are two possible causes for the trouble. One is that you used a stain containing stearate, a metallic soap that is incompatible with urethane. Not many stains contain stearate, but unfortunately there's no way of telling when they do.

The most likely cause of the trouble, however, is the presence of silicone on the original finish, due to the use of one of the silicone furniture polishes. Even when the old finish is stripped off with a chemical remover, enough silicone will be left on the wood to cause tiny bubbles and craters, known as "fisheyes", to form on the new finish.

I suggest that you sand the present finish again, then wash it down several times with petroleum solvent (mineral spirits) and clean cloths before applying another coat of urethane.

CLEAR FURNITURE FINISH

I have made a pine table and want to give it a clear, natural finish. I have seen some Scandinavian furniture with a water-white finish, not amber like varnish. How can I get a finish like this?

These very clear, colorless finishes are generally acrylic lacquer, which is only available for commercial use with special spray and drying equipment. Almost as colorless, however, are the brush or spray-can lacquers available at most paint and hardware stores.

REFINISHING CUPBOARDS

Our kitchen cupboards of golden ash were shellacked and varnished about ten years ago, and some of them are now quite worn and discolored. Can you tell me how to refinish them?

Strip off the old varnish with paint remover, then use methyl hydrate and some clean cloths to remove the shellac. You'll find it easier to do this if you take the doors off and lay them flat. Smooth the surface and remove any blemishes with #220 grit garnet paper or #0000 steel wool. Remove sanding dust and apply two coats of satin urethane varnish, allowing not more than 36 hours between coats.

KITCHEN CUPBOARDS

Our mahogany kitchen cupboards were finished with a wiped-off white primer and then a coat of varnish. They are now badly worn around the doorknobs, and oil has penetrated into the wood, which is rough and discolored. Can you tell me how I can refinish them?

It would be very difficult to patch up the worn areas and apply a new transparent finish. And if you tried to sand off all the old wiped-off paint finish and start again, you would probably sand right through the thin veneer.

I think the best thing to do is sand them down lightly, then apply a good enamel in the color of your choice. For something a little more exotic you could use one of the antique finishes—a flat base paint plus a wiped-on color toner plus a protective coating of urethane varnish.

DANISH OIL TOO THICK

At your suggestion I have used a penetrating Danish oil finish for several years on the furniture that I build—and as an occasional touch-up, when necessary. It is indeed the easiest type of finish to apply and maintain. Recently I started to use a partly filled can that had been on my workshop shelf for a year or so and found that it had become thicker. It was difficult to apply and didn't seem to sink in properly, so I removed it with petroleum solvent (mineral spirits). Can I use this to thin the Danish oil to the proper consistency again, or do I have to discard it and buy a new can?

No. Use lacquer thinner. The proper consistency is just slightly thicker than water. Filter the thinned Danish oil through a nylon stocking to remove any globules of finish that may have formed as the solvent evaporated. Keep the restored finish in a smaller, tightly sealed container.

DARK OAK FINISH

I have sanded down a light oak table to the bare wood, but am unsure how to finish it. I would like to give it a darker color, then a tough, stain-resistant finish. What would you suggest?

You can use a dark oak stain or even a walnut stain. Oil-based stains are most common, but water-based stains are also available. Test the stain first in an inconspicuous spot, such as the underside of the table (as long as this has been sanded like the top). When you have the color you want, brush or wipe the stain on the rest of the table to the density desired, wiping off any surplus with a cloth. If it's not dark enough, apply another coat of stain. Let this dry 24 hours, then apply two coats of satin urethane varnish, sanding lightly between coats.

DEEP FURNITURE FINISH

Can you tell me how to apply thick, heavy coats of varnish on furniture to get a deep-looking finish?

Furniture Finishing

The only way to get a thick finish is to apply a number of regular, thin coats until you build up the thickness you want. Brush them out thoroughly to get an even coat, and sand lightly between coats to roughen the surfaces slightly and provide a "tooth" for the next coat. As many as 40 coats can be applied in this way to get a deep finish.

A reguar varnish is better than urethane varnish for this type of finish, because of the way it sticks to itself.

Don't try to speed up the job by laying on thick coats of varnish. It won't dry properly this way and you'll end up with a soft finish that may also have unsightly drips and sags.

This slow process *has* been speeded up, however, by a 2-part plastic finish that is mixed and then simply poured onto the perfectly level surface, where it hardens in a smooth layer about 1/16" thick. It is sold at most paint, hobby, and hardware stores.

DISTRESSED FINISH

I would like to give our pine dining table a distressed finish. Can you tell me how this is done?

"Distressed" in this case just means marked and worn with age and use. These blemishes can be produced artificially in many ways. Small finishing nails laid on the tabletop and tapped with a hammer produce "worm holes". Random dents can be produced by beating the table with a length of heavy chain. Edges can be carved and sanded to imitate the wear of centuries. The surface is then rubbed with a dark pigment to darken and emphasize the distress marks, and finally given one or more coats of satin varnish, rubbed down with fine steel wool.

DRIFTWOOD FINISH

I have some nice driftwood that I would like to make up into a table centrepiece. How should I finish it?

Driftwood is usually varnished. Apply two or three coats of satin varnish, sanding lightly between coats. A simpler treatment is to wipe it with a solution made by melting beeswax and adding about half as much turpentine. Mop this on, then buff it to a soft sheen.

EASY REFINISHING

I have an old, painted washstand that I would like to restore with a natural wood finish, but

I have no idea how to go about it. Can you tell me a very simple, foolproof method?

There are a lot of ways to finish furniture, but here's a very easy one that seals the wood against oil and water stains yet leaves it looking natural.

Remove the old finish with a wash-off paint remover. Use a rubber spatula, a nylon scouring pad, some old rags, and a hose or a bucket of water to remove the softened paint. Do this outside or in the basement, because it's a messy job.

When dry, rub it down with fine steel wool, then wipe on a coat of a penetrating oil-resin finish such as Danish oil. There are several brands, and they come in wood stain colors as well as natural, so just choose the wood tone that you want. You wipe the oil finish on with a cloth, let it sink in for 15 minutes or so, and then wipe it off. Apply a second coat in 24 hours. That's it. You can add a wax gloss if you want, but it isn't necessary.

FRENCH POLISHING

The finish on some of our furniture was damaged while it was being moved. We called in an expert in such matters and he told us it should be stripped down and given a "French polish", for which he quoted an extraordinary price. Can you tell me what this expensive finish is, and whether I can do it myself? I have refinished a lot of furniture, and made a pretty good job of it, but don't know anything about this French polish.

French polishing is a very old, slow, tedious, and somewhat tricky method of applying a multi-layer shellac finish tempered with linseed oil. It has a rich sheen and takes a high polish, but shellac watermarks easily and is readily damaged by alcohol and related solvents. And it is not nearly as tough as modern finishes such as urethane. Unless you have valuable antiques that originally had a French polish finish and are worth the expense of authentic restoration, I would suggest a much cheaper and more practical finish such as satin urethane. And there's no reason why you shouldn't do it yourself.

FUMED OAK

I have a dining suite of fumed oak and want to make some matching leaves for the table. What exactly is fumed oak, and how can I duplicate the finish?

Fuming is an old wood toning process that

hasn't been used for many years. If your furniture is less than 50 years old, chances are it is simply *stained* to imitate the appearance of fumed oak. The old technique is too slow and cumbersome for today's production—it involved enclosing the piece of furniture in an airtight container, where it was exposed to the fumes of liquid ammonia for up to 24 hours. The tannic acid (tannin) in the wood was converted to ammonium tannate, a reddish pigment that gave the fumed wood a color tone ranging from light olive to a rich, deep brown, depending on the amount of tannic acid in the wood and the length of its exposure to the ammonia. Oak was the wood most commonly used, but any wood high in tannin, such as mahogany, walnut and chestnut, could be stained this way. This is hardly a practical process for the home handyman, however, so you'd have a better chance of matching the color of the fumed oak with a modern wood stain.

GREASE STAIN ON TABLETOP

The top of our old pine table was covered with a heavy layer of black grease before we stripped off the finish and sanded it down. There remains an area (about a foot square) where the grease soaked into the wood. Is there any way of removing this before we refinish the table?

Petroleum solvent (mineral spirits) or paint thinner will remove some of the grease stain, but I suspect that it has penetrated the soft wood too far to be removed entirely. The best thing to do is seal the remaining stain with a couple of coats of shellac before refinishing. But use a regular varnish, not urethane, over the shellac.

HAND-RUBBED FINISH

Our mahogany kitchen cupboards had a nice satin finish, but then they were painted with a high gloss varnish, which I don't like. Could the cupboards be sanded down and a coat of satin urethane varnish applied to give a softer look?

All you need to do to get a satin finish is rub the cupboards down with #0000 steel wool, in the direction of the grain. Keep a cross-light on the surface so that you can get an even, hand-rubbed finish over the entire area.

MAHOGANY CUPBOARDS

Our kitchen cupboards are mahogany with a

walnut stain and a very thin coat of varnish. Over the years they have got shiny around the door handles and I would like to refinish them. How should this be done?

Wipe them with petroleum solvent (mineral spirits) or paint thinner to remove any wax or oil film, then rub them with #00 steel wool or #60 sandpaper to remove the gloss and provide a "tooth" for another coat of varnish. A satin urethane varnish is recommended.

LIGHTEST WOOD FINISH

We are trying to refinish an old pine cradle. We have removed several layers of paint and sandpapered down to the soft pine. Now we want to apply a clear finish that will retain the light color of the wood. We tried regular and urethane varnishes on small hidden areas, but they darkened the wood too much. What should we use?

Anything you put on the wood—even water—will darken it to some extent. The lightest transparent finish, however, is lacquer. Various brands of brushing and spray lacquers are available at your local paint store. To make sure you've got a lacquer and not a varnish, see that the label says to use *lacquer thinner*, not paint thinner or turpentine, for dilution and cleanup.

Lacquer goes on very thin, and several coats are required to provide a durable finish, but this isn't much trouble since lacquer dries quickly. Spray lacquers are ready for a second coat in 15 or 20 minutes. Brushing lacquers are usually ready within an hour, so three coats can be applied in an evening. (In spite of the name, brushing lacquers should be brushed as little as possible. Load the brush generously and use it to flow the lacquer on to the surface. wherever possible, turn the piece so you can work on a horizontal surface.)

LIMED OAK

I want to apply a limed oak finish to a dining suite that has been stripped. How do I get this finish again after I have stripped down to base wood and sanded smooth?

The limed oak finish is usually achieved by wiping the wood with white paint, then wiping it off again with a coarse rag, leaving paint in the grain of the wood. Finish with at least two coats of satin varnish.

LINSEED OIL FINISH

I put two coats of boiled linseed oil on a new redwood garden table and benches several

111

weeks ago and it has never dried properly. The surface is still too sticky to use. Should I put something else on it or rub it down with something? I was only told to give it two coats of the linseed oil.

It sounds as if you brushed the linseed oil on each time like a coat of varnish. That was a mistake. The correct way to apply linseed oil is to dilute it with 1 part turpentine or paint thinner to 2 parts boiled oil, then brush or wipe it on the raw wood. Let it sink in for 15 minutes or so, *then use a dry cloth to wipe off any oil that remains on the surface.* Repeat 3 or 4 days later, again removing all surface oil. (Spread the cloths out to dry. Don't roll them up or stuff them away somewhere or they're liable to burst into flame as a result of spontaneous combustion!)

This is really a very poor finish. You could have done it better and faster with one of the penetrating oil-resin finishes.

FILLING MAHOGANY

We would like to paint our mahogany kitchen cupboards. They presently have a natural wood finish with a textured, open-grain surface. How can we seal the finish, to get a smooth surface for painting?

The characteristic open pores of Philippine mahogany, or lauan, can be filled with a material known simply as "wood filler," available at any paint or hardware store. This is a neutral-coloured mixture of linseed oil and fine mineral granules, with the consistency of thick cream when it is thoroughly mixed. It is brushed on with the grain of the wood, allowed to stand until it dulls (about 20 minutes) and wiped off across the grain with a pad of coarse cloth, such as burlap. Allow the filler to dry for 24 hours, then sand lightly and paint as desired.

FINISH FOR A MAPLE ROCKER

Could you please tell me how to finish a bird's-eye maple rocker? It has been sanded down to the bare wood and is very smooth. I would like to keep the natural color of the wood, and was thinking of just applying wax.

Wax, by itself, is not a good finish. It doesn't seal the wood properly, and no other kind of a finish can ever be applied over it.

For a sealing coat that leaves the wood looking almost untouched, I suggest using a penetrating oil-resin finish such as Danish oil. Simply brush or wipe on, allow to sink in for 15 minutes or so, then wipe off. A second coat can

be applied for more protection, if desired.

For a tougher, smoother, clear film finish, use a satin urethane varnish. Apply two coats, not more than 36 hours apart.

REFINISHING MISMATCHED WOOD

We have stripped down an old dining room suite for refinishing, but find that the wood is darker in some places than in others. Some of it has dark ribbons of color, and other parts are almost white. Is there any way we can get the wood tone even again?

You have two choices. You can stain the light wood to match the dark, or you can bleach the dark wood to match the light. Stain matching is trickier than bleaching, which can best be done with a 2-part commercial wood bleach. Try it on some inconspicuous spot first, such as the underside of a chair arm or the tabletop. Use as directed.

If the wood is now too light, you can darken it easily with an over-all stain application before applying a final finish, for which I would recommend two coats of a satin urethane varnish.

MISSION OAK

You explained what a fumed oak finish was; can you tell me what "Mission Oak" is, and how I can remove this dark finish in order to get rid of some heat marks on our dining room table?

This is just a fancy name for a dark stain finish. It can be removed with paint stripper and sanding, but this may not be necessary. Heat marks are usually just on the surface, and can often be removed with a mild abrasive such as automobile rubbing compound, available at any auto supply store. Rub only in the direction of the grain, and apply wax to restore the gloss, if necessary.

OAK TABLE

I have an old round oak dining table that I sanded down and finished with linseed oil and beeswax, hoping to get the same effect as seen on antique pine furniture. I'm disappointed with the result; it's slightly sticky and marks easily. What should I do?

Remove the wax by washing the surface down with petroleum solvent (mineral spirits) using several clean cloths. Then sand slightly, dust, and apply one or two coats of *satin* urethane varnish. This will give you a very durable, stain-resistant finish with a soft, hand-rubbed sheen. If you want a duller finish, rub it down with #000 or #0000 steel wool, in the direction of the grain.

REFINISHING OAK

We have an old solid oak table from which we've removed the varnish. The boards are uneven in color, and there are some nicks and dents that we'd like to fill. What kind of finish would keep the lovely oak grain and still be durable and easy to look after?

If you really want to even the color of the boards (it's not that important) you have two choices: you can apply a very light oak stain to the lighter boards, or you can apply a wood bleach such as oxalic acid to the darker ones. In both cases you will have to proceed carefully and slowly.

You can buy oak-toned filler to fill the nicks, but a few dents don't look out of place on old oak furniture. A lot of manufacturers go to considerable trouble to make such marks on their new furniture by hitting the wood with a heavy chain or the edge of a hammer. "Distressing," they call it.

The most durable finish is a satin urethane varnish, at least two coats, sanding lightly between coats. But an oil/resin sealer, or Danish oil, is sometimes preferred because it gives a more natural finish.

REMOVING FINISH
FROM CARVINGS

I have an old oak piano with quite a bit of carving and some intricate designs on the front. I would like to refinish it. How can I remove the old paint from the grooves?

Ordinary paint remover will do the job. Use a stiff brush to remove the old finish from the grooves after it's softened.

RESTORING AN ANTIQUE

My husband and I found a very old Victrola in my grandmother's attic. The works are in very good condition, and the mahogany cabinet is lovely, but the outside finish is very dull and warped and cracked in places. We would like to restore it and use it for a cabinet.

With a potentially valuable antique like this, it's best not to try to do too much to it. I would just rub the finish down with #0000 steel wool

and lemon oil. Warps and cracks I would leave; you can't do much about them anyway, unless you want to take the cabinet apart and rebuild it.

RESTORING WORN FINISH

We have a limed oak dining room suite, cream in color, that is roughly 25 years old. The finish is worn through in places, and there are some chips and stains. I don't expect to be able to restore the finish 100%, but is there some way we can redo the damaged areas?

I don't think it's practical to patch up a worn finish like this. I suggest that you cover it with one of the "antique" finishes. These consist of a colored base coat (I would use ivory, cream or off-white in your case) plus a dark pigment that is simply wiped on and rubbed off according to directions. Chips or deep scratches in the finish should be filled and sanded smooth before the antique finish is applied.

FURNITURE RESTORER

I understand there is a product that can be used to restore an old furniture finish. It is simply rubbed on with steel wool, and is supposed to fill in scratches, remove rough spots and level out any finish, even varnish. Can you tell me what it is?

It is essentially just lacquer thinner, and it will *NOT* work on varnish. But it works very well on 95% of old furniture for the simple reason that lacquer is the most common finish. The thinner dissolves the finish and the steel wool levels it out. If you keep applying the "restorer," it will eventually remove all the finish (and the stain, too), and you will be left with clean, smooth wood, ready to be refinished. You really can't go wrong.

But the best way to use this treatment is to apply just enough to soften the old finish, redissolving and spreading it around evenly to form a thin, protective coating on the wood. You can do this by brushing the lacquer thinner on the old finish, letting it stand for three or four minutes, and then rubbing it firmly in the direction of the grain with #0000 steel wool. Or you can apply the lacquer thinner with the steel wool.

Start with a light treatment first; it may be all you need. You don't have to do the whole piece at once. You can pick up where you left off, and it won't show.

If you want to add more finish, apply a clear brushing lacquer or a spray lacquer. You can

113

also use a regular, old-fashioned varnish, but don't use urethane.

But remember, this process only works on lacquer finishes. It won't work on any varnish.

REFINISHING A PIANO

We have a 50- or 60-year-old piano on which the finish is very rough and cracked. I've been told it can be restored by rubbing it with a cloth soaked in methyl hydrate. Is this true?

Only if the finish is shellac, and even then it's a tricky operation. If most of the finish is bad, we suggest you have an expert refinish the piano—it sounds like too valuable a piece of furniture to experiment on.

REFINISHING ROCK MAPLE

Some years ago we purchased a rock maple bedroom suite with a red maple finish. I decided I would like to refinish it in that light walnut shade that is in vogue now for Colonial furniture. After I had stripped the finish off I was dismayed to find that the stain I wanted to use won't color the wood. A local finisher tells me that I will have to have all the pieces "dipped to break the seal". This would be quite expensive, and I'm wondering if you have another solution.

You probably didn't get all the finish off, but I don't think dip-stripping is the answer. If you just used a paint remover, that is not enough. You must also sand the surface to remove the finish that has penetrated the surface and to get down to bare wood that will take a stain. Use very fine garnet or aluminum oxide paper, or #000 steel wool.

Different woods vary greatly in the amount of stain they will absorb. Rock maple is a very hard wood, so don't be surprised if it doesn't take up very much stain in one application. If it's not dark enough, let it dry and then give it a second application. It's a good idea to test the stain first on some hidden part of the furniture, but be sure it has been prepared the same as the surface you want to refinish.

FINISHING ROSEWOOD

I recently purchased a dining room table, removed the old finish with paint stripper, and put on a coat of satin urethane. This darkened the wood, and now I've been told that it's a rosewood table and I shouldn't have used urethane on it. I should either have used just wax, or another method of finishing that takes

a long time but does the best job on rosewood. I'd like to correct the mistake I made. Can you tell me the proper finish to use?

I'm afraid you've had some bad advice. Rosewood is supposed to be dark; it's one of the darkest woods around, and any finish you put on will bring out the dark color. Urethane varnish is a perfectly good finish for rosewood, but a penetrating sealer, sometimes called a Danish oil finish, is also very good, and a lot easier to apply.

Wax is a poor finish to put on raw wood. It doesn't seal the wood, and you can never put any other finish on top of it.

The finish "that takes a long time" is probably either a hand-rubbed linseed oil finish, which has nothing to recommend it today, or French polish, a shellac and oil finish that gives an excellent, high gloss, "piano" finish, but is easily marked by alcohol, water, and heat. It hasn't been used for years.

FURNITURE FINISH ROUGH

We refinished some dining room chairs, stripping and sanding them first. The wood was very smooth, but after the first coat of urethane was applied it felt rough. We are going to do an oak table next and I would like to know how to get a smooth finish.

The roughness was probably caused by using a final sandpaper that was too coarse, leaving a fine nap, like peach fuzz, that was brought up by the first coat of finish. An easy way to prevent this trouble is to thin the first coat of finish, let it dry, the remove the raised nap with #220 sandpaper or #0000 steel wool.

STAINING FURNITURE

I have a handmade, walnut bedroom set that has two different finishes. The bed is made of solid walnut and has a linseed oil finish. The dresser is made of walnut veneer and has a urethane finish. The problem is that the oil-finished bed is much darker than the urethaned dresser. Will time darken the dresser or is there some other way I can get them to match?

The dresser will darken somewhat with age, but if you don't want to wait you'll have to stain it. Until recently the only way to stain the dresser would have been to remove the present finish down to the bare wood and start again...a big job, and a tricky one where thin veneers are involved. But you can now buy a stain that can be applied *on top* of an existing finish. Only lightly tinted, it can be applied in several layers to build up the tone you require.

MAKING A TACK RAG

I am going to finish some furniture and was advised to clean it with a "tack rag" before varnishing. Can you tell me what this is and how to make it?

A tack rag is just a sticky cloth that is used to remove the last traces of sanding dust from the wood surface before it is finished. You can buy them at most paint stores, but it's easy to make one out of a 2'-square piece of clean, lint-free cloth such as cheese-cloth, sheeting or even a diaper.

Wet the cloth and wring it out well, then dip it in turpentine and wring it out again, but not quite so well. Spread the cloth out and sprinkle it generously with varnish dropped from a pointed stick. (Old-fashioned phenolic varnish works better than urethane varnish.) Knead the cloth to mix the varnish and turpentine evenly, shake it out until it dries slightly and becomes tacky, then fold the edges to the centre to form a hand-sized pad.

Add a few drops of turpentine and varnish as necessary to keep the cloth tacky, and store in a sealed glass jar.

STAINING OVER SHELLAC

I want to stain some unfinished furniture to match our other pieces, but the furniture was inadvertently given a coat of shellac. Is there any kind of a stain that can be applied over it?

You can't apply a wood stain on top of it, but the shellac can be removed quite easily with methyl alcohol. Wash the surface several times with wood alcohol (methyl hydrate) to remove all the shellac. Then start again—with the stain, this time.

USING FURNITURE STAIN

I have just finished staining a small dining room table that I had previously sanded down to the bare wood. The color is fine, but the stain shows brush marks in several places. I want to apply a clear varnish, but don't want to do this while the brush marks are showing. What should I do?

Stain should not be applied like paint and allowed to dry. It should be brushed or wiped on lightly, allowed to penetrate for a few min-

utes, and then wiped off. If the color is not dark enough, repeat. There is no way to remove the brush marks after the stain has dried, except by sanding. You'll have to sand the stain off back to the bare wood and start again. I suggest you use one of the new latex or gel stains. They're much easier to apply than the common pigmented oil stains.

VARNISH BEADING

I have been trying to refinish a table with satin varnish, but I can't get it to go on properly. I washed the tabletop first, and it seemed to be perfectly clean with no sign of grease or oil, but when I brushed on the varnish it beaded. What went wrong?

Paint experts know the problem as "fisheyes," and it is generally caused by the silicone used in many furniture polishes today. These are invisible and very hard to remove. Wet a cloth with turpentine and sprinkle it with a powdered detergent. Clean the surface thoroughly with this, then rinse several times with turpentine, using fresh, clean rags *each time* to prevent redepositing the silicone.

HOW TO VARNISH

Whenever I try to put a nice varnish finish on a piece of furniture, I am plagued with flecks and dust spots that mar the surface. How can I prevent them?

The two most common causes of failure in applying a varnish finish are using old brushes and old varnish. The surface to be varnished must be perfectly clean too, of course; the slightest amount of sanding dust left on the surface will show up in the finish. Wipe it down first with a damp cloth or a "tack cloth," which you can buy at most paint stores.

An old brush is all right if it's perfectly clean, but very few home handymen are willing to take the time and trouble to clean a brush thoroughly after every use. You're better off to buy a new, but inexpensive brush when you want to varnish furniture.

A can of old varnish usually contains tiny flecks of hardened varnish. You can screen it through a nylon stocking, but it's usually better to buy a new can for each refinishing job.

If you're using a satin or matt varnish, be sure to stir it well first. The additive that dulls the finish settles to the bottom of the can, and the remainder will be glossy. It isn't really necessary to buy a special varnish for a low-gloss finish; most experts prefer to rub down the final coat with very fine steel wool (#0000 grade) for a hand-rubbed, soft satin sheen. This also removes any tiny imperfections in the final varnish coat.

FINISHING WALNUT

I am making a coffee table out of black walnut and would like to know how to finish it to bring out the grain of the walnut but not darken the wood to any extent.

One of the most attractive features of American black walnut is its dark color, and most people want a finish that will bring this out. For this I recommend two coats of one of the penetrating oil-resin finishes such as Danish oil. Apply as directed.

But if you really do want a light-colored walnut finish, you will either have to bleach the wood first with a 2-part commercial wood bleach or use a primer-sealer-lightener such as Pryme, put out by the makers of Fabulon. This retains the natural color of the wood by preventing the finish from soaking into the fibres. For an even lighter finish, you can use both treatments—first the bleach, then the sealer-lightener.

You can't use an oil finish or urethane on top of this lacquer sealer, but you can use a regular varnish or lacquer.

REPAINTING WICKER

We have a number of pieces of old wicker furniture painted dark green and we'd like to have them a lighter color. What kind of paint should we use and how should it be applied?

A semi-gloss lacquer or enamel in a spray can is usually recommended for this job. If the paint is badly chipped, you should remove the old finish entirely with paint remover and a stiff-bristled brush. Otherwise, simply use a solution of one tablespoon of trisodium phosphate (TSP) in a quart of water to clean it and take off the gloss before applying two or more coats of paint.

REFINISHING WICKER

Can I re-varnish my wicker chairs?

You can use a brush and varnish if you have the patience, but we suggest you use a clear spray lacquer in an aerosol can. Sandpaper the chairs lightly before spraying to remove all loose varnish.

INFLATABLE FURNITURE LEAKS

I have an inflatable plastic chair that has a very slow leak. I've tried putting it in the bathtub but I can't find where it is leaking. Have you any suggestions?

With the tip of your finger or a small brush, rub some kitchen detergent along the seams of the chair. That's most likely where it's leaking, and you'll soon see bubbles forming at the spot. A leak in the middle of a seam is not easy to repair, but you may be able to fix it with patching material sold for use on beach balls, play pools, and blow-up toys.

"MELTING" FURNITURE

We have a fine bench table made by a leading manufacturer. The top is walnut, and the bottom looks the same, but when I dropped a cigarette on it, it immediately melted and bubbled like plastic. How can we fix it?

A lot of the "wood" decoration you see on furniture today is molded of foam plastic that is almost indistinguishable from real wood—until you touch a cigarette to it, that is. All you can do is fill the hole with something like plastic wood and paint it to match the rest of the piece.

POISONOUS POLISH

I have heard that lemon oil furniture polish is very poisonous, and that there is no cure if you drink it. Is this true?

Essentially, this is true, but there are a number of misconceptions about lemon oil that make this situation confusing. First of all, lemon oil doesn't come from lemons. The furniture polish is actually just a light grade of mineral oil, a petroleum distillate, perfumed with a few drops of an aromatic oil that smells like lemons.

The perfume oil, the so-called lemon oil, is not poisonous, but the mineral oil, like gasoline, lighter fluid, paint solvent, and similar petroleum distillates, can be quickly fatal *if it is drawn into the lungs.* You could swallow some without serious harm, as most people have done who have ever siphoned gasoline with a hose, but when the liquid gets into the lungs it causes a breakdown of tissue that is impossible to cure.

The problem is particularly serious with very young children because they may impulsively take a gulp of a strange liquid that an adult would cautiously taste. Then the action of the volatile liquid on the tongue causes them to gasp and draw the mineral oil into their very sensitive lungs. Never leave a bottle of furniture polish open near children.

REPAIRING FURNITURE VENEER

The bird's eye maple veneer on my desk has buckled and cracked. Can I repair this at home?

Unless you are an expert furniture maker, you will probably have to send it out to be repaired professionally.

You can try spreading white resin glue under the buckled parts with a hypodermic oiler (most hobby shops sell these for model work), then steaming the veneer with a damp cloth and a hot iron until it is flat. Hold it down with heavy weights until the glue has set.

GARAGE DOOR INTERFERENCE

I have a radio-controlled garage door that keeps opening to signals other than my own. I think they are CB radio signals from a nearby highway. Is there something I can attach to my radio control to cut out this interference?

You must have one of the older radio control units; they used to operate on the same frequencies as CB radios. The new units have a separate band of their own and are not subject to this problem. One remedy, then, is to put a new radio control receiver in the garage and a matching transmitter in your car. But before you do this you should try something a lot cheaper. Shorten the antenna wire on the receiver so that it doesn't pick up such distant signals but still responds to the unit in your car. Cut a little off at a time until you reach the required balance.

GARDENING—EVERGREENS DYING

How can I tell if my small evergreens are still living? I have pulled up some with yellowed needles, only to discover that the roots are still alive.

The best way to test a plant for life is to press your thumbnail into the bark and lift it gently. If the bark is dry and flaky right into the wood, then the stem is dead at that point. Keep working down the stem until you reach a point where the cambium layer under the surface bark is moist and slightly green. If there is no life in the cambium, the tree is dead and can be thrown away.

GARDENING—STUMP REMOVER

I remember reading somewhere about a chemical that removed stumps. You drilled holes in the top of the stump and poured this powder in, and it rotted the stump away. Can you tell me what it is?

It's a myth, that's what it is. There are chemicals that you can use in this way to *kill* a stump and prevent the growth of suckers (weed killers will work). There are also chemicals that make the wood more inflammable—saltpeter, for instance—so that it is easier to burn out the stump, but this is no longer permitted in most residential areas. There is nothing that will make a stump rot any faster than nature dictates, and that's a long, slow process. You will have to dig it out, tear it out or burn it out—or cover it with ivy.

GARDENING—HOUSEPLANTS UNHEALTHY?

My husband tells me it is unhealthy to have a lot of plants in the house, particularly in the wintertime. Is this true?

This is an old superstition. Plants do exhale a tiny amount of carbon dioxide (which is completely harmless) at night and a little more in winter than in summer, but they actually add more oxygen than carbon dioxide to the atmosphere and so are beneficial. There is no medical evidence whatever to support the suggestion that houseplants are harmful or unhealthy. If you lived in a greenhouse you would probably have a healthier environment than you have in the average home.

117

GARDENING—TREE SEEDLINGS

Lilac seedlings keep sprouting in my garden as fast as I can cut them down. What can I do to eradicate them?

Brush the leaves with weed killer, being careful not to let it touch other plants.

GARDENING—MOLES

I am having trouble with moles in my lawn and flower beds. What do you recommend?

Naphthalene flakes, or mothballs, tossed down the mole holes or into the tunnels will sometimes discourage them...but not always. It is said that moles will not stay where onions are planted. An old English trick is to plant castor oil beans in the area. The castor oil plant (Ricinus) is a tender annual, but quite attractive and easy to grow. The seeds are poisonous, however (which may be why the moles don't like it), and care must be taken to keep them away from children.

PLANTER DRAINAGE

I have a concrete block planter at the front of my house. Is it necessary to provide drainage holes in the sides of the planter?

Presumably the planter is just a concrete block wall sitting on the ground. In this case no other drainage is required.

GARDENING—BARK DAMAGE

We have a maple tree on our lawn, and the bark was damaged a year or so ago. It is not doing so well, and the bark seems to be curling away from the trunk. What should we do?

Cut back the damaged bark until you reach the point where it is still clinging to the tree. This may mean removing a lot of bark, but there is no alternative. Cut the edges clean and straight down to the trunk. Then paint the entire area, including the edges of the bark, with tree paint, available at any nursery.

GARDENING—TREE ROOTS vs FOUNDATION

I have recently bought an older home with mature trees front and back, one as close as 10 feet from the foundation. Some cracks are developing in the foundation, and I am afraid they are caused by tree roots. Could this be so?

It is unlikely that tree roots would crack your foundation walls. More likely the cracks are caused by the house settling. You can easily find out, in any case, by digging down outside the wall around one of the cracks. If you find any roots, you can dig back and cut them off. Or you can dig a trench parallel to the house, and cut off any roots that you meet. This "root pruning" will not harm the tree.

GARDENING—REMOVING A WILLOW

What is the best way to get rid of a weeping willow tree in our front lawn?

Cut it down, drill holes in the stump, and fill them with weed killer. This will kill the roots and prevent new shoots from developing. Next year, dig out the stump, or hire a stump grinder to cut it off below ground level.

DRILLING GLASS

I want to make a lamp out of a bottle, and would like to know how to drill a hole in the glass so that the cord can be hidden inside.

Use a special durium glass drill available at most hardware stores. If you use it in an electric drill, it must be one with a speed control; otherwise use a hand drill. Apply a light but steady pressure until the point of the drill breaks through the surface of the glass, then reduce the pressure to avoid breaking off glass chips. (If you're drilling a flat piece of glass, turn it over when the point breaks through, and finish the hole from the other side.) A few drops of turpentine, or a mixture of camphor and turpentine, should be used to lubricate the drill point as it's cutting. And it's a lot easier if you mount the drill in a drill press, instead of trying to hold it steady in your hand.

CUTTING GLASS

My teenaged daughter and I are attempting to

put mirror tiles on the wall of her room, but we need to cut some of the tiles and are having trouble doing it. We oiled the glass cutter but can't get it to make an even mark, even when we go back over it several times, and the glass usually breaks crooked. Can you tell us the trick?

It's just a matter of applying the right pressure to score the glass in one, clean stroke. A few practice strokes on a spare piece of glass should give you the feel of the cutter. When it works properly it makes sort of a tearing sound and leaves a hairline scratch.

It isn't necessary to oil the cutting wheel; in fact, heavy oil may interfere with its operation. But a drop of turpentine or kerosene will help. Place the glass on a flat surface padded with a towel or several layers of newspaper. Remove any dust from the surface. Use a ruler or other straightedge to guide the cutter, which should be held at right angles to the glass but tipped about 45° in the direction of the cut. Placing a piece of cloth under the straightedge helps to keep it from slipping around, a problem most beginners have.

A slow, steady cut with even pressure works best. Don't go back and forth over the line; this almost always causes an uneven break. Place the ruler underneath the glass at the edge of the cut (with the cut still on top) and press down gently on both sides. The glass should break easily and cleanly. After two or three tries you'll get the feel of it, and from then on it will be easy. If you still can't get the glass cutter to work, it must be dull; better buy a new one.

OBSCURE GLASS

I have a window 42" wide by 62" high that looks right into a window next door. I was thinking of replacing it with glass blocks, but this seems rather expensive. Can you suggest anything else?

There are spray-bomb paints that give the effect of frosted glass, and brush-on paints that dry in a translucent crystal pattern. You could also replace the clear glass with one of the many patterned glasses that are now available. You can also buy frosted, translucent vinyl with a self-adhesive backing that will stick to glass.

GLASS STOPPER

We bought a lovely blown glass decanter in Europe, but now I find that the ground glass stopper doesn't fit too well, and I fear that anything kept in the decanter will evaporate. Do you know of anything we can do to get the stopper to fit tightly?

Buy a can of fine valve grinding compound at an auto supply store. Rub some of the compound on the stopper, then put it in the neck of the decanter. Rotate the stopper to grind away the glass until it seats properly. Add more compound as needed. Wash thoroughly to remove the abrasive-oil-glass mixture. The whole job probably won't take you more than 20 minutes.

BOTTLE STOPPER STUCK

I have a lovely old crystal decanter that belonged to my grandmother. I used to keep sherry in it but after it was washed one day the ground glass stopper stuck and I haven't been able to get it out. I took it to a jewelery store but they told me there was nothing they could do. Have you any suggestions?

Hold the neck of the bottle under hot water. This expands the glass enough to loosen the stopper. There's a slight risk that the uneven expansion could crack the glass, but other than that it's a pretty reliable trick.

Vibration is another trick. Tap the neck of the bottle with a piece of glass, such as another bottle. Or press an electric razor against the stopper.

TEMPERED GLASS TABLETOP

We recently purchased a ½"-thick glass top for our dining room table. It was very expensive because we wanted tempered glass for safety. Unfortunately, someone has scratched the glass with a diamond ring. Is there anything that can be rubbed into this to make it less noticeable?

I don't think you received the tempered glass you asked for. A scratch from a diamond ring will usually cause tempered glass to shatter into thousands of tiny sections. Tempered glass is rarely used for tabletops, in any case. You probably have ordinary plate glass, which, in a thickness of ½" or more, is tough enough to stand up to normal use in this application.

A simple test for tempered glass is to put on a pair of Polaroid sunglasses and look at a daytime window reflected in the tabletop. If you move your head around to get the light reflected at different angles you should see a very distinct, bluish grid pattern in the surface of the glass. (You may have noticed this in car windows when you were wearing Polaroid sunglasses.) If you don't see such a pattern in the glass, the tabletop is NOT tempered.

A very light scratch can be removed by polishing the glass with a fine abrasive such as cerium oxide, but this is a slow and fairly expensive job and there are not many firms that do it. Check the Yellow Pages under Glass. A simpler trick you can try yourself is to touch up the scratch with one of the clear acrylic floor polishes, applied with a toothpick.

CHIPPED GLASSES

Due to careless washing, some tiny chips have been taken out of the edges of my fine crystal glasses, and now I'm afraid to use them. Is there any way I can restore them so they will be safe to drink out of?

All you need to do is rub the chipped edge with a very fine silicon carbide paper (#320). Wet the paper first, and wash the glass thoroughly afterwards. Small chips will virtually disappear.

CHECKING GRASS AND WEEDS

What is the easiest way of killing grass? We want to put a wooden deck over a 20′ × 30′ area of grass in our backyard, and don't want the grass growing up through it. Is there a chemical that would kill the grass and prevent it growing again?

There are a number of chemicals, including common salt, that will kill the grass, but they may also kill some of the garden plants you want to keep. Also, they are only temporary; grass and weeds will soon sprout again.

There's a much simpler method. When you're ready to build, cover the grass with black polyethylene sheet and a 2″ or 3″ layer of gravel. Nothing will grow through this. If necessary, apply soil first to fill up any depressions and slope the ground slightly so that surface water will drain off the polyethylene sheet.

REMOVING GROUT FROM CERAMIC TILES

How can I remove grouting cement from the face of glazed mosaic tile? When I was applying the grout to the tile I waited too long before attempting to remove the surplus, and now no amount of scrubbing with water seems to have any effect on it.

The grouting cement can be cleaned off the surface of the tiles with a solution of 1 part muriatic acid (any hardware store) to 10 parts water. Wear rubber gloves and keep the acid solution off everything but the tiles.

COLORED TILE GROUT

We recently re-tiled our bathroom with brown ceramic tile, and are now ready to grout the joints. We have white grout powder on hand but would like to tint it a light brown color in keeping with the tone of the tiles. What can we use to tint the white grout?

Special grout pigments are available from any tile supplier. The powdered pigment is very strongly colored and you won't need much to tint the white cement powder. It may be more economical to buy it from a hobby shop that sells mosaic tile work supplies. Mix up a small batch first and let it dry to check the color.

DISCOLORED TILE GROUT

A few months ago we installed ceramic tiles in our bathroom, and already the grout between the tiles around the tub is becoming discolored. Ordinary cleaners don't seem to do any good. Is there something I can do to whiten the grout again and prevent this black stain from forming?

The grout discoloration is a mold growth caused by continuing dampness. It can be removed by scrubbing it with a strong solution of chlorine laundry bleach—say 2 ounces to 1 cup of water. But the mold will return as long as the grout is allowed to remain damp for long periods. When it's dry, paint it with one of the silicone water repellents sold for use on shoes, and let this dry before steaming up the bathroom again. It would also be advisable, however, to put in a bathroom vent fan.

GROUTING PATIO SQUARES

Our concrete patio was poured in squares, separated by strips of wood. This wood rotted and had to be removed, leaving a ½" space between the concrete squares. We don't want grass and weeds growing between them; what can we use to fill the spaces?

You can make a cement grout by mixing one part portland cement with three parts of fine sand, and adding an oxide color pigment if desired. These ingredients are all mixed dry, and then brushed into the cracks. Tamp the grout into the cracks with a short length of ½" board, then refill and tamp again, slightly below the level of the concrete squares. Brush the surplus off the patio, then wet the grout with a fine spray from your garden hose.

REMOVING GUMMED LABELS

I bought a set of glassware to give as a wedding present, but I am having some difficulty removing all the labels. They are the common self-stick type with the gummy, rubber-like adhesive. I can manage to soak the paper label off, but can't find anything that will remove the adhesive.

You'll find that lacquer thinner or contact cement solvent works very well. These also remove cellulose tape adhesive and those self-stick vinyl decorations.

FINISHING DRYWALL PANELLING

I have paneled my basement recreation room with gypsumboard drywall and have taped and filled the joints to provide a smooth wall surface. I'm not sure whether I should paint it, paper it, or apply one of the textured, stucco-like finishes. Which one is best for drywall, and what kind of primer is required?

Drywall panelling makes a good base for any of these finishes, but the priming requirements are different. If you want to use a regular wall paint, either water-based or oil-based, use a latex primer—or a latex paint that is self-priming.

If you want to finish the wall with one of the heavy-textured paints, prime it first with an alkyd or other oil-based primer. Any of the enamel undercoats will do very well. The same kind of a primer is used if you plan to cover the wall with wallpaper. This will allow the new, dry-strippable wallpapers to be removed easily without damaging the paper face of the gypsumboard panels.

A word of warning about textured paints, however. They are almost impossible to remove if you want a smooth wall finish again.

DRYWALL BLEMISHES

I put up drywall panels in our recreation room and was careful to tape and sand the joints very smooth before I painted. Now I find that there are shiny strips on the wall where the joints were filled. Why is this?

You sanded the joints *too* carefully. The idea is to match the filled joint to the soft, slightly rough texture of the fibre-board face on the gypsum wallboard. This is best done by sanding the joint with medium grade, not fine grade, sandpaper. Your eye will show you when the joint surface is right.

HARDBOARD PANELS BUCKLING

We recently strapped and insulated our basement walls and applied polyethylene vapor barrier, then finished the walls with hardboard panelling in a simulated woodgrain. Now the panels are buckling and bulging in and out. Can you tell us what is causing this and how to correct it?

Hardboard panelling is very susceptible to changes in humidity, which causes it to swell and shrink. Before the panelling is applied it should be stood upright in the room for a few days so that it can adjust to the humidity. The basement is usually damper than the warehouse the panelling comes from, so if you nail it up too soon it will buckle as it absorbs moisture from the air. It it also recommended that you leave a slight gap between the panels to allow for a certain amount of lateral movement.

About all you can do now, however, is remove the panels and pile them flat on the floor with some weights on top and leave them for a few days. It's possible that this will flatten out the bulges.

HEATING

ADDING PUMP TO HOT WATER HEATING SYSTEM

We have an old-fashioned, gravity hot-water heating system. Would there be any fuel saving if we installed a circulating pump?

If your heating system works all right, warming all the rooms adequately, nothing would be gained by putting in a pump. This is only necessary if some of the radiators aren't receiving enough heat; it won't cut down on fuel consumption.

Your heating system must be at least 20 years old, so the pipes and the boiler will probably need replacing before too long. A modern burner, boiler, and closed circulating system would certainly be more efficient and reduce fuel consumption.

AIR IN HOT-WATER RADIATORS

We have a hot-water heating system, with old-fashioned, upright radiators. Air-locks constantly form in these radiators and we have to keep bleeding the air out of them almost every day. Where does the air come from? There is a pressure tank in the basement and we drain and refill it every fall.

The air is dissolved in the fresh water that is added to the system, and is expelled when the water is heated. After that very little air will be produced as long as the old water is used. It is a mistake to add any more water to the system than is absolutely necessary. It would be best if you could add none at all. This also reduces rusting and scale formations, caused by the oxygen and lime that are dissolved in the fresh water.

MORE HEAT FROM RADIATORS

We have a hot water heating system with old-fashioned, cast iron radiators. The wall behind the radiators is solid brick, and therefore uninsulated, and I'm sure we're losing a lot of heat that way. Is there any way we can keep this heat in the house?

Cut sheets of 1″ foamboard insulation the size of each radiator and cover them with aluminum foil, taped or stapled in place with the shiny side out. Lean them against the wall behind the radiators. If there isn't room to lean them, fasten them to the wall with double-sided adhesive tape. The foamboard will insulate the wall and the foil will reflect most of the radiant heat into the room.

AUXILIARY BASEMENT HEAT

We have a basement recreation room with three warm air registers. It is reasonably comfortable during the cold weather, but it gets quite cool during the spring and fall, when the furnace is seldom on. We are considering putting in either electric baseboard heaters or heating cable in the ceiling, under plaster. Which type would you recommend?

The electric baseboard heaters would be more suitable. I think, because these will provide a circulation of warm air over the cold outside wall, where it is needed. The heating cables in the ceiling won't warm the walls or the floor.

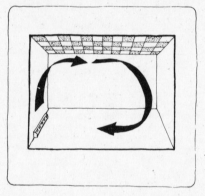

BASEMENT TOO WARM

We have a 2-storey house with a full basement and a warm air heating system. Our problem is that the unfinished basement is too warm and the bedrooms upstairs are too cool. We had the attic insulated and that helped a bit, but the top floor is still cool. Is there anything else we can do to correct this heat imbalance?

I assume you've already turned off the warm air registers in the basement, so that means that the heat must be coming mainly from the warm air ductwork in the basement ceiling. The first thing I would do is insulate the main duct or plenum from the furnace. This can be done by applying sheets of 1″ rigid fibreglass duct insulation to three sides of the ceiling plenum with mastic adhesive or special clips made for this purpose.

This may increase the air temperature in the upstairs ducts enough to correct the problem. If not, you may need a cold air return duct on the second floor to achieve better air circulation in the house.

CHIMNEY LINER NEEDED?

We have an old two-storey house with a coal furnace and a brick chimney. We plan to convert to natural gas, and have been told we must line the chimney or the gas will eat the mortar. How do we go about this?

Gas won't eat the mortar, but a gas furnace has a lower flue temperature than a coal or oil one. The exhaust gases also contain more water vapor, and this can cause condensation on the inside of a cold chimney. If the chimney is not lined, and the mortar is in poor shape, this condensation can soften it further.

The usual solution is to drop a double-walled metal vent down the inside of the chimney. The normal 9″ x 9″ flue opening will easily take a 6″ or 7″ metal vent, which is the most you will need.

COLD AIR RETURN DUCT

We are having trouble heating the second floor of our 2-storey home. There is no cold air return duct upstairs and I was thinking of running one down through a clothes closet on the main floor, using a flexible hose. Do you think this will solve the problem?

A cold air return duct from the second floor is the answer, but it should be 3¼″ x 12″ or larger, not a small, circular flex hose duct. Your local sheet metal shop can make up a duct to your requirements.

COLD FLOORS

Our apartment is heated with electric ceiling panels, and even though the floor is carpeted, I find it very cold around my feet and ankles.

I think the main cause of your cold floors is lack of air circulation. Without this, the cold air will fall to the floor and the warm air will rise to the ceiling. Try pointing an electric fan up at the ceiling to move the warm air around.

COLD FLOORS

I have a small bungalow with hardwood

floors that are always cold in the winter. My oil furnace blows hot air from vents in the ceiling. There are vents in the floor that go into the crawlspace, but I plug these up with fibreglass insulation in the winter. Should I put some insulation under the floor?

I don't think those vents in the floor open into the crawlspace. They are probably cold air return vents to the furnace, and they must be left open during the heating season so that the warm air can circulate as it is supposed to. They take the cold air off the floor and return it to the furnace. If you un-plug them, I think you'll find you get a lot more heat out of your furnace, and the floors will be much warmer. It would also be a good idea to put insulation batts under the floor.

COLD BASEMENT FLOOR

How can we keep our basement rec room floor warmer in the winter? It's presently covered with a thin indoor-outdoor carpet. Our warm air heating system seems to work very well except in the basement.

A common cause of cold floors in the basement is the lack of a cold air return vent at the floor level. A small vent in the bottom of the cold air return duct, where it enters the furnace, will draw the cold air off the floor and provide a *circulation* of warm air in the basement.

DOES IT PAY TO TURN OFF HOT WATER TANK?

When we go up to our cottage for the weekend, would it save money to turn the electric hot water tank off in the house while we're away? Or would it cost just as much to heat up the tank again when we get back?

In two days you would lose money on the deal. It takes about 2½ kilowatt hours of electrical energy a day to keep a 40-gallon tank of water hot, if it's not being used. So you'd save about 5 kilowatt hours in two days. On the other hand it takes 7 kilowatt hours to heat the water from 70°F. back up to 150 °F. again. But if you were away for a week, you'd save about 10 kilowatt hours, perhaps 20¢. Hardly worth the inconvenience of coming back to a house with tion, but the rest of the water should not be changed.

DRAINING AN EXPANSION TANK

We have an old hot water heating system with

an expansion tank over the furnace. Every couple of years the expansion tanks fills with water and I have to drain it to prevent the loss of water through the safety valve on the boiler. What causes this? Is it supposed to happen or is there somethiing wrong with my furnace?

When the expansion tank is filled it compresses the air inside it, and this keeps the hot water system at the required pressure for efficient operation. It also allows the water to expand and contract as it heats and cools. The air is gradually dissolved in the water, however, and after a while the tank gets full of water and there is no air cushion left. The tank is said to be "water-logged". Then when the water is heated and expands, it is forced out the safety valve.

This is a natural condition that requires occasional attention. When you feel the hot water close to the top of the expansion tank, all you have to do is drain it to let in some air. Some tanks have to be drained completely to do this (after shutting off the furnace and the water supply valve). Others are fitted with a special drain valve that lets air in as it lets water out. It should not be necessary to do this more than once a year. There are also expansion tanks that separate the air and water with a rubber membrane.

DRAINING HOT WATER HEATING SYSTEM

I bought an old house with a hot water heating system that didn't circulate properly to the radiators on the third floor. The plumber put an expansion tank on the boiler to cure this problem, but it didn't work. Now he says it's because I didn't drain the water out of the system last spring and put in fresh water. The water gets heavy after a winter's use, he says, and won't reach the upper floor. Is this true?

I've heard a lot of ridiculous excuses in my time, but that one deserves a special award for originality! It is nonsense, of course, to suggest that water gets heavy with use. His advice is quite wrong, in any case. Fresh water contains dissolved air that is driven off when the water is heated. This is the air that collects in radiators and must be bled off occasionally. And it is the oxygen in this air that causes metal to rust. After the air has been driven off, very little rusting will take place, so the water in a hydronic heating system should be retained as long as possible. Fresh water must be added occasionally to make up for evaporation, and this will add some air to the system, but the

water should only be changed if it is necessary to make plumbing repairs.

I suggest you call in another plumber to inspect your system and correct its problems. I wouldn't have much faith in the work your present plumber has done.

ELECTRIC HEATING

I am converting my summer home for year 'round living with insulation and wiring for electric heat. I can't decide, however, whether to install electric baseboard units in every room or an electric warm-air furnace. Can you tell me which is best?

As far as I know both systems are quite satisfactory and equally efficient. The baseboard heaters will probably cost less than a complete electric warm-air heating system, and they also permit separate thermostatic controls in each room, or even on each side of one room.

On the other hand, a warm-air circulating system permits the air to be filtered and maintains a more even heat throughout the house, particularly if the fan is left on all through the heating season. It also permits the installation of a central cooling and air-conditioning system, or even a heat pump, which appears to be the most economical way of heating and cooling with electrical energy.

ELECTRIC HEATING AND HUMIDITY

We are having a house built and plan on installing baseboard electric heating. Our builder says that with electric heat we will need two humidifiers, one upstairs, one down. The utility representative says that we won't need humidifiers at all, that, on the contrary, a dehumidifier will probably be required. Which one is right?

The utility rep is right, or almost right. Electrically-heated homes tend to have a higher humidity level than homes with a conventional furnace, mainly because they don't have the ventilation that comes from the operation of a furnace.

The excess humidity he speaks of will be evident only in the winter time, however, and an electric dehumidifier is not effective under those conditions. All you need to do is provide adequate ventilation to bring in fresh, dry air.

HEATING THE BASEMENT

We are finishing a recreation room in our

basement, and plan to put a cold-air return vent down there as you suggested, to get better circulation of the warm air. If the cold-air return is taken off the floor, should the warm-air supply ducts be brought down to floor level, too? We have been told this is the best place for them.

If the warm-air supply outlets are in the ceiling, as they usually are in the basement, then the cold-air return should be on the basement floor level. If you run the supply ducts down to the floor, then the cold-air return can be in the ceiling. One way works as well as the other as far as heat circulation is concerned; it's really a matter of which is most convenient to install. In many cases it's easier to put the cold-air return vent in the ceiling than on the floor, but then you have the problem of finding a spot where you can run the warm-air duct down an interior partition wall without too many sharp turns that will restrict the air flow. (If you run the duct down an outside wall you will lose a lot of heat). In general, I think it's best to leave the warm-air outlets in the ceiling and put a cold-air return vent on the floor.

BLOCKING COLD AIR RETURNS

With the cost of fuel oil going up, I've covered all the heat ducts in the basement, and would like to cover the cold air returns as well. Will this help?

You might as well just turn the furnace off. The heating system won't work at all if you close off the cold air returns. Turning off the basement heating ducts isn't going to help much, either, because the heat from the basement normally rises to help heat the upstairs. Without it, you'll just have cold floors and lower room temperatures, which will call on the furnace for more heat.

The best way to reduce heating costs is to add more insulation to the house . . . first in the upstairs ceiling, next in the basement walls, then in the upstairs walls. (See Insulation.)

COLD AIR RETURN

I have a closed-in porch and I want to heat it with a warm air duct from the furnace. Do I have to put in a cold air return duct too?

If you provide an opening between the porch and the rest of the house, you won't need a cold air return. But circulation of air must be provided; you can't push warm air into a sealed room.

FRESH AIR IN HEATING SYSTEM

I've heard that there's some way to introduce fresh, outside air into a warm air heating system that is beneficial and can even reduce heating bills somewhat. Can you tell me anything about it?

All you have to do is install a 5" duct from the outside wall to the cold air return plenum leading to the furnace. The outside opening should be screened, and the duct should be fitted with an adjustable damper that lets you control the amount of outside air that is introduced into the house. (See illustration on page 55.)

The main benefit of this system is that it reduces the humidity in the house and eliminates condensation problems. But it also removes cooking and smoking odors and keeps the house supplied with adequate fresh air without the customary cold drafts, because the cold, outside air is filtered and heated before it is distributed evenly throughout the house.

This is not going to reduce your heating bill, however.

FURNACE AIR DUCT

The outside air intake for our warm air heating system becomes covered with a thick coating of frost during very cold weather. This I can understand, but the difficulty comes when the frost melts and drips on to the basement floor. Our contractor wrapped the pipe with insulation, but that just gets wet. What can we do?

Wrap the insulation with polyethylene vapor barrier, and seal it with polyethylene tape to make it airtight. Don't leave any gaps for the moist household air to get through and contact the cold pipe.

FURNACE AIR SUPPLY

Our gas furnace has a vent pipe that brings outside air into the furnace room. The pipe goes down the back of the furnace and stops about two feet from the floor. I haven't seen another like it, and wonder if it is properly installed. A very cold wind blows in during the winter, and I've covered the opening, but don't know whether I should have. I would appreciate your advice.

That is an approved duct system, often used where the supply of fresh air to the furnace room would otherwise be inadequate. This air is essential for the efficient operation of the furnace, and the opening should not be covered during the heating season.

HEATING WITH HARD WATER

The water from our well is very hard, and we have a hot water heating system. Will the hard water cause any trouble?

The water in a heating system stays there for a long time, and what hardness it contains is soon deposited; after that, it's as good as soft water. There's no need to install a softener for the heating system. Just don't change the water.

HEAT MARKS

We have the old type of hot air registers in our home, and the walls above them are badly stained. Is this caused by excessive heat or by gas fumes, and how can I cure it?

Electrostatic attraction causes dust to adhere to surfaces around a hot air register, or even over a hot water radiator. It is worse with an old-fashioned gravity system (if that's what you have) because there are no air filters in these. You can clean the walls with a solution of trisodium phosphate (TSP) available at any hardware store.

HEAT RECLAIMER

I recently bought a heat reclaimer that fits into the chimney pipe just back of the furnace. It contains a small fan that blows air through the reclaimer and back into the house. We were told that 60% to 70% of the furnace heat is normally lost up the chimney, and that this device will recover most of it. Is it really that good?

It works, but not as well as you were told. To start with, a clean, well adjusted furnace should lose no more than 25% of its heat up the chimney. Even a very poor furnace is unlikely to lose more than 40%. And you can only recover part of this...perhaps one-quarter—so you can expect to gain something like 5% to 10% more heat from your furnace with such a device. If you can direct the recovered warm air into the main living area of the house, it can reduce your heating bills accordingly. But that air is more commonly used to heat areas that are inadequately heated by the present system, such as rooms in the basement or at the far end of the house.

HOUSE TEMPERATURE VARIES

We have an oil-fired warm air furnace that seems to give out plenty of heat, but our house cools down several degrees before it comes on again. We keep the thermostat set at 20° Celsius (70°F), but the temperature rises a degree or two above that before the fan turns off. A serviceman checked the furnace and said it's OK. What could be the trouble?

He should have checked the thermostat. It's not turning the furnace off soon enough and may be defective, but more likely it just needs a simple adjustment that you can make yourself.

A thermostat contains a device called an "anticipator" that is adjusted to turn the furnace off a short time *before* the room temperature reaches the thermostat setting. The heat that remains in the furnace will then bring the house up to the required temperature.

If you take the cover off your thermostat you should be able to see a small scale numbered from .1 to 2 amp. It may also have an arrow pointing to one end, marked "longer." This is the anticipator. Your furnace is running too long now, so you need to move the pointer on this scale in the "shorter" direction, or to the lower amps. Don't move the pointer more than one scale mark at a time, and wait 24 hours before moving it again. If you move it too far the furnace will cycle on and off too frequently. Watch the thermostat to see if the house temperature stays down to the level at which it's set. If not, move the anticipator pointer another mark on the scale. When properly set, the change in the room temperature between furnace cycles should be too small to be noticeable—certainly not more than 1°C (2°F).

DOES IT REALLY PAY TO LOWER THE HOUSE TEMPERATURE?

I keep reading that you can reduce heating costs by turning the thermostat down for a few hours a day, such as while you're asleep or away at work. But isn't the saving lost when the furnace has to work longer to bring the house back up to the temperature again?

A lot of people have this idea, but if you'll bear with me for a moment you'll see why it doesn't work that way. The amount of heat that is lost from a house in a given time depends on its temperature. A hot body gives off more heat than a cool body, in other words. So the furnace has to burn more fuel to maintain the house at 70°F (21°C) than to maintain it at 64°F (18°C).

The longer the house stays at the lower temperature, the more heat is saved, and the heat required to bring the temperature back up must always be less than the heat that would have been needed to maintain it at the higher temperature, no matter how short the period, or how well insulated the house.

ECONOMICAL TEMPERATURE

Will you please settle an argument regarding the most economical temperature setting for a home heating system? Our friends say it doesn't save any money to lower the temperature, that the same amount of fuel will be used to keep the house at a steady temperature whether it is 72° or 60°. I'm sure it must cost less to heat at a lower temperature.

You're right, of course. The amount of heat loss given off by the house is greater the higher its temperature is. A hot body gives off more heat than a cool one, in other words, and it is the heat loss of the house that you have to replace with more heat from the furnace.

HEAT vs HUMIDITY

Is it cheaper to heat a house with high humidity or low humidity?

As the humidity increases, the evaporation of body moisture slows down, and you feel warmer. You can therefore be comfortable at a lower temperature if the humidity is up. However, the cost of adding humidity to the air probably offsets the saving. As well, there's a limit to the amount of humidity you can have in the house without running into condensation problems.

FLOOR STAINS
FROM HEAT REGISTERS

Our house is about 25 years old, and the hot air registers, which are situated on the walls just off the floor, have discolored the hardwood in the bedrooms and the linoleum in the bathroom. We would like to put a light-colored carpet in the bedrooms but are afraid that the registers will stain it. How can we prevent this?

It will help if you put new grilles in the front of each warm air register to divert the air upwards instead of down on the floor. But it sounds as if the old ducts are dirty, and I think they should be cleaned. To do this properly you should disconnect them in the basement and use long brushes and an industrial vacuum cleaner. These can be obtained at most tool rental stores.

LOWER LEVEL COLD

We bought a new bi-level house three months ago and are having trouble keeping the lower level warm. There is only one cold-air return vent, and it's on the upper level, which is the main living area of the house. Downstairs, partly below ground level, there are four rooms—two bedrooms, a family room, bathroom and furnace/laundry room. The warm air outlets are in the ceiling and there is no cold-air return vent. Do we need one down there, and should the builder have to put it in?

A cold-air return vent near the floor of the lower level would definitely improve the circulation of warm air in that part of the house. This is not required by any building code that I know of, however, so I don't think you have any claim against the builder.

Another possible cause of the lower temperature on that level could be insufficient insulation in the walls. Ask your builder how much insulation has been installed. Some codes permit less insulation in the "basement" walls than upstairs, but in a bi-level home like this you really need the same insulation on both living levels.

POOR AIR CIRCULATION

Our townhouse has a central air conditioner that works through the warm-air heating system. In hot weather the upstairs is much warmer than the main floor, and in the winter the situation is reversed. What can be done to balance the air temperature on both levels?

I can think of two possible causes for this, and it's very likely that you have both of them. One is the lack of a cold air return vent on the upper level. Builders often try to cut costs by putting in just one cold air return vent on the main floor, somewhere near the stairway to the upper level. This isn't good enough.

The second cause could be insufficient insulation upstairs, particularly in the ceiling. Check the attic to see if you have at least 6".

HEATING SECOND FLOOR

The second floor of our two-storey house is

always much colder than the main floor. We have a forced warm air heating system and there seem to be plenty of ducts, but the heat just doesn't go upstairs. Is there anything we can do?

The ducts leading to the upstairs rooms are naturally longer than the lower floor ducts, and often have to follow a devious path with several right-angle turns. A heating system should be "balanced" when it is installed to overcome these differences. This is done by adjusting dampers located in each of the heating ducts near where they come off the warm air plenum. You can do this yourself, closing off the lower floor ducts to divert more of the warm air to the upper floor. Some cheap installations don't have dampers; in this case, you will have to make do with the controls at the registers, although this does not work as well.

You should also have at least one cold air return above the main floor; lack of this can keep the upstairs air from circulating properly.

Finally, make sure you have enough insulation in the upstairs ceiling.

WARM AIR CIRCULATION

My husband says that we will save money on heating bills if the furnace fan is only on for short periods, delivering fairly hot air. I think it would be more efficient if the fan stayed on longer. Who's right?

You're closer to the truth than he is. Warm air heating experts have found that the most comfortable and efficient system is to have the furnace fan on ALL the time during the heating season. The thermostat continues to turn the furnace on and off as required.

This eliminates the sudden rush of cool air when the fan first goes on, but more important, it provides a gentle, steady circulation of air throughout the house so that the temperature remains even from floor to ceiling and from room to room. Because the fan can be set at a slower speed for continuous operation, it is also quieter. And most people find steady, low-level sound much less disturbing than an intermittent one.

You can set your furnace to operate with constant air circulation simply by turning on the manual fan control button. One other adjustment is recommended. Have your furnace man set the fan to run a little slower, or do it yourself by adjusting the pulley wheel on the fan motor. You'll find that this wheel is in two parts. Loosen the set screw on the outer half and unscrew it so that the fan belt rides about ¼" farther down inside the pulley. (Turn the

furnace off while you're doing this, of course.) Readjust the fan belt tension after changing the pulley size; you should be able to move the belt about ¼" by pressing it with your finger.

Continual operation won't hurt the fan or motor. Most fans are permanently lubricated, but the motors normally require a few drops of oil two or three times a season. Do this once a month if you're running the fan all the time. The filter should also be cleaned or replaced once a month.

As to costs, it will add about $2.50 a month to your electric bill if the fan is running continually. But without the usual fluctuation in household air temperature, you'll find that the thermostat can be set down a degree or two, and the resulting saving in fuel will more than offset the added cost of electric power.

WARM-AIR VENTS

Recently I was in a house that had the warm-air heating vents near the top of the walls. In my house all the vents are in the floor at the base of the outside walls. Is there any advantage in putting them near the ceiling?

About 25 years ago this was the accepted method. It has since been discovered that the house is more comfortable if the vents are placed in the floor around the perimeter of the house, where the warm air can rise, keeping the walls warm.

For summer cooling, however, vents work better if they are near the ceiling, because cold air falls.

HOW TO ABANDON A HOUSE

We leave our house for the winter and go to Florida, but have always left the heat on here. With heating cost so high now, do you think it would be safe to turn off the water and the heat?

It's not quite as simple as that. There is the very important question of your house insurance. Some companies require that you notify them if you are going to be away from your house for more than four days during the winter, but all of them require that you either leave the heat on and have the house inspected by a responsible adult *once a day* while you are away, or else that you have the water turned off and drained by someone who knows how to do it—a plumber, for instance.

I don't recommend leaving the house

unheated through the winter. Dampness and mildew may ruin the rugs, drapery, clothing, and upholstered furniture—and this kind of damage is not covered by the standard homeowner's policy.

Leave the heat on, but turn the thermostat down to 50°. Disconnect the fridge and the hot water tank, and arrange with a friend or relative to check the house every day. If this isn't practical, you can hire a security patrol guard to inspect your house for about $5 a day...or something like $500 for the winter. That Florida trip may be more expensive than you expected.

HOUSE SAGGING

Why would one corner of my 50-year-old house suddenly develop a bad sag?

There are many reasons why an older home might sag. Underground water could be settling the earth under your house. Nearby excavating could do the same thing. A main supporting beam could be decayed or broken; the concrete foundation could be cracked and crumbling under the affected area; termites sometimes undermine beams, causing the house to sag. Most of these areas are exposed, so you may be able to find the cause yourself, or have a reputable contractor inspect them.

HUMIDITY

HUMIDITY vs TEMPERATURE

Is it true that we can save money on heating if we put in a humidifier?

I'm afraid not. A humidifier may eliminate such dry air problems as squeaking floors, shrinking furniture, sore throats, and static electricity, but it won't cut down on your heating bills. As a matter of fact, it will increase them, because it takes heat to evaporate water.

A humidifier installed in a warm air heating plenum lowers the temperature of the air passing over it quite significantly, and the furnace must burn longer to make this up. Even a portable humidifier cools the air around it.

Some experts claim that you can be comfortable at a lower temperature if the humidity is raised, but tests have failed to confirm this. Unless the humidity goes below 40% or above

70%, it doesn't seem to have much effect on comfort. I don't know of anyone who has lowered the room temperature because he put in a humidifier. Do you?

HUMIDIFIER INSTALLATION

I have installed a drum-type humidifier on my warm air furnace, but because of space limitations I couldn't put it in the way the instructions recommended. Instead of connecting the humidifier between the cold air return and the warm air plenum, I connected both ends to the side of the warm air plenum. Will it operate efficiently like this?

No. As you have installed it, there will be very little air flow through the humidifier—and therefore very little humidification. The reason for installing it as instructed is that there is a pressure difference between the cold air and warm air plenums on each side of the fan, and it is this pressure that forces air through the humidifier.

LIME DEPOSIT IN HUMIDIFIER

How can I eliminate the build-up of lime deposits on the evaporator plates and water tray of my humidifier?

Such deposits can cut the efficiency of a humidifier in half, according to the National Research Council, and the plates should be cleaned regularly and replaced at least twice a year. Any mild acid will dissolve the lime. Vinegar is readily available, but muriatic acid is a lot cheaper, and you can get it at any hardware store. Use one part muriatic acid to 20 parts water to dissolve the lime from plates or tray.

You can buy special tablets which you put in the evaporator tray to prevent the formation of hard deposits, but a tablespoon of washing soda, water conditioner, or even dishwasher detergent will do the job about as well.

SLIME IN HUMIDIFIER

I have a portable humidifier with a cloth wick and a metal tank, and I wash it out about once every two weeks. By that time, however, everything that has been wet is coated with a slime that is not only unpleasant but, I'm sure, cuts down on the efficiency of the humidifier. What causes this and what can I do about it?

The slime is a fungus growth fed by both the organic material in the air and the oxygen

129

supplied by the constant agitation of the water. The fungus spores are in the air, so you can't get rid of them just by washing out the humidifier.

There are several ways you can prevent the growth of fungus. One of the easiest is to put a piece of silver in the water tank, (a silver coin will do, or a silver-plated spoon.) As the water in the humidifier tank becomes slightly acid, a natural action, it dissolves a tiny bit of silver, which acts as a powerful fungicide.

Another thing you could do is add about a teaspoon of chlorine bleach to each gallon of water you put in the tank.

A pinch of potassium dichromate crystals per gallon will also kill the fungus. This has a fringe benefit: it inhibits metal corrosion in the tank. Since potassium dichromate doesn't deteriorate the way chlorine does, you only have to add it to the water in the tank very occasionally, and then only enough to give it the barest tinge of yellow. Your drugstore or photo supply dealer can get it for you.

SECOND DEHUMIDIFIER NEEDED?

We have a portable humidifier in the living room of our apartment, but I'm concerned about the air being dry in our bedroom. Do I need another humidifier there?

Probably not. Because of the physical laws of vapor pressure, humidity equalizes itself throughout the home very quickly, from room to room, even from one floor to another. You'll only need another humidifier if the present one isn't big enough.

BASEMENT HUMIDITY

Last year we installed a new forced air heating system which has a switch for summer use of the fan. We also have a dehumidifier in the basement as it is quite damp. Will the dehumidifier work when we are using the furnace fan to cool the house?

A dehumidifier only works in a confined area. It can't remove the humidity from the entire house, which it would have to do if the furnace fan is circulating the air through all the rooms. Insulating the walls is the best way to reduce the dampness in your basement.

DRY AIR

Why is the air in our house so dry every win-

ter? We get static shocks when we touch metal; our hair is frizzy and won't comb down; the floors squeak and our throats are dry. Some of our neighbors have the same trouble, even with humidifiers, but in other houses the air is so damp that the windows are steamed up much of the time. What makes one house so much dryer than another?

This is partly due to living habits. Some houses contain more people who take more baths and do more cooking and washing—all of which produce moisture. But the main reason for differences in the humidity levels of our homes during cold weather is ventilation, or air leakage.

If a house were sealed up tight, the humidity produced by normal household activities would soon become unbearable. During the winter, ventilation replaces humid household air with dry outside air—dry, that is, when it's heated up to room temperature. If there is not enough ventilation, then the house will soon be plagued with dripping windows and other condensation problems. But if there is *too much* ventilation (generally due to loose construction in an old house) the air will become much too dry.

Excess air leakage is the only reason for dry winter air in our homes. The first remedy, then, is to seal up the gaps with caulking and weatherstripping. Adding insulation in walls and ceiling will also reduce air leakage. The reduced ventilation will not only raise the humidity in the house, it will also cut down heat loss and lower fuel bills.

Some old houses can't be sealed up well enough to keep the humidity from dropping, however. For these, and for people who live in apartments that are centrally ventilated, a humidifier is the answer.

FRESH AIR vs HUMIDIFIER

I have always believed that it is important to have fresh air while sleeping. Now, after purchasing a humidifier, I have been told that fresh air will remove the humidity, and it will take all day to bring it back again. Do I have to choose between humidity and fresh air? Isn't the winter air damp?

The relative humidity outdoors is almost as high in the winter as it is in the summer. But when you bring the very cold air into the house and warm it up, the relative humidity drops and it becomes very dry in comparison to the household air. In fact, bringing in fresh air is the most efficient way to reduce the excess indoor humidity that causes condensation and other problems. So fresh air *will* soak up much of the humidity you get from the humidifier.

But that wouldn't make me give up fresh air; I'd settle for a little less humidity.

RELATIVE HUMIDITY

What is meant by relative humidity?

We all know that warm air will absorb more moisture than cold air. Relative humidity is a figure that shows how close the air is to holding all the moisture it can. If the relative humidity of the outside air on a zero day is 50%, that means it holds only half as much moisture as it's capable of holding. Bring this air indoors and heat it up to 70° and the relative humidity drops to 4%, because it's now able to absorb a lot more moisture.

MAKING ICE CUBES WITH WARM WATER

Can you settle an argument for me? My neighbor insists that warm water freezes faster in an ice cube tray than cold water. This doesn't make any sense to me, but I've heard it before so a lot of people must believe it. What's the truth?

Any scientist would tell you that warm water takes longer to freeze than cold water, but he could be wrong. There's a lovely story about an engineer whose wife insisted, like your neighbor, that warm water made ice cubes faster than cold water. To convince her she was wrong he put two trays on the freezer shelf, one with warm water, the other with cold. They check the two trays every half hour or so. To his amazement the warm water froze first! He thought he had made an important scientific discovery until he found out what was happening. The warm water was melting the frost on the freezer shelf and letting the tray come in contact with the cold metal, where it cooled faster than the other tray, which was insulated by the frost.

ICE IN THE VENT STACK

During extremely cold weather the vent pipe in the roof above our bathroom keeps plugging with ice. It's a big job to keep it clear. Our neighbors don't have this trouble. Can you tell me what's wrong?

Steam is the cause, and the reason you're having this trouble and your neighbors aren't, is that you're using more hot water than they are. This produces more steam, which makes more frost in the pipes. So one cure is to cut down on the amount of hot water you're using.

Another partial solution, if you have a sewer trap and breather tube outside your house (often in the front lawn), is to cover this with a cloth, forcing more ventilation through the house vent stack.

If your vent stack passes through the attic, you may be able to relieve or eliminate the problem by wrapping the pipe with insulation. This retains the heat and helps to melt the ice that forms around the top. You can also buy special insulating covers to fit over the vent pipe.

NON-POLLUTING ICE REMOVER

I've heard that there is a chemical I can use to melt ice that won't harm plants or grass and is non-polluting and non-corrosive. Can you tell me what it is?

The material is "urea", and it's commonly used as a fertilizer. Like other fertilizers, however, it *can* kill plants if applied excessively, so it must still be used with reasonable caution, but it's much less harmful to plants than common salt or calcium chloride. It also costs about three or four times as much, though, and is not effective at temperatures below 20°F (-4°C).

INSECTS

CARPENTER ANTS

Large, black ants have got into the walls of our cottage. They are nesting in the insulation and have eaten their way into some of the studs and beams, where I am afraid they can do considerable harm. I would be most grateful if you could suggest a suitable treatment.

This sounds like carpenter ants, and they can, indeed, do a great deal of damage. They don't eat the wood, but they tunnel through it to build elaborate, inter-connected galleries that can't be seen from the outside but can seriously weaken the wood. Little piles of sawdust, or frass, often point to the entrances to these nests.

As for other crawling insects, the best control is chlordane. This should be applied directly into the nest openings in the form of a 2% oil solution, or a 5% chlordane dust. Chlordane liquid is generally sold as a 40% concentrate; mix one part of this to 19 parts kerosene or petroleum solvent (mineral spirits) to make a 2% oil solution.

CARPET BEETLES

I've discovered some carpet beetles in our house. Where do they come from and how can I get rid of them?

They probably flew in the window. Carpet beetles usually spend their winged, adult life flying around the garden visiting the flowers, and it's a simple matter for them to fly inside and lay their eggs in a wool carpet or other material of animal origin, such as silk, which the larva eat when they hatch.

The best way to get rid of them is to apply a 2% solution of chlordane along the bottom of the baseboard in every room, and inside closets. This is a residual insecticide that kills any insect that touches it and remains effective up to two months. It's usually sold as a 40% solution, with instructions on the label for the proper dulution and handling. I recommend applying it with a paint brush rather than a spray, however. This way you keep it where you want it.

COCKROACHES

We have been shocked to discover cockroaches in our house. I have used up several cans of a common household insecticide but it doesn't seem to do much good. How can I get rid of them? Should we have the house fumigated?

You shouldn't be too surprised. Although most people don't talk about it, cockroaches are found almost everywhere, including some of our finest residential areas. A secretive, fast-moving, nocturnal insect, the cockroach has

been hiding from humans for thousands of years and has become very clever at it. Many homemakers are unaware that they have cockroaches until the infestation grows to serious proportions. Nests have been found in such unlikely places as the underside of kitchen drawers, inside electrical outlet boxes, the backs of picture frames, and even inside kitchen wall clocks. Locating and eliminating them is more a battle of wits than chemical warfare.

Good sanitation is the best control. Cockroaches like the same food we do, so spills, crumbs and scraps should be carefully removed and garbage should be well sealed. Most species also require a damp environment, so any such areas in the house should be given special attention.

Ordinary household insecticides kill only the insects they hit, so are not effective against a cockroach infestation. Residual insecticides, on the other hand, remain effective for several weeks and will kill any insect that touches them. Powders can be used, but sprays are more effective, less noticeable and can be applied to vertical as well as horizontal surfaces. Fumigation is not recommended because it, too, is a one-shot treatment and may miss nests or eggs in protected areas.

The best-known residual insecticide, chlordane, is no longer effective against cockroaches because they've developed a resistance to it. Diazinon is generally recommended for home use as a .5% or 1% solution or as a 2% dust. But rotenone (1%), propoxur (1%), lindane (.5-1%), and fenthion (.5%) are also effective, as is an old-fashioned remedy, powdered borax.

Government entomologists advise that the liquids be applied as a coarse spray, not a fine mist, to all hiding places and runways. For small areas, such as around the edges of cupboards and along the bottom of baseboards, a paint brush works best. Pay particular attention to cracks and crevices in woodwork and hidden spaces under sinks, behind refrigerators, etc. Remove kitchen drawers and spray inside the cupboard as well as under the drawers. Although cockroaches are most commonly found close to the kitchen, one species, the brown-banded cockroach, prefers high, warm spots and may be found throughout the house, often hiding in upholstered furniture and bedding.

A second application of residual insecticide to all the same areas in about six weeks will usually result in complete eradication.

STORING FIREWOOD IN GARAGE

I would like to know what insecticide I

should use on the firewood stored in my garage to prevent wood-boring insects from getting into my house.

It would be better to store the firewood in a separate shed, preferably a metal one. But if you must keep it in the attached garage, spray it liberally about every two months with a 2% solution of chlordane, available at all garden stores and most drug and hardware stores.

FURNITURE BEETLES

I noticed little flecks of powder on some of our walnut furniture which kept coming back after I had brushed it away. Then I found tiny holes on the surface of the wood. I'm afraid there are insects inside the furniture, eating it away. What should I do about it?

I'm afraid you're right. It's probably the furniture beetle, a relative of the common powder post beetle. The furniture beetle can actually digest the wood cellulose and is therefore able to live in old, dry wood devoid of sap or starches that other insects depend on. It's the grub-like larva that does the damage under the surface of the wood, where it lives for up to a year or more before emerging as a tiny beetle about $^3/_{16}$" long. The beetles push out the fine wood dust, or "frass", as they emerge through holes no bigger than a pinhead.

The only effective treatment for furniture infected with these insects is fumigation, which must be done by a licensed exterminator. (See the Yellow Pages under Extermination.)

MORTAR MITES?

The side wall of my house gets all the afternoon sun and is consequently nice and warm at night. But we've noticed that an insect of some kind likes to settle there and scrape out the concrete between the bricks. There are holes all over the wall and we're beginning to get concerned. We haven't actually seen the insects on the wall, but there are several in the garden that we think might be responsible.

There is no insect that eats or destroys concrete! It's just that the mortar between the bricks on that side of your house is crumbling due to weathering (and possibly an inferior bricklaying job to begin with). The loose mortar should be scraped away and the joints "pointed" again. (See repointing brickwork)

MOTHS

In the winter we keep our wool sweaters in our wardrobe closet, and in the summer we put them in a zippered container that we hang in a specially built, cedar-lined closet. Although the cedar smell is now very faint, our carpenter assures us that this should keep moths away. We continue to get moth holes in the sweaters, however, and are not sure whether the damage occurs in the summer or winter. I am allergic to mothballs and would like to know if there is some other way to stop the damage to our clothes.

As you probably know, it is only the larva or caterpillar stage of the clothes moth that does the damage. The moth itself never eats. The females lay eggs throughout the year, however, and the emerging larvae eat their way through wool and other fabrics for weeks or even months, so there really isn't a special season for the damage. But clothes that are being used regularly are rarely infected. Woolens that are stored, undisturbed, for the summer are much more likely to be damaged. The eggs also hatch much faster at this time.

Moth larvae also prefer woolens that are soiled, and one of the best ways to reduce damage is to have all your woolen clothing dry-cleaned before putting it into summer storage. There are a number of relatively odorless mothproofing sprays that can also be used at this time. If you are allergic to mothballs (naphthalene), try using paradichlorobenzine crystals. These are just as effective and don't have such a strong odor.

But don't put too much faith in the moth repelling power of cedar. Aromatic cedar has a very pleasant odor when it is fresh, but this doesn't last too long and is of questionable value as an insect repellent. Our Western red cedar has less smell and has never claimed to be a moth-killer.

PANTRY PESTS

I often find little bugs which later turn into worms in my kitchen cupboards. They turn up in boxes of rice, spaghetti, etc. Can you tell me what they are, how they get there, and what I should do to get rid of them?

Several kinds of insects that get into food products fit this description—weevils, grain and flour beetles, and larvae of the meal and flour moths. They can come with any of these foods, and once they are in they multiply rapidly. Throw away any food that is contaminated. Remove everything from the cupboards, wash them out thoroughly, then spray them with a household insecticide. Cover the shelves with clean paper and put back the contents.

133

Insects

PET FLEAS

About eight months ago I bought a kitten for my two little girls, who love animals. Shortly after that I noticed fleas in my basement. I got rid of the kitten immediately and tried various sprays to kill the fleas, but I still see them in the basement. What should I do?

Cat fleas can survive for weeks, or even a few months without blood food, but not this long, so unless humans or other animals are being bitten, I think you may be mistaking some other small insect for fleas. In any case, the remedy is to vacuum up, and immediately dispose of, all loose dust and debris in the area. Then spray the floor and part way up the basement wall with a kerosene solution of one of the following insecticides: ½% lindane, 2% chlordane, or 3% malathion. Concentrated solutions of these chemicals are available at most garden supply stores. Mix them with kerosene according to the directions on the label. Water can be used instead of kerosene, but it's not as effective. Some readers tell me that a Vapona or No-Pest strip will also get rid of any fleas that are in the house.

Pet fleas are easily controlled by the use of one of the many collars, tags, and powders that are available at pet supply stores. There was no need to get rid of the kitten just to get rid of the fleas.

POWDER POST BEETLES

I noticed some fine wood dust on the basement floor, and then found tiny holes in the main wood beam. The beam looks solid enough, but I gather that some kind of an insect is making tunnels inside it. Is this anything to worry about, and is there anything I can do about it?

That could be carpenter ants but it sounds more like the powder post beetle, which is not a serious pest but can cause considerable damage. The trouble is that by the time you see evidence of their work, they are usually well established and may have caused a great deal of damage that doesn't appear on the surface. An ice pick can be used to check the soundness of beams and other structural members. If you hit soft pockets, you'd better call in a pest control expert and have the damage assessed.

Fumigation is the best way to get rid of powder post beetles, but this isn't practical in all areas. The next best treatment is a 2% solution of chlordane *in oil*. Chlordane is generally sold as a 40% concentrate, and is available at all garden supply stores and most drug and hardware stores. Mix two ounces of this concentrate to a quart of stove oil or kerosene and apply it generously to all the beetle holes you can find. Repeat this treatment every two months for a year.

SILVERFISH

How can I get rid of silverfish and carpet beetles?

Chlordane and lindane are the best insecticides to use. Both are residual poisons, meaning that they remain effective for about four weeks in the case of lindane and eight weeks in the case of chlordane. Any insect coming in contact with the chemical during that time will be killed.

Chlordane should be used as a 2% solution. It usually comes in a 40% concentrate with instructions on the label for the proper dilution to use.

Lindane is used as a ½% solution. That's half of 1%, NOT half-and-half, incidentally!

The best way to apply either of these is with a brush, to avoid getting it around where you don't want it. Paint it along the bottom of the baseboard around every room in the house and inside the closets.

SOW BUGS

We had some firewood delivered and stacked in our garage. Ever since then we've been over-run with brown, flat, oval-shaped bugs in the garage and basement. They seem to gather where it is damp. We've sprayed with household insecticides but they don't seem to do any good.

They're called Sow Bugs and they're common around dead wood, usually burrowing under the bark. Like other crawling insects, they can be eliminated by brushing or spraying a 2% solution of chlordane around the areas where they're seen. In the house, brush it along the bottom of the baseboard around every room.

Unlike most other household insecticides, chlordane doesn't have to be sprayed on the bugs themselves. All they have to do is walk on it, and it will remain effective for up to two months.

Chlordane is available at garden, drug and hardware stores. It is usually sold as a 40% concentrate, with dilution instructions on the label.

TINY FLIES

We have recently noticed a number of tiny flies in our house. They look like the fruit flies that often come when peaches and similar fruit are kept around the house, but we haven't had any of those for several months. Can you tell me what these are and how we can get rid of them?

They are probably fungus gnats, a tiny fly that breeds in the rich organic soils used for house plants. This insect has become much more common in recent years because of the increasing popularity of potted plants. The larva spends about two weeks in the soil, where it attacks root growth and can seriously weaken the plants. Flies emerge to lay eggs in other plant soil, so the infestation spreads quickly.

The remedy is fairly simple. Just sprinkle a 2% solution of chlordane on the soil and work it into the top inch or so. Repeat in 10 days.

WASPS

Last summer Yellow Jacket wasps were getting under our shingles and into the attic of our house. A week ago my husband went up to check and found nests in the insulation, which he tore out and threw away. What can we do to keep them from coming back again this year?

When the wasp season comes, hang a Vapona Pest Strip or similar insecticide in the attic.

WASP NESTS

I read that bee stings can be fatal, and now I'm worried about the wasp nests that we have hanging in our carport. We've had a few stings, and I'd like to know how to get rid of them.

A strong solution of chlordane should be directed into the entrance of the nest with a squeeze bottle. Do this in the evening when all the wasps are home, and presumably asleep. Chlordane is sold by most drug and hardware stores in a 40% concentrate. Mix one part of this to 10 parts of water for the solution to squirt into the wasp nest.

WORM HOLES
IN HARDWOOD FLOOR

We have been in our new house for five months and have noticed a number of tiny holes appearing in the varnished hardwood floors throughout the house. The builder sent someone to fill the holes and says there's nothing to worry about because the worms are dead, but I've found more worm holes since. We only have a few months to get the builder to fix things up, so I would like to know what should be done about this problem?

This sounds like the work of the Powder Post Beetle or Furniture Beetle, which can attack even kiln-dried hardwoods such as oak flooring. The larvae (or "worms") feed on the wood beneath the surface and only make visible holes when they emerge as adult beetles. The holes are about the size of a pinhead and are generally surrounded with wood dust, or frass, but this is often blown away before it's noticed.

The larvae were probably in the wood when it was laid. Now that they have grown into adult beetles and are leaving, there is little likelihood of reinfestation through the varnished surface, but they can get into furniture and other wood. The only sure cure is to have the house sealed up and fumigated by a licensed exterminator.

INSULATION

ALUMINUM FOIL INSULATION

I want to insulate and panel my basement walls, and have been told that aluminum foil is the cheapest insulation and vapor barrier I can buy. Should this be applied to the concrete wall or on top of the strapping?

Reflective foil insulation like this was popular about 25 years ago, but tests conducted by the National Research Council and others have shown that it is not very effective and has some special problems.

A single sheet of aluminum foil has an insulation value of R2.73, which is only equal to about ¾" of mineral wool or plastic foam. But even that value isn't constant over the height of the wall. Because of air convection currents set up inside the wall space, the temperature of the bottom part of the wall can be much lower than the top part of the wall.

And in this type of application, aluminum foil is not really a vapor barrier at all, since condensation will readily form on the room side of the cold metal foil and run down inside the wall, causing all the problems that a vapor barrier is supposed to prevent. Aluminum foil can only serve as a vapor barrier if it is applied on top of insulation material, and polyethylene sheet is much cheaper and easier to use in this situation.

You would be better off to use a batt or foam insulation.

135

Insulation

ALUMINUM SIDING AS INSULATION

For extra insulation, we are thinking of having aluminum siding applied to our brick walls. Will this be sufficient, or should we have the walls insulated before the siding is applied?

Aluminum siding, even the kind that has an insulation board backing, is only equivalent to about ½" of fibreglass or foam plastic, which isn't very much. The main purpose of the backing board is to reinforce the metal siding.

You would be better off to apply 2 x 2 vertical strapping to the walls every 24", and put 1½" plastic foamboard insulation between the strapping...*then* apply the aluminum siding.

But if the walls are brick veneer on wood frame construction, and there is no insulation, you can have cellulose fibre blown into the hollow wall. This would probably be cheaper than applying foamboard and aluminum siding.

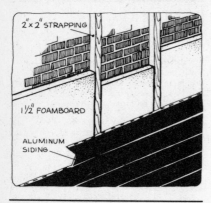

2" x 2" STRAPPING

1½" FOAMBOARD

ALUMINUM SIDING

LAYING AN ATTIC FLOOR OVER INSULATION

We have installed a pull-down, folding stairway to our attic because we want to use it for storage. We are going to put more insulation between the floor joists, and intend to lay a partial floor over that. But several people have told us that we can't put a floor over the insulation because it must "breathe". Wouldn't a partial floor be all right?

If there is no air space between the insulation and the floor, this might cause some condensation problems, particularly if full sheets of plywood are used. Boards would be better,

because they provide more channels for moisture to escape. The big question, however, is how thick the floor joists are. Some are only 2 x 4s, some are 2 x 6s, and a few are 2 x 8s, but even these are not thick enough to accommodate the R28 insulation that is now recommended for ceilings. This will make it difficult to put down a floor in the attic unless you build up the joists first by toenailing 2 x 4s or 2 x 6s to them. It is advisable to leave a ventilated air space of 1" or so between the insulation and the floor.

INSULATING THE ATTIC HATCH

We had cellulose fibre insulation blown into our attic but the hatch door in the ceiling is still very cold. My husband can't figure out how to insulate it.

He'll need one R20 insulation batt, a razor knife and some rubber cement. Tilt the hatch door and bring it down through the hole, then cut pieces of batt to cover the top of the door. Apply a few large dabs of rubber cement to the door and push the insulation in place.

That takes care of the insulation, but you should also do something to eliminate air leakage around the edge of the hatch door. The best way to do this is to apply strips of tubular rubber weather-stripping—the kind with a peal-off, self-stick backing—just inside the ledge on which the hatch door rests.

CHANGING ATTIC INSULATION

The people who owned our house before put 2" insulation batts between the rafters in the attic ceiling. There is no insulation in the floor, which is the ceiling of the finished rooms below. There are vents in the gable ends of the attic and it is very cold up there, so I was thinking of removing the batts from the rafters and putting them between the floor joists and then adding more insulation on top. The batts seem to have a paper vapor barrier on both sides. Must I take one of these off? And what kind of insulation should I put on top of the batts?

The present insulation in the attic is virtually useless. It's a waste of money to put insulation under the roof in a situation like this. It should be put between the floor joists. You will find that only one paper face of the batts is a vapor barrier, the one with a layer of black asphalt or plastic film in the centre. The other is plain kraft paper, which is permeable to moisture vapor.

The vapor barrier always goes on the warm side of the insulation; on the bottom, in this case. The insulation that you put on top of these batts should have no vapor barrier at all. Use friction-fit batts or any of the loose insulation materials. The present batts have an insulation value of about R7, and you should have R30 or more.

INSULATING AN ATTIC

I recently purchased a 2½-storey house. The top storey has two windows and a floor, but the rafters are exposed and the area is otherwise unfinished. I want to put in two bedrooms and a bathroom. How should the roof and the interior partition walls be insulated?

I assume there is room to have a small attic area above the horizontal ceiling section along the center. Large louvered vents must be provided at either end of this attic. The ceiling below it should be insulated with at least 6" batts. The sloping ceiling sections should also be insulated with batts.

The vertical walls on either side (knee walls) should have as much insulation as possible, and the floor of the space behind should also be insulated. This space should be ventilated too. When all of the insulation has been stapled to the studs and rafters, the entire inside of the upstairs living area should be covered with 4-mil polyethylene film as a vapor barrier (in addition to the vapor barrier on the insulation batts, if any). Interior partition walls do not require any insulation.

BASEMENT INSULATION

We are finishing our basement and have applied 1" plastic foamboard to the walls from floor to ceiling. Inside of this we have built a 2 × 3 frame wall. We read in your column that this is not enough insulation, and are wondering if it would be sufficient to add 2½" batts between the studs in the upper half of the wall.

One inch of the common foamboard has an insulation value of something less than R4, which is better than nothing but not nearly enough at today's fuel costs. There's no reason why you can't add 2½" batts and polyethylene vapor barrier, for a total insulation value of about R11, but since you were putting up a frame anyway, it would have been a lot cheaper and easier to have used 2 × 4 framing and 3½", R12 batts.

The insulation need only go down to 2' below the outside ground level provided it fits

tight against the wall. If there is any space behind the insulation, cold air will fall down into the empty wall at the bottom, creating a cold wall. For the small extra cost involved, it is better to run the batts from floor to ceiling.

INSULATING A BASEMENT WALL

I have nailed 1 × 2 strapping on my basement wall in preparation for panelling. What is the best kind of insulation to use?

Nominal 1-inch boards are really only ¾" thick, and there is no insulation of this thickness that would be adequate. You should have at least R10 insulation in a basement wall. Plastic foamboard ¾" thick has an insulation value of no more than R2.8.

I think it would be better to remove the strapping and build a conventional 2 x 4 stud wall in front of the concrete wall. This will permit you to use 3½" batts with an insulation value of R12. The strapping can be salvaged and used for something else.

BASEMENT WALLS

I want to finish my basement, but have had a lot of conflicting advice on how to insulate and panel the walls. Some say that plastic foamboard is best, others tell me to use fibreglass batts. Can you tell me the advantages and disadvantages of the different materials?

In my opinion, the best way to build an insulated, finished basement wall is to put up a 2 × 4 frame wall in front of it, add 3½", R12, friction-fit batts, then cover with polyethylene vapor barrier and the panelling of your choice.

An alternative method is to nail horizontal, 2 × 2 wood strapping along the top and bottom of the wall and at 2' intervals, then place 1½" plastic foamboard insulation between the strapping, attaching it to the concrete wall with panel adhesive. If common white foamboard is used, it will provide about R6 in insulation. Styrofoam (which is always blue, incidentally) will give R7.5, and urethane foamboard will give about R11.

But all of these plastic foamboards must be covered with a fireproof panelling such as gypsumboard. Plywood, hardboard and similar panelling should not be used. And foamboards are at least twice as expensive as batt insulation. Even if you use the cheapest white foamboard, the wall will cost about the same as using 2 × 4 studs and R12 batts, and have only about half the insulation value. With the other foamboards, it will be quite a bit more expensive.

137

Insulation

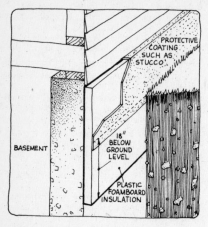

The best place to use foamboard insulation is on the outside of the foundation wall. Two-inch foamboard can be used here, applied directly to the concrete with panel adhesive and extending down to 24 inches below ground level. Where the foamboard is exposed above the ground, however, it must be protected with metal, wood, or hardboard siding, asbestos-cement board, or a stucco coat of cement plaster, which can be applied directly to the foamboard.

BATTS ON BATTS

I have batt insulation in my attic and would like to add more. Do I have to remove the top paper on the batts already there, or can I just lay new batts on top of them?

The backing paper on insulation batts is a plain, kraft paper that does not act as a vapor barrier. There is no need to cut or remove it. But you should not add batts that have a vapor barrier face; use only friction-fit batts. These will either have one plain paper face or no paper covering at all. If another vapor barrier is laid on top of the existing insulation, condensation could form between them, wetting the insulation and staining the ceiling underneath.

INSULATING A CATHEDRAL CEILING

Our cottage has a cathedral ceiling with exposed beams, a plank roof, and asphalt shingles. What is the best way to insulate it?

The most practical way to insulate a cathedral ceiling without losing the exposed beam effect is to apply foamboard between the beams and cover it with a vapor barrier and gypsumboard panelling. To leave as much of the beams exposed as possible, you should use a foamboard with a high insulation value. Urethane would be best, although it's not easy to find; it has an insulation value of R7 per inch. Styrofoam SM is rated at R5 per inch, and the common white foamboard or "beadboard", will give you R3.8 per inch. You should have at least R20 in the ceiling. This will take 3" of urethane foamboard, 4" of Styrofoam SM, or 5" of the common white foamboard.

Cut the foamboard to fit snugly between the beams, then fasten it to the ceiling with one of the panel adhesives. Urethane foamboard is available with a vapor-barrier skin of aluminum foil or polyethylene paper. Polystyrene foamboard acts as its own vapor barrier. Next cut panels of ½" gypsumboard to fit between the beams. Hold these in place with strips of quarter-round or square molding nailed to the beams. Joints can be taped and filled to provide a smooth ceiling surface for painting.

The only other way to insulate a ceiling like this is to put the insulation on top of the roof, under the shingles. Special rigid insulation boards are made for this purpose. Most of them have a vapor barrier on the bottom. If not, you'll have to use polyethylene film.

The 2" plank deck should be covered with overlapping layers of 15-pound roofing felt. The insulation board, in 2' x 4' panels, is then tacked in place. Shingles are applied in the usual way, but you'll have to use shingle nails that are long enough to penetrate at least 1" into the wood decking.

CEILING INSULATION

I have an electrically heated bungalow with 1,500 square feet of ceiling that is presently insulated to R20 with 6" batts. I am thinking of having 3" of cellulose fibre blown in on top of the batts. Would this be practical and will it save me any money on heating costs?

Yes to both questions. Three inches of cellulose fibre will provide an additional R12 insulation and reduce the heat loss through your ceiling by a little more than one-third. Since you are probably losing about 15% of your heat through the ceiling now, this means a saving of about 5% on your annual heating bill—forever. You can figure out how long it will take you to recover the cost of the additional insulation at today's electricity rates. After that the savings go in your pocket, and they're likely to be a lot bigger than they are today.

Just make sure the installer doesn't block the opening between your rafters from the attic into the roof overhang. Ventilation is required here to prevent condensation problems in the attic.

CEILING INSULATION

An insulation salesman tells me that 60% of the heat in our house is lost through the ceiling, and he can cut out heating bills by 40% just by blowing insulation in our attic. We only have a couple of inches up there now. I can afford to have more insulation put in if it will save that much money, but I don't know whether to believe him or not.

It's a good idea to add more insulation to your ceiling, but the salesman's claim is wildly exaggerated, as many of them are these days, I'm afraid. Heat loss through the ceiling rarely exceeds 25% of the total. In some homes it is as little as 5%. The most you can expect to save on your heating bill in one year is about 15%. However, at today's fuel prices this is still a good investment.

ADDING MORE CEILING INSULATION

We have wood shavings for insulation in our ceiling. I want to put some more insulation on top of it, but the manager of our local lumber yard says that you can't combine different kinds of insulation. I must remove the shavings and put in all new insulation, he says. That doesn't sound right to me.

Or to me, either. Insulation is insulation, and any number of different materials can be combined. The standard method of calculating insulation value and heat loss is to add the figures for each of the materials in the wall or ceiling to arrive at the total insulation value for the structure. Plaster, wood, insulation, sheathing, siding, shingles all contribute to the total value.

INSULATING GARAGE CEILING

We have an unheated garage below our bedroom, which has been very cold as a result. I removed the gypsumboard from the garage ceiling and put in 2 layers of 4″ batts. Unfortunately, I think I put them in upside down; both batts have the vapor barrier on the bottom. The gypsumboard was replaced. Should I take this off again and reverse the batts?

There should only be one vapor barrier, on the warm side of the insulation, so your present installation is incorrect. There is a good chance that this won't cause any trouble, however, and if I were you I would leave it and just watch for water stains on the garage ceiling. If you don't see these, everything's okay. If you do, it means that condensation is forming within the insulation. Remove the ceiling and both layers of insulation. Put one back in with the insulation on top, facing the bedroom floor, and the other with the vapor barrier and stapling tabs on the bottom. Staple these to the joists, then take a razor knife and cut long, diagonal slashes in the vapor barrier face. Replace the gypsumboard ceiling.

INSULATING A SLOPING CEILING

I want to insulate the upstairs bedrooms in our 1½″-storey house. I'm going to remove the panelling and put 3½″ batts in the walls, but have been told I can't put these batts between the 2 x 4 rafters in the sloping ceiling because of condensation problems. If that's true, how can I insulate this part of the ceiling?

Building codes are getting tough about ventilation in ceilings because of problems with condensation. They once called for ventilation in walls, too, but have since decided that insulation is more important. When does a sloping wall become a ceiling? Nobody knows, but most experts now agree that a sloping ceiling like this should be insulated like a wall. Fill it with insulation batts and cover it with an airtight vapor barrier extending down over the wall to the floor.

CHECKING INSULATION

How can I find out if there's any insulation in our walls?

Remove the cover plates from wall switches and outlet sockets to expose the metal junction boxes. These usually fit rather loosely in the wall, and you can often see any insulation material around them. A short length of coathanger wire can also be bent and used as a probe—*outside* the junction box. Don't put your fingers or any metal object inside the box unless you have taken the precaution of turning off the electric power supply to the circuit.

INSULATING A CINDER-BLOCK HOUSE

Our bungalow, built in 1949, has concrete

block walls with a stucco finish. Does this have much insulation value? What can we do to increase it?

Assuming you have strapping and plaster on the inside, the insulation value of your walls is probably about R4. This is much less than the insulation required today.

The most practical way to add more insulation is to apply foamboard on the outside, then cover this with one of the siding materials . . . lumber, aluminum, steel, or hardboard. Apply 2 × 2 strapping vertically to the walls, spaced 2' apart, using concrete nails. Glue 1½" foamboard to the wall between the strapping, then apply the horizontal siding.

Urethane foamboard has the greatest insulation value, about R10 in 1½" thickness. Styrofoam SM (blue) is next, with R7.5. The common white foamboard will give you about R5.5.

INSULATING CLOSET WALLS

The clothes closets in our back bedrooms are built on the outside wall of the house. They are cold and musty in the winter. Would you please tell me how to insulate them?

The easiest way is to glue 1" or 2" foamboard directly to the outside wall at the back of the closet with panel adhesive.

INSULATING COTTAGE FOUNDATION

I am building a cabin at the lake. I have poured the concrete foundation walls, which are about two feet high, and now I want to insulate them before I put the floor down. My plan is to glue 2" of plastic foamboard to the inside of the foundation walls, instead of the outside, which seems to be the more common method. Will this give me the same insulation value?

If I understand you correctly, the low foundation walls will enclose a crawlspace, not a full basement. You can either insulate the walls, as you suggest, or you can put insulation under the cottage floor. It depends on whether you want a heated or unheated crawlspace. If you insulate the walls with foam board, this should extend down to 2' below ground level. If you decide to insulate the floor, you can either staple kraft-faced batts between the joists before the subflooring is laid down, or push friction-fit batts up between the joists afterwards, holding them there with wire screening or 16" lengths of coathanger wire. Batts should also

be wrapped around water pipes and heating ducts in the crawlspace.

COMPRESSING INSULATION

I have heard that you can compress 6" insulation batts to fit in a 2 × 4 wall without any loss of insulation value. Is this true?

No. The *total* insulation value is reduced, but the insulation value *per inch* increases. Sounds confusing, but here's how it works: A 6", R20 batt compressed to 3½" (the thickness of a 2 x 4 wall) will have a total insulation value of only R14. This works out to R4 per inch, compared to its original R3.33 per inch. But 3½", R12 batts cost about half as much as 6" batts. The slight increase in insulation is not worth the extra cost.

In any case, it is not a good idea to compress batt insulation this much inside a wall. The pressure may cause the wall panelling to bulge or come away from the studs entirely.

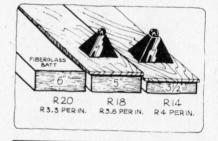

FIBERGLASS BATT

6"	5"	3½"
R20	R18	R14
R3.3 PER IN.	R3.6 PER IN.	R4 PER IN.

INSULATING CONCRETE BLOCK WALLS

The exterior walls of our house are made of 8" × 8" × 16" concrete blocks. I was thinking of insulating them with 1" plastic foamboard glued directly to the concrete (which has never been painted) and then applying an exterior latex paint. Can this be done?

Not according to most building codes. Foamboard is required to be attached to the concrete mechanically, such as with special fasteners that are made to fit an explosive nail gun. These can be obtained from a tool rental shop.

Also, paint doesn't provide enough protection for the plastic foamboard. It must be covered with something much stronger, such as stucco or siding. If you use siding, you'll have to attach 2 x 2 vertical strapping to the wall first, again using a nail gun. Easiest for do-it-yourself application would be premixed exterior stucco, available at most building supply stores. This can be trowelled directly over the foamboard.

I suggest that you use thicker insulation, too. One inch of common white foamboard has an insulation value of less then R4. You should have at least 2" and preferably 3".

The foamboard should extend down to 2' below ground level. But it can simply be glued to the wall there, and doesn't have to be covered with a protective coating.

INSULATION AND CONDENSATION

We had more insulation put in our ceiling last year, and during the winter the windows began steaming up for the first time. Does this mean we need more ventilation in the attic?

No. It means you need more ventilation *in the house* during cold weather. The condensation on the windows is caused by excessive humidity in the house, which is partly due to the fact that the insulation in the ceiling has reduced the amount of air leakage into the attic. But it may also be due to some change in your household, such as a new baby or other addition to the family, leading to more baths, washing, cooking, etc. Or perhaps you have had a humidifier installed, or have had the windows and doors weatherstripped. Any or all of these changes would result in increased humidity in the house, which would lead to condensation on cool surfaces like walls and windows during winter weather. A little more ventilation is the answer.

INSULATING A CRAWLSPACE

Can you tell me what to do about the crawlspace under the house? Should it be ventilated all year or closed during the winter? And where does the insulation go, under the floor or on the walls of the crawlspace? Is there anything we can do to reduce the dampness?

Since you must have water and drain pipes down there, and perhaps heating ducts, too, it's better to insulate the walls of the crawlspace and close off the ventilation. This can be done by hanging fibreglass batts down the walls from the header joists. Lay 6-mil polyethylene film over the earth first, and extend the batts out over them about two feet.

Although the crawlspace will receive some heat from the floor of the house, pipes and heating ducts should also be wrapped in batt insulation.

If it is impractical to put insulation in the crawlspace, foamboard can be applied to the *out-*side of the foundation wall and down two feet below ground level. Above the ground it must be protected with stucco, siding, or asbestos cement board.

COVERING FOAMBOARD INSULATION

We have purchased a 10-year-old house and have a problem. The basement walls have been insulated by gluing 1" panels of white foamboard directly to the concrete. The plastic foamboard, which I understand is very inflammable, has been left uncovered. One building supply dealer tells me we can glue gypsumboard panelling directly to the foamboard. Another says we must cut strips out of the foamboard so we can nail 1 x 2 strapping directly to the concrete, then cover the wall with a vapor barrier and nail the gypsumboard to the strapping. Which is right?

The first method. The second method is complicated and unnecessary. Also, 1 x 2 strapping is only ¾" thick, while the foamboard is 1" thick, so it won't provide a firm nailing support behind the gypsumboard. And foamboard is classed as a vapor barrier itself, so you don't need another one.

FOAMBOARD INSULATION

The recreation room in our new home has plastic foamboard insulation from floor to ceiling on three walls. Is there some way we can finish these walls with paint or paper, rather than panelling them?

This type of insulation is inflammable and should be covered with a fireproof panelling such as gypsumboard. When the panel joints are taped and filled, this provides an excellent surface for painting or papering.

FOAMBOARD vs FIBREGLASS

Can you tell me how much foamboard insulation would be required to equal 6" of fibreglass?

The common white plastic foamboard has an insulation resistance value (R) of 3.7 per inch of thickness. Fibreglass batts have an R value of about 3.3 per inch, or R20 for 6". It would take 5½" of the common foamboard to equal this. But fibreglass blowing wool only has an insulation value or R2.2 per inch, or R13 for 6", so it would only take 3½" of foamboard to match it.

INSULATING A FLOOR

You recently suggested insulating a cottage floor by pushing friction-fit batts up between the joists from the crawlspace. Out cottage is partly on a rock shelf. We can insulate the living room floor from underneath, but the bedrooms are right on the rock. I was thinking of putting 1″ plastic foamboard on top of the present floor, then covering this with ¾″ plywood. Would this work?

Yes, but 1″ of the common white foamboard doesn't really provide very much insulation—only about R3.7, whereas you should have at least R10. This will take 2½″ to 3″ of the common foamboard, plus the plywood. This is fine if you have enough space under the doorways and elsewhere to allow you to raise the floor that much. If not, you should consider using an insulation material with a higher R value per inch such as urethane foamboard.

You can save a little space by using ½″ plywood instead of ¾″. Buy the special floor sheathing plywood with a tongue-and-groove edge joint. Nail it through the foamboard into the existing flooring, using ringed flooring nails spaced 6″ apart around the edges and 12″ across the face. Then cover with tile or carpeting. (The latter will add a little more insulation.)

INSULATION DIDN'T REDUCE HEATING COSTS

Last fall we put R20 friction-fit batts on top of the R10 batts in the attic of our 20-year-old home. In comparing the heating bills with previous winters, however, we find there has been very little improvement, if any. We were told there would be a major saving. Can you explain this?

Not without knowing more about the size, shape and construction of your house. If, for example, you have a 2-storey house with no insulation in the walls and much air leakage, it is quite possible that you were only losing 10% of your heat through the ceiling. The addition of another R20 in the ceiling would cut this heat loss by ⅔, or about 6%. If you check the total degree-days in your area this past winter, you may find that it was 6% colder than previous winters. This would counterbalance the modest improvement in your insulation.

Contrary to popular opinion—encouraged by most insulation contractors—the ceiling is NOT the major area of heat loss in a house. It's just the easiest and cheapest place to add more insulation. Walls, basements and single-glazed windows each account for more heat loss than ceilings in most homes. If you want to see a big reduction in fuel consumption, you'll have to do a complete insulating job.

INSULATING HEATING DUCTS

I would like to know what type of insulation would be safe and economical to use on the forced air heating ducts located in the crawlspace under our house.

Use regular, friction-fit fibreglass or mineral wool batts, the kind without any paper facing. Wrap the batts around the ducts and hold them in place with masking tape, thin wire, or cord. The small, round pipes will be easier to wrap if you cut the 15″-wide batts in two, lengthwise. The ductwork temperature is far below the combustion point of paper or string, so these materials can be used on the outside of the insulation without any worry.

INSULATING HOT AIR DUCTS

Would it improve the heating efficiency of our warm air furnace if we wrapped the exposed heating ducts in the basement with some kind of insulation? Since the ducts are hot to the touch, it seems there must be a certain amount of heat loss in the basement.

The heat is not being lost; it is warming the basement, and this, in turn, warms the floor above. But if the basement is too warm this would save a little fuel. It would do more good to insulate the basement walls, however.

HOW MUCH INSULATION?

I had 3½″ of fibreglass insulation (R10) in my ceiling and added another 3½″ to bring it up to R20. What advantage, if any, would there be in adding another 3½″? Is there a limit to the heat saving you can get with insulation? Does the insulation value decrease for each additional inch of insulation?

The value of the added insulation stays the same, but the *percentage* of the heat you save diminishes. Let's say you lost $90 worth of heat through the original 3½″ of insulation. When you doubled this you cut the heat loss in half, to $45. If you add another 3½″ the heat loss will be reduced not by one-half again but by one-third, to $30. A further 3½″ of insulation will only reduce the heat loss by one-quarter, to $22.50.

So you saved $45 when you added the first layer of insulation, $15 when you added the next layer, and $7.50 when you added the last. Whether or not it would pay you to provide this additional insulation would depend on how much it cost and how much you pay to heat your house.

But remember, the added insulation only reduces the heat loss through your *ceiling*. In a 1-storey house with a basement, less than 20% of the heat is lost through the ceiling; in a 2-storey house, it is only about 10%.

INSULATING WITH LOGS

We are planning a retirement home in a wooded area of the country, and have been thinking about the possibility of log construction. We like the look of a log house but are concerned about the insulation value, since the area we are building in gets very cold. How do logs compare with the conventional forms of construction in this respect?

By today's standards, wood isn't a very good insulation material. Most softwoods have an insulation value of around R1.25 per inch, or about one-third the value of common white foamboard. Cedar is somewhat better—perhaps R1.5 per inch—but you still need a log wall with an average thickness of 10" to achieve the total insulation value of R16 that is now considered a minimum in cold areas of the country. And to get a wall this thick you would have to use logs with a diameter of at least 12".

But if you are going to have a good supply of inexpensive firewood, and will not be totally dependent on oil, gas or electricity to heat your home, the relatively small difference in heat loss between standard frame construction and a good log home would not be significant—and will probably be far outweighed by the satisfaction you get from living in it.

NEWSPAPER INSULATION

To increase the insulation in my ceiling I have been laying folded newspapers over the loose fill insulation between the joists in my attic. Do you think this is a good idea?

Newspaper is a very good insulation material. It has a value of R2.5 per inch, which is better than vermiculite, sawdust, or wood shavings and only a little less than fibreboard insulation.

The only problem is weight. A cubic foot of newspapers weighs about 32 pounds, while a cubic foot of fibreglass only weighs about 12 ounces. A 2" layer of newspapers, with an insulation value of R5 weighs 5 pounds per

square foot. Evenly distributed over the ceiling, this weight might not be a problem, but it could crush fibreglass batts or loose wool, and reduce their insulation value. (Vermiculite would only be slightly compressed, however.)

COMPARING INSULATION PRICES

We are planning to have more insulation put in our attic, and have been quoted a wide range of prices by different contractors. But the type and thickness of insulation to be put in varies in each case, so I don't know how to compare them. One company, for instance, will put in 4" of cellulose fibre with an insulation value of R16 for $224. Another company will put in 6" of fibreglass blowing wool with an insulation value of R13 for $117. Other materials and prices vary the same way. How can I determine which is the best price for the job?

All you're buying is insulation value. It doesn't matter what type and thickness of insulation is used to achieve it. The companies are quoting on the same area, so all you have to do is divide the price by the insulation value to get the comparable cost. The $224 price for R16 works out to $14 per R (224 ÷ 16). The $117 price for R13 costs $9 per R, and is therefore a much better buy. Do the same with the other bids to get a true cost comparison.

KEEPING PIPES FROM FREEZING

I wish to know if there is any way to insulate a water pipe under the house to keep it from freezing. The black plastic pipe runs on the ground in the crawlspace under the house.

This sounds like a cottage installation. If the water is being used all winter, then a heavy wrapping of insulation should keep it from freezing. But if the house is not occupied for days or weeks at a time, then this would not be enough, and the only solution would be to wrap the pipe with an electric heating cable.

INSULATING AROUND PIPES

You advised insulating basement walls to eliminate a major source of heat loss. We started to do this but don't know what to do about the water pipes that go up against the walls. Would they freeze if they were covered?

Where possible, push fibreglass insulation behind them. Otherwise just leave them uncovered. The heat loss from such a small area would be negligible.

**INSULATING A ROOM
OVER A GARAGE**

I plan to build a spare room over the flat roof of my garage, laying 2 × 8 floor joists over the tar-and-gravel roof. I intend to put 6-inch fibreglass batts between the 2 × 12 roof joists of the garage. My carpenter insists that I vent the area between the garage roof and the floor of the new room "in order to prevent a musty smell." Is this correct?

No. If you ventilate the space between the insulation and the floor of the room you will end up with a cold floor and defeat the purpose of the insulation. Put the insulation between the 2 × 8 floor joists of the new room, then cover this with 4-mil polyethylene vapor barrier before laying the subfloor. Although it isn't essential, it would be a good idea to ventilate the space *under* the insulation by putting vents in the blocking at the ends of the floor joists.

SAWDUST INSULATION

Our house was built in the Twenties and has about 4" of dry sawdust insulation in the attic. We would like to add more insulation but I get different advice on what to do about the sawdust. Some people say it must be removed; others say we can just put new insulation on top of it.

There's no need to get rid of the sawdust. It has an insulation value of about R2.4 per inch, so

you have about R10, which is equivalent to 3" of mineral wool batts. You can simply add batts or loose fill insulation on top of the sawdust. But if you use batts, they should be the friction-fit kind, without any vapor barrier. Just make sure there is plenty of ventilation in the attic, at least one square foot of screened vent for every 300 square feet of ceiling.

INSULATION UNDER SIDING

I intend to put aluminum siding over the existing clapboard on an old 2-storey frame house. To get some insulation in the walls, I was thinking of covering the clapboard with a softboard sheathing instead of strapping before applying the new siding. Will this give me enough insulation?

No. Softboard sheathing 1" thick only has an insulation value of about R2.7, and you need at least R12 today. It would be better to have cellulose fibre or mineral wool blown in the walls first. Insulation sheathing can then be applied for additional insulation.

INSULATION UPSIDE DOWN

I have 2½" insulation batts between the floor joists in my attic and I want to add some more. But the present batts have been installed upside down, with the paper vapor barrier on top. I've been told I must turn these all over before I add more insulation. Is this right? And then should I place the new batts with their vapor barrier to the top or to the bottom?

This is probably just a plain paper face, not a vapor barrier. To be safe, just take a sharp knife and cut two or three slits lengthwise through the paper. Then add new "friction-fit" batts, the kind without a paper face, on top of the present batts. Add at least 6".

INSULATING WALLPAPER

Do you know of a wallpaper or similar decorative wallcovering that has some insulation value? I'm enclosing a newspaper clipping from Germany about a wall material that has an R value "equivalent to 17 centimetres of natural stone".

That may sound impressive, but 17 centimetres (6.7") of stone only has an insulation value of .5R, which is equal to about ⅛" of foamboard—hardly worth bothering about.

There is no wallpaper or similar covering that has any significant amount of insulation value.

INSULATING WALLS

We have a 60-year-old, 2 storey brick-veneer house with about 6″ of blown fibreglass insulation in the attic floor and no insulation in the walls. There is a 3½″ air space in the frame wall behind the bricks, and I can think of three ways to insulate it: blow in fibreglass or urethane foam, or pour in vermiculite. I'm afraid fibreglass would settle; I hear that urethane is inflammable, and I'm not sure that vermiculite would pour in properly. What do you suggest?

First of all, 6″ of blown fibreglass has an insulation value of only about R14, so I think you should start by adding another R14 in the attic. This should cut your heating cost by about 5%. Next insulate your basement walls, where about 25% of the heat will be going. R12 insulation here (3½″ fibreglass *batts*) should cut your heat loss by 15% or 20%. Then do the walls.

Neither vermiculite nor urethane foam are recommended for use in hollow walls. Blown fibreglass will give you about R8 insulation in the stud wall—not up to present building standards, but a lot better than nothing. There aren't many firms doing this work, however. Your best choice is cellulose fibre, which will give you R12 or more in the 3½″ wall. A lot of firms are using this for attic insulation, but only a few are putting it in walls, which are a lot more trouble. Some insulation companies and a number of tool rental shops will sell you the insulation and rent you the blowers for do-it-yourself installation, however. Check the Yellow Pages and phone around.

INSULATING WALLS

In order to save fuel, and money, we would like to add more insulation to our old house. At present there is only about 2″ or 3″ of insulation in the ceiling, and I don't think there's any in the frame walls. Will you please tell me how I can add more insulation without tearing the house apart?

If you can get into the attic you can add insulation to the ceiling very easily with batts or loose fill materials. If you use batts, they should be the friction-fit type, with no vapor barrier. The loose insulation materials can be poured or blown in. Among the best, and certainly the cheapest, is cellulose fibre, made from recycled newsprint.

Walls are more of a problem. In some types of construction, such as solid masonry with a gypsumboard interior finish, there is no space to put insulation inside the wall. It must be added on the inside by gluing foam plastic foamboard insulation to the wall and then covering this with gypsumboard. The problem here is how to fit it around window and door frames. Even with 1½″ insulation board, which is about as thin as it is practical to use, you still have a new wall that projects out 2″ farther than the window frame.

If you have hollow walls, however, such as wood frame or brick veneer, there are a number of ways insulation can be put in. The most common way is to make holes in the top of the wall (outside, if possible) and blow or pour in loose fill insulation.

Firms who do this work can be located in the Yellow Pages under Insulation Contractors. If you want to do the work yourself, blowers can sometimes be rented where cellulose fibre insulation is sold. It isn't quite as simple as it sounds, however, and considerable care must be taken to do a good job. Some hollow stud walls have horizontal cross-braces or firebreaks halfway up, which means that another opening must be cut in the wall to fill the space below the obstruction. The same applies to the space under windows. A plumb-bob should be used to locate obstructions in the stud space.

A brick veneer wall is difficult, but bricks can be removed from the top and holes drilled in the sheathing behind to provide access to the stud space. If the wall is blocked halfway up, more bricks will have to be removed, and this becomes rather tricky.

Aluminum siding can't be opened without damaging it, either, so it's usually better to cut holes in the inside wall in such cases. You need at least one 1½″ hole every 16″ to fill all the stud spaces, so this will make a mess of the wall. Patching and repainting will repair it, however.

Insulation can sometimes be blown up into the wall from the basement.

Insulation

WALL INSULATION

We are living in an unfinished house. The outside walls have R12 batt insulation between the 2 × 4 studs, but no vapor barrier or panelling yet. We are wondering if it would be a good idea to apply 2 × 2 strapping to the walls and add another R7 or R12 insulation before panelling. Our ceiling is R20 at present; should we increase this, too?

With recent and predicted fuel price increases, the more insulation you can put in now the better. It is difficult and expensive to add it later.

Two-by-two strapping is 1½" thick, and this will allow you to put in R5 in fibreglass batts. Apply a 4-mil polyethylene vapor barrier to the walls before they are panelled. I suggest you bring the ceiling insulation up to R30. And don't forget the basement walls; a lot of heat can be lost there.

INCREASING WALL INSULATION

Our house was built 15 years ago and there is only 2½" of batt insulation in the frame walls. They are plasterboard on the inside. We would like to increase the insulation. Would it help to cover the walls with polyethylene vapor barrier, then another layer of plasterboard? Or do you have a better suggestion?

I'm afraid there is no practical way to add insulation to these walls. The panelling you describe would not provide enough insulation to be worth the trouble, and there isn't enough space left inside the wall to justify blowing in more insulation.

SHOULD WALLS BE INSULATED?

I would appreciate your advice on an insulation problem. One company recommends blowing cellulose fibre into our frame walls and adding 10" to the 6" of mineral wool insulation we already have in the attic. Another company says we should leave the walls alone, that the 1" insulation sheathing and the air space behind it is all we need.

The sheathing and the air space provide very little insulation—perhaps R3 at best. If you already have 6" of insulation in the ceiling, most of your heat loss is through the walls, and you should have them insulated first, then put more in the ceiling.

HEAT LOSS FROM WINDOWS

We are planning to build a house with dou-

ble-glazed, floor-to-ceiling windows along the south wall of the living room, but now I am concerned that there may be too much heat loss through this large glass area. Should we reduce the size of these windows to conserve heat?

Even double-glazed windows have very little insulation—less than R2, compared with R12 or more in a frame wall. Until recently it was assumed that this resulted in a substantial heat loss. But studies by G.P. Mitalas of the National Research Council have shown that much depends on which way the windows are facing. Even in the coldest areas, double-glazed windows facing *south* result in a net heat *gain* due to the solar radiation they capture and retain in the house. Windows facing southwest and southeast show only a slight heat loss. Only on the north side of the house do windows create a substantial heat loss.

So your big living room windows will actually *reduce* heating costs. For best results, however, the drapes should be closed at night, and on overcast days if possible, during very cold weather.

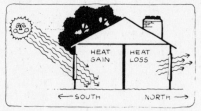

RESTORING AN IRON BED

A friend recently gave us an old iron bed that has obviously been painted many times. The paint is chipping badly, and we can see that there are some brass fittings that we would like to restore. The iron parts we will repaint. Do you have any advice on how we should proceed?

Any paint remover can be used to take off the old paint. If there are several layers, you may have to apply more than one coat of remover. Tarnished brass parts can be cleaned with #0000 steel wool, then sprayed with clear lacquer. It isn't necessary to use a metal primer on the iron parts to be repainted; consumer laboratory tests indicate that paint holds just as well if it is applied directly to the metal. Any interior enamel can be used.

REFINISHING
KITCHEN CUPBOARDS

The kitchen cupboards in our 8-year-old home are beginning to show signs of wear, particularly around the door handles. The doors are apparently made of pressed particle-board covered with a thin, plastic laminate in a woodgrain finish. This woodgrain surface is worn through in places. Can this surface layer be removed and replaced, or is there some other way to restore the finish?

It's not possible to remove the woodgrain laminate, and the worn spots can't be patched. Some building supply dealers sell a lightweight plastic laminate that can be applied on top of the present surface. It comes in 2′ × 4′ sheets, in plain colors and woodgrain patterns, and is easier to cut and handle than the regular countertop material. It is applied the same way, however—with contact cement.

If you don't want to go to this much trouble you could use one of the peel-off, self-stick, decorative vinyls like MacTac or Contact, which also come in realistic woodgrain patterns. Or you could simply sand the surface of the doors lightly and then paint them.

VENTING A KITCHEN FAN

I want to install a kitchen exhaust fan in our 1½-storey house. It would be very difficult to vent this outside, so I am thinking of connecting it to the chimney, which is very close. The concrete block chimney serves our gas furnace and hot water heater in the basement. Would the vent fan disturb the operation of the furnace?

Yes. It is unsafe to connect the kitchen exhaust fan to the furnace chimney. This could easily cause the furnace flue gases to back up into the house. You will either have to run the exhaust duct through the upper floor to the roof, or through an outside wall.

COLD DRAFT FROM KITCHEN VENT

During cold weather I am troubled by a draft that comes down the kitchen exhaust fan vent. This is vented through the attic to the roof, and when the wind is in the wrong direction the draft is very strong. What can we do to stop it?

There should be at least one, preferably two back-draft dampers in the exhaust fan duct, but some workmen don't bother to put these in. There is also the chance that your damper is stuck. If you remove the fan you should be able to see a damper right above it. If it's there, check to make sure it isn't stuck and that it fits tightly when it's closed. A strip of felt or sponge plastic weatherstripping can sometimes be applied to make it fit tighter.

REPAIRING KNIVES

I have some sterling silver bread-knives with mother-of-pearl handles. Several of the handles have come off or are loose, and I don't know what adhesive to use to repair them.

You can buy epoxy putty at any hardware store. It comes in two foil-wrapped sticks. You cut off an equal portion of each and knead them together until they're soft. Use the prong of the knife to push two or three small wads of the putty down inside the handle, then push it firmly in place. If any putty squeezes out, remove it. The putty sets very hard in about half an hour.

SEALING A KNOT

Can you tell me what to put on a knot in wood to prevent it from bleeding through paint?

A coat of aluminum paint.

REPAIRING LEAK
IN LAUNDRY TUB

Can you tell me how to stop my concrete laundry tub from leaking? Years ago you could buy something that you just painted on to seal hairline cracks, but I can't find it anymore, probably because the new tubs are made of plastic.

That was probably waterglass, or sodium silicate. It was once used for preserving eggs, and you can still find it at some rural grocery stores. If not, any drug store can order it for you. Dilute the syrupy solution with three parts water and brush it on the inside of the tub, paying particular attention to the cracks. Allow 24 hours to dry, then apply a second coat.

REPAIRING LAUNDRY TUB

I would like to know how to repair a small hole in a plastic laundry tub.

If it is one of the fibreglass-reinforced plastic tubs, it can be repaired with a fibreglass patching kit available at any auto supply store. But if it's made of polypropylene you'll have to buy a new tub; there is no patching material that will work on this plastic.

APPLICATION TO LEASE

If I sign an application to lease, am I bound to sign the lease itself or can I still change my mind?

The "offer to lease" document is as binding as any other contract, once it has been signed by both parties...subject, of course, to whatever terms it contains. There is usually a clause that indicates a time limit for acceptance of the offer, and you can fill this in to suit yourself. In other words, you can give the landlord so many days in which to accept your offer, and the offer will terminate if you do not receive a signed acceptance within that time. Up to that time, however, your offer is irrevocable. You can also include any other conditional clauses you want in your offer, such as permission to select any colors you want, have pets, or whatever. In the event that you do change your mind after signing the offer to lease, you will almost certainly have to forfeit your deposit; you may be required to pay rent until the landlord can find a new tenant to take over the payments.

SCRATCHES ON A LEATHER CHAIR

I have a pedestal armchair and ottoman made of rosewood,and black leather that has given great comfort for many years. The leather has been scratched in a number of places by a cat that lived with us briefly, and the white marks aren't very attractive. I thought of using black shoe polish on them, but I'm afraid this might come off on clothing. How can I cover the scratches?

Blacken the scratch marks with a fine-tipped felt pen—the kind made for writing, not sign-painting. Let the ink dry thoroughly, then apply a coat of leather dressing or neutral paste wax.

LONG-LIFE BULBS

The bulbs in my light fixtures burn out too often for my liking. Should I use special long-life bulbs?

Long-life light bulbs give less light and cost more to burn than ordinary bulbs of the same rating. They operate at a lower temperature, too, so the light is a little more yellow. They are rated at a higher voltage than ordinary bulbs—125 to 135 volts, instead of 120. They are useful for some hard-to-get-at areas, provided you

put in a high enough wattage to compensate for the lower light value.

LIGHTNING PROTECTION

We are in the process of building a new home in the country. It's at the top of a hill and very exposed with no large trees within, perhaps, 200 yards. We are concerned about the possibility of lightning, and wonder if we should have lightning rods or some other protection installed. Or have modern wiring and plumbing systems made these obsolete?

While the chance of a house being struck by lightning is very slim in most areas, it happens more often than most of us realize in places where lightning storms are common. Lightning is ranked sixth out of the 18 most common causes of home fires, just behind hot ashes, coals, and open fires, and far ahead of matches, petroleum products, and defective chimneys.

Modern plumbing and wiring systems are no protection. As a matter of fact, above-ground wiring connected to the house is often the source of lightning damage, since it can carry very heavy electric currents induced by nearby lightning discharges. In a normal installation, there is no ground connection between the hydro pole and the house, but you can have a "surge protector" installed for about $50.

Lightning rod protection probably isn't worth the cost (about $800) for a city home, but it is certainly sensible for a country home in an area where lightning storms occur.

DOES IT PAY TO LEAVE THE LIGHT ON?

Is it true that an electric light uses a lot of power when you switch it on?

This idea has long been popular as an excuse for leaving lights on, but it doesn't work that way. While it's true that any electric light or appliance uses 8 to 10 times as much current when it starts as it does when it's operating, the surge only lasts a fraction of a second—about 20-thousandths of a second, to be exact. And your electric meter doesn't react that fast, so you don't pay for it, anyway. It always pays to turn out a light, no matter how short a time it's going to be off.

LIME SCALE IN HOT WATER TANK

My electric hot water tank has a build-up of lime scale on the inside. It keeps gurgling and popping and some of the loose scale comes through the hot water taps. Can I get rid of

this by emptying the water tank and putting in a gallon or so of vinegar to dissolve the lime?

It's a good idea to drain and flush the tank a couple of times to get rid of any loose lime scale, but it's not practical to use vinegar or other mild acid to dissolve the deposit. Theoretically this will work, but there are several problems.

One is how to get the acid solution in the tank. You would have to fill the tank with vinegar to dissolve all the scale. Then there is the problem of a build-up of gas pressure in the tank while the acid is working. Another is how to keep the acid out of the household water lines. There is also the difficulty of determining when the lime deposit has been completely removed.

I can think of other problems, but that should be enough to convince you that it's not a very practical idea.

LIQUID SANDPAPER

Is there a product on the market that I can use to take the glossy finish off my painted walls before repainting, or do I have to do it the hard way, with sandpaper?

Most paint and hardware stores sell products called "liquid sandpaper" to do this job. But you can make your own with 2 heaping tablespoons of trisodium phosphate (TSP) in a quart of warm water. Wash the walls down with this, rinse and dry before repainting. It won't take off all the gloss, but it will dull it enough to provide a "tooth" for the next coat of paint.

LOG CABIN

We bought an old log house that's in good shape except that the white mortar between the logs is coming loose, and we'd like to take it all off and replace it. Can you tell me how this was done in the old days?

The traditional material used to chink up the logs was oakum, made by unravelling old rope. This was jammed between the logs, then a mortar of one part cement to three parts sand was applied. Strips of mineral wool insulation work just as well. For white mortar, use white cement and white sand. Today the mortar can be mixed with a liquid latex concrete additive to improve the bond. Chicken wire or expanded metal lathing can also be tacked in the joint to reinforce the mortar.

WEATHERPROOFING LOG CABIN

I am building a log cabin from reasonably straight trees and would like to know what to use to chink between them.

The proper way to build up a log wall is to V-notch the underside of each log so that it will fit over the log below. This is done with a scriber and a chain saw. The notch is then packed with fibreglass as the log is laid to make a thick, tight, insulated joint. Just piling the round logs on top of each other produces a thin joint that is difficult to insulate, although some fibreglass can be packed in and covered with one of the latex-cement patching compounds that are available at any building supply dealer.

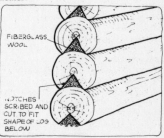

FIBERGLASS WOOL

NOTCHES SCRIBED AND CUT TO FIT SHAPE OF LOG BELOW

LOG ROUNDS FOR TABLE TOPS

I would like to make tables out of 2" thick log rounds. When I tried to dry some last year they cracked badly. Can you tell me how to dry them so they won't crack?

There is much less tendency for the wood to split if the tree is felled in winter. And the rounds will dry out more evenly, I'm told, if they are packed in salt and wrapped in burlap. A commercial trick is to soak the green wood in a 30% solution of polyethylene glycol 600 for several weeks before it is dried.

Polyethylene glycol, or PEG, is produced by Union Carbide and Dow Chemical, but is not generally available to the consumer market. Some drug and chemical supply companies do carry it, however.

REPAIRING BROKEN MARBLE

Somebody broke the corner off our lovely marble mantlepiece over the fireplace. It was a clean break, and the piece fits perfectly; is there any way I can put it back on?

Epoxy glue works very well in this situation. Use the fast-setting type, sometimes referred to as "5-minute epoxy." Mix the two parts carefully according to the manufacturer's instructions, then brush a very thin coat of the mixture on one of the surfaces. Press the pieces tightly together and hold firm until the epoxy sets. Use a razor blade to remove any excess glue before it hardens completely, which usually takes a few hours. Heat from a reading lamp or similar source will speed the setting and provide a stronger joint.

MARBLE STAINS

I have acquired several fine pieces of furniture with marble tops that have been marked with glass rings and various stains. How can I remove these?

First clean the marble thoroughly. If it has a glossy, polished surface, use warm water and a few drops of a mild, hand-safe detergent. If the marble has a dull, matt, or satin "honed" finish, you can clean it with any of the household cleaning powders.

Always wet the entire surface with clean hot water before applying detergent or cleaning powder. This will help to avoid a patchy cleaning job. If stains remain, cover them with a poultice made of talc, whiting, or chalk mixed with one of the following stain removers:

For organic stains from such things as leaves, tea and fruit juices, make the poultice with 20% hydrogen peroxide bleach and a few drops of household ammonia, or with one part chlorine bleach to four parts water. Apply the poultice to the stain, allow it to dry, then brush off. Repeat if necessary.

For green stains left by copper or bronze, mix one part sal ammoniac (ammonium chloride) with four parts of whiting or talc and moisten with ammonia to form a thick paste.

Oil and grease stains can be removed with a poultice made with petroleum solvent, cleaning fluid or lacquer thinner.

For ballpoint ink stains, mix a poultice with rubbing alcohol or a few drops of one of the special ballpoint ink solvents sold at stationery stores. Regular fountain pen ink stains can be removed by first covering the spot with a piece of blotter soaked in alcohol, then with a blotter soaked in ammonia. Any remaining stains can be removed with a hydrogen peroxide or chlorine bleach poultice.

For rust stains, dampen first, then sprinkle with sodium hydrosulphite (the color remover sold with household fabric dyes). Allow to stand for 15 or 20 minutes, then apply a solution of sodium citrate (drug store). This should convert the rust stain to a colorless compound, which can then be removed by washing with clean water.

The above treatments can be applied to either polished or honed marble. Surface stains on the latter, however, can sometimes be

removed simply by rubbing with a very fine emery paper, #300 grit or finer. Try this before going to the trouble of the poultice method, but *don't* try it on polished marble.

Marks on polished marble that appear *lighter* than the rest of the surface are generally not stains at all; they're surface etching caused by such common acid liquids as soft drinks and fruit juices. If more than a few square inches are involved, send the piece out for commercial repolishing, but small areas can be done at home if you have the patience: Sprinkle tin oxide polishing powder on the surface and rub briskly with a dampened cloth pad. You can buy tin oxide at any hobby shop that handles lapidary or rock polishing supplies.

PAINT STAIN ON MARBLE

I have a beautiful old marble fireplace that someone had covered with several coats of paint, for some reason or other. I was able to remove most of it with paint remover, but the bottom coat, which was red, seems to have soaked into the white marble and given it a reddish tinge. A friend suggested muriatic acid, but I'm not sure this is safe to use on the marble.

Don't use muriatic acid, for heaven's sake; this will dissolve the marble. I would try chlorine laundry bleach, diluted one part to three parts water. Mix this with chalk or whiting (any hardware store) to make a paste, and apply this to the marble about half an inch thick. When it dries, brush it off, and if you're lucky, the stain will go with it.

PROTECTING MARBLE

We have just built a fireplace and used a lovely old piece of marble as a mantel. I would like to know what I could use as a sealer to protect it from stains. Would varnish do?

There is a special sealer available for commercial use, but it's not on the retail market. Some protection can be achieved, however, by using a clear paste wax or one of the liquid acrylic floor polishes. But don't use a varnish or plastic finish.

REMOVING MASKING TAPE

When we painted our house we used masking tape to keep paint off the aluminum window frames. Now we can't get the masking tape off.

Can you suggest something?

Although manufacturers never bother to tell anybody, masking tape should be removed as quickly as possible, certainly within eight hours. After that it begins to dry and eventually becomes extremely difficult to get off. Petroleum solvent, available at any service station, will help, however. So will contact cement solvent.

METER READING

Could you please tell me how to read my electricity and gas meters?

Nearly all gas and electricity meters use a series of four or five small "clock" dials to record consumption. Each dial is numbered from 1 to 0(10). There are also one or two small test dials which are not used in taking the meter reading.

All you have to do is start at the righthand dial and write down the number that the pointer has just *passed*. (You'll notice that each succeeding dial turns in the opposite direction to the dial preceding it.)

Continue reading the dials from right to left, and writing the number down in the same way, noting the number that each pointer has passed. The accompanying illustrations show two typical meters and give the proper reading in each case.

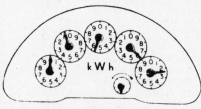

The reading on this 5-dial electric meter is 00562 kilowatt hours.

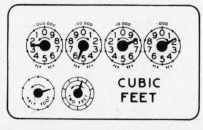

This 4-dial gas meter reads 258100 cubic feet.

To find out how much electricity or gas was used in a certain period, you simply subtract the reading taken at the beginning of the period from the last reading.

Gas meters show the number of cubic feet of gas used. Regardless of whether they have four or five dials, the dial on the right is numbered in 100s of cubic feet, the next one in 1,000s, and so on. To get the total number of cubic feet used, you add two zeros to the reading shown by the dials. There are a few old meters around that read in 1,000s of cubic feet, but they are rare, and the dials are clearly marked.

MICE

How can I get rid of mice in my cottage?

See if you can find where they are coming in, then cover the holes with metal. A generous sprinkling of moth balls when you close the cottage for the winter will also discourage mice and other rodent pests. There is poisoned seed on the market, but this is dangerous when there are pets and young children.

MILDEW

MILDEW IN CLOSETS

Last winter we discovered that mildew was developing in two of our bedroom closets that are located on an outside wall. The mildew even got into shoes that were stored in boxes. Would this be caused by poor insulation, or what? We would like to correct the problem before next winter.

There are two basic causes for the condensation that produces mildew growth—insufficient insulation in the closet walls, and too much humidity in the house. Either or both can be changed to remedy the problem. The closet walls can be insulated by applying plastic foamboard to them with a bead of panel adhesive around the back of each sheet. The humidity level of the house can be reduced by bringing in more fresh air.

Increasing the ventilation and temperature in the closets will also help. You can buy small plug-in heaters for closets, but just keeping a light bulb burning in them will often do the job. Closet ventilation can be improved by using louvered doors, or trimming ½" or so off the top and bottom of solid doors.

Mildew

MILDEW ODORS

One of the most common problems I have received is one that I cannot answer: how to eliminate the musty mildew odor from mattresses, trunks, furniture, rugs, shoes, etc., that once were stored in a damp basement.

Getting the mildew smell out of the basement itself is another problem, but one solution is to wash it out with a 9½-ounce can of lye dissolved in a pail of water, something you cannot do with the other items mentioned.

There is really no way to eliminate mildew odor from items that cannot be laundered or dry-cleaned. The smell is reduced once the items are thoroughly dried, of course, but it can still be detected by a sensitive nose, and generally reappears at the first sign of dampness.

Remedies like mothballs and household deodorants merely mask the mildew smell with something stronger that doesn't last as long. It is a temporary cure, at best.

We invited readers to send in their suggestions for eliminating mildew odors. While a number of ideas were offered, it does not appear that any of them is 100 per cent effective. Until some better ideas come along, however, here is a summary of the possible solutions:

CLOVES: A number of readers suggested that these be used, either whole or powdered, to mask mildew smells in suitcases, clothes closets, etc. They should be renewed every month, apparently.

LYSOL: A great many readers found this very effective in hiding mildew smells. It is also claimed that this product kills mildew fungus, which it probably does, but that will not prevent further growth if damp conditions remain.

WINTERGREEN: An ounce of oil of wintergreen added to the laundry wash water was recommended to eliminate mildew odors from clothes.

CHARCOAL: Pieces of charcoal, briquettes or lumps, placed in cupboards, suitcases, furniture upholstery, and so on, were suggested by other readers as a method of preventing mildew odors in damp places. Place several briquettes, loosely wrapped in paper, among the clothes you want to protect.

MUSTARD: Another material recommended to remove mildew smells from old trunks or the insides of refrigerators is dry mustard. Just sprinkle on a dry cloth and rub on.

MILDEW ODOR IN BASEMENT

We have been in our new house about a year and have stored a lot of books and other things in cardboard boxes in the basement. Although the basement is perfectly dry there is a strong smell of mold and mildew. Is there a chemical that we can use in the basement to kill the mildew and remove the odor?

The basic cause is dampness. It takes about a year for the moisture in fresh concrete and new wood to dry out completely. During this time it is not advisable to store mildew-prone things like books, leather and cotton fabrics down there, even if the basement appears to be dry. Unless the article can be washed or dry-cleaned, it is almost impossible to get rid of the mildew odor; it tends to recur at the first sign of dampness. If the smell lingers in the basement I suggest you brush the walls with a solution of one 9½-ounce can of lye to a pail of water.

MILDEW ON BAMBOO SHADES

This past summer we bought roll-up bamboo shades for our sunporch. They are ideal for this purpose because they provide ventilation along with shade. But after the wet weather we find that a black mildew has formed on the part that was exposed. How can we remove this and what can we do to prevent it happening again?

Scrub them with any good household cleaning compound to which a generous amount of liquid chlorine laundry bleach has been added. Rinse, let dry, and then apply a pentachlorophenol wood preservative. This should prevent the mildew from recurring.

MILDEW ON BOOKS

We stored some books in a damp basement and now they have developed mildew stains and smell musty. Can you tell me how to get rid of these?

Mildew, a mold growth, can be killed by placing the books in a plastic garbage bag along with a saucer of paradichlorobenzene crystals, available at any drug store. Stand the books up and open them so that the fumes can reach the pages. Tie the bag and leave for 48 hours. Remove the books and brush off as much of the mildew growth as you as you can. Stains can be removed with a strong solution of chlorine laundry bleach, but if the books are valuable, take them to someone who specializes in the restoration of old books. Your library can direct you.

Store the books in a dry, warm, well-ventilated room.

MILDEW STAINS

There are some mildew stains on our canvas tent that I can't seem to remove. Do you know of anything that will take them out?

Mildew stains can sometimes be removed by moistening them with lemon juice, sprinkling them with salt, and spreading the material out to dry in the sun. A strong solution of chlorine laundry bleach also works.

MILDEW STAINS ON PAINT

The paint on our house is still in pretty good condition, but there are a number of dirty black patches along the lower edges of the siding and under the windows. I've tried washing it off but it doesn't do much good. I hate to have to repaint the house. Do you have any suggestions?

The black patches sound like mildew. There's a simple test. Apply a few drops of full-strength chlorine laundry bleach to the stain. If it bleaches out in two or three minutes, it's mildew. If the bleach doesn't affect it, it's dirt.

Small spots of mildew can be removed with a wet cloth and any household scouring powder. Large areas should be scrubbed with a solution of one cup of chlorine bleach and ¼ cup of dishwasher detergent (not sink detergent) to one quart of water. Use a long-handled brush and rinse thoroughly.

The mildew should be removed before you repaint, in any case, otherwise the fungus will grow through and stain the new paint.

MILDEWED WALLS

Our plaster walls are spotted with mildew. I want to paper them; how do I stop the mildew from coming through?

Excessive moisture in the house is causing the mildew. Increasing your ventilation will help reduce this.

Scrub the mildew spots with a solution of two ounces of liquid chlorine laundry bleach to a quart of water, then paint the walls with glue size and allow to dry before papering.

MILDEW UNDER FOAM MATTRESS

Is there any way of preventing mildew from forming between our 4" foam mattress and the plywood platform?

The mildew is caused by the lack of ventilation under the mattress. The problem is compounded if the plywood is unfinished, because the soft, porous wood holds moisture like a blotter. Drill ½" holes in the plywood about 3" apart, then apply at least two coats of varnish.

CARE OF MIRRORS

I have heard that a mirror shouldn't be hung facing a window. Is there any truth in this?

There was once. The paints that were used to back the silver coating on mirrors would sometimes bubble and flake away with extended exposure to direct sunlight. You've probably seen this in old mirrors.

Paint used today doesn't do that, and now you can hang a mirror any place you want to.

MARKED MIRROR

My large mirror over the fireplace developed a discoloration which, after having it re-silvered, is showing up again. What could cause the marking?

If your mirror still shows spots after being re-silvered, I would say that your mirror man did a poor job and that you should have him re-do it.

RESTORING A MIRROR

I have a beautiful, antique mirror in an oval frame. Some of the paint is beginning to flake off the back of the mirror, exposing the silver coating. What kind of paint can I use to protect these spots from tarnishing?

The silvering on my dresser mirror has discolored. Is there any way I can re-silver it myself?

When we were moving someone scratched the back of a fine old mirror that has been in the family for many years. How can I touch up these scratches so they won't be noticeable?

It is not practical to re-silver a mirror yourself. And unless the mirror is very valuable or very unusual—engraved, painted, etched, bevelled or curved—it would probably not pay you to have it re-silvered.

There are some things you can do yourself, however. A good quality "silver" paint (actually aluminum paint) from an art supply store can be used to touch up scratches. This won't hide them completely, but they will be far less noticeable.

If the protective paint on the back of the

mirror has chipped or peeled off, and the silver coating is still in good condition, some protection against tarnishing can be provided by touching up the spots with a dark-colored latex paint.

MIRROR TILES

We wanted to put mirror tiles on a cork wall, but had trouble removing the cork, so my husband covered the wall with plywood, to which we applied the tiles with the adhesive tape provided. A couple of months ago they started falling off. What did we do wrong and how can we correct it?

The plywood should have been painted first, because adhesive tape doesn't stick very well to bare wood. If you can remove the remaining tiles without breaking them, apply a coat of primer and then a coat of enamel to the plywood. Remove the adhesive tape from the mirrors and apply 12" strips of double-sided adhesive tape to the back of the tiles. Peel off the protective layer and press the tiles onto the painted plywood.

If some of the mirror tiles can't be removed, leave them in place and paint around them.

REMOVING MIRROR TILES

Can you tell me how to remove mirror tiles from a gypsumboard wall without damaging it or them? I don't know how they are applied but they are on there very firmly.

The superintendent of a large apartment building who has faced this problem many times tells me the best remedy is to cover the mirrored wall with new gypsumboard applied with panel adhesive. When the joints are taped and filled, this creates a smooth new wall ready for painting or papering.

But another reader told me he had removed and re-used mirror tiles several times using a flexible strip of galvanized metal about 20" long and 3" wide. He heated the end of the strip with a propane torch and then slid it behind the tile, where the hot metal easily cut through the self-stick adhesive pads that hold the four corners of each tile to the wall. Petroleum solvent (mineral spirits) was then used to remove any adhesive that remained on the wall. The tiles were re-applied somewhere else with squares of double-sided carpet tape.

LEVELLING A MIRRORED WALL

I want to cover one wall of my living room

with 12" square mirror tiles, but the wall is bowed out in the middle and the mirror reflection will be distorted. How can I correct this?

Apply 1×2 or 1×3 strapping vertically to the wall every 12", with blocks or shims behind the straps to bring them out level. Start by drawing a string horizontally across the wall over the point of maximum projection. Mark this distance on the end walls, and nail a block of wood of this thickness to the wall at each end.

Drop a plumb line in each corner, just touching the wood blocks, and measure the distance of this out from the top and bottom of the wall. Nail wood blocks of this thickness to the wall. Nail a length of strapping to the blocks at each end of the wall. You now have two vertical straps or "furring strips" marking the ends of a perfectly level wall.

Fasten a length of string between them across the top of the wall, another one across the centre, and another across the bottom. Every 12" across the wall apply a vertical 1×2 or 1×3 strap, shimming it out with pieces of plywood or wood shingle to the level of the string. Note that the straps should be *centred* every 12" out from the end of the wall so that the mirror tiles can be glued to them with the recommended adhesive.

MORTAR

MORTAR FALLING OUT OF CHIMNEY

My house is only about 15 years old and we have a natural gas furnace. I have discovered that the mortar is falling out of the top 12 courses of bricks on the chimney, and I can even see daylight between some of them. What should I do?

If you can see daylight through the bricks, you apparently don't have a flue lining in the chimney. I suspect your trouble is at least partly caused by condensation inside the top of the chimney—not uncommon with gas furnaces because the flue gases are relatively cool and contain a lot of moisture. The best remedy for this is to have an insulated metal flue installed inside your chimney. Any chimney expert can do this for you. Have the mortar joints repointed at the same time.

FLAGSTONE MORTAR DIDN'T WORK

Last summer I put in a flagstone patio. The base was a concrete slab four inches thick, on top of which I spread a layer of mortar made with one shovelful of mortar mix, three of sand and one of hydrated lime—plus water, of course. The stones were pushed down into this mortar layer. I find now that the mortar hasn't set at all; it is crumbling like loose sand. What did I do wrong?

You got your formulas mixed up. "Mortar mix" is a ready-to-use mortar that is simply mixed with water. It's sold for small jobs like brick pointing. Adding sand and lime to this only weakens the mixture.

If you wanted to mix your own mortar, you should have used one part portland cement and one part hydrated lime to six parts sand—or one part *masonry cement* (a mixture of portland cement and lime) to three parts sand.

You'll have to remove the flagstones and the crumbling mortar and start again, I'm afraid.

FROSTPROOF MORTAR

I want to repoint the mortar joints in a stone wall this winter. I understand that I can add salt to the cement so that the mortar can be used below freezing temperatures. How much salt should I use?

Salt should not be used. A special masonry cement is made for mortar. This contains a foaming agent that makes it resistant to freezing, as well as hydrated lime to make a more workable mixture. All of the dry mortar mixes sold in deep frost areas are made with this special masonry cement. It's best not to attempt this job while the temperature is below freezing, however.

LIGHT-COLORED MORTAR

I have exposed an old brick wall on the inside of my living room. The mortar joints need patching, but they are very light in color and I can't get a mortar mix to match. One part cement to 3 parts sand is much too dark. What can I use?

Replacing half the cement with hydrated lime will lighten it and also make a smoother, more workable mortar. If this is not light enough, use white cement instead of regular portland cement. For a really white mortar, use white silica sand instead of the usual sand.

HOLES IN MORTAR

We have a brick home about 16 years old. Last year I began to notice holes in the mortar. Some are quite large, but most are perfectly round, as if they had been drilled. Is some kind of a bug doing this? What can I do about it?

The round holes are caused by bubbles or gaps in the mortar, not by insects. The mortar is beginning to deteriorate and should be replaced to prevent moisture from penetrating the wall. Scrape out all the loose mortar and chip it back to a depth of about ¾", using a hammer and chisel if necessary, then replace with fresh mortar.

You can buy sacks of prepared mortar mix at any building supply store. To reduce shrinkage, add just enough water to produce a damp mixture that will hold its shape when squeezed in the hand. Allow this to stand for an hour, then add enough water to bring it to a smooth working consistency. Wet the mortar joints and the brick. Hold the mortar on a "hawk," a square piece of wood or metal with a handle in the centre, and use a narrow pointing trowel to place the mortar in the joints, forcing it in well.

In about 15 minutes, or when the mortar no longer appears wet, smooth the joints with a short length of ½" copper pipe bent in a shallow S-curve to form a concave mortar joint that will shed water. Wash off any mortar that has stained the brick.

LOOSE MORTAR

I have had the chimney of my home pointed twice, but the mortar keeps falling out. What is wrong with the chimney?

Nothing, but something is wrong with the work you have had done. It is obvious that a poor grade of mortar was used, and most likely the old mortar was not cleaned out and cut back far enough to provide a key for the fresh mortar.

MISMATCHED MORTAR

The front of our new house is faced with sand-colored brick. Half of it was laid in one day, and the other half the next day. The mortar used on the second day is much lighter, and the combination looks terrible. Our builder tells us that the color difference was due to a change in the weather, and that it will go away within a few months. Is this true?

Large brick buildings are built through all kinds of weather, and the mortar still matches. The only reason for the difference in your case is that the second day's mortar was not mixed properly to match the first day's. A sloppy masonry job, in other words.

It's an old trick to say that a problem will disappear in time. The only thing that will disappear in time is your one-year warranty.

Unfortunately, there isn't anything the builder can do to remedy the mistake now. He can't scrape out the old mortar, and it isn't practical to paint it. If you're mad enough, though, you might take legal action to get a refund for faulty work.

MORTAR STAINS

The builder left bits of mortar on our red brick fireplace. How can we remove these and clean up the bricks?

Chip off any blobs of mortar. Any remaining blemishes or stains can be removed with a solution of 1 part muriatic acid to 10 parts water. Apply with a stiff brush, but be careful to keep the solution off your skin, clothes, metal, paint, and anything else you value.

MOTHPROOFING WITH CEDAR

I've had my heart set on a large, cedar-lined closet for clothes, linen, and blankets, but it will cost four times as much as an ordinary closet, and my husband questions whether it's worth it. I can't find any information on the value of a cedar lining. Is it really necessary in order to keep out moths?

The advantages of a cedar lining are largely imaginary, although there was probably a time when this was the best thing available. A pleasant smell is about the only advantage today, and that doesn't last very long. It is doubtful if the smell has any effect on moths. Sealed plastic bags and a handful of moth flakes are much better protection. Ordinary cedar won't do, by the way; it has almost no smell. You have to use aromatic cedar from the southern United States, and this, as you've found, is very expensive.

MURIATIC ACID

I've read in several places that a 10% solution of muriatic acid—one part to nine parts water—is used to clean concrete and brick. But the label on the bottle of muriatic acid I bought at the hardware store says to mix one part to two or three parts water. This sounds like an awfully strong solution. Is it right?

It could simply mean that the muriatic acid in the bottle has already been diluted. But if it's the standard strength (usually given as "20° Baume"), the strongest solution recommended for removing efflorescence, mortar stains, and other discolorations from brick or concrete, is one part muriatic acid to nine parts water. This is also a safe strength to use on the acid resistant baked enamels found on modern bathtubs and sinks. I've even heard of it being used to clean the logs in an old cabin.

It's not advisable to use acid on light colored clay bricks, however, and it should NEVER be used on marble, imitation stone, or sand-lime brick. Sandstone and some other building stones contain minerals that may be discolored by the application of a strong acid, but a 1:9 dilution of commercial muriatic acid is usually safe. It's best to test a small area first, however.

Always add the acid to the water when diluting it, never the other way around. Wear rubber gloves and take other precautions to keep the acid off your skin, eyes, clothes, and anything else you value.

MURIATIC ACID vs SHRUBS

We purchased a new house last summer and the concrete porch is badly stained. I was advised to scrub it with a muriatic acid solution, but hesitate to do so because of the shrubs around the porch. Would the acid harm them?

If the muriatic acid solution (1 part acid to 9 parts water) is kept on the concrete until it stops foaming, it will be neutralized and can be safely hosed off without harming the plants.

NAILING A WOOD DECK

I built a sundeck last summer, using 2 × 4s spaced ¼″ apart. I covered the nailheads with putty and then applied two coats of paint. Now the paint and putty are peeling off the nailheads and rust is staining the paint around them. What went wrong and how can I fix it?

It sounds as if you used common (flat-headed) steel nails. These can't be countersunk enough to be covered with putty. You should have used hot-dip galvanized finishing nails. The small heads can be countersunk, and the zinc coating will prevent them from rusting.

I can only suggest that you sand the rust off the nailheads and then paint them with one of the rustproofing paints that are now available.

NAIL-POPPING

We have a 2-year-old, custom built house with drywall problems. A number of the nails have popped out, pushing a dab of plaster with them. Can you tell me what causes this and what we can do about it?

The most common cause is the use of green (wet) framing lumber, which shrinks as it dries and pushes the nails out. The remedy is to drive the nails back with the rounded end of a ball-peen hammer, then drive in a new nail about 1½″ above or below the popped nail. Use 1³/₈″ annular-ringed drywall nails, and drive them below the surface of the panel by striking them with the ballpeen hammer to dimple the surface of the gypsumboard. Fill all the depressions with premixed spackling compound or plaster filler. For a perfectly smooth finish, fill each depression three times, sanding lightly between applications. Then repaint.

NAIL SIZES

I have some plans for a woodworking project that call for "2d" nails. I'm told this stands for "two pennyweight", but what's a pennyweight, and what does it have to do with nail sizes?

A pennyweight is 1/20th of an ounce, and it's an English measurement for nails that is still commonly used in the United States. A 2d nail is a 1″ nail (either common or finishing); 3d is 1¼″, 4d is 1½″; 5d is 1¾″; 6d is 2″, and so on, ¼″ per pennyweight. This isn't really what they weigh, but it's the way they're measured, anyway.

NEWSPAPER FIRELOGS

Can you give me the formula for making firelogs out of newspapers? I think they have to be soaked in a solution of bluestone and salt, but I don't know the proportions and I think there may be other chemicals involved.

It isn't necessary to soak newspaper logs in any solution to make them burn. Chemicals are only used to color the flames, and they are now very difficult to obtain in small quantities. It also takes weeks to dry the rolled-up newspaper.

If you want to make cheap firelogs out of your old newspapers, just roll them up, snug but not too tight, into logs about 2½″ in diameter. Tie them with soft iron wire or garbage bag twist-ties. Don't use string. If you have a lot of newspapers, you can make yourself a simple roller. Buy a 20″ length of 1″ dowel and saw a 16″ slot down the centre of it. Just slip a section of newspaper in the slot and start rolling, adding another section of newspaper when the first one is half rolled. Continue until the roll is the desired size, then pull out the dowel.

Newspaper logs burn quite well when added to a wood or manufactured log fire, but not well enough to start a fire.

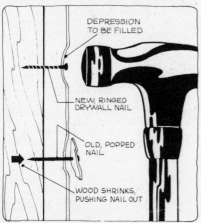

DEPRESSION TO BE FILLED

NEW, RINGED DRYWALL NAIL

OLD, POPPED NAIL

WOOD SHRINKS, PUSHING NAIL OUT

NOISE

AIR CONDITIONER NOISE

What is the quietest air conditioner I can buy? I want to put one in my bedroom window, which is quite close to my neighbor's window. And is there anything else I can do to reduce the noise level from an air conditioner?

Although noise level standards do exist for central air-conditioning units, there are none as yet for window air conditioners. So there is no way to determine the noise level of a particular model before you buy it.

But I do have a few suggestions. First, compact units tend to be noisier than larger units of the same capacity. Second, most manufacturers put out high, medium, and lower-priced units—and generally speaking, the higher priced units tend to be quieter. And third, it is claimed that the new, rotary-type compressors are quieter than the conventional piston-type compressors.

Other than getting a quiet unit, there seems to be nothing else you can do to reduce the outside noise from an air conditioner. If your unit is going to be very close to your neighbor's window, any model may be too noisy.

ALUMINUM SIDING NOISES

We have been living in a new townhouse for almost a year. During the hot weather we were disturbed by a rather loud crackling sound in the wall on the east side of the house, which is wood frame construction with aluminum siding. The noise occurs mainly in the morning when the sun is on that side of the house. Why is it only on one side, and is there anything we can do about it?

This is almost certainly due to expansion of the aluminum siding, probably because the siding was nailed too tightly on that side. Aluminum siding has nailing slots instead of round holes to allow for a slight amount of expansion and contraction. Nails are supposed to be centred in the slots and left loose enough to allow some movement, but an inexperienced applicator could easily make the mistake of driving the nails too tight. All that can be done is to take the siding off and reapply it.

NOISY VENT FAN

We had a bathroom installed in our basement,

with a ceiling fan that vents through the bedroom closet above. There is no window in the bathroom, so the fan comes on automatically when the light is turned on. The problem is the noise, which is very loud in the bedroom upstairs. What can we do to reduce the noise?**

Most vent fans have propeller-type blades, but the best and quietest models have a squirrel-cage type fan—a revolving drum rather than blades. This moves air faster and quieter than the propeller-type fan.

It would help if you wrapped the fan housing and the vent duct with fibreglass batts. But don't expect too much; a fan in the floor of a bedroom is bound to make quite a bit of noise. It would have been better to put the exhaust fan in the basement wall and vent it directly outside.

SQUEAKING CARPET

Last summer we had wall-to-wall carpet laid in three rooms, and during the winter the floors started to squeak in all of them. The carpet dealer says it isn't the fault of the carpet or the rubber underpad, but it sounds to me as if that's where it's coming from. Have you ever encountered this problem?

I've encountered the problem of squeaking floors many times, but it has always been traced to the wooden floor or, more correctly, the subfloor, which shrinks in the dry, winter air, and moves up and down on the nails when it is walked on. I don't think there is any way this could be caused by the carpet or the underpad.

You can verify this yourself if you can see the underside of the floor in the basement. Look for movement of the subfloor when someone steps on a squeaky spot upstairs. Driving a thin wooden wedge, such as a piece of shingle, between the subfloor and the joist at this point will stop the movement and eliminate the squeak.

NOISY ELECTRIC CLOCK

I like electric clocks because they are so quiet, but after a while ours began to sound as though a little man were inside playing the bongos. What causes the noise and what can I do about it . . . other than buy a new clock?

The gearbox of an electric clock is packed at the factory with a lifetime supply of grease. With heat and use, however, the grease softens and settles to the bottom, and that's when the bongos start.

The cure is to turn the clock upside down in

a warm place and run it for a few days to give the grease a chance to settle back where it belongs. This usually works for a while, anyway. Unfortunately there's no way to put in more grease, so you eventually have to replace the clock . . . or the motor, which is a lot cheaper.

SQUEAKING FLOORS

We bought a 1½-storey, older house last fall and during the winter we discovered that the hardwood floors squeak badly in several places. We plan to put down wall-to-wall carpeting, but would like to do something about the noisy floors first. What should we do?

The squeaking is caused by the subflooring riding up and down on the nails that have been pushed up due to shrinkage of the floor joists. If the basement ceiling is unfinished you will be able to see the subflooring moving when someone steps on it from above. The solution is to wedge or block the subfloor to prevent this movement. This is easy to do if you can reach the floor from underneath. Thin wedges, made from pieces of wood shingle, can be driven between the joist and the subfloor. Or you can nail a short length of 1x2 along the top of the joist, parallel with the floor and tight against it. Another remedy is to use a caulking gun to apply a bead of elastomeric adhesive along both sides of the joist directly under the floor.

Where the underneath of the floor is not accessible, such as in your upper level, you will have to drive 2½" spiral steel finishing nails down through the floor into the joist at the point of the squeak. The trick is to find the joist. The best way to do this is by tapping on the floor and listening for the solid sound that indicates a joist. Joists usually run at right angles to hardwood flooring and are spaced every 16". Countersink the nailheads with a nailset and fill the holes with plastic wood or a similar filler matching the floor finish.

HUM IN FLUORESCENT LIGHT FIXTURES

The fluorescent light fixture in our bathroom has started humming very loudly. Is there any way we can stop it making this noise?

All fluorescent fixtures produce a slight hum, caused by the action of the alternating current, but sometimes this is amplified by a loose part inside the fixture. Tightening the loose part will stop the noise. More often, however, a loud hum indicates that the heavy ballast or transformer in the fixture is defective. It's generally cheaper and less trouble to replace the entire fixture than to put in a new ballast.

THE SOUND OF COLD

I live on the top floor of a 4-storey apartment building. During very cold weather the building sounds like an army firing range, with loud shots going off at odd hours during the day and night. What causes this and what can we do about it?

These sounds are usually caused by ice cracking on a flat roof, but it can also be caused by the expansion or contraction of the building structure itself due to sudden changes in temperature. As far as I know there is nothing that can be done about it, except moving to a quieter building.

NOISY FURNACE

We have a hot water heating system equipped with a circulating pump that runs continuously. Our problem is that whenever the oil burner is on, there's a light tapping or drumming noise throughout the whole system. We've had two plumbers in to investigate, but they say they can't stop the noise. This is difficult to believe, and I'd appreciate your advice.

It's difficult to pinpoint the source of a noise by mail, but from your description there would appear to be two possibilities. The noise could be coming from the expansion of the pipes inside the walls. This sometimes causes a chattering sound where a pipe rubs against the woodwork or a metal support bracket. Such sounds *can* be traced and eliminated, but if the trouble is inside a wall it may not be practical to cure it.

If the noise is heard all the time the burner is on, it's more likely that the source is in the furnace itself. The burner unit may be vibrating against some part of its housing, for instance. You would hear this as a distinct metallic noise coming from the furnace. If it's more of a deep-throated rumble, the trouble is probably due to lack of sufficient chimney draft. You can sometimes cure this yourself by simply propping open the viewing port located above the burner. This lets a little more air into the combustion chamber. If this doesn't work, a burner mechanic may fix the trouble by reducing the size of the flame slightly, so that less draft is required.

HUM IN HOT WATER HEATING SYSTEM

We recently had our old gravity hot water heating system converted to a pump circulation system. While the pump itself seems reasonably quiet, there is a persistent hum in the pipes that we can't track down. The furnace man says it's just something we'll have to put up with, but he doesn't have to live with it.

The sound of the pump may be amplified by the hot water pipes touching the framework of the house. This can be remedied by packing some padding between the pipe and the wood.

More likely, however, the problem is "velocity noise" in the pipe, caused by the fact that the old gravity pipes are too large for the pump. Adding some basement radiators frequently helps by slowing down the flow of water. But the best solution is to replace the impeller in the pump with a smaller one, in order to cut down the pressure. It is not necessary to buy a new pump; your heating man can simply change the impeller.

HUM IN OIL TANK

When the burner in our oil furnace is running there is an annoying hum in the fuel tank, located in the basement. The noise seems to be louder when the tank is half empty. The serviceman says this is a common occurence, but he doesn't know of anything that can be done about it. Can you help?

The hum comes from the pump gears inside the burner and is transmitted through the fuel line to the oil tank. If you put your ear to the tank you can actually hear the gears turning. The cure is quite simple, and your serviceman should have known it. All pumps have an anti-hum device made to eliminate this very problem. Some of the older pumps must be replaced entirely when this device fails, but most pumps in use today have a plastic anti-hum diaphram that can be replaced in a few minutes.

HUM IN FURNACE RELAY

All winter the relay or stack switch in our furnace made a high-pitched hum that could be heard throughout the house. We had a new relay switch installed, a new burner motor, and a new thermostat, but the noise persisted. We'd like to get this fixed before next winter. Can you tell me what is wrong?

This is probably caused by vibration in the 24-volt transformer in the relay—very much like the 60-cycle hum you sometimes hear in an electric clock, only louder. If you take the cover off the relay, you'll see the transformer made of many laminations of sheet metal wound with wire. When these laminations get a bit loose they vibrate with the alternating current and transmit this noise to other parts of the furnace. Pushing a toothpick or a thin piece of cardboard between the end laminations will generally stop the hum.

NOISE IN FURNACE PIPES

Can you tell me what causes our heating ducts to bang when the heat comes on, and again when the heat goes off? I've asked our heating man but he said he didn't know.

It's caused by the expansion and contraction of the ducts with the temperature change, causing curved sections of the sheet metal to snap in and out. If you can find the spot where the sound comes from, it can usually be stopped just by bending the side of the duct slightly at that point. The cure is simple, but it's often difficult to find the right spot.

NOISY WATER TANK

We have a gas-fired hot water tank that bangs and cracks whenever the heat comes on. What can we do about it?

This is probably caused by a build-up of lime scale on the bottom of the tank, but a high temperature setting will contribute to the problem. Drain a pail of water out of the tank to see if you can flush out some of the scale, then try lowering the temperature setting on the tank thermostat. It shouldn't be any higher than 140°F.

RADIATORS

Can you please tell me the cause of the thumping and knocking in our steam radiators whenever the heat starts to circulate?

This can be caused by water that has gathered

in pools at the bottom of the radiators or in pipes that sag or slope the wrong way. The usual treatment is to put small wooden blocks, say ¼" thick, under the feet of the radiator to slope it towards the intake valve and raise the pipe under the floor.

NOISY REFRIGERATION

We just purchased a new refrigerator. It works fine but is much noisier than the old one, and makes a loud, pulsating noise that can be heard in our bedroom at the other end of the house. The serviceman tells us that the new motors run faster and noisier than the old ones and that there's nothing that can be done about it. Do you have any suggestions?

The new compressors *are* noisier than the old ones, but not objectionably so, and there's no reason why you should have to accept a noisy refrigerator. There are adjustments that can be made by the serviceman, such as adjusting the mounting brackets. If this doesn't work, the store should either replace the compressor unit or the entire fridge.

But before you call the serviceman back, make sure the floor underneath it is not loose or springy, and that all four feet (two of them are adjustable) sit firmly on the floor. The noise could be caused by something as simple as the fridge wobbling a bit on one leg.

SQUEAKING BED

We have a wooden bed that's several years old and has started squeaking. We've tried oiling it, but that doesn't seem to work. Do you have any suggestions?

Sometimes just increasing the humidity in the house will do the trick. Otherwise, take the bed apart and rub a stick lubricant (available at any hardware store) on all parts that fit together.

SQUEAKING STAIRS

What can be done to stop stairs from squeaking, even when our youngest child walks on them?

The problem is often caused by excessively dry air; the squeaks disappear after a humidifier has been installed.

But if the problem is structural, the easiest solution is to remove the molding along the back of the treads (the horizontal part of the stairs) and hammer in wooden wedges coated with glue. If the staircase is open on the underside, check the triangular blocks or wedges to see if they are fitted tightly; condensation, heat

and movement sometimes loosen the blocks. If this is the case, they should be driven tight and nailed. Often there is only one row of blocks down one side, but there should be two—one on each side.

If the staircase is plastered or covered in, you might try driving spiral finishing nails through the front of the tread into the risers below. Nail holes can be filled with plastic wood and stained to match the existing stairs.

NOISY SINK

I may be over-sensitive, but I find the noise of the dishes rattling in our stainless steel sink very annoying. Is there anything I can do to remedy this?

You could put a rubber dishmat in the bottom of the sink. It's easy to cut one of these to size and make a hole for the drain.

You could also reduce the noise somewhat by painting the underside of the sink with automobile underbody coating, available at any auto supply store.

"KNOCKING" IN DRAIN PIPES

My problem is a loud knocking sound in the drain pipe whenever the sink, tub, or toilet in the upstairs bathroom are drained. I replaced the faucets in the sink, put new washers in the bathtub, and had a new flush valve unit put in the toilet tank, but the noise continues. Could this be an air lock in the drain pipe?

This trouble is not unusual; I have it in my house. It's caused by the expansion and contraction of the cast iron drain pipe when hot or cold water runs down it. This causes the pipe to rub against the wood or other support at some point with a jerky motion that sounds like someone knocking on the wall. The only cure, I'm afraid, is to open the wall and pack some padding around the pipe wherever it's rubbing. Most of us just live with the noise.

HISSING NOISE IN TAPS

Would you please tell me how we can get rid of a hissing sound every time we turn on the taps. Putting new washers in the taps didn't help. The toilet also makes this hissing sound, and is very slow to fill. When we asked our plumber about this trouble he just shrugged and said, "I guess you've got air in your pipes," but didn't offer any solution. Is there anything we can do?

Noise

The noise is almost certainly due to the water passing through a constricted opening. The most likely place is at the end of one of the thin, flexible, chrome-plated copper supply pipes connected to the taps or the water closet. Either the plumber has used a cutter that has reduced the opening of the pipe (he should have used a reamer) or he has pushed the supply pipe too far inside the fitting. In both cases the water is forced through a narrow opening, which produces a hissing sound that is transmitted through the pipe. These mistakes are very simple to rectify.

NOISY TOILET

Our toilet makes a loud whining noise while it is filling up after it has been flushed. What can we do to stop it?

You probably need a new washer in the ballcock valve at the end of the float arm. Turn off the water supply to the tank, flush the toilet to empty it, and unscrew the wing nuts that fasten the float arm to the ballcock. When the arm is removed, lift out the ballcock valve and unscrew the washer from the end. Take this to your hardware store and ask for a replacement. Or buy a ballcock valve washer kit before you start the job. This includes a packing washer that fits in a groove around the plunger. You might as well replace this, too.

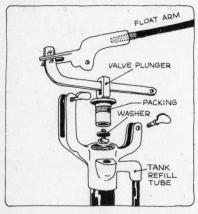

FLOAT ARM

VALVE PLUNGER

PACKING
WASHER

TANK
REFILL
TUBE

SCREENING TRAFFIC NOISES

We have just learned that the road at the back of our house is going to be widened to four lanes, bringing cars about 25' closer to our

property line. Could you tell me the best kind of a fence to build to keep out the noise? The new road will be about 6' below the level of our back yard.

Weight and surface texture are the most important qualities of a sound barrier. The most practical and economical material for the homeowner to use is an 8" x 8" x 16" hollow concrete block with a rough-textured or anglecut (faceted) face. The textured or patterned surface should face the source of the noise. The wall should be high enough so you can't see the cars. It should be as close to the road as possible.

TRAFFIC NOISES

I live in an apartment facing a busy street and find the traffic noise at night very annoying. Have you any suggestions for cutting down on the noise? Would weatherstripping around the window help?

Weatherstripping, storm windows and heavy drapes will all help.

NOISY TV ANTENNA

I have a rather unusual problem, but hope you may have some suggestions. Last Fall I installed a 30' TV tower and 10' antenna according to instructions. The concrete base is 4' in the ground and the tower is fastened to the house about 15' up. My problem is that the tower vibrates even in a gentle breeze and produces an annoying, low-pitched hum. Can you offer any advice on how to correct this problem?

I notice that the anchor point is exactly halfway up the tower, and it would appear that this creates a resonance between the two sections of the tower, like a violin string stretched over a bridge. I think the vibration could be eliminated by adding another connection to the house, say about 8' from the ground and/or by attaching a guy wire to the top of the tower. A little experimenting should give you the best location for these connections.

DUCT NOISE

The warm air ducts in our heating system make a lot of noise—whistling and blowing whenever the fan is on. Can we remedy this by wrapping the ducts in insulation to deaden the sound?

You would have to put the sound insulation

material *inside* the ducts to absorb the noise, and that is not practical in a home heating system. The trouble is almost certainly caused by undersized ductwork and poor layout, and the best solution is to have a new duct system installed.

It may help, however, to reduce the speed of the fan. You can do this by removing the fan belt and adjusting the pulley on the fan. You will find a screw inside that loosens one side of the pulley, allowing you to open it slightly so that the fan belt will fit deeper in the V.

VIBRATING WATER PIPES

Can you tell me how to stop my water pipes from vibrating and hammering when I use my garden hose. The noise is strongest when I turn the hose partly on, and it goes away when the water is turned on full.

It sounds as if you have a loose washer in the hose faucet. Try putting in a new one.

ODORS

SMELL FROM BASEMENT FLOOR DRAIN

We are having trouble with the smell of sewer gas coming from our basement floor drain. Our house is still under its one-year warranty, and if there's something wrong I'd like to get the builder to fix it, but he says there's nothing he can do.

There should be a trap in the drain line under the floor, a U-shaped piece of pipe that remains filled with water and prevents sewer gases from getting back into the house. Now, there are three possibilities: 1) Your drain has never been used, and so the trap contains no water to block the gas. Answer—Pour some water down the drain. (Plumbing codes generally call for a special fitting that runs a little water into the floor drain every time the laundry tub is used.) 2) The trap may be cracked, allowing the water to leak out. An-

swer—Dig up the floor and replace the faulty trap. 3) The builder may have neglected to put a trap in this drain line. Answer—Dig up the floor and put one in.

My guess is that the answer is No. 1.

PLUMBING PROBLEM

We bought an old house in the country and have been having a lot of work done on it. One of the biggest jobs was having plumbing installed and a septic system put in. There is a full bathroom upstairs and half bathroom on the main floor. Our problem is an objectionable odor from the upstairs bathroom. I have noticed that there is no breather pipe on our roof, as other houses have. Could this be the cause of the trouble?

Very likely it is. The plumbing code requires that all toilets and other drain fixtures be connected to a vent pipe extending above the roof. Every fixture has a U-shaped trap in the drain line, and this retains enough water to block the pipe and stop sewer gases from entering the house. The vent pipe prevents the traps from being siphoned dry when the fixtures are drained, which is probably what's happening in your case.

DOG SMELLS

For several years our pet dog spent the winter months in the garage, and there is now a strong odor from the concrete floor, particularly during damp summer weather. Is there any way we can get rid of the smell?

Wash the concrete with a solution of lye, one 9½-ounce can to a pail of water, but use a plastic or enamel pail, not an aluminum one. Just brush it on with a stiff brush, then rinse the floor thoroughly. Be careful not to get the solution on your skin, clothes, or any painted surface. If you do, wash it off quickly.

BAD ODOR IN FRIDGE

When we were away on a trip our refrigerator failed and food went bad in it. Now I can't get rid of the smell. Do you have any suggestions?

There are a couple of things you can try, but I don't offer much hope. Powerful smells like this penetrate into places where you can't get at them, and they outlast anything you can use to mask them.

First, of course, wash the fridge out thoroughly with a solution of baking powder

Odors

and water. Ammonia can also be used. Put things back and then place an open bowl of granulated garden charcoal (not barbecue charcoal) in the fridge. Charcoal has an amazing ability to absorb stray molecules, including those that cause food odors. This ability can be repeatedly restored by heating the charcoal for half an hour or so in an oven at 450°.

Leaving a box of baking soda in the fridge is also said to remove odors, but I have more faith in charcoal.

Other people claim they have got rid of the odor by leaving a can of paint open in the fridge for a few days, placing a dish of ground coffee on the shelf, or putting a few tablespoons of vanilla extract in a saucer.

CISTERN WATER

We have a rainwater cistern that holds approximately 1,850 gallons of water. Sometimes it seems to have a bad smell, and I have been told I can put bleach in the water to stop it. Is this safe, and how much should I use?

It is perfectly safe to use a household bleach as a disinfectant and deodorizer in water. This is essentially what is done to municipal water supplies. For 1,850 gallons, you can safely add 24 ounces of bleach to start, then more if this is not enough. You really need a testing kit, however, to determine when you have reached the correct level. Such kits are sold by swimming pool supply stores.

Before you use the bleach, however, try just lifting the cover off the cistern for a few days. This often does the job.

MOTHBALL ODOR IN CEDAR CHEST

I recently purchased a very old but very good cedar chest. I intended to refinish it as the outside had been badly scratched. My problem is that the previous owner used mothballs in the chest and I would like to know how to get rid of the smell.

You will get rid of much of the smell, I think, when you remove the old finish and sand the wood. Putting the chest out in the sun for a few hours will also help. Finally, two coats of satin urethane varnish should complete the process.

DAMP COTTAGE

Our summer cottage sits on concrete posts about three feet off the ground. Last spring I covered the front and two sides with plywood, leaving the back open for ventilation. We have since noticed a damp, musty smell in parts of the cottage. Is this because we closed it in?

I would think so. Closing the crawlspace in on three sides doesn't really provide very much ventilation. It would be a lot better to have large, screened vents on at least two opposite sides. It will also help if you cover the ground underneath the cottage with polyethylene sheet held down by stones or a few shovelfuls of gravel.

MUSTY SMELL FROM BATHROOM SINK

We are having a problem with a very strong musty odor coming from the overflow of our bathroom sink. We have tried various disinfectants with very little effect. A wire probe doesn't reveal any sign of blockage. Can you tell us how we can cure this problem?

Anything you pour into the overflow runs out into the drain so quickly that it doesn't have time to do much good. Nor will it always reach the problem area. In most sinks the overflow openings in the outlet are above the metal strainer, where you can plug them with pieces of cloth. If you can do this, pour a couple of tablespoons of lye into the overflow and add water until it just about reaches the top. Leave it there for about half an hour, then remove the cloth plugs from the strainer outlet to let it pour out. Pour more water into the overflow to flush it out. This should get rid of the smell. If not, repeat with a stronger lye solution.

FURNACE OIL SMELL

I have a big, old-fashioned coal furnace (hot water) that has been converted to oil. Every time the furnace starts up there is a momentary smell of oil in the house. I called a serviceman and he changed a strainer of some kind, I think it was, but the smell continues. Do you have any suggestions?

There are a number of possible causes, but if the oil smell only appears at the time the furnace starts up, then it is most likely due to delayed ignition. In other words, the oil sprays into the combustion chamber a fraction of a second before the spark ignites it with a small explosion that blows oil fumes out the vents in the front of the furnace.

An incorrect draft setting, improperly placed burner electrodes and a build-up of soot in the heat exchanger can all contribute to the trouble. Your serviceman should be able to correct it.

PERFUME SMELL

A perfumed candle was placed in our dining room hutch, which is made of pecan wood. Now we can't get the perfume smell out of it. Do you have any suggestions?

There is no sure way to get rid of odors, but one trick that may work is to leave an open bowl of charcoal inside the hutch for a few weeks. Use the pea-sized granulated charcoal that is sold at nurseries and garden supply stores for use in potting soil, not the charcoal briquettes used in barbecues.

WELL WATER SMELLS BAD

We have a country home where the water supply comes from a well. It used to be all right, but recently it has developed a bad smell, like rotten eggs. We had it tested and they said it's perfectly safe to drink, but the odor is very unpleasant. Is there something we can put in the well to eliminate the smell?

This is caused by the presence of sulphur in the water, in the form of sulphates. These are broken down by bacterial action and release hydrogen sulphide, the rotten egg gas. It is not harmful but it can corrode pipes, tarnish silverware, and spoil the taste of food.

You can buy a water conditioner that removes the sulphur by treating the water with chlorine bleach, then filtering out the precipitated sulphur and the chlorine to give you pure, odor-free water. Check the Yellow Pages under Water Treatment Equipment.

WOOD IN OIL TANK

In trying to measure the amount of fuel oil we had on hand, I dropped a stick about four feet long into the underground tank. My husband says this will deteriorate and plug the fuel line to the furnace. If so, what can I do about it?

I don't think a piece of wood in the oil tank is going to cause any trouble. As a matter of fact the oil will help to preserve the wood, which will probably last a lot longer than the steel tank.

PAINT

ALLIGATORED PAINT

After 25 years of repainting the interior of our house without any problems, we are now experiencing a serious case of "alligatoring" on the walls. The previous paint, a different color, shows through the cracks and makes the deteriorated finish look even worse. Can you tell me what caused this and how I can fix it? My letter to the paint manufacturer wasn't even answered.

Alligatoring is caused by the failure of the top coat to bond properly to the paint underneath, perhaps because this was greasy, too shiny, contained too much thinner, or was incompatible with the type of paint being applied over it. There is always the possibility, of course, that the last paint was defective, but this is very unlikely.

Whatever the cause, the remedy is a lot of work. The alligatored paint will have to be removed by sanding or scraping before the wall can be repainted. A chemical paint remover could be used, but this is an expensive way to do it and the fumes can be hazardous in a confined area.

COVERING ASPHALT PAINT

The concrete foundation walls of our house were painted with an asphalt waterproofing compound on the outside. Unfortunately, this extends above the ground level and looks very unsightly. I've been told it will just bleed through paint. What can I do to cover it?

It won't bleed through aluminum paint. Apply one or two coats of this as a sealer, then cover with an exterior latex paint. This can be applied over the rest of the concrete as well.

RESTORING OLD PAINT BRUSHES

I have some old paint brushes that were not cleaned properly and are now as solid as a board. Good brushes are expensive today; is there some way I can restore these?

Just boil the paint brushes in vinegar for about 15 minutes to soften the paint, then remove it with a metal comb or a wire brush.

EXTERIOR PAINT CHALKING

The hardboard siding on our house needs to be painted. The original paint is chalky and some of it has come off. Do I need a primer? What kind of paint is best?

Hardboard siding is made of compressed wood fibre and is painted like any other wood product. Scrape off any loose paint, then wash the chalk dust off with a solution of ¼ cup of trisodium phosphate (TSP) to a gallon of water. Allow to dry, then use any exterior house paint. Some call for a primer, others are self-priming, but two coats will probably be needed over the bare spots, anyway.

CONCRETE FLOOR PAINT

I painted our basement floor about a year ago with a well known brand of concrete floor paint. Now it has started to bubble and lift off in many spots, apparently caused by a white powder that is attacking the paint. I cleaned the floor thoroughly before painting, but now I've been told that I should have etched it with acid first. What should I do now?

Although etching might have helped, the problem is primarily caused by moisture that is coming up through the slab. This is what lifts the paint off. The white powder (efflorescence) is simply salts that have been dissolved out of the concrete and left on the surface when the water evaporates.

Before you can apply any type of floor finish—paint, tile, wood, or carpet—you will have to do something about the lack of drainage around your foundation footings.

This may be due to a blockage in the drain tile system, which can be expensive to repair, or something as simple as a broken downspout that directs water down the outside of the wall instead of away from it. If you can't find the source of the trouble yourself, call in a drainage contractor to have a look at it and give you a quote on repairs. Better still, get quotes from three companies.

When the floor is dry, use a wire brush to remove any loose paint, or apply a strong solution of lye (one 9-ounce can to a quart of water) to get it all off. Wash off, then etch with a solution of muriatic acid, following the directions on the label. (Usually it's 1 part to 10 parts water, but some brands may already be partly diluted.) Then repaint the floor.

CRACKING PAINT

I am having trouble with the paint on my living room walls cracking in a spiderweb pattern. This happened before, so I filled the cracks and sanded them down before repainting, but the cracks appeared again after about six months. The ceiling has no cracks. Can you tell me what's causing this?

This is usually caused by painting over a gloss paint without sanding it first. If you examine one of the cracks closely you may be able to see a shiny paint at the bottom of it. Try filling the cracks with a vinyl-based spackling compound instead of one of the plaster compounds.

MOLD ON BATHROOM PAINT

I used a flat latex paint in my bathroom, and now it is spotted with mildew and peeling in places. I have been told that I'll have to scrape it all off and use an oil-based paint. Isn't there something I can use to kill the mildew and then just repaint?

Yes, there is, but you'll have to remove all the loose paint first. Then wash the walls down with a strong solution of chlorine laundry bleach, say 1 part bleach to 4 parts water. When dry, paint with a semi-gloss enamel.

Your trouble is mainly due to extreme dampness in the bathroom, however, and it would be advisable to install a vent fan to reduce the condensation on the walls and ceiling.

ALKYD AND OIL-BASED PAINTS

I was told to use an oil-based paint, but the salesman in the paint store tried to sell me an alkyd paint instead. What is the difference?

The term "oil-based" is misleading, because linseed oil and other drying oils that once were the basis of all paints have now been almost completely replaced by synthetic alkyd resins, which are not oils at all. But they do resemble oil-based paints in that they must be thinned or cleaned up with petroleum solvents (mineral spirits) in contrast to the latex paints, which are thinned with water, of course. It would be more accurate to describe the two main types of paint as "water-thinned" and "solvent-thinned" rather than "latex" and "oil-based."

OIL-BASED PAINT ON CONCRETE

I have used an oil-based paint on the interior walls of my house. Can I use this on the concrete walls in the basement, too?

No. The alkalis in concrete break down the oils into a form of soap that is water-soluble and doesn't make a very good paint. You should use an exterior latex paint or a paint that has been formulated especially for use on concrete. There are several types, both water-based and solvent-based, but all do a good job if they are properly applied. Read the directions carefully.

PAINTING RADIATORS

We have just bought a house with hot water heating. The cast iron radiators have several coats of paint on them now, and need to be done again, but we were told that the layers of paint will keep the heat from getting out. Paint remover will take it off but leaves a rough surface, and some places are hard to reach. Is it really necessary to take off all the old paint? And, if so, how should it be done?

Paint remover is the only practical way to take off the coats of paint, and that isn't an easy job, as you've discovered. I don't think the paint layers have any significant effect on the temperature of the radiators, however, and that's what determines how much heat you get out of them.

PAINT PEELING FROM MASONRY

I have painted the outside of my concrete block foundation wall twice with a well-known brand of exterior masonry paint (latex), but it keeps peeling. Can you tell me what would be causing this? The basement is unfinished.

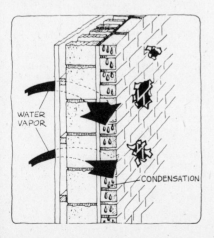

WATER VAPOR

CONDENSATION

This is probably due to moisture vapor passing through the block wall due to the lack of a vapor barrier on the inside wall, and perhaps to excess humidity in the house. If you are also troubled with dripping windows during cold weather, this is almost certainly the cause. The answer is to increase the ventilation of the house to replace the humid household air with relatively dry outside air.

It will also help if you finish the basement with 2 × 4 frame walls, 3½" batts, polyethylene vapor barrier and panelling.

PEELING SOFFITS

We have a wide overhang around our house and the paint keeps peeling off the soffit underneath it. We have to repaint it every year. Can you tell me what causes this and what we can do about it, if anything?

There are two possible causes. One is that ice dams form in the eavestrough during winter, forcing water to back up under the shingles and run down into the soffit. This may indicate that you don't have enough insulation in your ceiling. Another remedy is to put electric heating cables along the edge of the roof.

The second possible cause of paint failure in this situation is heavy chalking of the paint film. All exterior paints chalk or powder away; this helps to keep them clean and prevents an excessive build-up of paint. But the paint under soffits and porch roofs never gets washed off by the rain, so the new coat of paint is being applied on top of this powdery surface. Latex paint is particularly susceptible to failure under these conditions.

The remedy is to scrub the paint with a solution of one tablespoon of trisodium phosphate (TSP, any paint or hardware store) to a quart of water before repainting.

BLEEDING PAINT

Our 10-year-old house has always been painted white until last year, when we changed it to dark blue. Now I have noticed that pitch is bleeding through the painted siding in a number of spots. Why would this happen?

The change to a darker paint has increased the temperature of the siding, and this has caused pitch pockets in the wood to melt and bleed through the paint. Remove the paint from these patches, then soak the wood with petroleum solvent (mineral spirits) to dissolve the pitch. After this has dried, apply two coats of shellac and repaint.

167

Paint Removing

ROUGH PAINT

We painted our new plaster walls with interior latex paint, and when it dried it had a rough surface just like sandpaper. I can't even clean it with a cloth. We used a semi-gloss alkyd paint in the kitchen, and the surface is fine.

This trouble is probably due to the use of paint that had been allowed to freeze at some time or other. This causes the emulsion to break down and the pigment to form tiny granules. These aren't apparent when you mix the paint and brush it on, but they produce a rough, sandpaper finish when the paint dries.

Sometimes this will happen with old latex paint, too. Manufacturers don't recommend using a latex paint that is more than three years old, although most paints will last much longer than that if they're properly stored.

If you have any of the paint left, take it back to the store and ask for a replacement or a refund.

You'll have to sandpaper the walls smooth and remove all the paint dust with a damp cloth before you repaint.

WHITEWASH

I remember when whitewash used to be considered a good, cheap paint for concrete and wood, but you never hear of it anymore. Can you tell me how to make it?

Although it isn't as durable as modern paints, whitewash is still a very practical paint to use on fences, curbs, trellises, greenhouse roofs, tree trunks, and similar outdoor projects. If you add glue and coloring to whitewash, it becomes calcimine, once a popular pastel paint for interior walls and ceilings. Best of all you can make whitewash for about $1 a gallon!

The basic ingredient is lime paste—hydrated lime or calcium hydroxide—which turns to calcium carbonate, or chalk, on exposure to air.

To make one gallon of lime paste, soak 8 pounds of hydrated "spray lime" in 3 quarts of water. Hydrated lime is sold by some garden supply stores and *all* farm supply dealers. But be sure to get hydrated lime, and not the crushed limestone used for dressing lawns, etc. You can't make whitewash out of this.

For a general purpose outdoor whitewash, dissolve 2 pounds of salt in 2½ gallons (10 quarts), of water and add this to 1 gallon of lime paste. Stir and add water as required to make a thin paint.

An interior whitewash, or calcimine, can be made by dissolving half a pound of animal glue in 1 quart of water, and stirring this into 1 gallon of lime paste. Add water as required.

The calcimine can be tinted with universal paint pigments.

STAIN BLEEDING THROUGH PAINT

When we bought our house two years ago it was freshly painted. Apparently the white paint had been applied over a dark-stained cedar siding, and now this stain is bleeding through. How can we prevent it from coming through the next coat of paint?

A coat of aluminum paint will seal the stain. If only a few spots are bleeding, it might only be necessary to seal these areas, but it would probably be safer to cover all of the siding with aluminum paint. The siding can then be finished with any exterior paint, although an oil-based alkyd paint is recommended.

PAINT REMOVING

DISSOLVING FURNITURE

I was using paint remover to take the finish off a small chest that I wanted to refinish, and it dissolved some of the decorative wood molding. Is there something wrong with the paint remover I used?

No, there's something wrong with the wood. A lot of the decorative carving and fancy moldings on today's furniture isn't wood at all, but plastic, and it's realistic enough to fool anyone but a wood worm. Paint removers will dissolve many of these plastics, and there is usually a warning about this on the label. I know of no practical way to remove the finish from such furniture without damaging these plastic parts, although you might manage it with very careful hand sanding. You can't remove the finish from the plastic parts, however.

RESTORING A PAINTED BALCONY

I live in a high-rise apartment, and I painted the floor of my balcony green. Now I am leaving and the management tells me I must restore the balcony to its original condition. How can I do this?

I include this letter in my column not because I have an answer, but as a warning to other apartment residents who may be thinking of doing the same thing.

There are only two things that will remove paint from concrete—commercial paint remover, or a concentrated solution of lye. And I don't recommend that either of these be used on a high-rise balcony where they would almost certainly drip on the balconies below.

My advice is to leave the paint there and pay whatever penalty is assessed. And be wiser next time.

REMOVING PAINT FROM BRICK FIREPLACE

My niece recently purchased an older house that has a beautiful brick fireplace in the sitting room. Unfortunately, the previous owners had painted the brick, and my niece would like to know how to restore the original brick surface. We don't know what kind of paint it is.

Tell her to apply paint remover, then use a stiff brush to take off the softened paint. She will have to be very careful, however, to keep the paint remover from being spattered on the floor or other finished surfaces. This system doesn't always work too well because the paint tends to stay in the textured surface of the brick, but I don't know of any other way to do it.

PAINT ON CLOTHING

Could you please tell me if there is anything I can use to get paint out of clothes after it has dried?

Only paint remover will soften paint once it has hardened. This can be safely used on pure wool or cotton, but not on some of the synthetics. If in doubt, test it on some inconspicuous part of the garment first.

REMOVING PAINT FROM CONCRETE

A few months ago we spilled some navy blue oil-based house paint on our cement sidewalk. Is there any way we can get this off?

A strong lye solution will remove it. Dissolve one 9½-ounce can in a quart of water (but not in an aluminum container) and brush it on with a string mop. Brush and hose off the softened paint. Be careful to keep the solution off skin, clothes, and anything else you value.

REMOVING PAINT FROM VARNISH

The solid mahogany door frames, baseboards and trim in my apartment were first varnished, then covered with several coats of paint. Is there anything I can use to remove just the paint, and leave the varnished wood?

No. You'll have to strip off all the finishes down to the bare wood with paint remover (it'll probably take more than one application), then sand lightly and apply fresh varnish.

PAINT ON VINYL TILES

When repainting my kitchen cupboards I spilled some on the vinyl-asbestos tile floor. Now it has hardened. How can I remove it without damaging the floor?

Paint remover can be used safely, but try to keep it on the painted spots. Remove the softened paint with a piece of wood as a scraper to avoid scratching the tiles. Rub with a piece of burlap, rinse well and wax when dry.

REFINISHING LACQUERED CUPBOARDS

Our kitchen cupboards are peeling and I want to refinish them. I'm told that they are finished with two coats of lacquer. How do I get these off?

You could dissolve them with lacquer thinner, but this is very inflammable and you'd be better advised to use one of the many noninflammable wash-off paint removers. Refinish with two coats of satin urethane varnish.

REMOVING WHITEWASH

I'd like to know how to get whitewash off bricks and wood beams inside a building I'm renovating.

Whitewash is made of slaked or hydrated lime, and it usually washes off very easily. If it's mixed with sizing (when it becomes "calcimine") it may be a little more difficult to remove. But a dilute solution of muriatic acid, about one part to 20 parts water, should dissolve the lime.

REMOVING PAINT WITH LYE

I have just bought an old table that is covered with many coats of paint, but I suspect there may be some nice wood underneath. Someone told me that lye would be a good paint remover to use on something like this. Can you tell me how to mix this?

In an 8-ounce glass jar, dissolve 2 heaping tablespoons of lye in 4 ounces of cold water. In another container stir 1 level tablespoon of cornstarch in half a cup of cold water, then add this to the lye solution while stirring. It will thicken to a paste-like consistency almost immediately.

Take the table outside and brush this paste on the paint. Wear rubber gloves and be careful to keep the lye solution off of everything but the paint. Use a putty knife to scrape off the softened paint. More than one application may be necessary to remove several coats of paint, but as soon as you get down to the wood, wash the lye solution off quickly to keep it from softening the surface.

This work should only be done outdoors or in a basement with an unfinished concrete floor and good drainage.

Unused lye solution can be stored in a covered jar.

REMOVING TEXTURED PAINT

The previous owners of our house used a rough-textured paint on the living room walls. We don't like it and want to have smooth, painted walls again. How can we remove the textured paint?

These textured paints can be very attractive in some situations, but they have one serious weakness—and you've just found it. Once they're applied, you're stuck with them. If your walls are only slightly textured, you may be able to sand them down somewhat, but it's unlikely that you will get them level enough for a good, smooth paint job. If they are deeply textured, all you can do is cover them with gypsumboard panelling applied over horizontal strapping. Tape, fill and sand the joints to get a smooth, new wall surface suitable for painting or papering.

TEXTURED PAINT OVER GYPSUMBOARD

Our house is being built with drywall panelling, and to save money we are thinking of finishing the walls and ceilings ourselves with a rough-textured paint. Do the gypsumboard

walls have to be treated with something first?

Yes. They should be given a coat of latex primer before the textured paint is applied. But this is a relatively expensive way to finish the walls, because textured paints go on much thicker than regular paints and therefore cover a smaller area. Some have a coverage of as little as 60 square feet per gallon, compared with 500 feet or more for most interior latex paints. It would be more economical, and perhaps more attractive, to use textured paint on the ceiling and a standard flat latex paint on the walls.

TEXTURED PAINT OVER WALLPAPER

We are planning to put interior stucco on our living room walls, and would appreciate some advice on its application. The walls are drywall gypsumboard with two or three layers of wallpaper on top. Can the stucco be applied directly to this, or is some special treatment required?

Because these textured, plaster-like finishes go on very thick and contain a lot of moisture, there's a good chance that they will soften the adhesive backing of one or more layers of the wallpaper. An alkyd primer can be used successfully in some cases, but I really don't think it's worth the risk, myself. You should remove the wallpaper, and all the adhesive, before applying this type of finish. Follow the manufacturer's instructions regarding the treatment of the gypsumboard.

PAINTING

REPAINTING ALUMINUM SIDING

The embossed aluminum siding on my house is 14 years old and the color is fading. It has also peeled in a few places. I'd like to repaint it a different color. What kind of paint should I use and what preparation is required?

Special paints are available, but any exterior house paint can be used. The new finish won't last as long as the original, factory-applied coating, however.

As with any surface to be painted, make sure the aluminum siding is clean, dry, and free of loose material. Use a wire brush to remove any loose paint, and sand the edges smooth. Spot prime any areas where the bare metal is exposed. If these are just small spots, use the paint that you are going to apply. If there are any large areas of bare metal, however, these should be treated with a phosphate "wash primer" recommended for aluminum. A boat supply dealer may be the best source for this.

PAINTING ALUMINUM WINDOWS

I want to paint my aluminum storm windows to match the aluminum siding. What is the proper way to paint aluminum?

Aluminum requires special treatment before it can be painted. At one time it used to be washed with a 10 per cent solution of phosphoric acid, but today there are a number of special aluminum primers that do a better job and are easier to use. Most of them consist of zinc chromate in a varnish base, and they are widely used for painting aluminum boats, among other things, so the best place to find them is in the paint department of a marine supply store.

Wash thoroughly to remove grease and dirt before applying. A steel wool soap pad does a good job. Apply primer, let dry, then apply the finish coat of regular paint.

PAINTING ASBESTOS SIDING

The outside of our house is covered with asbestos siding in a shade of pink. Some of the pieces of siding that were broken have been replaced with new pieces that don't quite match. Instead of replacing it all, I would like to paint it, but understand that a special kind of paint must be used. Can you tell me what it is?

Asbestos-cement siding can be painted with any exterior latex paint.

PAINTING ASBESTOS SHINGLES

About 20 years ago my mother's home was re-roofed with white asbestos shingles. They're looking rather grey and dingy now, and my mother is thinking of having them painted. Is this practical? What kind of paint should be used? Or is there some other way to clean up the roof?

Asbestos shingles can be painted with any exterior latex house paint, but I don't think it's a very wise thing to do. No paint will last forever, and the roof will almost certainly have to be repainted every two or three years.

I think it would be much better to have the roof scrubbed down with a solution of ¼-cup of trisodium phosphate (TSP, at any paint or hardware store) to a gallon of water. Don't let this solution drip down onto painted surfaces below, or it will leave clean streaks and you'll end up by having to wash the entire house. Hose the roof off thoroughly after it has been cleaned.

REPAINTING A BASEMENT FLOOR

The previous owners of our house seem to have painted the basement floor with ordinary enamel, which is badly worn in spots but otherwise in good condition. We would like to repaint it. What should we use?

If the old paint shows no sign of peeling or flaking, moisture is obviously no problem, so you can use any floor paint you like. I suggest that you avoid red, however. My mail indicates that a lot of people have trouble with red paint coming off on shoes and marking up carpets and floor tiles throughout the house.

BLACK WOOD STAIN

I've been unable to find a really black wood stain. They all turn grey when they dry. What should I use?

A stain, by its very nature, is somewhat transparent. You can get transparent colors, but have you ever seen transparent black? The only thing that will give you a solid jet-black color is an opaque black paint.

PAINTING A COTTAGE

We have recently purchased a cottage that appears to have two coats of yellow paint on the outside. We would like to change this to a red stain. Is it necessary to remove the yellow

171

paint, or can we seal it with something and then use a stain?

You can't use a stain on top of paint. If you want to use a stain, you'll have to soften the paint with a propane torch or electric paint remover and then scrape it off with a putty knife. Sand off the scorch marks and any remaining paint, *then* apply the stain.

It would be a lot easier to use red paint or one of the so-called "opaque" stains, but this will have to be re-done every couple of years.

PAINTING—CONCRETE DRIVEWAY

We have a concrete driveway that was painted with latex house paint. This is chipping and peeling in places. How can I take off this paint, and what is the proper kind of paint to use?

You can remove the paint with a strong solution of lye—one 9½-ounce can to a quart of water. Apply it with a string mop, preferably on a hot day. Scrub the softened paint off, then wash the concrete down with a solution of one part muriatic acid to ten parts water. Both the lye and the acid should be used with caution. Wear rubber gloves and keep the solutions off clothes, metal, plants and anything else you value.

There is no paint that will last very long on a concrete driveway.

CONCRETE FLOOR PAINT

We are having trouble with our basement floor. It had been painted some years ago, but the paint was badly worn and we refinished it with two coats of a well-known brand of plastic floor paint. After about three weeks the new paint developed bubbles about the size of a quarter. When these broke they left a white powder.

An expert from the paint store says that moisture was the cause of the trouble, but the floor always seemed perfectly dry and we never had this problem with the original paint.

In spite of the fact that the floor didn't appear to be damp, there are two facts that indicate that this is the cause of the trouble . . . the fact that the paint came up in bubbles, and that these contained a white powder. The powder can only be efflorescence, a deposit of salts leached out of the concrete by moisture, and left on the surface when the water evaporates.

Perhaps the dampness only developed in the last year or two, and since the paint was badly worn, the moisture simply evaporated and you didn't notice it. If you had put down a rubber mat for a few days before you painted, you might have seen the evidence of dampness when you lifted it.

Some paints will adhere to a slightly damp concrete better than others, but there are none that can hold back a serious moisture problem caused by faulty or inadequate drainage around the outside of your foundation. This must be checked and repaired before you paint the floor again.

PAINTING CONCRETE STEPS

How can I stop the paint lifting and peeling from my concrete porch and steps? Last summer I removed as much loose paint as I could before repainting with a well-known brand of concrete paint. Now it is flaking and peeling again. Perhaps it would be better just to get rid of the paint entirely. How can this be done?

A good concrete paint, properly applied, should last longer than that, but none of them survive very long outdoors. The remaining paint can be removed with a strong solution of lye, one 9½-ounce can to a quart of water. (Don't mix this in an aluminum pan, and be careful to keep the caustic solution off your skin and clothes and everything else but the concrete.) Apply with an old brush or a string mop.

Scrub the softened paint off with a stiff brush on a long handle, then hose it away. If you want to repaint, etch the surface of the concrete first with a solution of 1 part muriatic acid (any hardware store) to 10 parts water. (Be careful with this solution, too.)

PAINTING CONCRETE FLOORS

I am going to paint the concrete floors in my basement and garage. Would it keep the paint from peeling if I went over them first with boiled linseed oil and paint thinner?

I wouldn't recommend using linseed oil as a primer on your concrete floors. There are several good concrete floor paints on the market, and the best preparation for any of them is to clean and etch the concrete with a solution of 1 part muriatic acid (any hardware store) to 10 parts water. Just brush this on, then rinse it off when it stops foaming. Wear rubber gloves and keep the solution off everything but the floor. But if it does splatter on something, including yourself, just wipe it off quickly with a wet cloth.

CORK WALLS

One of the concrete walls in our basement has been covered with ½"-thick cork panels in a dark brown color. We want to finish the room in a lighter color. Can we just paint the cork? And will this give us enough insulation?

The open-textured surface of the cork will leave voids in the paint, which may not look very attractive. The cork is not providing much insulation in any case—only about R2. R12 is recommended today. I suggest that you build a 2 × 4 frame wall in front of the foundation wall, then use 3½", R12, friction-fit batts, plus polyethylene vapor barrier and the panelling of your choice.

PAINTING AN APPLIANCE

I have a white dishwasher and would like to paint it Avocado Green to match my fridge and stove. What kind of paint should I use?

Any good enamel can be used, brush or spray. There are several brands of spray-on appliance enamels. The color range is limited, but all brands contain the currently popular Avocado Green. It's not likely that you'll find an exact match for your other appliances, however. Rub the present enamel down with fine sandpaper or steel wool to provide a "tooth" for the new coat.

PAINTING A DOOR

Our front door has been stained and varnished. I would like to paint it white. Do I have to take off the varnish first? And what kind of paint should I use?

There's no need to remove the varnish. Just rub it down with medium grade sandpaper or #00 steel wool to remove the gloss and provide a "tooth" for the paint. Any good exterior enamel can be used.

PAINTING FORMICA

Can I paint my plastic countertop?

It's possible, but not advisable. The paint won't last too long. The hard, glossy finish of plastic laminate should be roughened with fine garnet paper or steel wool to provide a "tooth" for the paint. Then use a primer coat and two finishing coats of a good alkyd enamel.

PAINTING GALVANIZED METAL

I am having trouble getting paint to stick to my galvanized metal eavestroughs. I scrape off the old paint every year, wash the surface with vinegar, apply a metal primer and a good quality exterior trim paint. By next spring it's hanging in shreds again. Can you tell me what I'm doing wrong?

In spite of what a lot of old-time painters say, vinegar does not improve the adhesion of paint on galvanized metal. The best cleaner to use is toluene or lacquer thinner, but you can also use petroleum solvent (mineral spirits).

And I would guess that you're using the wrong kind of primer, too. You should use a primer labelled as being made specifically for galvanized metal. Ordinary metal primers are not suitable. There are a number of brands on the market, but you may have to shop around to find a paint store that carries one.

FILLING HAIRLINE CRACKS

The paint on my front door has developed a lot of hairline cracks, and I've been told I'll have to strip off all the paint in order to refinish it. Is this true?

If it's an old door that has been painted several times, that would be the best way to refinish it. If not, the cracks can be filled with spackling compound or one of the premixed crack fillers. You can also use ordinary putty mixed with a little of the oil-based paint you are going to use on the door, but this must be allowed to set for 24 hours before being painted. The other materials are ready for painting inside of an hour. Sand the door lightly before painting to provide a "tooth" for the next coat.

Painting

PAINTING HARDBOARD TILE

Our bathroom walls are finished with hardboard imitation tile. We would like to paint this another color. Is there any special material we should use?

Any enamel can be used, but the surface should first be roughened with fine sandpaper to remove the shiny finish and provide a "tooth" for the paint. It's not going to be so easy to paint on the imitation grout lines, however. If you haven't got a very steady hand, you'll have to use a lining tool or buy several rolls of white vinyl tape used for stripping automobiles.

PAINTING HOT CONCRETE

Last summer I painted a concrete wall and a month or so later the paint turned to powder and just dusted off. I used an exterior latex paint that was supposed to be right for concrete. And I painted the wall on a hot, sunny day, so moisture can't be the problem. I think I got a bad batch of paint. What do you think?

I think you should have cooled the wall down with a hose before you painted it or waited for a cloudy day. When concrete is exposed to the direct sun for a few hours, it gets so hot that a water-based paint will evaporate before it has time to form a film. Wetting the surface will cool it and also make the paint easier to apply.

PAINTING A KITCHEN FLOOR

The linoleum on my kitchen floor is getting worn in places and I was thinking of just taking it off and painting the floor with a high gloss floor enamel. What can I use to remove the linoleum adhesive from the floor before I paint it? Do you think a painted floor will last?

I don't think that paint is a very good surface for a floor that must take as much traffic as this one will. If the linoleum is firmly attached, I would lay a sheet vinyl floor on top of it, attached according to the manufacturer's instructions. The linoleum should be sanded if adhesive is to be applied.

If the linoleum is not firmly attached, then it would be best to remove it, sand the floor, and lay new sheet or tile flooring.

PAINTING MAHOGANY

Our kitchen cabinets and the window trim throughout the house are mahogany with a natural finish. We would like to paint them, but have been told that the uneven wood grain will not take paint. What do you suggest we do?

If the surface of the mahogany shows the open grain of the wood, you will have to apply a filler, available at any paint store. Simply brush it on in the direction of the grain, allow it to set for about half an hour, then wipe it off across the grain with a rough cloth, such as burlap. Let the filler dry for 24 hours, sand lightly, then paint.

But if the mahogany has a smooth varnish finish that does not show the texture of the grain, this need only be rubbed down with #00 steel wool to provide a "tooth" for the paint.

PAINTING MASONRY

The chimney outside our house was painted white several years ago, and now it's peeling badly. What is the proper way to repaint this, and what kind of paint should I use on the stucco of the house?

Use a wire brush to remove the loose paint from the chimney, then apply any exterior latex paint. This is the kind of paint to use on stucco, too.

PAINTING METAL CUPBOARDS

The metal cupboards over the stove in our kitchen are pebbled and discolored and have been badly touched-up with porcelain paint. How can we refinish them?

Rub them down with fine sandpaper to take off any loose paint and to roughen the surface to provide a "tooth" for a new finish. Then simply paint with any good enamel. If this is done carefully, and two coats applied if needed, it should look as good as new. But it won't be as durable as the original baked-on finish.

PAINTING OIL SPOTS

My 3-year-old son got his hands on an oil can and squirted it all over the playroom walls. I've tried to clean it off but I'm afraid to repaint in case the oil seeps through. Is there anything I can do?

The new paint wouldn't adhere to the oily surface, anyway. Wash the oil spots several times with Varsol or other petroleum solvent. When dry, seal the spots with a coat of shellac before painting.

OIL PAINT OVER LATEX

The outside of our house is painted with a latex paint, but we want to re-paint it with an oil-based paint. Is there a special primer that we should use?

No special primer is required, but most experts don't recommend the application of one kind of paint on top of another. This is believed to be one of the causes of paint peeling. As in most fields, however, there is a broad difference of opinion on this matter between the experts, so the decision is really up to you.

Whatever kind of paint you decide to use, I strongly recommend that you first scrub the walls down with a long-handled brush and a solution of half a cup of trisodium phosphate (TSP, available at any hardware store) to a bucket of water. Rinse off with a hose and let dry.

PAINTING OVER GLOSS ENAMEL

We painted the inside of our house with latex, and are very pleased with the results everywhere but in the kitchen, where it was applied over a high gloss enamel. It has chipped and flaked in many places where it has been rubbed or bumped. As we are planning on painting again, we would appreciate any suggestions you might have on how to prepare the kitchen walls and what kind of paint we should use this time.

A high gloss paint should always be roughened with fine sandpaper to remove the shine and provide a "tooth" for the next coat—regardless of what kind of paint you're using. The trouble now is that you don't have a firm film to paint on, since the present latex paint is not holding very well to the gloss enamel. No matter how well the next coat goes on, the latex undercoat may still chip off if it is hit.

The proper thing to do is sand off all the latex paint down to the enamel, then apply any gloss or semi-gloss paint you want—oil, alkyd, or latex. That's a lot of work, but anything less will be a gamble.

PAINTING OVER KNOTS

I put several coats of paint on an old pine bookcase I had, and some months later brown circles began to appear on the paint. I presume these are pitch stains coming through from the knots. What should I do to keep these from coming through the next coat of paint?

Sand off the stained areas and wash the wood with petroleum solvent (mineral spirits) or paint thinner to remove the surface resin. Then seal the knots with a coat of aluminum paint before re-painting.

PAINTING OVER SILICONE

My house has concrete block walls. When I bought it a few years ago I cleaned it carefully and applied a good brand of masonry paint. Since then I have had to do it every year because the paint flakes off so badly. When I spoke to the builder about it, he recalled some kind of a finish being put on the concrete blocks, but couldn't remember what it was. I was thinking of applying a coat of cement plaster this time, instead of paint. Do you have any other suggestions?

I believe your builder is referring to a silicone treatment that was once commonly applied to masonry to make it water-repellent. Unfortunately, silicone also repels paint, and it may also make it difficult to apply a cement parge coat or stucco directly to the concrete block. You would have to remove all the old paint by sandblasting, in any case. The only alternative I can suggest is aluminum or other siding.

PAINTING OVER VARNISH

I have some old varnished furniture that I would like to paint for my little girl's bedroom. If the varnish is in good condition, can I paint over it, or must it be removed? Can latex paint be used on furniture?

There is no need to remove the varnish, but it should be sanded to cut the gloss so that the paint will adhere better. Latex paint can be used, but enamel is generally preferred for furniture; it is harder and does not soil as easily.

PAINTING OVER WALLPAPER

We have an old home in the country and want to fix up a spare room as easily as possible. We would like to paint it, but it is now wallpapered . . . just one layer, though, because we stripped the old paper off a few years ago.

Painting

Can we paint on top of the present wallpaper? What kind of paint should we use? Will the seams show? Will the wallpaper pull away?

It would be better to remove the wallpaper, which is probably a dry-strippable type if it was put on in the last few years. However, any paint can be applied over wallpaper, and the joints don't usually show if they were tightly made. A self-priming interior latex paint is probably easiest to apply, but you may still need two coats if the wallpaper pattern is very bold.

Wallpaper does not make a solid base for paint, and it is very likely to peel off at some future date, after two or three coats of paint have been applied. It will be more difficult to remove then than it is now.

PAINTING OVER WATER STAINS

Our roof leaked two years ago due to an ice dam forming in the eavestrough. The water ran down inside the wall and made brown stains. We've tried painting over these water stains, but they keep bleeding through. What kind of paint can we use to cover them, or must we use wallpaper?

If you seal the stained areas with aluminum paint or shellac, you can use any kind of paint.

PAINTING OVER WAX

Our kitchen cupboards were given one coat of stain and then several coats of wax. Now we want to change the color in our kitchen and would like to refinish the cupboards in an antiqued blue. I was going to use wax remover and then apply the antique base paint, but I'm told that there will still be wax in the wood and that the paint won't stick. Is this correct?

Yes, but there's an easy remedy. After you have removed as much wax as possible with petroleum solvent (mineral spirits) apply a coat of aluminum paint to seal the surface of the wood. After this is dry (about half an hour) you can apply your antique base coat.

PAINTING OVER WHITEWASH

Would you please tell me how to paint over whitewash?

If the whitewash is firmly bonded to the wood, you can paint over it with either alkyd or latex paint. It's more likely to be powdery, however,

and in this case you should seal the surface of the whitewash with an application of ordinary varnish, diluted to about half strength with paint thinner. Then paint as usual.

PAINTING OVER STAIN

The wood siding on our house is stained dark brown. It is in excellent condition, not cracked or peeling, but we would like to paint it white. Can we paint directly over the stain, or do we have to use a special primer to prevent the colour bleeding through?

It depends on what kind of stain was used. Creosote-based stains will bleed through most paints, and so will some of the early oil-based stains. Either of these can be sealed with a coat of aluminum paint. In recent years, however, exterior wood stains have been made with an alkyd base, and these can safely be painted over without bleeding through. You'll probably need two coats of white to cover the dark brown.

PEELING PAINT

Last summer we bought an old wood frame house with clapboard siding. The paint is peeling badly, mostly on the shady side of the house. I've been told this is due to the fact that the wood was wet when it was painted, that it was painted too late in the day, or that the paint was put on too thick. Could any of these reasons be correct? The paint is curled and chipped and very thick; I've tried taking it off with a scraper, sandpaper, a wire brush, even a propane torch. What is the best way to get this off and repaint the house to prevent further peeling?

First, there's no such thing as a permanent paint job. Any paint will peel, flake, and chalk away in time. It may just be that your house hasn't been painted for many years. Any or all of the suggested reasons for paint failure may also apply—plus another one: the lack of a vapor barrier on the inside of the walls, permitting warm, humid household air to pass through the walls and condense under the siding. The fact that most of the peeling occurs on the cold side of the house suggests that this is the most likely cause.

Unfortunately, there's no practical way to add a vapor barrier now, but you can reduce the humidity in your house by increasing the ventilation during the winter.

Remove all the old paint by softening it with heat from a hot air gun or an electric paint stripper. Then apply a latex paint and the recommended primer—three coats altogether. Latex paint has less tendency to blister because it allows moisture vapor to escape.

PAINTING PLASTIC TILE

Can I paint over plastic wall tile?

Yes, if you roughen the surface first with coarse sandpaper, to give the paint something to stick to.

PAINTING NEW PLASTER

I understand that new plaster must age or be specially treated before it can be painted. How long must I wait and what must I do?

The high alkali content of new plaster will react with oil-based paints to produce a soft and tacky film. It takes about six months for the plaster to neutralize in the air, but this process can be speeded up by painting the surface with a solution of zinc sulphate, after which oil-based paints can be safely applied.

Latex paints don't have this problem; they can be used on plaster even before it is completely dry. (They should NOT be used if the surface has been treated with zinc sulphate, however.) And if you want to use an oil-based paint, all you have to do is use a latex primer first.

PAINTING A PLASTIC ROOF

The roof over our patio is made of a translucent plastic, but when the sun shines it's so hot underneath that we can't enjoy it. Is there some kind of paint or insulation we can use?

You're a victim of the familiar "greenhouse effect". The plastic lets the short infrared rays through, but traps the long heat rays that bounce back from the patio. Anything that keeps the light out will reduce the heat. An exterior white latex paint will do the job.

PAINTING A PLENUM

I am building a rec room in our basement and am having a problem with the main warm air duct. This is quite low, and I don't want to have to box it in as is usually done. Would it be all right just to paint it white to match the ceiling tiles? And if so, what kind of paint should I use?

This is a perfectly good idea. I've seen it done and it looks fine. Few people even notice it. Use two coats of any flat latex paint.

BEST COLOR FOR RADIATOR

What is the best color to paint a hot water radiator so it will give off the most heat? I think I read somewhere that radiators should be painted white, but a friend tells me that dark colours are better.

Dark colors radiate heat better than light colors, and matt surfaces are better than shiny ones. So the most efficient color for a hot water radiator is flat black, and the poorest is glossy white. The difference in the amount of heat given off can be as much as 10%. This isn't going to cut down on your heating costs, however, because you'll still pay for whatever heat you use. But if you're having trouble keeping some rooms warm, this may help.

Don't be confused by the fact that light colors *reflect* heat better than dark ones. They don't *radiate* heat as well as dark colors do.

PAINTING RADIATORS

We are going to paint our living room with a satin latex paint. Can we paint the two hot water radiators with the same paint?

Yes. Any interior house paint can be used on a hot water radiator. The radiator should not be painted while it is hot, but the temperature is not high enough to cause any problems after the paint has dried.

IRON RAILING RUSTED

The paint on the iron railing surrounding our porch has chipped off and the metal is rusting. What is the best way to refinish it?

Use a propane torch to soften the paint so it can be scraped off with a putty knife. Sand it smooth. Use a wire brush or silicon carbide paper to take the rust spots down to bare metal, then apply a coat of metal primer and repaint with any exterior enamel. Or use one of the rust-proofing paints that require no primer.

PAINTING OVER SAP BLISTERS

The siding on our 12-year-old house continues to ooze sap that bubbles out under the paint.

Can these spots be sealed, or must we remove the defective siding?

If there are large pitch pockets in the wood, about all you can do is cut them out and fill them before repainting. Small sap pores, however, can be sealed with shellac or aluminum paint. This should have been done before the siding was painted. You can do it now by removing the paint over the sap spots, sealing them, then repainting.

SEMI-GLOSS OVER FLAT LATEX PAINT

The walls and all the woodwork in my bathroom and kitchen have been painted with a flat latex. I would like to put on a gloss or semi-gloss paint that is easier to clean and more resistant to moisture. I would also like to apply a natural wood finish to the baseboards. What would you recommend I use?

I would suggest a semi-gloss alkyd paint for the walls and a gloss alkyd for the woodwork.

If you want a natural wood finish on the baseboards you will have to strip them with paint remover first, sand down to the bare wood, then apply two coats of urethane varnish.

PAINTING SHOWER FLOOR

The shower in my basement has a cement base, and I can't keep paint on it. After a few showers the paint starts to peel off. What can I do?

You will have to remove the old paint and soap fats from your shower base. A good scrubbing with trisodium phosphate and a stiff wire brush is recommended. Scrub all parts thoroughly, then remove all the paint with a non-wax, non-inflammable paint remover. Next etch the concrete with a solution of muriatic acid, 1 part to 10 parts water. Leave on for about 5 minutes, then rinse thoroughly with clear water. (Wear rubber gloves and eye protectors; keep solution off clothing, paint, and metal.) Allow at least two days to dry before repainting.

Probably the best idea is to leave the shower base unpainted, for the etched concrete has a good non-skid finish. Or you might use one of the porcelain shower pans or rubber mats that are available. If you do want to paint it, use a 2-component epoxy paint. No paint can be guaranteed to adhere permanently to concrete, however. Sometimes inexpensive paints give excellent results; sometimes the most expensive materials fail.

"SOLID" WOOD STAINS

The paint on our wood siding has cracked and peeled in a few places and we want to redo it. The salesman at the paint store suggested that we use something called a "solid color stain," which he says won't peel or blister like paint. Is this the right thing to use?

A "solid color stain" makes about as much sense as an "opaque window." The word "stain" has always meant a transparent or semi-transparent surface treatment that adds color to wood but does not hide the grain or other natural markings. These so-called solid color stains are not stains at all, in my opinion, just another kind of paint, very similar in appearance to a flat latex paint.

Like the latex paints, they are porous to water vapor (but not to water) and are not as subject to blistering as the oil-based paints. But this only works if they are applied to bare wood. They won't prevent blistering if applied on top of another paint.

In any event, it isn't a good idea to put one kind of paint on top of another. For best results, use the same kind of paint—latex or oil-based—that you have on now. If you don't know what kind you have, use one of the alkyd paints. These seem to be the most compatible with other paints.

You'll have to remove all the loose paint first in any case, and sand down the edges to provide a smooth surface for the new paint.

PAINTING ROUGH-TEXTURED CEILING

I would like to know if it is possible to clean or repaint a very rough-textured plaster ceiling. Brushing just knocks off little pieces of the plaster.

You should be able to paint it with a thick pile lamb's wool roller.

PAINTING A TILE FLOOR

What kind of paint can I use on a resilient tile floor?

There's no paint that will adhere properly to such a surface.

PAINTING VINYL SIDING

We have green vinyl siding on our house and I would like to paint it brown. Can you tell us

what kind of paint to use?

Even the manufacturers of vinyl siding don't have any suggestions about how to paint it. They can't understand why anyone would want to, since no paint will adhere for very long and it will just result in a great deal of maintenance work.

That's my view, too, but if it's terribly important that you change the color, I suggest that you roughen the vinyl surface with coarse steel wool or medium grade sandpaper, then use any exterior house paint.

WASHING WALLS BEFORE PAINTING

Our apartment hasn't been painted for four years. What should I use to clean the walls before painting them?

Washing walls is more work than painting them. And since it often leaves them looking blotchier than they were before, it may even make them more difficult to cover. Except for kitchens, where grease film can be a problem, walls are almost never washed before painting. They should be dusted, however, and any grease spots removed with a heavy-duty household cleaner. Marks left by adhesive tape can be taken off with lacquer thinner. Nail holes should be filled with one of the plaster patching materials.

PAINTING WINDOW FRAMES

We had new windows installed two years ago. The carpenter told me to paint them outside at that time but I was unable to do so. I intend to paint them this spring. What is the best way to do it? Do I need a primer?

If the wood has been unpainted for two years I suggest that you sand it down lightly with fine sandpaper before painting to remove the raised grain and any mould growth that may have started. Then select an exterior trim paint that you like and follow the instructions on the label. Some paints require a primer, others don't.

SPRAY-PAINTING METAL CUPBOARDS

Our enamelled metal kitchen cupboards need refinishing. Would you recommend painting them with a brush or with an aerosol spray can?

Spray cans are a lot trickier to use than a brush, and generally result in a messy finish with many sags and drips. They also produce a fine spray that gets on everything else in the room. You can do a much better job with a brush.

PAINTING WOOD GUTTERS

There doesn't seem to be any paint left on the inside of our wooden gutters, and I am afraid they will rot. What should I paint them with?

First, clean them out thoroughly with a wire or stiff-bristled brush, then paint them on the inside only with a bitumen waterproofing paint, available at building supply stores. The outside of the gutters should be painted to match the trim of your house, of course, so be careful not to spill the bitumen on the outside, or it will bleed through the paint.

PAINTING SHINGLES

We have bought an old farmhouse in the country and the old shingle siding needs painting. My husband thinks it would take too much paint because the shingles are so dry.

The most common treatment is shingle stain. It is relatively inexpensive and available in many colors, but none of them lighter in color than the shingles themselves. For lighter colors you would have to use paint, either oil-based or latex. At least two coats will be required but the job can be speeded up considerably by using a soft-textured roller or a spray gun. The paint itself is the cheapest part of the job, so don't try to cut costs there.

PANELLING

CEDAR PANELLING IN A BATHROOM

I am going to remodel a 50-year-old bathroom and plan to strip the walls down to the studs, then apply gypsumboard and cedar panelling. Is there a waterproof grade of gypsumboard I should use? What is the best finish to seal the tongue-and-groove cedar, particularly around the tub/shower enclosure?

All manufacturers of gypsumboard make a waterproof grade. This is meant primarily as a backing for ceramic wall tiles, but it would be a good choice for use behind the cedar panelling.

I'm a great admirer of cedar and have often seen it used in bathrooms, but I don't recommend it for shower walls because there's no practical way to waterproof the tongue-and-groove joints. The wood is certain to become stained. It would be much better to use a completely impervious material such as plastic laminate or one of the premolded plastic tub/shower enclosures.

Elsewhere in the bathroom the cedar can either be left unfinished or given a coat of penetrating oil-resin sealer such as a Danish oil finish, or two coats of satin urethane varnish.

DARKENING PANELLED WALLS

We have just purchased a house in which the kitchen has two walls panelled in a light-toned wood with a clear finish. We would like to stain this a darker color to blend with our maple furniture. Is there any way we can re-stain the wood a darker shade without having to remove the present finish and start from scratch?

Until a few years ago the answer would have been No. But now there is a new type of urethane stain-finish that can be applied over an existing finish. It comes in light shades of various wood stains. You simply apply as many coats as required to reach the tone you want. See your paint dealer.

INTERIOR WOOD FINISH

We are building an A-frame cottage and are going to panel the inside walls with tongue-and-groove white pine and red cedar. I would like a finish that will be easy to keep clean, won't have to be re-done every year, and will maintain the natural look of the wood. What would you suggest?

There are a number of finishes you can use, but basically there are just two types—clear film finishes and penetrating sealers. The first gives more physical protection to the wood and is easier to clean. It does, however, cover the wood with a smooth, transparent film that to some extent changes the natural appearance and texture of the wood. Urethane, regular varnish, and most multi-coat lacquer finishes belong in this category. I would recommend a satin urethane finish in your case.

A penetrating sealer, on the other hand, is absorbed into the surface of the wood, where it hardens and provides a relatively waterproof finish. This protects the wood against oil or water stains, and makes it fairly easy to keep clean, but it doesn't cover the natural grain texture or put a new plastic surface on the wood. Danish oil finish, "plastic in oil", teak oil, boiled linseed oil and turpentine, and thin lacquers belong in this category. I think one of the Danish oil finishes would be best.

Any of these finishes will darken the color of the wood slightly. The only way to keep the wood looking really natural is to leave it alone. There's no reason why this shouldn't be done if the wood is not going to be touched or handled frequently, otherwise finger marks will be a problem. Architects commonly leave cedar panelling unfinished in order to preserve its prized color and patina.

PANELLING A PAINTED WALL

We would like to put hardwood plywood panelling on the painted plaster walls in our bedroom. Can we glue this directly to the wall, or do we need to apply a vapor barrier first?

There is no need for a vapor barrier, but panel adhesive may not adhere well to the paint—or the paint may not adhere well to the wall. In either case the panelling will come loose. The proper procedure is to nail 1 × 2 strapping horizontally to the wall, then nail or glue the panelling to this. The strapping should be nailed through to the studs along the top and bottom of the wall and about every 16'' between. Where panel edges butt together, short lengths of strapping can be glued to the wall behind them as blocking. Nail the panelling to the strapping with colored, 1'' panel nails.

SCRATCHED PANELLING

We purchased a used mobile home recently. My problem is that the interior wood panelling has been scratched and scarred in a

number of places and I don't know how to get rid of the marks. I've tried the special wood conditioners that are supposed to be for panelling, but the results are only temporary. I'd like to know how I can refinish my panelling.

This may not be wood panelling at all. It is more likely to be hardboard panelling with a printed woodgrain overlay. Some of these look very realistic. Unfortunately, however, it is impossible to remove scratches and other scars from such panelling.

Even if it *is* wood, it will be a very thin veneer, too thin to permit the sanding that would be required to remove the scratches.

I think the best you can do is hide the scratches with a wax touch-up stick that comes in many wood tones and is available at most hardware stores. Or use a child's colored wax crayon in a matching color, then buff with a soft cloth.

REFINISHING WOOD PANELS

I was unhappy with the finish on the wood panelling in our family room, and applied a coat of urethane varnish. It is too shiny and has started to peel in spots. How can I remove it without damaging the panelling?

You should have sanded the old finish lightly before applying the urethane—and you should have used one with a satin finish instead of a high gloss.

Use a paint remover to strip the finish off the panels down to the bare wood, then start again. Put plenty of newspapers on the floor to protect it from the paint remover. And make sure the room is well ventilated.

MAINTAINING WOOD PANELLED WALLS

We just bought a house with finished birch panelling in the family room. What should I use on it to preserve the wood—lemon oil or teak oil?

Lemon oil is only petroleum solvent with a little lemon perfume added. It's a cleaner and it helps to remove dust, but it does nothing to preserve the wood. Teak oil is just thinned linseed oil, and it should only be used on porous, open-grained wood with an oil finish, such as teak. It should not be used on wood that has been given a smooth, film finish, which is what you probably have on your birch panelling.

Properly finished wood needs nothing to preserve it. Just dust it regularly (lemon oil on the cloth helps pick up the dust) and clean it occasionally with a damp-dry cloth and a drop of detergent. Waxes and other polishes are only required if you want a higher shine on the finish.

FADED WOOD PANELLING

The natural wood panelling in my living room has darkened where it is exposed to the light, leaving the areas behind the pictures, the chesterfield, even a potted plant, lighter than the surrounding wall. Is there any way this can be prevented? And what can I do to match up the light areas?

This is a very common problem; and there isn't anything you can do about it. Wood darkens with exposure to light. You can't prevent it, and there isn't any way to darken the light areas to match the rest of the wall. Even if you strip off the present finish, you would find that the wood itself has darkened where it was exposed. The only remedy is to paint it.

END Panelling

PARTICLE BOARD DOORS

I am replacing my kitchen cupboard doors with ½″ particle board to which I've glued ⅛″ plywood. The edges are covered with vinyl molding. Both sides of the door have been varnished. Now that I'm half-finished, I've been told by the salesman at the lumber yard that the particle board doors will warp because they're heavier on one side. I find this hard to believe but will not continue until I hear from you. If it is true, would plywood doors be better?

Particle board is less likely to warp than plywood, but there is always a chance of warping if one side of the door can absorb moisture more easily than the other. As long as both sides are sealed with two or three coats of varnish, I don't think you have anything to worry about.

FADED PHOTOGRAPH

We have an old photograph that is badly faded. Is there any way we can have it strengthened again?

If it's a black-and-white picture, you can have it copied, and strengthened in the process. Your photo dealer can handle this for you. If it's a color photo, there isn't any way you can restore the original colors after they have faded.

PICTURE HANGERS

I am moving into an apartment, and have quite a number of paintings. Since I understand that you are not allowed to put nails into the walls of an apartment, what can I use to hang them?

Most apartment owners accept the fact that tenants are going to hang pictures, and the truth is that a tiny nail driven into the plaster causes less damage than those glue-on hooks and other alternatives. The little hole can be easily filled with a dab of plaster patch when you leave, and this will be covered when the apartment is repainted for the next tenant.

PIGEONS

I am bothered by pigeons that roost under the roof overhang outside my bedroom window and keep me awake at night. I'd be grateful if you could tell me how to keep these pesky critters away.

Those little plastic windmills on a stick that they sell at fairs, circuses and toy stores will sometimes do the trick. Tack them as close to the pigeon roost as you can and face them into the wind to keep them spinning. Of course you may find the noise of the little windmills as annoying as the pigeons.

FINDING A BURIED WELL PIPE

When we had a house built in the country a few years ago, they drilled a deep well and put in a submersible pump. Before I could note the exact location of the well the contractor graded over it and laid sod. I'd like to know where it is in case it ever needs servicing, but I don't want to do any more digging than necessary. Do you have any suggestions?

If the pipe running from your house to the well isn't buried any more than 4' or so, you can trace its course with a metal detector. The best type to use is one that has a small radio transmitter that attaches to the pipe being traced (where it enters the house) and uses a radio to pick up and follow the signal. Some tool rental shops have these. They are used to trace wires and plumbing in buildings.

PLASTER

BULGING PLASTER

A small area (about 6" x 8") of the plaster wall in our bathroom has cracked and is bulging outwards. It's just below the shower head. Can you tell me what might have caused this, and how I should repair it?

It sounds very much as if you have a leak in the shower pipe behind the wall. You'll find out when you start to repair it, in any case, because the first thing to do is remove all the loose plaster. When you do this, you'll be able to see if water has been getting in from behind. If it has, you'd better call in a plumber and be prepared for a fairly expensive repair job. He'll have to knock out more of the wall, and then you'll need a carpenter and a plasterer to repair it.

If there's no sign of moisture behind the bulge, it may simply be a faulty plastering job. Remove all the loose plaster and enough of the surrounding plaster to make a rectangular hole that can be patched with a piece of gypsumboard. Nail this in place, then tape and fill the edges with drywall joint compound. Sand when dry, then apply two more thin coats, feathering them out beyond the edge of the patch.

CRACKED PLASTER

We have an 18-year-old brick house with a concrete foundation and a medium-sized, L-shaped living room. We have developed a bad crack in the plaster which seems to be travelling right across the ceiling and is now about a quarter of an inch wide. What do you think might be the trouble?

With a house that old and a crack that big, it's obviously not the natural settling and drying of the roof framing. The trouble is probably in your basement. Check for cracks in the foundation. Also examine the main supporting beam under the floor to see if it is sagging or warped. If you suspect a basic foundation problem, call in an expert to examine it.

CRACKING PLASTER

We have a 30-year-old, Spanish-style bungalow with solid concrete walls that have a stucco finish outside and a textured plaster finish inside. During this past winter cracks have developed in the walls in almost every room. Some of them are just hairline cracks, but a few are ⅛″ wide. My husband says that all we have to do is fill them and repaint, but I'm afraid the walls are going to come down. In one room the wall is bulging where the crack is. What should we do?

It's just the plaster surface on the inside wall that is cracking, not the wall itself, so you needn't worry about the house caving in. Plain cracks can be patched as your husband suggests. There are many plaster patching materials on the market, or you can use one of the drywall joint-filling compounds. Where the plaster is bulging away from the wall it will have to be broken off, and this will be more difficult to patch without special plastering tools. If such areas are very large, it might be better to call in a plasterer.

PLASTER CEILING

In the upstairs bedroom of our 1½-storey house, a double chimney from fireplaces in the living room and the basement passes behind the plaster wall. The plaster is disintegrating in the ceiling where it meets the chimney, and down part of the wall. We've had the roof checked, and it's OK, but I don't think we have much insulation. Could this be the problem?

This doesn't sound like an insulation problem to me. It's probably a leak. Water must be getting into the plaster either through the flashing around the chimney, where it goes through the roof, or through cracks in the mortar joints in the chimney itself. Or, if the chimney isn't lined with ceramic flue tile, rain water could be leaking through the bricks and mortar from inside the chimney.

Check the flashing for possible leaks, and seal all the joints with caulking compound. Look for loose or cracked mortar, and patch with mortar mix or concrete patching compound. If there's no flue lining in the chimney, it would be a good idea to have a chimney cap put on to keep out the rain.

PLASTER CRUMBLING

The chimney of our brick house runs outside the wall of our bedroom. During cold weather the bedroom wall gets very damp in this spot, and the plaster is getting soft. The wall seems to be dry during the summer and fall, however, even when it's raining. The problem started when we switched from oil to gas. We have been told that a new roof, chimney and eavestroughs will correct the problem, but that's a

very expensive solution. Isn't there anything else we can do?

The dampness comes from condensation inside the chimney, a common problem with gas furnaces because they operate at lower flue temperatures than oil furnaces do. They don't waste as much heat up the chimney, in other words, but the lower stack temperature can cause moisture vapor to condense inside a cold chimney.

I suspect you have an old house with no flue tile lining in the chimney, so that the condensation soaks through the bricks and mortar into your plaster walls. If the plaster is soft it will have to be replaced.

The best remedy would be to have an insulated metal vent installed inside the brick chimney. Any chimney repair company can do this for you.

PLASTER—GAP AROUND BATHTUB

Our problem concerns the ugly "line" where the plastered wall meets the rim of the built-in bath. The wall is painted with white enamel. Over the years the plaster has slowly disintegrated leaving a ¼″ gap along the rim. We do not wish to tile. Have you any suggestion?

If your plaster has not disintegrated more than ¼″ or so, you can cut the soft plaster away and fill up the resulting gap with a silicone rubber caulking compound. If the gap is larger, I am afraid you would have to cut out the bad plaster and refill the affected parts. If the plaster is backed by gypsum lath, check to make sure this has not deteriorated also. When re-plastering, leave ¼″ space between the plaster and the tub and caulk this with the silicone rubber to prevent further trouble.

PANELLING ON PLASTER

Is there any reason why I can't attach hardboard or plywood panelling directly to a plaster wall?

The best way is to nail 1 x 2 strapping to the wall vertically at 16″ or 24″ centres, and horizontally top and bottom, and attach the panelling to this with mastic adhesive. You can glue it directly to the wall, however, if it is smooth enough, using one of the panel adhesives sold for this purpose.

HOLE IN PLASTER WALL

We have a 3″ hole in our plaster wall, and the

wall is empty behind it. How can I patch the hole?

You take a piece of ¼" wire screen ("hardware cloth") about 1" bigger than the hole. Attach a piece of wire or string to the centre of the screen then roll it up so you can push it into the hole. Hold on to the string and juggle the screen around until you have pulled it open against the back of the hole.

Now, with your third hand, or the help of a friend, fill the hole roughly with patching plaster, forcing some of it through the screen at the back. Put a pencil or a larger piece of wood over the hole and tie the string to it tightly to hold the screen against the back of the hole until the plaster sets. Then cut the string, remove the stick, and fill the hole flush with the surface. When this is dry, sand lightly and apply another coat of patching plaster feathering it out over the edges of the hole.

PATCHING PLASTER WALLS

Our plaster walls keep cracking every year, and I'm getting tired of patching and repainting and then having the cracks open up again. Is there any way I can stop the house heaving, or at least apply some kind of a permanent patch?

Changes in temperature and humidity keep a house in constant motion, but it's usually too slight to cause any trouble. There's no way to stop it, in any case, but there is a way you can patch the cracks that will last much longer. Instead of filling them with plaster, you apply a layer of adhesive over the cracks, and then cover this with a strip of open-mesh glass fab-

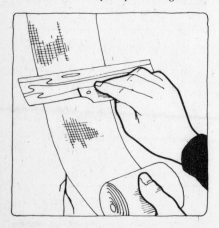

ric. This is pressed in place and then covered with another layer of the special cement, feathered at the edges to hide the tape. Properly done, such a repair is almost invisible once it's painted, and it's flexible enough to give when the wall moves. The patching material is available at any hardware store or building supply dealer.

REMOVING PLASTER FROM BRICK WALL

How can I remove the plaster from my kitchen wall to expose the brick that is behind it?

You just go at it with a ballpeen hammer. This fractures the hard, thin finish coat of plaster on the surface and exposes the softer base coat, which is usually grey. A wire brush is used to remove this from the brick, but you may have to use a chisel to get it off the mortar joints.

Sometimes you'll find that the base coat has been applied over strips of wood lath that are fastened to nailing strips embedded in every sixth course of bricks. This is easier to remove because a prybar can be used to rip off large areas of lath and plaster.

But any way you do it, it's going to be a dirty job. Seal off the rest of the house as best you can to prevent brick and plaster dust from getting everywhere. And don't be surprised if the brick wall itself is pretty rough. Any kind of brick that was cheap and handy was used as a backup for plaster walls, because it was never meant to be looked at. The random appearance has a charm of its own, however.

REPAIRING OLD PLASTER WALLS

Oil paint has been applied over the wallpaper on the walls of my mother's old frame bungalow. The plaster underneath is badly cracked and there are several holes under the paper. What is the best way to remove the wallpaper and restore the plaster walls?

The best thing to do in this situation is to forget about the wallpaper and the broken plaster and simply apply gypsumboard panelling to create a new wall surface. If the walls are smooth enough, you can glue the panelling directly to the walls with panel adhesive. If not, then apply horizontal 1x2 or 1x3 strapping to the top and bottom of the walls and approximately every 24" in between, nailing it through to the studs, then nail or screw the gypsumboard to this. When the joints are taped and filled you will have a smooth new wall surface suitable for painting or papering. Believe me, this will be a lot easier, and better, than trying to restore the old plaster wall.

SOFT PLASTER UNDER WINDOW

The plaster gets soft and the paint peels under each corner of one of our bedroom windows. I replace it every time I paint, but it keeps recurring. Condensation is not the problem.

It sounds to me as if water is leaking in around your window frame. Apply a caulking compound all around the outside of the frame.

PLASTER SPILLS

Can you tell me how to remove plaster from a brick fireplace, a bathtub, toilet, and water pipes?

Sounds as if you had a sloppy plasterer. Since plaster is easily softened with water, this is the usual treatment for removing it from hard, non-porous surfaces like bathtubs and pipes. It will scrape off quite easily after it has been softened.

It is more of a problem to remove it from rough, porous surfaces like brick. Muriatic acid is the usual treatment here. Use 1 part acid to 10 parts water, applied with a stiff-bristled brush. If that doesn't seem to work fast enough you can strengthen the solution up to 1 part muriatic acid to 4 parts water. But be careful not to get the solution on skin, clothes, paint, metal, or anything else you value.

PLASTER vs DRYWALL

We will be building a new home shortly. The builder wants to use gypsumboard drywall, but I always thought that plaster was better. Could you give us your opinion?

"Wet" plaster is rarely used today. I have had houses built for me both ways, and I've seen a lot of others, of course. In my opinion plaster is no better than drywall, and sometimes not as good. It takes a lot of skill to do a good plaster job, and there aren't many experienced plasterers around any more. Drywall application is much easier and faster, and generally produces a smoother, flatter wall surface. It is also quite a bit cheaper than wet plastering.

REPLACING LAMINATE COUNTERTOP

I want to replace a plastic laminate countertop. Can you tell me how to cut the new laminate to fit?

Plastic laminate can be cut with any fine-toothed saw, or it can be scored and cracked in the same way that you cut a sheet of glass. Draw a line with a metal scriber or a sharp awl, then place the line at the edge of a firm support, such as a table, and snap off. A special hand tool that also squares and bevels the edges is available at most hardware stores.

PLASTIC LAMINATE FOR CUPBOARDS

We would like to change our kitchen cupboard doors and drawer fronts, and were considering replacing them with a natural wood veneer. Is there a better material to use, something that would be tough and easy to clean?

The plastic laminate used for countertops can be used for this purpose, but not over a painted surface. A better material is a thinner grade of plastic laminate made especially for cabinet and furniture use. It also comes in smaller sheets. There's no need to replace your present door and drawer fronts; just cover them with the laminate, applied with contact adhesive.

REGLUING LAMINATE

The plastic top on our kitchen counter has lifted around the edge. How can I reglue it?

Prop the edge open as far as it will go and apply contact cement to the underside of the top and the top of the counter. When the adhesive is dry to the touch, press the top down firmly. This should hold it, but for extra strength, place a board on the edge of the counter and clamp it down for 24 hours.

PLASTIC LAMINATE ON PLASTER WALL

About six weeks ago I applied a thin grade of countertop laminate (Formica) to the bare plaster wall between the kitchen counter and the cupboards. I used contact cement. It looked all right for a while, but now it is bulging in places. Should I have sealed the plaster first? What should I do now?

A sealer might have helped, but laminate manufacturers do not recommend the application of this material to either a plaster or gypsumboard base. There are two ways to apply plas-

tic laminate to such surfaces. 1) Nail ½"
plywood or particle board to the wall and then
apply the laminate to this with contact cement.
2) Back the laminate with the plywood first,
using contact cement, and they apply the
plywood to the wall with panel adhesive.

If you're careful you can remove the laminate from the wall by squirting or brushing
contact cement thinner under the edge and
gently peeling it off.

WRONG PLASTIC LAMINATE

**We asked a carpenter to panel one wall of our
dining room with satin-finished plastic laminate in a walnut pattern. When he had done it
we realized that he had used the high gloss
laminate by mistake. It looks terrible but,
since it has been put on with panel adhesive,
the carpenter says he can't change it. Is there
any way we can remove the shine without
ruining the plastic?**

It could be done with fine (000) steel wool, or
cutting compound used for automobile finishes, but it is a lot of work and would be very
difficult to get a perfectly even satin finish over
the entire surface. The carpenter could remedy
his mistake by applying the proper laminate
panels on top of the shiny ones.

PLASTIC WALL TILE

**The plastic wall tiles in our bathroom have
lost their shine. Is there anything we can do to
bring it back?**

The use of harsh scouring powders or other
abrasives will take the gloss off plastic tiles. If
they're not too bad, you can restore the shine
with one of the acrylic, "self-polishing" liquid
floor waxes.

PLUMBING

ACID IN SEPTIC TANK

**We want to paint our concrete laundry tubs
with one of the paints sold for this purpose.
Instructions call for etching the concrete with
an acid first, and I would like to know if this
would be harmful to our septic tank.**

The addition of a small amount of acid will
probably be beneficial. Septic tanks tend to get
too alkaline because of the chemicals contained
in dishwasher detergents and other cleaners.

PLUGGED DRAIN

**The sink drain in our basement bathroom is
plugged. I've tried various drain cleaners and
even removed the trap under the sink, but
can't find the trouble. The bathtub works
fine. Is there anything I can do other than call
in a plumber?**

You can buy a plumber's auger or snake at any
hardware store for a couple of dollars. Push
this down the sink drain to locate and clear the
obstruction. It can't be far away if the bathtub
drain is working properly.

DRAIN PIPE PLUGGED
WITH PLASTER

**Our laundry drain has been plugged solid with
plaster of paris that was mistakenly dumped
down the sink. Is there an acid we can use to
dissolve the plaster?**

Water will soften it eventually, but it would be
better to remove the drain trap under the sink.
If you're lucky, that's where the blockage will
be. You can either chip this out or replace it
with a new one. Use a plumber's "snake" to
check the rest of the drain.

DRAINS BACKING UP

**When I drain the dishwater from the kitchen
sink, some of the water and suds come up into
the bathtub. Is there any way I can stop this?**

There are a number of possible causes, but they
all boil down to interference of some kind with
the flow of waste water.

The drain pipe may be partly plugged with
soap, dirt, and hair, for instance. Clean out both
drains with heavy-duty cleaning compounds.
The kind sold for regular household use may do
the job, but plumbers prefer to use stronger
types, usually referred to as "hot shot", or "tri-
ple strength" cleaners, available at plumbing
supply companies and some hardware stores.

Another common source of trouble is excessive use of high-sudsing detergents. Turbu-
lence in the drain water where it is diverted
past the bathtub drain can cause it to foam up
and restrict the flow of water, which then backs
up into the tub. Try cutting down on the

amount of detergent you're using in the kitchen sink.

And if those tricks don't cure it, the trouble is probably in the plumbing installation. The drain pipes may be too small or the wrong kind of connecting pipes may have been used...a T instead of a Y, for instance. Or there may not be enough slope or "fall" in the drain pipe to carry the waste water away properly. All these will require the attention of a plumber.

DRAIN PROBLEMS

Whenever we flush the toilet our bathtub rumbles, and sometimes a sewer smell comes up the drain. What causes this and how can we stop it?

The problem is in the venting of your bathtub drain line. Most likely the vent is plugged. When a toilet is flushed or a sink or bathtub drained, the air pressure changes momentarily in the drain line. Unless there is an air vent to equalize this pressure, the water can be sucked out of sink traps, allowing sewer smells to enter.

Better get a plumber to check your system and see if the vent pipe is plugged or if you need a new one.

DRIPPING FAUCET

Our bathroom tap continues to drip even after I've replaced the washer. What else could be wrong?

It sounds as if the valve seat is damaged or worn. Most faucets are now made with replaceable seats, and it's very easy to put in a new one. You can see the seat down at the bottom of the tap when you remove the valve stem. If it has a hexagonal hole in it, it means it's removable. All you have to do is insert a hexagonal (Allen) wrench of the correct size down inside the valve and then unscrew the seat and screw in a new one.

Just one word of warning. If you're like me, you usually undertake a job like this at night or on Sunday when all the hardware stores are closed. Make sure you have a selection of valve seats (they come in three sizes and cost about 25¢ each) and the wrenches to fit them, on hand before you start.

LEAKY FLAP VALVE

I put a new flap valve in the bottom of our toilet water tank because the old one was sticking open. This one doesn't stick, but it leaks slightly and the water keeps running into the toilet bowl. Did I get the wrong flap valve?

I don't think so. If you will turn off the water, flush the toilet, and remove the flap valve again, you'll probably find that the foam plastic stopper has a little ridge on both sides, where it came out of the mold. If you remove these ridges with a piece of sandpaper I think you'll find that it seats properly and doesn't leak.

FREEZE-PROOF TAP

Is there any kind of an outside tap I can install that can be used all winter without freezing?

A device called a non-freeze hose bib is what you want, I think. The faucet and handle are on the outside of the house, but there is a long stem that controls a valve located inside the house. It is often used in commercial buildings, but rarely in homes, although there's no reason why it shouldn't be.

HAMMERING WATER PIPES

Our water pipes make a hammering noise when we turn off the water. How can we remedy this?

There are several possible causes of this noise. Often it is simply a loose washer in the tap. Turn off the water supply, undo the tap, and tighten the washer or put in a new one. Look to see if the washer seat is damaged; if so, you can buy an inexpensive reamer at your hardware store to fix it. Another possible cause is a loose water pipe that bangs against its support bracket when the water pressure is released. If you find this, simply tighten the support bracket or add a new one.

Most likely, however, the trouble is "water hammer," due to the lack of, or malfunction of, an air cushion in the water line. An air cushion is simply a vertical piece of pipe about 18" long, capped at the top, placed in the main water supply line. Air in this pipe absorbs sudden changes of pressure in the line as taps are closed, and prevents the hammering noise.

HOT WATER SLOWS DOWN

I have a strange problem with my hot water tap, and I can't seem to cure it. After I turn it on it gradually slows down to a trickle. I have put

187

in a new washer, but that hasn't done any good. What's the cause and what's the cure?

The problem has been caused by the new taps, and the higher water temperatures and pressures in today's homes. Old-fashioned taps required several turns to open fully; some of the new tap designs require only a part-turn to obtain full water flow. When the water gets hot, the tap spindle expands very slightly, but this is enough to close the small opening in some taps.

High water pressure contributes to the problem by reducing still further the amount you have to open the tap, and high water temperature causes greater expansion of the spindle.

There are three possible cures. One: Change from a bevelled washer to a flat one; this provides a larger opening at the valve seat when the tap is turned on. (Sometimes the trouble is caused in the first place by installing the wrong kind of washer.)

Two: Lower the water temperature—20° the first time, then 5° at a time. Wait about two days between each change to be sure the hot water supply is adequate at the lower setting.

Three: Turn down the hot water shut-off valve under the sink. This will reduce the pressure at the tap and allow you to open the tap further when you turn the water on. If you don't have a shut-off valve under the sink, you'll have to install one.

LAUNDRY DRAIN

The water is not draining away fast enough from the automatic washing machine in the basement. I've been told that the weeping drainage tile in the floor drain has probably been broken, and that this will cost several hundred dollars to repair. Is there another solution?

Like your sinks, bathtub, laundry tubs, etc., the washing machine should drain into the sewer, not into the weeping tile system under your foundation. Normally it drains into the laundry tub, which is connected to the sanitary sewer. Ask your plumber to advise you how the proper connection can be made.

LEAKING FAUCET

We recently bought a portable dishwasher. It works fine, but the swivel faucet in the sink has now started to leak a little around the base when the dishwasher is in use. How can I correct this?

The base of the swivel faucet is sealed with a rubber O-ring, but this is not designed to withstand a full head of water pressure, which it must now do when the faucet is connected to the dishwasher and the hot water tap is opened. The rapid, hammer action of the solenoid valve in the dishwasher adds to the problem.

Faucet manufacturers have asked the dishwasher manufacturers to use a different kind of valve, but they reply that the faucet makers should find a solution. The way it stands now, it's strictly a consumer's problem.

All you can do is remove the faucet (it unscrews in various ways) and replace the O-ring.

(See next item.)

LEAKING FAUCET

Our kitchen faucet is leaking. This is the kind with a single swivel faucet in the middle and the taps on either side. I know how to put new washers in the taps, but this leak is around the base of the faucet, where it swivels, and I don't know how to fix this.

Unscrew the collar that holds the faucet to the "deck," then lift out the faucet. (You don't have to turn off the main water supply to do this, just make sure the two kitchen taps are closed.) If you look inside the collar you'll see a rubber gasket down at the bottom. That's an O-ring, and you need a new one. They come in many sizes, so take the whole thing down to your hardware dealer and get him to pick out the one you need. He'll get all of ten cents for his trouble, but you're probably a good customer, anyway.

Pry out the old O-ring with an awl or the point of a knife, push the new one in place, being careful not to damage it, and then replace the faucet and screw the collar back on. Tighten it just enough so the faucet will swivel easily. If all this works the way it's supposed to, the leak will be cured.

O-RING

LEAKING TOILET

There is a rusty discoloration around the base of our toilet bowl, and an unpleasant smell. I

can't detect any drips or condensation on the outside of the bowl. Can you tell me what the trouble is?

It sounds as if the seal around the bottom of the toilet bowl may be leaking slightly. Vibration, rough use, or poor installation sometimes loosens the nuts that fasten the toilet to the floor. Check to see if it's loose. If so, remove the porcelain caps that cover the four nuts around the base of the toilet, and then tighten them gently . . . but be careful not to crack the bowl.

If the toilet is not loose, then the trouble may be caused by a deteriorated seal, or closet flange gasket, under the toilet bowl. You have to remove the toilet to replace this, but otherwise it's not a difficult job.

NOISY HOT WATER TANK

Is there any way to stop our gas-fired hot water tank and adjoining pipes from banging and cracking when the heat comes on?

Scale that has settled to the bottom of the tank is the probable cause of this. It can usually be cured by draining a couple of gallons off the bottom of the tank once or twice a year.

The problem will be aggravated by having the water temperature set too high. Try lowering the temperature.

NOISY DRAINS

I'm having trouble with all my sinks and the bathtub. After the water drains out, a gurgling and dripping noise continues for some seconds. I've used various types of drain cleaners, but they don't do any good. Can you tell me what the trouble is?

It sounds as if the drain water is syphoning the water out of the traps under the sinks. This suggests that the vent stack is blocked or has not been properly installed. You'll have to get a plumber to check this.

NOISY TAP

A few months ago the hot water tap in our bathroom started to shudder when it was turned off. Can you tell me what causes this and what we can do about it?

It is caused by a loose tap washer. Turn off the water and remove the handle. Sometimes the screw is visible on the top, but on most models it is hidden under a snap-fit disc that can simply be pried off with the point of a knife or similar tool. Remove the chrome-plated bonnet, if there is one, and then use a wrench to unscrew the packing nut that holds the valve stem in the faucet. Take out the valve stem as if you were opening the tap. On the bottom of the stem you will see a screw that holds the tap washer in place. Just tightening the screw might cure the trouble, but the washer is probably worn anyway, so it's better to replace it. Take the old one to a hardware store and get a few replacement washers exactly the same size and shape. Put everything back the way it was removed, then turn on the water.

Some modern taps come apart a little differently, but the general procedure is the same. The idea is to remove the valve stem so you can get at the washer and replace it. Usually this can be done with nothing more than a screwdriver and a monkeywrench.

NOISY TAPS

Our bathroom taps were dripping so I put new washers in them. Since then the taps have made a singing, whistling noise whenever they are turned on. What did I do wrong?

You probably put in the wrong kind of washers. Most taps take flat washers, but tapered washers are the kind most commonly seen in the stores, for some reason or other, and that's the kind most people buy. A tap will usually work with either kind, but tapered washers constrict the valve opening and sometimes cause the water to make a lot of noise as it passes through. It should stop if you replace the tapered washers with flat ones.

PHOSPHATES vs SEPTIC TANK

Since our water softener went out of operation, we've been using a water conditioner powder with a high phosphate content in the laundry, bath, and dish water. Although we had no trouble with our septic tank before this change, we had to have it pumped out about 18 months after beginning the use of this material. Could the phosphate in the water conditioner be harmful to the function of the septic tank?

Actually, phosphate is a nutrient for the bacteria that make a septic tank function. But it's also a strong alkali, and when there's too much of it the water in the tank becomes excessively alkaline and the bacteria are killed. Authorities recommend at least a 500-gallon septic tank to handle the output of today's automatic

Plumbing

washers, but many are smaller than this, and that's probably your trouble.

Theoretically, you could adjust the alkalinity by putting acid in your waste water, but that's impractical. The best answer would be to repair your water softener or get a new one.

PLUMBER vs PLASTER

If a plumber breaks into a plaster wall when making repairs, is it his responsibility to have the wall repaired?

Unless the plumber states in writing that his price includes plaster repair, the answer is usually no. A plumber is not a plasterer and so he would not be familiar with the trade. If you wish him to include the plaster repairs in his charge, he would have to get a plasterer in and give you a complete price on both plastering and the plumbing. Always have these details stipulated in writing.

FIXING A POP-UP DRAIN

We have a pop-up drain plug in our bathroom sink, controlled by a lever behind the faucet. It won't stay closed any more, but pops up as soon as we let go of the lever. It's very difficult to wash your face with one hand while holding the drain plug closed with the other! Is there any way we can fix this?

The lift rod behind the faucet is connected to a horizontal lever that enters the drain pipe just under the sink. As this is moved up and down it opens and shuts the drain stopper. The lever moves on a ball joint that fits in a socket and is held there by a retaining nut. This nut has slackened, allowing the ball joint to become loose. All you have to do is tighten this nut just enough to hold the drain plug in place when the control rod is lifted.

PUTTING NEW WASHER IN BATHTUB FAUCET

I have put new washers in our kitchen and bathroom sink faucets several times to stop them dripping, but I can't figure out how to do it in the faucets that are located on the bathtub wall. I have taken off the handle and unscrewed the top nut I find there, but I can't get the valve stem out. A brass washer inside seems to be holding the stem in place. There must be a simple way to do it. Can you tell me what it is?

Bathtub faucets are tricky to work on because

they're usually recessed into the wall. What you have removed is the packing nut, which does not release the valve stem of a bathtub faucet as it does in most sink faucets. To remove the stem *you must leave the packing nut in place* and unscrew the entire valve assembly (the larger nut behind the packing nut). You may be able to do this with an adjustable wrench, but more likely you'll need to buy or rent a special socket wrench. Use the tips of a pair of scissors to measure the size of the nut.

REPAIRING SHOWER HEAD

A hard, white deposit has formed around the small holes in the spray-head of our bathroom shower. The shower doesn't spray properly any more. How can I get rid of this deposit?

It is simply a build-up of calcium or lime from the hard water, and it can be dissolved with any mild acid. Unscrew the shower head, take it apart, and put the pieces in a bowl of vinegar until all the deposit has been removed, then reassemble.

COLD SHOWER

I live in a condominium apartment that has one annoying problem—the shower shocks you with an icy spray whenever someone in another apartment uses the hot water. Is there some device I can have installed that will keep the temperature constant?

Yes, it's called a pressure-balancing valve, and any plumber can install one in place of your present tub-shower control valve. There are several makes on the market.

SMELL FROM FLOOR DRAIN

The smell of sewer gas is coming from our basement floor drain. Our house is still under its 1-year warranty, but the builder says there's nothing he can do about this smell.

There should be a trap in the drain line under the floor, a U-shaped pipe that remains filled with water and prevents sewer gasses getting back into the house. There are three possibilities: 1) Your drain has never been used, and so the trap contains no water to block the gas. Answer: pour some water down the drain. 2) The trap may be cracked, allowing the water to leak out. Answer: Dig up the floor and replace the faulty trap. 3) The builder may have neglected to put a trap in this drain line. Answer: Dig up the floor and put one in. The builder would be responsible for 2 and 3, but my guess is that the answer is No. 1.

Most plumbing codes now require a special fitting on the laundry tub taps to run some water into the floor drain whenever the tap is used. This is usually enough to keep the drain trap full and prevent odor from backing up into the house.

SLOW SINK

We have just completed a new house. The sink in the main bathroom drains very slowly, and releases a big bubble as the last of the water flows out. Our plumber can't seem to help us. Can you?

It sounds like a plugged drain or a faulty vent pipe. But these are hardly likely in a new house, so we asked our plumbing expert for some advice. Almost certainly, he says, the trouble is in the strainer outlet in the sink...something the plumbers call a P-and-O, or plug-and-overflow connection. The crossbars in the strainer should be made of rounded cast metal, but some are made of stamped, flat sheet metal. These often trap a bubble of air beneath the strainer, which prevents the water from draining out of the sink.

You can test this by putting a soda straw down through the strainer when the sink is draining slowly. As you break through the bubble, the air will be released and the water will flow away.

The best solution is to have your plumber replace the P-and-O outlet with one that has smaller, rounded crossbars. An alternative is to take a triangular file and file down the crossbars to make the drain opening larger. You can even remove one of the crossbars entirely, leaving just one bar across the strainer.

FREEZING TOILET

The toilet in our cottage froze up last winter and we had to replace it. Is there anything I can put in the water to prevent this happening when we leave the cottage unattended again this winter?

Yes, automobile antifreeze. After you turn the water supply off, flush the toilet to empty the water closet, then pour about two cups of antifreeze into the toilet bowl.

LEAKING TOILET BOWL

Here's a strange problem. Our toilet flushes properly, but the water won't stay in the bowl afterwards. It slowly drains away, leaving just a puddle at the bottom. Can you tell us what is wrong and what we can do about it?

There are three possibilities. The vent pipe that goes from the toilet drain to the roof may be plugged with leaves, a bird's nest, or whatever, causing the water to be siphoned out of the toilet bowl. The cure for this is fairly easy; put the nozzle of a garden hose down the vent stack and turn it on to flush out the obstruction.

The second possibility is a crack in the bottom of the toilet bowl. You should be able to see this as a fine hairline, but it may be hidden. You wouldn't see the water on the floor, because it just goes down the drain. The cure is expensive: a new toilet.

The third possibility is that you've somehow dumped a cloth down the toilet. This can get stuck on the rough, unglazed surface of the trap, where it acts like a wick and drains the water away. You can probably locate and remove it with a length of coathanger wire.

CRACKED TOILET TANK

My china toilet tank has a crack. Is it possible to repair this? I cannot get a new tank to match the bowl.

You may be able to repair it if you can drain the tank and let it dry for a few days. Use coarse steel wool or a scrubbing brush to clean the inside surface around the crack. Squeeze a bead of silicone rubber bathtub caulk or ceramic adhesive along the crack inside the tank. Rub it into the crack with your fingers. Cover the crack with a second layer of the silicone rubber. Allow this to dry for 12 hours before filling the tank.

TOILET DOESN'T FLUSH PROPERLY

The new toilet we had installed in our bathroom about a year ago has never worked properly. The water just swirls around in the bowl and the toilet must be flushed several times. Is there anything we can do to remedy this?

First check to see if there is a partial blockage in the drain. If not, either the water tank isn't filling completely or it's not emptying completely. You can check this simply by taking the lid off the tank.

If the water isn't coming up to the level

marked inside the tank, the float arm should be raised by turning the adjusting screw at the pivot end or by bending the float arm itself. (Toilet tanks without a float arm will have another means of adjusting the water level.)

If the water level is high enough but the tank doesn't empty completely when it's flushed, then the flap valve in the bottom of the tank is closing too quickly, probably because the chain that connects it to the flushing lever is too long. Try shortening it a couple of links; it should be just long enough to let the flap valve close when the handle is at rest.

Some toilets use a different system, however. The flap valve is controlled by the rate at which water empties out of a black cylinder on top of the valve. If the hole in the cylinder is too large (which has happened occasionally) the valve will close too quickly. The solution is to replace the flap valve assembly, available from any plumbing supply store.

TOILET TANK TROUBLE

Our toilet tank was taken off when our bathroom was tiled about a year ago, and it hasn't worked properly since. The plug in the bottom of the tank doesn't quite shut the water off unless you push it down. Is this difficult to repair?

No. Turn off the water under the toilet tank, then flush it to empty the tank. Check the wire stem that holds the stopper ball over the valve in the bottom of the tank. It may just be bent slightly and need straightening. Or the lift arm on the flush handle may be sticking, and not letting the stem fall down to the "off" position. A little plumber's grease around the handle bushing may be the answer. Or the ball valve seat may be dirty and scratched. Lift the ball and smooth the seat with sandpaper.

If these adjustments don't work, I suggest replacing the stopper ball with a soft rubber flap valve, which you can buy at any hardware store.

LEAKING TOILET

The water main on our street broke and was repaired a few days ago, and since then both our toilets keep running and won't shut off properly. I've called the municipal water department but they say they can't do anything about it. What should I do?

By the time you read this, I think the problem will have cured itself. It is caused when fine silt, stirred up by the repair work, lodges in the

water closet. This usually washes away in a few days. If it doesn't, turn off the water, flush the toilet, and check the flush valve stopper in the bottom of the water closet. Wipe off any dirt that may be keeping the ball or flap from fitting tightly.

If leaking continues, then it must be in the ballcock valve located at the end of the float arm. Turn off the water, flush the toilet, and then take the valve apart by unscrewing the hinge pin and lifting out the valve plunger. Take this to your hardware store and get a ballcock repair kit with new washers to fit it.

VENT STACK PROBLEM

My problem concerns the water level in our upstairs toilet bowl. When the toilet on the lower floor is flushed, the water level drops in the upstairs toilet. I have spoken to two plumbers about it and they say they don't know what the cause can be.

The drain line from both toilets is supposed to be connected to a vent pipe that is open to the roof. This would prevent the siphoning action that is drawing water from the upstairs toilet. Either this is not properly vented, or the vent pipe is clogged. You can test it by putting a hose in the vent pipe on the roof and turning it on. The water should run down the pipe and into the drain freely. If the water backs up and runs on the roof, the vent pipe is plugged. If the water runs away properly, then there is something wrong with the connection to the upstairs toilet—and any plumber should be able to fix it.

VENTING A SINK

I don't know why, but my kitchen sink and the laundry tub below it in the basement are not connected to a roof vent the way the other plumbing fixtures in the house are. As a result, a gurgling sound can be heard in the kitchen when the laundry tub is used, and sometimes there is a sewer smell from the sink. It would be very difficult to install a vent pipe inside the finished wall and up through the roof at this stage, so I was thinking of running a 1½" pipe up to the eaves outside the wall. Would this be satisfactory?

It would work, but there's an easier solution. Hardware and plumbing supply stores can sell you something called an "automatic plumbing vent". This small plastic device contains a one-way valve that admits air into the drain line behind the trap, breaking the suction that causes the gurgling sound and can empty the trap, permitting sewer gases to enter the house through the sink drain. The device costs about $6 and is simply attached to a short, upright extension pipe connected to the drain line under the sink.

Plumbing codes do not permit the use of this vent valve as a substitute for a vent pipe in new construction, but there's nothing to stop you using it in an existing home to overcome a venting problem such as yours.

LOW WATER PRESSURE

Our house is very old and the water pressure is very low. I opened one length of galvanized pipe and found it was plugged with a white deposit and only had a small hole in the center for the water to pass through. Is there a chemical I can use to dissolve this deposit?

There is no way to remove the lime deposit from the pipes. All you can do is replace the piping.

PIPE DIAMETER AND WATER PRESSURE

I will soon be replacing my galvanized water pipes with copper. The supply line coming into the house is ½". If I connect a ¾" pipe to this and then drop back to ½" supply lines to the fixtures will it increase the volume of water at the taps?

Very slightly. A ¾" pipe offers a little less resistance to the flow of water than a ½" pipe, so theoretically there would be some improvement, but probably not enough to notice. If you want a larger service line to the house you'll have to contact your local water department.

FILLING PLYWOOD CRACKS

The plywood panels in our kitchen cupboard doors have small, vertical cracks in the surface that still show after three coats of paint. How can I cover these?

If the cracks are big enough to see, paint won't cover them. They must be filled first with a spackling compound or one of the ready-mixed crack fillers. Apply with a putty knife. Sand lightly when dry, then paint. Two coats will probably be necessary.

PREVENTING PLYWOOD FROM CHECKING

I have noticed that fir plywood used for outdoor construction sometimes checks very badly. Is there some way I can treat it to prevent these hairline cracks from appearing?

This problem is caused by moisture getting into the face veneer of the plywood. The best preventative is to give it at least two coats of a good exterior paint. The edges should also be sealed with a prime coat to keep water from seeping into the wood.

Any checking that does occur should be sanded and filled with spackling compound and then re-painted to prevent water penetration that will cause further checking.

If a smooth surface is very important, you can buy plywood with a plastic-impregnated paper overlay that will not check or crack. It is widely used for building concrete forms, and any building supply dealer should be able to get it for you.

PLYWOOD EDGES

I want to build some bookshelves out of plywood. What's the best way to finish the edges so the laminations will not show?

If you're going to paint the bookcase, you need only fill any gaps in the laminations with wood filler, then sand smooth before priming and painting. Apply at least two coats of enamel, sanding lightly between coats.

If you want a natural or stained woodgrain finish, you should cover the edge of the plywood with ¼" x ¾" strips of solid wood, or with ¾"-wide strips of wood veneer. Both are available at building supply dealers, and both are applied with contact cement.

DYEING POLYESTER

The fabric dyes that are sold for home use are not recommended for use with polyester fabric. Can you tell me what kind of dye can be used on this material?

One of the big advantages of polyester fabric is that it doesn't absorb moisture. Unfortunately, this also means that it doesn't absorb dyes, either. There are commercial processes for dyeing polyester, but they are impractical for home use.

PORCUPINES AND PLYWOOD

Porcupines are eating the plywood on our cottage. Why do they do this and how can we stop them?

This is a common problem, but no one really knows why the porcupines are attracted to plywood. Some experts believe it's the glue. Others think that plywood simply makes an effective grindstone for honing down the porcupine's teeth, something he must do regularly to keep the teeth in cutting condition.

No one has found a good remedy, either, other than getting rid of the porcupines. The most humane way to do this is to drive them away by putting naphthalene flakes in their nests, if you can find them. They're probably not far away.

Painting the plywood with one of the common wood preservatives—creosote, pentachlorophenol, or copper naphthanate—is sometimes effective, but there's no accounting for a porcupine's tastes.

REPAIRING BROKEN POT

Could you please tell me what adhesive I should use to repair a broken pottery plant container from Mexico? It's about 15″ deep, 12″ across, and the walls are 1″ thick.

A fast-setting, 2-part epoxy glue would be best. Mix the two ingredients in the proper proportions (usually equal amounts) and blend them carefully, then apply quickly to one surface of the break and press the two parts together. Bind tightly with string, wipe off any surplus glue that squeezes out, and put the pot in a warm place for 24 hours. Properly done, the repair will be as strong as the rest of the pottery.

HOMEMADE PUTTY

Years ago I used to make my own oil-base putty, but I can no longer find the whitening that this is made with. The putty I buy gets brittle very quickly and I have to keep redoing the windows. Can you help me?

Putty is just a mixture of linseed oil and powdered limestone, or chalk, generally called "whiting" . . . about a pound of chalk to 9 ounces of oil. For glazing, the raw linseed oil is better than the boiled, because it stays soft longer.

Putty is not nearly as good as the non-hardening glazing compounds that are now available, however.

CARE OF QUARRY TILE

I'm going to have a red quarry tile floor put down in our entrance hall. What is the proper way to finish this for easy maintenance?

The tile should be cleaned with a general purpose liquid cleaner. Use a scrubbing brush, remove the soiled solution with a damp mop and rinse thoroughly.

After the tile is dry, a sealer should be applied. The type you use depends on how readily the tile absorbs moisture. A simple test is to sprinkle water on the tile; a porous tile will absorb the water within a minute or two. On this type of quarry tile, one coat of a solvent-based sealer should be used. On relatively impervious tile, use two coats of a water-based sealer. Both types of sealer are available from any tile supplier. Apply as directed.

For easy maintenance, finish the floor with two coats of a clear acrylic floor polish. Additional coats can be applied when necessary, or the entire finish can be removed with an ammonia-based stripper and a new finish applied.

The above treatment will prevent quarry tile from absorbing stains and provide a soft shine that is very easy to maintain.

CREOSOTED RAILROAD TIES

Last year we hired a contractor to do the landscaping around our country home. He was very fond of railroad ties and used them for retaining walls, steps, and a pathway to our front entrance. The trouble is that all of the ties have been treated with creosote, and many of them are so heavily impregnated that they bleed whenever the weather gets warm, and the black, sticky stuff is tracked into the house. We tried scrubbing them with gasoline but that hasn't helped.

Your contractor made the mistake of using new, pressure-treated ties, which, as you can see, are unsuitable for paths, steps or other surfaces that will be walked on. Only old, weathered ties are suitable for such construction.

Washing the wood with petroleum solvent (mineral spirits) may help, but I think you will have to replace the ties in the pathway and steps—either with old ties or with something else. It should not be necessary to replace the ties in the retaining walls, however. If the top ties get any foot traffic, just nail a 1 x 6 board along the top. (This could be done with the steps, too, but it wouldn't look very good.)

The landscape contractor should have

known better than to use heavily creosoted ties for this kind of work, and I think you would have a legitimate claim against him to replace them.

UNVENTED RANGE HOOD

The range hood in my kitchen is not vented to the outside, but contains two filters. One is a metal gauze screen, and behind that is a filter containing a lot of small black granules in a ½" layer between two metal screens. How do I clean this filter? How effective is this type of a range hood?

The granules are activated charcoal, which can't be cleaned, but can be reactivated to some extent by baking the filter in an oven for about an hour at the highest possible temperature. Other than that, you must buy a new one from the manufacturer.

An unvented range hood is of questionable value, and should be used only where an outside vent is impossible. The activated charcoal is only effective for a few months at most, and the filter system does a very poor job of removing grease, smoke, and cooking fumes—and it's incapable of ventilating the room or removing the steam and moisture vapor that cause condensation problems in the house during and after cooking.

If there is any way you can vent the hood to the outside you should do so. Remove the charcoal filter, but keep the other one, which serves as a grease trap, and clean it regularly in hot water and detergent.

MOVING A REFRIGERATOR

I want to take a refrigerator up to our cottage, and am going to rent a trailer to carry it in. Is there any reason why I can't lay the refrigerator down on its side? It would be much easier to carry it this way.

There are a couple of good reasons why you shouldn't do it. For one thing, the sealed compressor unit contains a quantity of oil that can leak into the evaporator if the unit is turned over for any length of time. Some of the newer models have special valves to prevent this, but you have no way of knowing whether yours does or not, so it's best not to take the risk. (Any model that has been tipped over should be allowed to stand upright for several hours before being used.)

There is also a chance that the copper tubing or some of the connections could be damaged if the refrigerator is transported on its side.

BUILT-IN FRIDGE

I want to build a refrigerator into a brick wall in our kitchen. Do I have to make any special provision for ventilation?

You certainly do. The heat that is extracted from the food inside the fridge is transferred to the condenser coils that are located on the back of the fridge. Unless there is a constant movement of air over these coils to dissipate the heat, the fridge won't get cold. You need a ventilating grill 4" to 6" high both above and below the fridge.

ROOFS

BLISTERS ON ASPHALT SHINGLES

I had my roof re-done with asphalt shingles a couple of months ago, and now I notice that blisters about 2" or 3" across have formed on some of the shingles, particularly on the sunny side of the roof. The roofer says this is caused by moisture from the house and is not his responsibility.

This is almost certainly due to undersaturation of the felt with asphalt when the shingles were manufactured. The roofer can probably get them replaced by the manufacturer (unless he bought them as "seconds"), but he would have to take off all the shingles and replace them with new ones. I wouldn't want to bet on your chances of getting this done.

To be honest about it, I wouldn't be too concerned about this. The blisters are unlikely to cause any trouble because there are still two layers of shingles under the one you see.

BUBBLES ON SHINGLES

The black asphalt shingles on our year-old house are blistering in places. The blisters are about 1½" in diameter and are mainly on the sunny side of the roof. The roofer says this is caused by moisture from the house, but the wood frame house has a good vapor barrier and the attic is ventilated by soffit and roof vents. What do you think can be the cause, and what should I do about it?

Roofs

Since your house has been built to present building codes that assure adequate attic ventilation as well as a good vapor barrier, it is unlikely that moisture from the house is the cause of the trouble. The delamination of the shingles is almost certainly due to faulty manufacture, probably undersaturation of the felt with asphalt. This fault should be covered by your new home warranty. The best remedy would be a new roof, but it's also possible just to replace the damaged shingles.

Another remedy would be to break off the top of the blisters, then apply a thin layer of roofing cement and cover this with matching granules obtained from the manufacturer, or scraped off some spare shingles.

BUCKLING SHINGLES

We had a new addition put on our house a few years ago, and now the asphalt shingles on this section are all buckling up. On the older section, they still lay flat. Is there anything wrong?

I suspect that wet, "green" lumber was used under the shingles, instead of plywood. The lumber shrinks as it dries, causing the shingles to buckle. It's not likely to get any worse, and shouldn't cause any trouble unless someone walks on the roof, which could crack the shingles. The only remedy is to have the shingles taken off and re-laid.

CURLING SHINGLES

The asphalt shingles on the roof of my house are curling up at the corners, some as much as ¾" above the underlying shingle. I have tried to stick them down with various adhesives, but none of them seem to work. As I see it, the only solution left is to nail the corners down but I hesitate to do this in case the nail holes leak.

You can cover each nailhead with a dab of roofing cement, but if you have many to do this isn't going to look very attractive. There is also a good chance that one or more of the nail holes might still leak. The best answer is a new roof, I'm afraid.

REJUVENATING OLD SHINGLES

The asphalt shingles on my roof are beginning to curl and split, and some of the colored surface granules have come off. Is there anything I can brush or spray on to restore them?

There are some asphalt-aluminum paints that can be applied to an asphalt shingle roof to change or renew its color, but this will not flatten them out or seal up cracks. The color range is also very limited.

Various plastic sprays have been developed to put a colored, waterproof membrane over a shingle roof, but none of them have been too successful. The best are rather expensive if they are properly applied. It takes something like 30 gallons to apply a 20-mil layer on a 1,500-square-foot roof, and this costs about as much as a new shingle roof. It doesn't rejuvenate the old shingles, anyway; they have to be stapled down before the spray membrane is applied.

But watch out for a new roof repair racket. Salesmen are offering to restore old asphalt shingles with a cheap spray treatment that is nothing more than asphalt driveway sealer thinned with gasoline or petroleum solvent. It does the roof no good at all, and actually causes the shingles to curl and crack even more, but not until after the salesmen have collected their money and disappeared.

Re-roofing is the best solution to your problem.

REPLACING CEDAR SHINGLES

How do you replace cedar shingles that are curled, split, or otherwise damaged? I know how to lay shingles from scratch, but I can't figure out how to extract and replace one or a few shingles in the middle of the roof. How to get the nails in under the shingles is the problem.

Professional roofers use a tool called a shingle lifter, but you can do the job with a flat crowbar or nail-puller. The procedure is quite simple. Starting 4 or 5 courses ABOVE the shingle you want to replace, you slide the bar under a shingle and raise it enough to lift the nails out about ¼". Then you move down to the next course and lift this shingle enough to pull the nails out about ½" to ¾". Move down to the next course and repeat the procedure, lifting the shingles a little higher. When you reach the damaged shingle you'll find you can lift it up enough to remove the nails entirely. (Actually, you can't do this just by lifting one shingle all the way down. Because of the way shingles are laid, you'll need to lift the 2 shingles above the damaged one, then 3 shingles in the next row, and so on. This will be obvious when you start to do it, however.)

When you put in the new shingle, start the 2 nails where they will be covered about 1½" by the next row. Put the shingle in position, then

slide your shingle lifter between the head of
the nail and the shingle above. If you hold the
bar firmly and hit it with a hammer just below
the top shingle, you'll be able to drive in the
nail very easily. Just repeat this until all the
shingles have been re-set.

BUBBLE ON FLAT ROOF

We had the flat roof on our house re-surfaced
about a year ago. The roofer used hot asphalt
and 15-pound roofing paper. There is no
gravel on the roof because he said it isn't necessary if the asphalt is heated to the right temperature. Water running off the roof into the
eavestrough is dark brown in color, and if you
run your hand on the dry roof it comes off
black. In one place there is a bubble about 18"
square; the builder says this is normal for this
kind of roof. I don't know very much about it
but it doesn't seem right to me. Can you give
me some advice?

A bubble like this is definitely not normal. It
should be repaired by cutting it open and applying a heavy coat of rubber-asphalt sealing
compound, replacing the flaps and applying
another coat of the same material along with a
fibreglass fabric patch extending about 9"
beyond the bubble area.

Although there is a cold asphalt roofing system that does not require a gravel cover, the
hot asphalt process your roofer has used must
be protected from sunlight and heat with a
coating of gravel. The dark brown deposit
coming off the surface of the roof now is oxydized asphalt. This may not cause any serious
problems yet, but it will in a few years.

So I suggest you get the roofer back to repair
the bubble as described and to put on the layer
of gravel that is necessary to protect the asphalt.

ICICLES

We have more and bigger icicles than anyone
else on our block. They hang from the eavestrough over the concrete walk along the side
of the house, and I'm afraid somebody's
going to get hurt. Why do we have so many,
and what can we do about it?

Your roof must be warmer than anyone else's,
and there could be several reasons for that
...too high a temperature in the house...not
enough insulation in the ceiling...inadequate
ventilation in the attic.

You'll know if the first is true, but you'll have
to get up in the attic to check the other two

possibilities. You should have at least 6" of insulation in the ceiling, and it should extend right
out to the edges.

Ventilation is necessary to keep the attic cool
and remove any humidity that gets into it from
the house. You'll need one square foot of
screened vent for every 300 square feet of ceiling.
Half of this ventilation should be near the top
of the roof—in the gable peak, for instance—
and the other half should be along the lower
edge of the roof, under the eaves.

All of the above will reduce the amount of
melting on your roof, and should pretty well
eliminate your icicle problem. If low temperatures keep the gutter and downspout frozen,
however, you may have to install an electric
heating cable in them to maintain drainage.

NEW ROOF BRINGS ICICLES

About two years ago we had a new roof put on
our 40-year-old house. The original cedar
shingles and a second roof of asphalt shingles
were removed and replaced with roofing paper
and new asphalt shingles. Every winter since
then we have had enormous icicles form on the
eaves on both sides of the house. I can't see
how a new roof could have caused this, but it
apparently has, and I would appreciate your
advice on what to do about it.

There was probably a lot more air leakage
through the wood shingles than you are getting now, and the reduced ventilation has
increased the temperature in the attic, causing
more melting on the roof, which produces the
icicles. More ventilation in the attic is one
answer; more insulation is another.

INSULATING ROOF

We have black asphalt shingles on our roof and
4" of insulation in the floor of the attic. Since
the black shingles absorb a lot of heat, would it
be a good idea to put insulation batts between
the roof rafters in order to keep the attic cooler
during the summer?

No. A much better way to keep the attic (and
the house) cool is to increase the ventilation in
the attic and put the additional insulation in the
floor. Attic ventilation is required all year—to
prevent condensation during the winter and
keep the attic cool during the summer—so
insulation under the roof would be wasted. You
should have at least one square foot of screened
vent for every 300 square feet of ceiling.

Roofs

LEAKING ROOF

We have a problem with water leaking through the roof and down the walls of the bedrooms. I also notice that ice is forming in the eavestroughs. This is an old house that was completely renovated two years ago. The walls and ceilings were re-panelled and the roof was reshingled. There is no way to get in the attic to see if there is any insulation, but I can see that there is no ventilation up there. What should we do about the roof leak?

There are two possible causes. It may be due to a buildup of water behind the ice dam in your eavestroughs. Increasing the insulation and ventilation in the attic would reduce the ice dam. Another solution is to run an electric heating cable along the lower edge of the roof to keep the ice dam open.

But the apparent leak in your roof could actually be due to condensation in the attic, caused mainly by the lack of ventilation up there. To find out which it is you'll have to cut a hole in the ceiling and install a hatch. Inspect the attic for frost under the roof; this could be the source of the water. Also check the insulation; you should have at least 6" between the ceiling joists. Then put in gable or roof vents as well as soffit vents along the lower edge of the roof to provide a circulation of air through the attic. You should have at least one square foot of screened vent for every 300 square feet of ceiling.

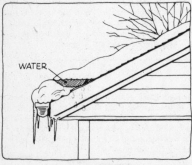

WATER

ROOF LEAKING

During mild winter weather and the first days of the spring thaw, our roof seems to leak. It's all right the rest of the year, even during heavy rains, but every spring we get water stains in one or two spots on the bedroom ceilings. A roofing man tells us we should have a new roof put on, but the house is less than ten years old and the roof seems to be in good condition. What do you suggest?

I don't think you need a new roof. In fact, I don't even think your roof is leaking. It sounds to me more like frost in the attic. This is caused when humid air from the house is trapped in the attic during the winter, and then condenses and freezes under the cold roof. When this melts it drips on the ceiling below and looks very much as if the roof were leaking.

The problem is really in the attic, where more ventilation is needed to get rid of the humid air. You should have one square foot of *open* attic vent for every 300 square feet of ceiling. Check, too, to see if you can find where the warm, humid air from the house is leaking into the attic.

MOSS ON ROOF

Moss is growing on the shady side of our asphalt shingle roof. Is there some way I can kill this and prevent it coming back?

Any wood preservative or garden fungicide will kill the moss, but won't remove it. You will still have to scrape it off with a square-ended shovel or similar tool, so there's not much point in killing it first.

Strips of galvanized metal, aluminum or zinc placed along the top of the roof are said to prevent moss, but all they seem to do is stain the roof. The truth is that moss will continue to grow wherever conditions are right—shade, dampness, and nearby trees. It doesn't seem to harm the asphalt shingles, anyway, but it doesn't look very attractive. (It does promote decay in wood shingles, however.)

REMOVING OLD SHINGLES

We have two layers of shingles on our roof now, but it needs to be done again. How do I take out the nails, and what do I do about the holes these will leave in the roof?

The easiest way to remove old asphalt shingles is with a *flat* garden spade. Just drive it up under the shingles to shear off the old nails. Start at the top of the roof. It may help if you sharpen the edge of the shovel with a file.

Don't worry about nail holes in the roof sheathing. This isn't meant to be waterproof, anyway. The shingles do that.

RESHINGLING A ROOF

Some years ago I had asphalt roofing applied

over old cedar shingles. Now they have curled and cracked and some of the gravel has washed off, so I need a new roof again. Should I just remove the asphalt shingles and replace them, or do I need to remove the old cedar shingles, too, as one contractor suggests.

It would be best to remove all the old shingles and start again. Wood shingles are sometimes laid on sheathing boards spaced several inches apart. If this is what you have on your roof, you will either have to use cedar shingles again or have the sheathing filled in to provide a solid surface for asphalt shingles. The former provides better attic ventilation.

SHAKE ROOF LEAKING

The shake roof on my house is only 12 years old, but it's leaking badly. The shakes seem to have split and the rain comes through in several places. Why would this have happened, and is there something I can paint on to remedy it?

Incorrect application is the only explanation for this problem. Such a simple mistake as using three nails per shake instead of two can cause them to split down the middle when they get wet and expand (which is normal), but even this is unlikely to cause leaks unless the shakes were applied too thinly. They should not be laid with more than 5" exposed to the weather for every 12" of length—that's a maximum of 10" for a 24" shake, 7½" for an 18" shake. This provides two layers of shakes for each nailing point. Perhaps your roofer skimped on the number of shakes he used. You can easily check by measuring the length and overlap of the shakes at the edge of the roof.

If the shakes have too much exposure (not enough overlap), all you can do is take them off and re-do the roof, adding more shakes as required.

I know of nothing that you can paint on the roof to seal it.

REROOFING IN SUMMER

We're going to have a new roof put on our house, but have been told that asphalt shingles shouldn't be applied during hot weather because walking on them when they are soft could do some harm. Is this true?

No. They're more flexible and easier to lay when they're warm. There's more danger of damage if asphalt shingles are laid during cold weather, when they're brittle.

RE-ROOFING

The asphalt shingle roof on our house is about 20 years old. It looks all right, doesn't seem to be cracked or curled, and isn't giving us any trouble, but I'm afraid something might happen and I think it might be advisable to have it re-done. Do we have to have the old shingles taken off first?

If your roof isn't leaking and still looks all right, I see no reason why you should have it re-shingled. Age alone is certainly not a good reason; there are many perfectly good roofs around that are a lot older than that. If and when it does leak, call in a roofer and have new shingles laid on top of the old ones. There's no need to take them off.

ROOFING PAPER

My father wants to put new asphalt shingles on his 20-year-old house. He plans to remove the old shingles and the tarpaper, but has been told that he should use polyethylene film instead of roofing paper under the new shingles. He thinks this won't breathe like tarpaper and may cause condensation. (He's a Scottish stonemason and wants to do a thorough job.) Your advice would be appreciated.

It isn't necessary to remove the old shingles and roofing paper at all. It actually makes a better job if the new shingles are applied on top of the old ones—in which case, of course, no roofing paper is required.

TAR-AND-GRAVEL ROOF

I am considering putting a tar-and-gravel roof on our house, and I would like to know how this should be done. Does the gravel serve any purpose other than to stop the tar from running in hot weather?

This is no job for an amateur. Call in a roofer. Roofing tar will not run in hot weather; the gravel is only there to screen it from the ultraviolet rays of the sun, which will deteriorate it.

TARPAPER UNDER SHINGLES

We are going to have two layers of old asphalt shingles removed from our roof before the new shingles are put on. Is it necessary to put tarpaper down first?

No. This was once common practice, but it is no longer required under asphalt or cedar shingles. The only exception is cedar shakes, each course of which should be overlapped with 15-pound roofing paper. In cold areas, however, it is a good idea to apply a strip of 6-mil polyethylene film at least 3′ wide along the lower edge of the roof under the shingles. A strip of rubberized asphalt is even better. The purpose of this waterproof membrane, which should extend at least 12″ beyond the inner edge of the outside wall, is to keep water from backing up under the shingles and leaking into the house if ice dams form in the eavestroughs.

CUTTING ROOF TRUSSES

The pitch of our roof is rather shallow so there isn't a great deal of room in our attic. There are also a number of 2x4s connecting the rafters and the joists, most of them running at angles that make it very difficult to move around up there. We would like to use the attic for the storage of trunks, luggage and other rarely used items. Can I remove a few of the 2x4 uprights to make more room?

No way! Like most homes built in recent years, your roof is supported by trusses instead of the traditional rafters and joists. Prefabricated trusses are designed like a bridge, with a carefully engineered pattern of light-weight structural members capable of supporting a large load over a long span. But the entire truss assembly operates as one unit; removing a single part can seriously weaken it.

There's nothing wrong with using the attic for light storage, but under no circumstance should the roof trusses be cut or altered in any way.

WOOD SHINGLES OVER ASPHALT

I still have the original asphalt shingles on my 20-year-old house. I'd like to replace them with cedar shingles, but don't know how this should be done. One roofer says he will apply the new shingles directly over the old ones, which are still in fairly good condition. Another roofer says the correct way to do it is to apply 1 x 3 nailing strips first. This is more expensive, of course. Which is right?

Both methods are widely used, but the Cedar Shingle Bureau recommends the use of nailing strips to provide ventilation under the wood shingles. Most roofers, however, apply the

wood shingles directly to the asphalt shingles unless they are in very bad condition, in which case they simply remove them.

ROOF DECK

We have a 2-storey house with a door from the upstairs hall that opens on to the flat roof over the family room. The roof is tar-and-gravel, and it's not very comfortable to walk on. Is there some way we can pave this?

The only practical thing to do is cover the roof with slatted deck panels. These should be about 4′ square, made of 2 x 4 frames covered with 1 x 3 or 1 x 4 boards spaced about ¼″ apart so that water will drain through them. Cedar is the best material, and it should not be painted, although it would be a good idea to treat it with a colorless wood preservative.

ROOTS IN SEWER LINE

Our sanitary sewer line has started backing up because of tree roots in the pipe. Is there anything we can do short of replacing the pipe or removing the tree?

This problem only happens to old sewer lines that have cracked or whose joints have come loose. The materials and methods called for in modern building codes are impervious to tree roots. Having the sewer line cleaned out with a mechanical "sewer snake" is the most practical remedy. Some municipalities provide this service for a moderate fee. In other areas you must call in a sewer contractor. You'll find them listed in the Yellow Pages.

This will probably have to be redone every few years. A better remedy is to have the sewer pipe joints repacked, or the entire line replaced, but this is expensive. It is generally cheaper to have the pipe reamed out every three years than to have it dug up and repaired once.

ROTTENSTONE

You suggested using something called "rottenstone" as a gentle abrasive for removing white watermarks from furniture. I have tried several drug stores but they have never heard of it, and say it is not listed in their reference books. Does it have another name?

Rottenstone is a decomposed siliceous limestone, also called Tripoli, that is softer than pumice and is commonly used to give fine furniture a hand-rubbed, satin finish. It is available from any well-stocked hardware store.

PROTECTING RUBBINGS

I made some brass rubbings in Britain and want to hang them in our home, but don't want to go to the expense of framing them under glass. Is there any other way I can protect their surfaces?

You can buy a plastic "fixative" spray at any supply store that will seal the rubbing to the paper. Be sure to clean up the rubbing and erase all undesired marks before fixing, however.

RUST SPOTS ON SHOWER STALL

Some years ago we installed a shower cabinet of steel with a baked-on enamel finish. Rust spots have appeared in the floor pan and part way up the walls. What can we do to stop these from rusting through?

Remove the rust spots down to the metal with steel wool, then apply metal primer and a porcelain touch-up paint.

RUST RING IN TOILET BOWL

There is a rust ring around the inside of our toilet bowl, and I can't remove it with scouring powders, steel wool, or bleach. Is there anything that will take this off?

As regular readers to this column will know, the magic formula for removing rust stains from just about anything is a concentrated solution of oxalic acid crystals, available from any drug store. You'll have to empty the toilet bowl to apply it. Turn off the valve under the water closet and then flush the toilet. Sprinkle oxalic acid crystals around the rust ring and let them dissolve there. In 15 minutes or so the stain should begin to bleach out. Use a damp rag to rub the oxalic acid solution around the ring, adding more crystals if necessary.

SHARPENING SCISSORS

I have a good pair of sewing scissors that I use a lot. I've often heard that I can sharpen these by cutting a piece of emery paper with them. Is this true?

I've heard and read this many times, but never believed it. This time I got in touch with one of

the world's leading manufacturers of scissors and shears, J. Wiss & Sons. They say that scissors CANNOT be sharpened by cutting emery paper or sandpaper, and that this should not be tried with a good pair of scissors. Have them sharpened professionally.

LOOSE SCREWS

The screws holding the hinges of our back door to the door jamb have become loose. Please tell me if there is some way to remedy this without having to change the position of the hinges. That's a job I don't want to try.

There are a couple of easy ways to cure this trouble. One is to fill the screw holes with pieces of toothpick. Push in as many as you can, and just break them off at the top. Another trick that works very well is to stuff the screw holes with steel wool. Using screws that are slightly fatter and longer than the present ones will also help.

BATH OIL vs SEPTIC TANK

I have bought some rather expensive bath oils, and my husband claims that they interfere with the action of our septic tank. I have put them away until I hear from you. Is he right?

A lot of things interfere with the bacterial action in a septic tank, including soap, detergent, bleach, and oils. But in normal quantities, they do no harm to a properly designed septic tank with an adequate disposal field.

You probably put a lot more oil down the drain in the form of fat, cooking oils or hair oil than you do with a little bath oil.

Ordinary soap is very bad for a septic tank, but it manages to operate anyway. Ideally, a septic tank would serve the toilets only, with all other waste water going to a rockpit or similar drain, but plumbing regulations do not usually permit this.

CARE OF SEPTIC TANK

We have bought a new cottage with a septic tank and disposal field. I'm sure this is properly built, but I've never used such a system before and am worried about what special care or attention is needed. Is it safe to use bleach or drain cleaner, for instance? Do I have to add anything to the water to keep the septic tank active? How often will it have to be cleaned?

Septic Tanks

A septic disposal system is surprisingly efficient and durable if it is properly installed. Normal amounts of grease, soap, detergent, bath salts, and other common household chemicals will not harm it. Even bleach and lye—in moderate quantities—will not hinder the bacterial action in the septic tank.

There are a number of products on the market that are said to accelerate or improve the action in a septic tank, but government studies have shown that these are unnecessary. All the bacteria needed for the operation are already contained in the sewage entering the system.

How often the tank needs to be cleaned out depends on its size and the amount of use it gets. Once every three or four years is usually enough, but many systems go a lot longer than that. It is advisable to have the tank inspected once a year, however. Excessive buildup of the sludge in the tank may clog the disposal field and require its complete replacement.

BAD ODOR FROM SEPTIC TANK

We have a new summer cottage that is served by a septic tank disposal system, like every other cottage in the area. We are experiencing a problem with ours, however, and that is a bad odor that comes from the vent pipe on the roof. The prevailing winds blow this towards our patio, and it is very unpleasant. Do you know of any way this can be remedied?

It is the practice in some areas to build septic tanks with an inlet pipe or baffle that is open at the top. This allows sewage gases to flow back up the main waste pipe and escape through the vent pipe on the roof. The inlet pipe should be fitted with a closed elbow that discharges below the liquid level, so that no gases can escape.

If you have an open inlet pipe, the simple solution is to block the top opening with a heavy sheet of metal or a piece of concrete. Your local septic tank service company can do this for you.

SEPTIC TANK

I have just had my septic tank pumped out but it is still not working right. The toilet does not flush properly and the water stands on the ground over the tile bed, especially near a weeping willow tree close to the tank.

The tile bed is probably plugged with roots from your tree and will have to be dug up. You may also have to cut down that willow tree.

DISUSED SEPTIC TANK

They are installing sewers in our town and we would like some expert advice on what should be done with our septic tank. We keep getting different opinions on whether it has to be dug up and removed, whether the tile bed can be left in, and so on. Can you tell us what we should do?

All you have to do with a disused septic tank is make sure no one can fall into it. Concrete tanks with concrete lids can simply be abandoned, but metal tanks or tanks with wooden lids should be opened, pumped out, and filled with earth or gravel. The tile bed, too, can simply be left where it is, unless it's near the surface and you want to cultivate and plant there.

SEPTIC TANK vs GARBAGE DISPOSAL UNIT

We have just bought a house in the country that has a septic tank. We would like to put in a garbage disposal unit, but don't know if this can be done.

It depends on the size of the tank. If a garbage disposal unit is to be used, a septic tank must be 20% larger than otherwise required. A 3-bedroom house, for instance, normally requires a 600-gallon septic tank, but if a garbage disposal unit is to be used, you would need to move up to a 750-gallon tank.

WATER SOFTENER vs SEPTIC TANK

Is a water softener harmful to a septic tank? I'm concerned that the salt and other chemicals washed out in the regenerating cycle may kill the bacteria.

Scientific opinion, research, and a considerable amount of practical experience indicate that neither softened water nor the regenerative chemicals have any harmful effect on a septic tank. There is evidence, in fact, that the very dilute solutions of calcium, magnesium, and sodium chloride stimulate bacterial action in the tank.

INTERIOR SHINGLE FINISH

We are building a new home and are planning to finish one wall of the bathroom with cedar

shingles. What treatment should we give the shingles to prevent them being water-stained?

To seal the shingles without losing the natural texture and appearance of the wood, give them a coat of a penetrating oil-resin sealer such as Danish oil.

LEAKING SHOWER WALL

Every time we have a shower, water leaks into the basement underneath, but I can't see where it's coming from. The tub/shower enclosure is panelled with those small ceramic tiles, and none of them are missing.

There are several places that could be leaking, but the most likely spot is the joint between the wall and the top of the tub. There are a number of bathtub caulking compounds that can be used to seal up the crack that commonly develops as the bathtub settles.

The next most likely source of the trouble is the cement grout between the tiles. There may be gaps in this, or cracks where two panels meet, such as in the corner. These can be filled with a slurry of white cement and water. (White cement is available at all hardware stores.) Mix it about the consistency of soft butter and wipe it over the tiles. Use a rubber spatula to force it into cracks and gaps. Wipe it off the tiles with a damp cloth, but leave it in the joints. After the grout begins to set, wipe the tiles off with a wet sponge, and clean any drips off the bathtub. A toothbrush handle makes a handy tool to smooth the grout in the joints between the tiles. Keep the grout damp for at least 48 hours.

SHOWER TILE LEAKING

The tile around our bathtub and shower is leaking badly and the water has stained the ceiling below in two places. We have been advised to remove the tile and replace the crumbling plaster behind it with cement mortar to prevent further trouble, but were thinking of using plywood instead. Which do you think would be better?

I wouldn't use either. A much better solution to your problem is to cover the existing tile with one of the molded plastic bathtub enclosure kits that are available from plumbing suppliers, hardware and building supply stores, and other retail outlets. These are easy to install and can be adjusted to fit different tub and shower enclosure sizes.

GREEN SIDEWALK

Our front sidewalk has some sort of green fungus growing on it. Do you know of any way I can stop this from happening?

The green stuff is algae. A strong solution of chlorine laundry bleach will kill it.

TIRE MARKS ON SIDEWALK

One of our son's friends revved his car on our driveway and took off in a "drag" start that left black tire marks on our sidewalk. We tried taking them off with gasoline, but that only made a larger stain. Do you know of anything we can use to clean up this mess?

A solution of 1 part muriatic acid (available at any hardware store) to 5 parts water should do it. Brush on, let foam, then rinse off. Repeat if necessary. Follow the safety instructions on the label.

ALUMINUM SIDING CHALKING

White aluminum siding was put on our house about 18 years ago. Now it is beginning to chalk quite badly and on one side of the house it has turned grey. Can you tell me how to refinish the siding?

The grey is probably mildew, which can be removed with a solution of one quart of chlorine laundry bleach, such as Javex, to three quarts of water. The addition of two-thirds of a cup of trisodium phosphate (TSP) or borax will also remove the chalky film from the old paint. All the siding should be scrubbed with this solution and then rinsed thoroughly and allowed to dry before repainting.

According to aluminum siding manufacturers, any exterior house paint can be used, although it won't last as long as the original factory finish. There are flexible urethane-latex finishes made especially for repainting metal siding, however.

DENT IN ALUMINUM SIDING

A wayward baseball made a dent in my aluminum siding. Is there any way I can take this out?

There's no practical way to remove the dent but it's not difficult to take out the dented section and insert a new piece. Use a razor knife and a metal straightedge such as a carpenter's square to make a vertical cut through the siding

203

on either side of the dent and across the top, just under the lower edge of the strip of siding above. Don't press too hard; use several strokes of the knife to cut through the soft metal. Remove the damaged section.

Cut a piece of matching siding 2" longer than the piece you removed. Bend the locking tab at the top back and cut it off as close to the top as possible. Slide the new piece up under the lip of the siding above and snap the bottom tab in place. Drive a couple of aluminum nails or screws up under this lower edge to hold the new piece of siding in place.

ALUMINUM vs WOOD SIDING

My husband and I purchased a home from the builder's display model. This had cedar siding, but the builder has advised us that he will be using aluminum siding instead. We tend to think that aluminum siding cheapens the appearance of the house, and we'd like your opinion on whether this change is to our advantage or not.

There is usually a clause in the builder's sales contract that allows him to substitute materials "when necessary". Shortages in construction materials pop up overnight, so changes like this are becoming common.

I would prefer wood siding myself, but I know that aluminum siding is perfectly satisfactory, and actually requires less maintenance. It's used on some of the most expensive homes these days, so I don't think it has an inferior status anymore.

REFINISHING OILED SIDING

On the outside of my house I have some vertical tongue-and-groove wood siding that was finished some years ago with linseed oil and turpentine. The areas that are protected by the roof overhang are in fairly good condition, but the lower parts are badly weathered. I want to remove the present finish and apply a darker stain. The weathered areas sand off easily enough, but the sheltered parts gum up the sandpaper almost immediately. Turpentine or paint remover don't seem to work. What do you suggest?

I'm afraid there is no easy way to remove the old finish, and that's why I don't believe in using linseed oil as an exterior wood finish. It will have to be sanded, scraped, or burned off . . . well, not really burned, just heated with a propane torch or an electric paint remover until it softens and bubbles, but it's still a lot of work to scrape off.

Even when you get the old oil finish off, a wood stain won't be able to penetrate the way it should. You will have to use a heavily pigmented exterior stain.

NEW SIDING OVER ARTIFICIAL BRICK

Our house is faced with an artificial brick siding that is similar to asphalt shingles in composition. Insul-Brick, I think it is called. We want to cover it with aluminum, vinyl or stucco siding, but can't get a straight answer as to whether or not the present siding can be left on for added insulation and lower installation cost.

It is common practice to leave the old siding on. If metal, plastic, wood or hardboard siding is to be applied horizontally, vertical 1 x 3 strapping should be nailed every 16". For vertical siding, the strapping is applied horizontally. If stucco is to be applied, metal lath or wire mesh is put on first, then the stucco.

Since your frame walls probably contain no insulation, you should consider having cellulose fibre blown in.

SILICONE ON WINDOWS

I recently had my brick house cleaned with a chemical solution, then sprayed with a silicone water repellent. The silicone got on the windows and I'm still trying to remove the streaks from the glass. Do you know of any solution that will take these off?

The silicone can be removed fairly easily with petroleum solvent (mineral spirits) if you catch it within two or three weeks. But after the silicone film cures, it is very difficult to remove. There are special industrial solvents that will dissolve it, but these are not available in consumer quantities or through retail outlets.

The only practical way to remove a cured silicone film from glass is to scrape it off with a razor knife.

REMOVING SILICONE RUBBER

My application of silicone rubber caulking compound around my bathtub didn't turn out like the pictures. The bathtub and sink are now edged with a corrugated mess. Is there any solvent I can use to remove it?

There are industrial solvents for silicone rubber, but they're available only in commercial quantities. The best way to remove it is with a razor knife.

MAGIC SILVER CLEANER

I saw someone demonstrating what he called an "electronic" silver cleaner. It was a small sheet of metal that you placed in an enamelled or glass dish with a hot solution of washing soda. When tarnished silverware was placed in contact with the metal plate, the tarnish disappeared. The metal plate cost about $5. Can you tell me if this would be safe to use for my good silverware?

This trick has been around for many years, and it really works, but the magic metal is nothing more than a piece of aluminum, worth about 2¢. A piece of aluminum foil will do the same thing, if it is placed in a glass or enamelled dish and covered with a solution of 1 tbsp. of washing soda to 1 quart of boiling water. Electrolytic action between the silver and the aluminum converts the tarnish back to pure silver.

This method should never be used on silverware with a carved or raised design that is accented by a dark, oxydized, or "French" finish. The electrolytic action will completely remove this and spoil the sculptured effect.

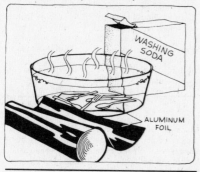

WASHING SODA

ALUMINUM FOIL

REMOVING PROTECTIVE FINISH FROM SILVER

We have some silverware that has a protective coating of some kind on it. It has begun to tarnish under this coating and I would like to be able to remove it so I can polish the silver again. It is too expensive to send the silverware back to the factory to be refinished.

A number of different coatings have been developed to produce "tarnish-proof" silver, but they must be treated with special care to avoid damaging the finish. Instructions usually say to avoid cleaning the silverware in very hot water or strong detergents, which is the most common cause of the trouble you have had.

Most of these finishes can be removed with lacquer thinner, available from any paint or hardware store. Either dip the silverware in the thinner or apply it with a clean cloth. Repeat several times to make sure all of the lacquer finish has been removed, then buff with silver polish to remove the tarnish.

CLEANING A SILVER TEAPOT

Can you tell me how to clean the inside of my silver teapot? The opening in the top is too small to let me get my hand in to buff it with regular silver polishes.

Put a piece of heavy aluminum foil—a small foil muffin tin or a section cut out of a TV dinner tray—into the teapot and then fill it with a solution of 1 heaping tablespoon of washing soda to a quart of boiling water. In a few minutes the tarnish will have transferred quite magically from the silver to the aluminum. Empty the teapot and rinse thoroughly.

REPAIRING SOAPSTONE CARVING

I have an Eskimo soapstone carving that has been broken. It's a very nice piece with special sentimental value, and I'd like to be able to repair it. How can this be done?

Very easily, I'm happy to say. Use a 2-part, quick-setting epoxy glue. Mix this according to directions, apply sparingly, then press the pieces together. Wipe off any excess glue that squeezes out, and hold the pieces together for about 5 minutes. Then set the carving aside carefully and allow 24 hours for the glue to harden completely. If it's done properly, the join will be almost invisible and about as strong as the stone.

SOUNDPROOFING

In our townhouse we can hear the people talking and running around next door just as if they were in our house. What can we do to soundproof the wall between us?

My son plays drums, and we want to build him a soundproof room in the basement.

We live in a duplex, and the noise from the apartment overhead is getting on our nerves. How can I soundproof my ceiling?

Trying to soundproof a house after it's built is

like trying to waterproof a wicker basket. Sound doesn't just travel through walls and ceilings. It travels through studs and joists, and along beams. It follows heating ducts and piping, and sneaks through holes cut for ceiling fixtures and other electrical outlets. Hidden joints at the top and bottom of walls let sound leak through like water from a cracked jug. And the tiny gap around a door will ruin a carefully soundproofed room.

Sounds that originate in your own house can generally be controlled at their source, either by cutting them down or by filling the room where they originate with soft, porous materials such as carpets, heavy drapes, upholstered furniture, and acoustic tile. These soak up sound like a sponge, absorbing as much as 90% of the sound that hits them. Even flocked wallpaper will absorb a lot of sound, as does coarse-textured cork. Or you can use inexpensive ½" softboard covered with perforated pegboard. Like acoustic tile, however, these only absorb the sound waves that come to them directly through the air; they don't do much to reduce the *transmission* of sound through the wall itself. Sound-absorbing surfaces like this won't cut down noise from an adjoining house or the apartment upstairs, in other words.

You can cut sound transmission in half simply by applying gypsumboard panelling to a wall by means of horizontal metal furring strips spaced about 2' apart. The resilient metal channel isolates the gypsumboard from direct contact with the common wall and also provides a ½" air space that helps to deaden the sound. After the new gypsumboard panelling is screwed to the furring strips and the joints taped and sealed, it should be carefully caulked where it joins the ceiling, floor, and end walls. (The panelling should not quite touch these surfaces.) Resilient metal channel is available from any drywall manufacturer or supplier.

SOUNDPROOFING DOOR

Is there any way to soundproof a plywood door?

Most sound comes around a door, not through it, so it is almost impossible to soundproof one unless you're going to put an interlocking, felt-lined, weatherstrip edge around all four sides. Sound-absorbing materials like acoustic tile and sheet lead can be applied to the surface of the door, but they should be on the side facing the noise. There are also special doors built with soundproof construction, but they're rather expensive.

SOUNDPROOFING AN AIR CONDITIONER

Our neighbors have central air conditioning and the noise from the compressor unit outside their house bothers us a great deal. They have agreed to put up a sound barrier, but don't know how to build one. Can you give us any advice?

Although it may be necessary to put up a sound barrier eventually, there are several simpler and less expensive remedies that can be tried first. If it's really the compressor that's making the noise, and not the fan, this can be covered with a fibreglass-lined metal shroud available from the manufacturer of the air conditioner. Most likely, however, it's the fan that's making most of the noise, and this can be reduced by putting in a thermostatically-controlled 2-speed fan that runs at a slower speed when the air temperature drops at night.

If the compressor is located close to the wall of your neighbor's house, this is probably reflecting the sound towards your windows. Anything that will give the wall a rough-textured or perforated surface will absorb and scatter the sound. An ivy-covered lattice works quite well but stucco is a lot faster.

Where the only solution is to build a sound barrier wall between the compressor and your house, it should be made of something heavy and rough-textured, such as "rug" or "bark" brick, or split-faced, ribbed, or fluted concrete block. The textured side of the wall should face the compressor and the wall should be high enough to hide the unit from view from any of your rooms.

PRESSURELESS SPRAY CANS

My cans of spray starch peter out before they're empty. I don't use them too often, but I always rinse off the nozzle after it's been used. Is this a general fault with aerosol spray cans, or am I doing something wrong?

This is a common complaint, but it's not the fault of the spray cans. It's due to incorrect use. The way an aerosol spray can is constructed, it must be held at least partly upright when it's being used. If held at or below the horizontal, the liquid freon propellant will escape without spraying out the contents. When the freon is gone, there's nothing to push out the remaining spray material.

Instructions printed on the can clearly state that it should be held upright when used, but many people overlook this. If you make sure you use your aerosol spray can correctly, we don't think you'll have any more trouble.

PREVENTING SQUIRREL DAMAGE

For several years we have been plagued by squirrels tearing the shingles off the edge of our roof to get behind the faciaboard to nest. When we cover the holes with metal they just move to another spot. Now we have to reshingle the roof and I would appreciate any advice you can give us on how to get rid of the squirrels.

I can only suggest an unusual remedy that was told to me by a well-known wildlife photographer. He claimed to have solved this problem by building a squirrel house under the peak of the gable and fitting it with old carpet and other squirrel comforts. The idea is that one family of squirrels takes up residence here and then proceeds to protect its territory, keeping all other squirrels away from the house.

If you stop to think of it, this makes sense, but I didn't like to ask him what happens when the new brood grows up and goes looking for a home near mom and dad. Do you start building a squirrel subdivision? As a temporary solution, however, it may be worth a try.

POLISHING STAINLESS STEEL

I have a very good set of stainless steel flatware, which we use regularly. Over the years it has become scratched and dulled. Is there any way I can restore the polish? Ordinary polishes don't seem to do any good.

It's not difficult to restore the polish on stainless steel if you have the right abrasives. Polishes used for silver, copper, or aluminum are not hard enough for steel, which requires abrasives like silicon carbide or aluminum oxide.

The trick is to do the job in three steps, using three progressively finer grades of abrasive. For the first, you can use coarse automobile valve-grinding compound. Follow this with fine valve-grinding compound. (Coarse and fine are sold in one, double-sided container, available at any auto supply store.) For the final polishing, use white rouge or Tripoli, available from any jewelry supplier.

Apply the abrasives with cloth or felt pads, using a different pad for each grade of abrasive and cleaning the flatwear between each application. Use the coarse abrasive until the scratches have been removed and an even, matt finish can be seen. Then use the finer abrasive to give softer satin finish. A final polishing with white rouge will give a high shine.

If you have an electric drill and a drill stand,

you can do this work much faster with felt buffing wheels. Use a different wheel for each grade of abrasive.

If the handles of your stainless steel flatware have a satin finish, use just the coarse valve-grinding compound, or #240 grit emery or silicone carbide paper on this part.

TESTING STAINLESS STEEL

I bought a set of stainless steel tableware which I now think is not very good quality. Is there any simple test for good stainless steel?

If you have a small magnet of any kind around the house, you can test it very easily. High quality stainless steel is non-magnetic; it won't stick to the magnet. Low quality alloys will.

STAINS

SANDSTONE ACID STAINS

We recently cleaned our sandstone fireplace with full strength muriatic acid. It turned brown and went quite blotchy. Is there anything we can do to restore it?

You should have diluted the muriatic acid, one part to ten parts water, and rinsed it off thoroughly. What you have are "acid burns". They can usually be removed with a concentrated solution of oxalic acid, available at any drugstore.

BALLPOINT INK STAIN

I have a ballpoint ink mark on my light-colored vinyl upholstery. Can you tell me how I can remove it?

Rubbing alcohol works pretty well. So does hair spray, believe it or not. There are also a number of ballpoint ink removers on the market, available at most stationery stores.

STAINS ON BATHROOM CEILING

I have a very annoying problem with the ceiling in our bathroom. My husband takes a lengthy shower every morning and I take one every day later on. The trouble we are having is that our painted ceiling has brown water spots all over it and I can't wash them off.

The brown marks are mold or mildew, and they can be removed with a fairly strong solution of chlorine laundry bleach. But they'll keep coming back unless you do something about the humidity. The proper solution for this problem is to install a vent fan in the bathroom to remove the steam and reduce condensation on the walls and ceiling.

BROWN STAINS ON CARPET

I cleaned our light green, wall-to-wall carpet with a special carpet cleaner. I put the foam on very generously and soaked it in well, then vacuumed it when dry, as instructed. It came up a lot cleaner, but some brown patches have appeared on the carpet, and further cleaning won't remove them. What do you suggest?

It sounds to me as if you used too much water and too much foam. The trick in these home cleaners is to use a very dry foam, and apply it just to the surface. It should never be allowed to soak down through the fibres and into the backing, because these often contain dyes that bleed up into the carpet fibres when they get wet. I think that's what happened in your case. A commercial cleaner may remove some of the discoloration, but I don't think you'll be able to get rid of it entirely.

CURRY STAINS

My husband and I are fond of curry dishes, but we can't remove the stains from placemats or napkins.

The stain is probably caused by turmeric, one of the spices used in curry powder—and,

unfortunately, one of the strongest natural dyes. You have to catch the stains very quickly, and soak them in ammonia or alcohol. If some stain remains, try bleach (but not on colored materials, of course).

DYEING A RUG

There are some spots on our off-white Indian wool rug that the professional carpet cleaners can't remove. They suggest that we have the rug dyed in order to hide them. Do you think this a good idea?

Not necessarily. What often happens is that the stains get dyed a darker color too, so they still show up. The only cure would be to bleach the stains out first, then dye the rug.

DYE STAINS ON FURNITURE

The three felt pads on the bottom of an ashtray left green dye stains on my walnut coffee table when they were placed there damp one day. How can I remove them?

Dampen a small piece of cloth with a dilute solution of chlorine laundry bleach (about 1:10), wrap it around your index finger, and rub it gently on the dye spots.

EGG STAIN ON STUCCO

Some young vandals threw eggs on our stucco house a couple of years ago, and we have been unable to remove the stain. Do you have any suggestions?

Try a strong solution of ordinary household lye . . . one 9½-ounce can to a quart of water. Mix this in a glass or enamelled pot (NOT aluminum). Wear rubber gloves and be careful to keep the caustic solution off everything but the stucco. Apply with a string dishmop.

This may leave a "clean" stain, of course. If it does, you will have to wash the entire stucco wall down with a solution of 1 part muriatic acid (any hardware store) to 10 parts water. Hose off.

FILLER STAIN ON FLOOR TILE

We dropped some prepared wall filler on our kitchen floor tile and it has left spots that we can't remove. What's the answer?

Some of the instant fillers that come in a tube contain a solvent that will etch the surface of a vinyl tile. If this is the case, there's nothing you can do to remove the spots, short of replacing the tiles.

GLASS STAINS

We have a dishwasher and a water softener, yet all our glassware is getting streaked with what appear to be dirty marks. The marks can't be removed with any household cleaner or scouring powder, even steel wool, and the problem is driving us nuts!

Your glassware isn't dirty, it's etched, and there is nothing you can do to remove the marks. Glass manufacturers tell me that this common problem is caused by the strong alkalis used in dishwater detergents. Combined with the very hot water used in dishwashers, these alkalis are quite capable of etching the surface of most household glassware. Some glasses seem to be more susceptible than others, but crystal and Pyrex are not affected. The only way to prevent it is to wash your glassware by hand, using a mild detergent or plain soap.

GRASS STAINS

How can I remove grass stains from clothes?

Most grass stains can be removed with methyl alcohol. Always test colors first to see if they are affected. If a stain remains on white material, use a mild solution of sodium perborate, chlorine bleach or hydrogen peroxide.

GREASE ON CONCRETE

Someone put a bowl of popcorn on our concrete hearth, and the butter has left a stain that won't seem to wash off. What do you suggest?

Grease stains like this can be removed from concrete with a poultice made of petroleum solvent (mineral spirits) and powdered chalk, both of which you can buy at any hardware store. Mix the solvent and the chalk to make a paste, and spread it thickly on the stain. When it is dry, brush it off, and if you're lucky, the stain will go with it. If not, repeat.

You can also use one of the de-greasing compounds sold at automobile supply stores.

GREEN BATHTUB STAIN

What causes the green stain around the drain in my bathtub, and what can I do to remove it?

The stain is caused by copper salts deposited by a dripping tap. First replace the washer in the faucet, then remove the stain with household ammonia, applied full strength, or wet the stains and sprinkle them with oxalic acid crystals.

GREEN STAIN ON WOOD DECK

The north side of the wood deck at the back of my house is turning green. How can I remove this and keep it from coming back?

That's a form of moss or algae that grows on any damp material that is near trees and continually in the shade. Apply a strong solution of chlorine laundry bleach—say one part to four parts water—and scrub with a stiff brush. Rinse and dry, then apply a non-staining wood preservative such as 5% pentachlorophenol. This will discourage the growth of algae.

HAIR DYE STAINS

Please tell me how to remove stains on curtains caused by hair dye.

You can use the lighteners or bleaches recommended by the hair dye manufacturers, but the spots left by the bleach will probably be as bad as the spot left by the dye.

INK STAINS

I am renovating an old oak desk, and have progressed to the point where all the old finish has been removed. Unfortunately there are still some large ink stains that I have not been able to get off. They seem to have penetrated into the wood and I would have to sand very deep to get them out. Can you suggest any alternative?

A fairly strong solution of chlorine laundry bleach will work on some ink stains. So will hydrogen peroxide. If these don't do the job, try one of the ink removers that are available at all stationery stores. But if it's India ink, I'm afraid you're out of luck. This is made from lampblack, or carbon, and there's nothing that will bleach that out.

Stains

MILDEW STAINS ON LINEN

Is there any way to get mildew spots out of dinner napkins? I sent them to the cleaners but they came back just as bad.

If the napkins are not colored, a fairly strong solution of chlorine laundry bleach can be used to remove the mildew stains.

MUSTARD STAINS ON VINYL TILE

Because our children like hot dogs and eat them in the kitchen, I now have some colorful mustard stains on the white vinyl tile floor. Ordinary cleaners won't take them off and I'm afraid to try anything exotic for fear of ruining the tile, which otherwise looks beautiful. Can you tell me what to use?

Remove any wax or other protective finish from the stained area, then apply a 5% solution of hydrogen peroxide, leaving it on for several minutes, or until the stain is bleached out. A few drops of household ammonia will increase the bleaching action. Then rinse, dry, and apply your usual polish.

OIL STAINS ON CONCRETE

How can I remove grease and oil stains from the concrete floor under our car?

First scrape off as much of the greasy dirt as possible. Buy a pound of trisodium phosphate (TSP) crystals from a hardware store. Wet down the concrete and sprinkle the TSP generously over the greasy spots. Brush lightly with a stiff-bristled brush to dissolve the TSP and work the solution into the area. Let stand for 15 minutes or so, then brush vigorously until all the grease is removed. Flush with clean water.

Oil stains can also be removed from concrete with one of the washable degreasing compounds sold at automobile supply stores.

A coat of boiled linseed oil, diluted with an equal quantity of turpentine or paint thinner will seal the surface against further oil penetration.

OIL STAIN ON SIDING

Our oil tank has overflowed on the stone-grey asbestos-cement siding. How can I remove the oil stain?

Spray it with one of the degreasing compounds sold at auto supply stores, then hose off.

PERSPIRATION STAIN ON CHAIR

There are white stains on the back of my walnut dining room chairs caused, I believe, by perspiration when the chairs were used during the hot summer months without jackets being worn. What can I use to remove these stains?

Such stains are usually just on the surface of the finish and can be removed by rubbing in the direction of the grain with any gentle abrasive, such as No. 0000 steel wool and a few drops of lemon oil; automobile rubbing compound (available at any auto supply store), even toothpaste. If this dulls the finish slightly, the gloss can be restored with paste wax and buffing.

PRINTER'S INK STAIN

I left some wet newspapers on our kitchen floor all night, and now I can't get the ink stains out of the tiles.

Rub the spots gently with a cloth moistened with petroleum solvent (mineral spirits).

SPOTTED PRINTS

I have found some old engravings that I want to frame, but they are badly marked with brown spots and some even have brown water stains. Is there any way I can get rid of these marks?

The brown spots are called "foxing", and are caused by mildew. Provided the prints are only black ink, and are not colored, you can remove the stains and restore the bright, original sparkle of the engravings just by soaking them for a few minutes in a solution of one part chlorine laundry bleach to 20 parts water, and then laying them out to dry. But I repeat, *don't* try this if the prints are colored.

STAINS ON STAINLESS STEEL

I was given an expensive set of stainless steel tableware about a year ago, and now the pieces have become discolored and pitted. I thought stainless steel was really stainless; what could be wrong?

There are several grades of stainless steel, and some are more resistant than others. Even the best grade, however, is not entirely immune to corrosion. There are several reasons why tableware becomes marked in normal use:

Iron in the water is capable of staining stainless steel. In areas where the water is soft and somewhat acid, the use of copper pipes in the household plumbing system can also cause stains. And under certain conditions, acid in foodstuffs can mar stainless steel. So can strong salt solutions.

Corrosion can be caused by the minute electric currents that are set up when two different metals are placed in the same chemical solution—if a mixture of stainless and silver cutlery are washed in a detergent and left to dry by themselves, the washing-up water will act as a conductor. The most chemically active of the metals, the steel, will start to dissolve and, while it won't be evident right away, in time it may even produce deep pits in the stainless.

Another problem is that modern detergents wash too well. Old-style powders left a trace of grease on the surface of the metal, and this helped to protect it.

There is no harm in using detergents to wash stainless steel, but it should be used in moderation and the cutlery should be rinsed thoroughly in clean water. Most important, it should be dried as quickly as possible after it has been washed.

RUST MARKS ON STONE

We have a split fieldstone fireplace that was built about a year ago. Recently we began to notice what appear to be rust spots on the stones. They're about ¼" in diameter and the stone dissolves into a powder inside the spot. You can push a nail in about ¼". What can we do to prevent the stone from deteriorating in this way?

There is iron in a lot of our native stone, and when the stone is cut and the new face exposed to dampness, these pockets of iron absorb moisture and turn to rust powder. The stone itself isn't going to deteriorate, however, just the few spots where the iron is located. And there isn't anything you can do about it, anyway, I'm afraid.

RUST SPOTS ON LAUNDRY

We recently moved into a country home with a good supply of clean, clear well water. We put in a water softener, but I am still having trouble with brown rust spots on my laundry. My husband also notices a metallic taste in our tea. What is wrong, and what can we do about it?

You have too much iron in the water. It's dissolved, so you can't notice it until it precipitates out in the laundry or forms bad tasting compounds with the tannins found in many common beverages. Chlorine laundry bleach causes the iron to precipitate out, so one cure is to stop using this.

A water softener will remove a certain amount of dissolved iron, but obviously not enough in your case. You can buy a separate unit to remove the dissolved iron. It does this by precipitating the iron with chlorine (laundry bleach) and then filtering out both the iron and the chlorine.

The spots that are now on your clothes can be removed with a concentrated solution of oxalic acid crystals, available at any drug store. Lemon juice and salt can also be used. Moisten the spot with lemon juice, sprinkle with salt, and hold over steam from a boiling kettle.

RUST STAINS ON STONE

There are rust stains on our stone steps around the bottom of the iron railing supports. I can't seem to get them off with anything I try. Do you know how to do it?

Rust stains on stone—or concrete, or ceramic tile, or porcelain enamel, for the matter—can be removed quite easily with a concentrated solution of oxalic acid crystals, available at any drug store.

RUST STAINS ON SIDING

There are rust marks on the white siding on our house. How can we remove them?

These are caused by nailheads which have not been recessed into the wood. Buy a nail set and punch the nails a good ⅛" below the surface, then fill the holes with putty. The rust stains can be removed with a steel wool soap pad.

SCORCH STAINS

Can you tell me how to remove ironing scorch stains from a pair of washable cotton slacks?

Washing will often remove superficial scorch marks. Hydrogen peroxide can be used on more stubborn stains. Sponge on full strength, add a few drops of household ammonia, then rinse. But if the material is colored, check first for color fastness; hydrogen peroxide is a mild bleach.

SINK STAIN

There's a nasty yellow stain where the water has been dripping into my sink. I've tried bleach and scouring powders, but none of them work.

This sounds like a rust stain, which can be removed quite easily. Sprinkle it, when wet, with oxalic acid crystals, available at any drug store. This is handy stuff to have around the house, anyway, because it can also be used to remove rust stains from clothing, as well as black water stains from wood.

OXALIC ACID

STAINED VINYL FLOOR

The sheet vinyl floor in our kitchen has been stained by a colored floor mat. Floor cleaners, wax removers, even steel wool have been tried without success.

Have you tried liquid laundry bleach?

BLACK TOILET BOWL STAINS

There are black stains coming down from the flush ring around my toilet bowl. What causes these and how can I get them off?

These black marks are sometimes caused by an old rubber ballcock stopper valve in the bottom of the water closet. Remove the surface stain with scouring powder, and then replace the stopper valve. You can buy these at most hardware stores.

WATER STAINS ON FABRIC

The rain blew in an open window in our living room and soaked the bottom of our pale green curtains. Water stains were left when the curtains dried out, and washing doesn't remove them. Do you know of any way to remove water stains from fabric?

Such stains can often be removed by soaking them in a solution of 1 cup of salt to 1 quart of water. Scrub the spots thoroughly, then rinse thoroughly with clean water.

WAX ON NYLON DRESS

Is there any way of removing wax spilled on a black nylon jersey dress?

Sandwich the wax stain between several layers of paper towelling and press with an iron set at low heat. Repeat until most of the wax is absorbed by the towels, then send the dress to the cleaners—they'll remove the rest.

WHITE WATER MARKS

We have a nice little dog who a few weeks ago had a few accidents on my hardwood floors. This has left some large, white water marks, and nothing I've tried will remove them. I don't want to have to refinish the whole floor. Do you have any suggestions?

White water stains like this are usually just on the surface, and can be removed with a mild abrasive such as automobile rubbing compound or even very fine steel wool (#0000 grade). Rub in the direction of the grain, and use paste wax to restore any lost gloss.

STAIR DIMENSIONS

I want to build a flight of stairs and would like to know the proper measurements for the steps.

These are partly determined by the pitch of the stairway, but a tread depth of 11" and a rise of 7¼" is generally considered ideal. The tread normally overhangs the riser by about 1". For main stairs the rise should be no more than 8" and the tread width no less than 9¼". The maximum rise and minimum tread width for other stairs is 9". (Note that the width of the tread *decreases* as the height of the rise *increases*.)

SQUEAKING STAIRS

We recently purchased an old house with stairs leading from the kitchen to the bedrooms. We would like to carpet these stairs when we do the kitchen, but they squeak badly and we want to cure this before we carpet them. Can you tell us how to do it? Under the stairs is a stairway to the basement, so we can reach the underside of them quite easily if necessary.

Drive two or three 2½" spiral finishing nails through the front of the treads into the riser (the vertical board at the back of each step) and one or two nails through the side of the treads into the stringers or cleats that support them. From below, nail the back of each tread to the bottom of the riser above it. Since you're going to carpet the stairs, there's no need to countersink the nails and fill the holes; just drive them flush.

TILING BASEMENT STAIRS

Our basement stairs have been painted for years, and now I would like to tile them, but I've been told that tile won't stick to a painted surface. Is this true?

Tiles that are applied with adhesive are not recommended for painted surfaces, but you can use any of the self-stick tiles with the peel-off backing.

WATER FOR STEAM IRON

Is it safe to use rainwater instead of distilled water in my steam iron? It would be much cheaper.

Yes. Rainwater isn't the purest water these days, because of atmospheric pollution, but it's certainly soft, and that's the requirement for use in a steam iron. In other words, it won't leave a buildup of hard lime deposits behind when it evaporates.

Another easy source of water safe for steam irons is the water that collects when you defrost your refrigerator. That's distilled water, too, and probably cleaner than rain water these days. But be sure the defrost water is not contaminated with blood or food particles from the fridge.

Water from a dehumidifier can also be used.

SOFTENED WATER IN STEAM IRON

We've had a water softener installed in our house. Is it safe now to use softened tap water in my steam iron?

I'm afraid not. In a water softener, the "hard" calcium and magnesium salts are simply replaced with soluble sodium salts. This results in "soft" water, but it still contains dissolved salts that would be left inside the steam iron as the water boils away.

STEEL STUDS

I have heard that builders are now using steel framing instead of lumber, and that it is a lot easier to use. I want to build some rooms in my basement and would like to know if I can use steel studs instead of 2 × 4s. Would this be economical?

Steel framing has been used in commercial construction for a number of years, and quite a few house builders are also using it for interior partition walls. For a while it was actually cheaper than lumber, but prices fluctuate with changing demand.

Steel framing has a lot of advantages besides price, however, and it is an excellent material for the handyman builder. It's very light—you can carry enough to finish a basement under one arm. It doesn't warp or shrink. And it can be put up in about a quarter of the time it takes to construct a wood frame wall. Only the top and bottom track have to be fastened in place; the studs just snap in position.

On the other hand, you can't nail anything to steel studs; adhesives or special self-taping screws must be used. Also, the material itself is not that easy to find. Very few building supply stores carry it yet, although it is available from drywall suppliers, and any gypsumboard manufacturer can tell you where to get it.

CRUMBLING STONE WALL

We have a very old house with basement walls made of stone. The mortar is crumbling away, and even the cement plaster coat we had put on the wall is beginning to fall off. Must I have a new wall built?

Poor drainage outside the foundation walls would seem to be your main problem. Fix this and your stone wall won't give you much trouble. The mortar will have to be repaired outside as well as inside, anyway, so while you're there you can check and repair the drainage. Call in a stonemason to check the work and give you an estimate.

BUILDING A STONE WALL

I want to build a stone wall with rocks on my property. What is the best way to split rocks, and what is the correct mortar mix to use?

A 12-pound sledgehammer is the best tool to use, plus a smaller, 2-pound hammer for shaping. Very large boulders are usually split by drilling a ¾" diameter hole in them with a star drill and hammer and then driving a set of wedges called plug-and-feathers into the hole.

Use mortar composed of 1 part portland cement to 3 parts sand, and enough water to make a fairly dry mix that just sticks together when you squeeze it. Make sure each rock is well supported on a bed of mortar when you lay it, then fill in the gaps with more mortar and smooth with any improvised pointing tool.

CRACKED CROCK

I have an old, glazed, stoneware crock that I like to use to put cut flowers in, but it has developed a hairline crack. Is there any way I can fix it?

Old-fashioned waterglass, that grandmother used to preserve eggs, will sometimes work. Dilute the syrupy liquid with an equal amount of water and paint it on the crack, getting as much as possible to sink in. Then wipe the surface clean with a damp cloth and allow to dry.

It's not easy to find waterglass these days, but some drug stores and grocery stores carry it.

STUCCO

BLOTCHY STUCCO

The top floor of our new, 2-storey house has a stucco outside finish that has dried unevenly and looks blotchy. Also the color isn't quite what we wanted. We have been told that it can't be painted because the surface is too rough. What do you suggest?

The blotchy color is probably due to incorrect mixing of the stucco. There's no reason why you can't paint it any color you want. Any exterior latex paint can be used. This goes on best if you dampen the surface of the stucco first, then use a brush or a lamb's wool roller.

CEMENT WASH FOR STUCCO

Part of my house is covered with stucco, and I would like to give it a "cement wash." I've seen this done with a mixture that is about the consistency of paint, applied with a whitewash brush. Can you give me the formula for this?

It's simply a mixture of portland cement powder and water. White cement is commonly used. Wet the stucco and let the surface water be absorbed before you apply the cement wash. Use a fine spray to keep the surface damp for a couple of days to allow the cement to harden properly.

CLEANING STUCCO

The white stucco on the outside of our house is dirty and stained. We don't want to paint it, because it has glass chips in it that sparkle in the sunlight. How can the stucco be cleaned?

Stucco can be cleaned with a solution of ½-cup of trisodium phosphate (TSP, from any paint or hardware store) to a gallon of water, plus a generous squirt of any household detergent. Apply with a stiff brush, then hose off.

In very stubborn cases it would be worthwhile to rent a high-pressure, hot water spray cleaner from a tool rental shop. You can add detergent and TSP to the spray. For best results, hold the nozzle at a low angle to the surface of the stucco.

CRACKED STUCCO

The stucco finish on our 6-year-old house is

beginning to look shabby and has a few cracks in it. I don't want to spend a lot of money and would like to fix this myself, if I can. Is this a practical project for a home handyman?

I think so. Large cracks can be filled with any of the latex-cement, concrete patching materials available at hardware and building supply stores. Fine cracks can be filled by brushing on a thick paint mixture of plain Portland cement powder and water.

The stucco should be dampened thoroughly with water before either of these materials is applied, and should be kept damp for three days afterwards so that the cement will cure properly. This can be done with an occasional fine spray from a garden hose.

It is unlikely that the patching coat will match the old stucco, so you will probably have to paint it. Any exterior latex paint can be used.

HAIRLINE CRACKS IN STUCCO

We recently had our house stuccoed. The applicator put wire mesh on the plywood siding first, then put on two coats of white stucco. Within a few days I noticed that it was covered with fine, hairline cracks. The applicator says this is natural and I shouldn't worry about it. Is that true?

No. It is probably due to improper curing. Stucco, like any other portland cement compound, must be kept damp for at least three days to set properly and minimize shrinkage. In hot, dry weather the fresh stucco must either be sprayed frequently or covered with polyethylene film to keep it from drying out too soon.

If the applicator didn't want to do this himself, he should at least have told *you* to keep the surface damp for a few days.

The best remedy now is to apply a cement "wash" coat, which is nothing more than a soupy mixture of white portland cement and water. Dampen the stucco first, brush on the cement mixture, let it set for a few hours, then keep it damp with a fine hose spray for three days.

APPLYING STUCCO OVER SIDING

The outside of our house is finished with 10″ bevelled wood siding and we are tired of having to paint it every three years or so. We don't like the idea of aluminum, steel or vinyl siding, however, and are thinking of having stucco applied. Would this adhere to the painted siding? How long would it last?

The painted surface would not provide a good base for cement stucco. The standard method of applying stucco over wood siding is to apply vertical 1x3 strapping, then exterior sheathing. Chicken wire or metal lathing is stapled to this as a support for the stucco. It would be best to use one of the foamboard insulation materials as sheathing.

A good stucco job will last for many years but it does get dirty and may require painting periodically. Check other houses in your area to see how this finish stands up, then get bids from several contractors.

INTERIOR STUCCO

Our living room walls are faced with imitation wood panelling. We would like to cover them with one of the stucco-like finishes that you mix with water and apply like paint. Can this be applied to this type of panelling?

It sounds as if you have one of the decorative hardboard panels with a printed paper face in a simulated woodgrain pattern. This material swells and buckles when it absorbs moisture, so I would not recommend using this kind of paint on it.

STUCCO vs BRICK

I am getting ready to build a house, and was planning to use stucco on wood frame. Now I'm told that stucco doesn't provide as much insulation as brick veneer, and that moisture will penetrate it and rot the framework. Is this true?

There is very little difference between the insulation value of stucco and brick; both are equal to no more than ¼" of fibreglass. You will have batt insulation inside the frame walls anyway, but for additional insulation, foamboard sheathing can be applied on the outside before the stucco is put on.

Some moisture will penetrate the stucco, but a waterproof building paper is used behind both stucco and brick veneer to protect the wood. Either material is perfectly good. The choice is a matter of personal taste, and budget.

EMERGENCY SUMP PUMP

Our house is in a very wet area and the sump pump in the basement floor runs at least once a day. Twice in the last ten years the pump has failed and flooded the basement. Is there such a thing as a double pump or other back-up system that will prevent this?

One solution is to put in a high water alarm that will let you know when a pump has failed. This has a float switch and an alarm bell that warns you of trouble, but you would still have to repair or replace the faulty pump very quickly to keep the basement from being flooded.

Duplex pump systems for residential use are available but expensive. You can achieve the same result much cheaper simply by enlarging the sump to take two conventional pumps, and raise one a few inches higher than the other so that the second pump will only come on when the first one fails. If both pumps are connected to the same drain hose, you'll have to put a check valve in each of them to prevent water from flowing back into the sump.

DISCHARGING SUMP PUMP

We have a sump pump in our basement that discharges to a low spot in our back yard. This area gets wet and swampy, and I would like to know if there is some way to improve the drainage.

The best solution, I think, is to put a rock pit, or dry well, in this spot and run the sump pump line to it, 12" or more underground. The size of the pit depends on the porosity of the soil, but a pit about 4' deep and 5' in diameter filled with random-sized rocks and topped with coarse gravel, earth and sod, will probably be big enough. It would be a good idea to dig a percolation test hole first with a posthole auger. Fill

the hole with water and time how long it takes to drain away. Anything under 5 minutes per inch will give you good drainage. If it's more than that you'll need a larger rock pit, or one in a different area.

NEIGHBOR'S SWIMMING POOL

My next door neighbor is installing an in-ground swimming pool. Instead of making it level with the ground, he's going to have it about a foot above the ground, and the surrounding concrete deck will slope away from it, directing any run-off toward us. I'm afraid that next spring we will have a lake in our back yard and a pool in our basement. What do you think we should do to prevent this?

I really don't think you have anything to worry about. When the pool is in use it's not going to cause any noticeable amount of water to run on to your property. There would be more run-off from watering the lawn than from a swimming pool in normal use. The only time there would be any extra water is when your neighbor drains the pool, or lowers the level a bit for winter. At that time he will pump the water out through a hose, and will have to dispose of it in a way that doesn't disturb his neighbors. If a problem arises then, that's the time to take it up with him. But until that happens, I don't think you have any cause to worry.

SWIMMING POOL COLLAPSING

We bought an older house last year with an in-ground vinyl liner swimming pool that had been installed several years ago and apparently never gave any trouble. During a very heavy rainstorm some months ago, however, we noticed that one wall of the pool was beginning to bulge in slightly, as if the earth was collapsing. Do you know of any way we can restore and reinforce this?

An in-ground vinyl liner pool should have strong supporting walls of poured concrete, concrete block, or metal, although the floor need just be sand. When these pools were introduced some years ago, many of them were simply placed in earth excavations, but the trouble you are having was not uncommon, and the vinyl liner pools got a bad reputation. Then they started building them with strong supporting walls. Evidently you've got one of the old ones, and it's done well to last this long. The only remedy I know of is to have the pool rebuilt.

HANGING TAPESTRY

I have a tapestry about 6′ by 3½′ that I would like to hang in my living room. How do I put it up so that it will not sag?

The best way to hang a rug or tapestry on the wall is to use what carpet-layers call "tackless edging," or "smooth-edge." This is a wood strip with a row of closely-spaced steel pins projecting at an angle. Get a piece of this tackless edging, as long as your rug is wide, from a carpet company. Nail it to the wall where you want the top edge of your rug to be, then simply hang the rug on the row of projecting pins, which will support it evenly along the full width. This also makes it easy to take the rug down for cleaning.

MATCHING TEAK FURNITURE

We bought a teak coffee table a few years ago, and now want to buy end tables to match. However, we find that the new teak tables are much lighter in color than our coffee table. The salesman says that the new tables will darken in a few months, but this doesn't sound reasonable to me. Can we strip the finish of the coffee table and sand the teak to restore the original color?

The salesman is right. The new teak table will darken after it has been rubbed with linseed oil or teak oil a couple of times and exposed to light. Within a year I doubt that you would notice much difference in color between the old and new pieces.

You might lighten the old table slightly by sanding it, but this would be very risky to try because of the thin veneer on the top.

TEAK OIL

Could you please supply me with a formula for making Teak Oil? I understand the basic ingredient is linseed oil, so I think I should be able to make up my own much cheaper than the ones available in the stores.

Teak Oil is a mixture of boiled linseed oil and turpentine. (Be sure to buy the boiled linseed oil, not the raw oil.) The proportion isn't critical, but 50:50 is about right.

Remember, never leave a wet film of oil on the surface of the wood. It should be given about 15 minutes to sink in, then buffed off completely with a dry, soft cloth. Oil that is left on the surface will become sticky, and is very difficult to remove.

LONGER LIFE FOR TEFLON

I have bought a lot of Teflon-coated frying pans in my time. They work great for a while, but after a few months the food begins to stick and I have to buy a new one. Is there any way I can make them last longer?

Teflon loses its non-stick quality with extended use. Like anything else, it wears out in time. Heat is the main cause of deterioration, and you will find that your Teflon pan will last a lot longer if you are very careful not to let it get overheated. If it's hot enough to cause fat to smoke, it's too hot for the Teflon, so just be sure to keep it cooler than that.

When food does begin to stick, here's how to clean it properly. Mix 2 tablespoons of baking soda and ½ cup of liquid laundry bleach with 1 cup of water. Boil this solution in the pan for five minutes, then wash thoroughly and dry. Before using again, wipe the Teflon surface with cooking oil.

This cleaning solution may lighten the Teflon somewhat, particularly where it removes the stain, but this does no harm. And it will at least partly restore the non-stick surface.

TEFLON RE-COATING

Food sticks to my favorite frying pan. Can I coat the inside with Teflon?

You can't apply Teflon yourself, and it's not easy to have one frying pan done commercially. Some firms will do it however. Check the Yellow Pages under "Coatings-Protective."

There are sprays on the market that will prevent food from sticking for a little while, anyway.

SCRATCHED TERRAZZO

How can I remove some scratches from the terrazzo floor in our entrance hall?

The best way to remove them is to call in a terrazzo expert to repolish the floor with power equipment. If there are just a few small scratches, however, you can remove them with silicon carbide paper. Begin with #180 or #220 grit, and use successively finer grades, ending up with #400 or finer.

TILE GROUT

I put down a new floor in my bathroom using 8″ octagonal Italian quarry tiles laid on ¾″

plywood. I purchased the white grouting powder from the same company where I bought the tiles, but it didn't work very well. The first time I used it, it flaked out of the joints and had to be patched. I bought a different brand that seemed to stay in better, but now the whole floor looks patchy. Both brands are soft, porous and very difficult to clean.

Tile grouting is one of those simple jobs that requires a great deal of experience and skill to do it properly. I suspect that you: (a) mixed the grout too thin—it should be about the consistency of soft butter; (b) did not force it into the joints well enough; (c) did not choose the right time to strike it off—it must be allowed to set just hard enough so it can be rubbed smooth, and only experience can tell you when it's right; (d) did not keep it wet for 48 hours so that the cement could set properly.

Grout is white portland cement plus certain bonding agents and plasticizers. Properly applied, it will make a hard, smooth, almost glossy joint that does not absorb dirt and is as durable as the tile itself. But very few amateurs, and not all professionals, have the knowledge or patience to do it right.

And a ceramic tile floor really needs a solid concrete base topped by a bed of mortar. Wood-frame house construction, even with a ¾" plywood sub-floor, is too flexible. Hairline cracks are likely to form in the joints, letting water seep through into the wood.

All things considered, I think ceramic tile is a poor choice for a bathroom floor. A good sheet vinyl is a lot better.

REMOVING CERAMIC TILE

We would like to remove the ceramic tile around our bathtub and put up heavy vinyl paper. Is this practical?

It's practical, but messy, and its success depends partly on how the tile has been applied. Generally the tile is applied with adhesive spread on the drywall (gypsumboard) panelling. In this case you only have to worry about scraping off the old adhesive after you've removed the tiles. A sanding disc in an electric drill sometimes helps. Paint remover, or heat from a hairdryer will also soften the adhesive so it can be scraped off.

But another way ceramic tile is applied (and it's the best way) is in a bed of mortar on a wire grid attached to a rough plaster wall. In this case some of the mortar may break away with the tiles, and that will have to be patched with latex-cement patching compound. And even if the mortar doesn't break off, the surface will be too rough and uneven to take a vinyl paper;

you'll have to sand it down first.

It would be a lot easier to cover the tile with gypsumboard panelling applied with adhesive, then paper over this.

RESILIENT OVER CERAMIC TILE

The ceramic tiles on our bathroom floor are beginning to crack, and it is impossible to get new ones to match. Can a resilient tile floor be laid on top of the ceramic tiles?

The joints of the ceramic tile will show through any resilient tile you put down. Why not put down one of the new bathroom-kitchen carpets?

TINNING COPPER UTENSILS

We bought a set of Portugese copper cooking utensils, and after a couple of months' use the silver metal lining is beginning to wear off two of the pots and the copper is showing through. Is it safe to use them like this? And if not, what can we do about it?

The "silver" lining is a coating of tin, which is put on to prevent the formation of green corrosion on the copper. Even in minute quantities this can effect the taste of food, and anything more than that can be quite toxic.

As long as the copper is kept scrupulously clean, you could probably cook in it safely, but I don't think it's worth the risk. Restaurants and hotels that use copper utensils have them re-tinned regularly. Look in the Yellow Pages under "Tinning" to see who does this work in your area.

TOILET BOWL CLEANER

Can you give me a simple formula for an effective toilet bowl cleaner I can make myself? The commercial products are getting rather expensive.

Before these products came on the market, lye was commonly used for this purpose, and it still works just as well. Shake a tablespoon of household lye crystals into the bowl and let them dissolve, then clean the bowl as usual with a long-handled brush. Or you can simply pour a dollop of liquid drain cleaner (which is really just a concentrated lye solution) into the bowl.

A milder but somewhat slower acting toilet bowl cleaner can be made by mixing 1 pound of washing soda with 3 tablespoons of lye. This can be mixed and stored in a glass jar with a plastic lid, then used like the commercial products, as needed.

Lye is a very strong caustic and must be handled with care. If you get any on your skin or anywhere else you don't want it, wash it off quickly with plenty of cold water.

TOILET PROBLEM

I wonder if you can tell us why our toilet doesn't flush properly. When we press the lever the water from the tank doesn't come down with enough force to siphon out the bowl. It just swirls around for awhile and then stops. The drain is not plugged because when I pour a pail of water into the bowl it flushes away rapidly. Is there some adjustment I can make to remedy this problem?

Either the water tank isn't filling enough—which can be adjusted by raising the float arm (bend it if there is no screw adjustment on the valve end)—or the flap valve in the bottom of the tank is closing before the tank has been emptied. You can check this by taking the lid off the tank and watching the water level as it flushes. If the tank is not emptying completely, perhaps the flap valve (or ball valve in some cases) isn't being lifted high enough; try shortening the chain or wire that lifts it when the flush lever is pressed. If that's not the problem, the flap valve may be waterlogged or otherwise defective. Replace it.

FREEZING TOILET

The toilet in our cottage froze last winter and we had to replace it. Is there anything I can put in the water to prevent this happening again this winter?

Yes, automobile radiator antifreeze. After you turn your water supply off in the cottage for the winter, flush the toilet to empty the water closet, then pour about a pint of antifreeze into the toilet bowl.

WATER SURGING
IN TOILET BOWL

During high winds the water in our toilet bowl upstairs rises and falls. During one bad storm recently, the water was completely drained from the bowl. What causes this and what can we do about it?

The drainpipe is connected to a vent stack that extends up through your roof. Wind blowing down the vent causes the water level in the toilet bowl to change. Freak gusts of wind sometimes create low pressure, or partial vacuum, inside the drainpipe—enough, in this case, to suck all the water out of the bowl.

A sheet metal shop or plumbing supply house can sell you a cone-shaped cap with spring clips that fit inside the top of the vent stack. This should stop the trouble.

SUPPORT FOR TOILET TANK

I had a new toilet put in the upstairs bathroom. When it was installed, the tank was sitting 3″ or 4″ out from the wall. I felt that the tank needed the support of the wall, but the plumber assured me that this was unnecessary. I recently heard of a toilet tank breaking and causing a lot of water damage, and I'm worried about mine. Should I have it changed?

No, the plumber is right. The water tank of a modern toilet rests entirely on the back of the bowl, and no other support is necessary. Don't worry about it.

DANGEROUS TREE LIMBS
OVERHANGING PROPERTY

My next door neighbor has a very large tree on his property that has been partly eaten away by insects. One large branch hangs over my garage and I worry that it may come down in a storm. Can I make him cut this branch off before it causes damage?

You can ask him to remove the offending branch, but you can't make him. On the other hand, you have the right to cut off any branches that overhang your property.

The recommended procedure is to notify the owner of the tree, in writing, that the overhanging limb represents a danger to your property and you would like him to remove it. If he refuses, notify him (again in writing) that you are going to have the overhanging branch removed yourself. You will have to pay the cost of this, of course, and you must be careful not to cut the branch off on his side of the property line; or to cut it in a way that harms the tree.

ROOTS vs DISPOSAL FIELD

We have a large lot with a septic tank and disposal field at the back of the house. About two years ago our neighbor planted a poplar tree on his side of the property line, just about 7′ from our disposal field. The roots from this tree are getting into the tile bed. Can we make him remove the tree? Or is there a chemical we can use to remove the roots from the tile bed?

Any chemicals strong enough to remove the roots would interfere with the operation of your septic tank, so that's out. And you can't make your neighbor cut down his tree, either. But you *can* cut off all the roots that extend into your property. (This won't harm the tree, incidentally). Dig a ditch between the tile field and the tree, on your side of the property line, and cut off all the roots you meet. This should be done every two or three years to keep the roots out of your tiles.

TREE ROOTS

Our house is surrounded by trees and the roots grow through the pipes that lead to our septic tank. Is there a chemical that can be put in the tank to kill or dissolve the roots?

The roots can't get into the pipes that lead TO the septic tank, because they're solid and tightly sealed. And they can't get into the septic tank, either. The only place that the roots can cause any trouble is in the weeping tile lines that run through the disposal field. There is no chemical that will dissolve them. The only remedy is to dig up the weeping tiles, clean out the roots, and re-lay them. Then dig a ditch between the trees and the tiles and cut off any roots you encounter.

TREE ROOTS vs POOL

I am installing a concrete swimming pool on my property this summer, but I am concerned about the large poplar trees that are growing nearby. I planted these seven years ago, but now I want to know how to kill them in case they interfere with the pool structure in later years.

The pool companies I have spoken to about this problem tell me they have never heard of tree roots damaging a reinforced concrete pool. The leaves can be a problem, but most pool owners find the shade and beauty of ornamental trees worth the extra work in keeping the pool clean.

There's only one way to get rid of the trees, and that's to cut them down. To prevent regrowth, the stump and roots must either be removed or poisoned with weed killer poured in holes drilled in the stump.

FRIENDLY MAPLES

I have a male and female maple tree, which are growing close together. I would like to cut the female tree down to make room for a driveway, but understand that the male tree will die if I do. Is this true?

Maple trees are bisexual, so you can't have a male and a female. Removing one will probably improve the other if they are growing close together.

CANDLE WAX ON UPHOLSTERY

I would like to know how to remove red candle wax from an upholstered chair covered in an off-white, slub wool fabric.

Chill the wax with an ice cube to harden it, then break and scrape off as much as you can. Cover the spot with a folded paper towel and apply a hot iron to melt the remaining wax and soak it up into the paper. If any stain remains after you have removed all you can this way, rub the spot gently with a clean cloth dampened with petroleum solvent (mineral spirits)—or use one of the spray-on, powder-type spot removers.

URETHANE

URETHANE ON FRONT PORCH

Last year I painted our front porch with polyurethane varnish on the advice of friends who assured me that the surface would stand up for years. Now it is badly scratched with ordinary use and is peeling badly in spots. Will it help if I put ordinary varnish on top? If not, how do I remove this plastic finish?

I don't recommend the use of *any* varnish on an exterior surface like this. They all crack and peel in time, and are very difficult to refinish when they do. Paint works much better. Urethane varnish can be taken off with any paint remover, but for a large surface like this it would be better to use a floor sander. If only a few small areas are peeling, these could be sanded down by hand and the rest of the floor just sanded lightly to roughen the surface and provide a "tooth" for the paint.

URETHANE OVER LATEX

We have painted our inside walls with latex paint, and I was thinking of applying a coat of urethane varnish over the baseboards so that they will be easier to keep clean. Can I do this on top of the latex?

Urethane varnish can be applied over latex, but this has an amber tone, remember, so it will change the color of the paint to some extent. It would be better to use a matching enamel.

BLISTERING URETHANE FINISH

Eighteen months after moving into our new home, the finish on our black walnut kitchen cupboards began to blister and peel. The painter says he shellaced the cupboards and then used a satin urethane varnish. Other built-in cabinetwork is beginning to do the same thing. What do you recommend?

Urethane varnish should never be used on top of shellac, and any professional painter should know this. All you can do now is to use a paint remover to strip off all the present finish and then refinish with urethane only.

STAIN/URETHANE FLOOR FINISH

I want to sand my hardwood floor and give it a dark walnut finish. I plan to use a walnut stain followed by a clear urethane. Is this the way to do it?

Yes, but check with the manufacturer of the urethane floor varnish as to what stain to use. Some stains contain stearates that prevent urethane from adhering properly. The manufacturer probably puts out stains to be used with his floor finish.

PEELING URETHANE FINISH

Several years ago we had our hardwood floors finished with urethane varnish, and they were beautiful. I waxed the entrance hall and other traffic areas. Then one day my husband decided to touch these areas up with more urethane without first removing the wax. Now the floors are peeling and blistering. Is there any way we can remove this touch-up coat and refinish the areas again?

You'll have to sand the floor down to the bare wood in these areas, and then start again with a 2-coat urethane finish. You really need a heavy-duty power sander for this job, and I think it would be safer to have this done professionally.

Although the wax may be the cause of the trouble in this case, chances are that the touch-up coat of urethane would have peeled even if the wax had been removed. Ordinary varnish can be re-coated at any time, but urethane varnish should not be applied after the last coat has completely hardened. Instructions on the label indicate the maximum time that can be allowed between coats . . . usually 36 hours or less . . . unless the first coat is sanded.

RECOATING URETHANE

In a recent column you said that not more than 36 hours should elapse between coats of polyurethane varnish. I painted outdoor steps with polyurethane enamel, and after the first coat (on new wood) a spell of bad weather prevented me from putting on the next one. Would you please tell me why there is a time limit between coats of urethane, and what should be done to apply another coat after a long delay?

Urethane is weak in what paint chemists call "recoatability", which simply means that it doesn't stick to itself very well after it has hardened completely. It will go on all right, of course, but it's likely to peel prematurely. This problem can be overcome simply by sanding the last coat lightly to remove the gloss and provide a "tooth" for the next coat.

CARE OF VACANT HOUSE

We are planning to close our house for the winter and intend to turn off the furnace and water and drain the system. Are any other precautions necessary to protect our furnishings from cold and dampness?

There's the matter of insurance coverage that must also be considered. To retain your water peril protection you are generally required to notify your insurance company if your house is going to be unoccupied for more than 4 days during the heating season. They will require either that the water be shut off and drained or that the premises be checked by a responsible adult at least once a day to make sure the heat is on.

My own recommendation is to leave the heat on and the thermostat set at 50°. Without any heat at all, I think there is a good chance that dampness and mildew might get into rugs, upholstery, drapes, clothing, etc. This would ruin the furnishings, and it is NOT covered in the standard homeowner's insurance policy.

This means, however, that you will have to make arrangements to have your house checked every day while you are away. If you have it done by a security patrol service it will cost from $5 to $10 a day.

If you plan to be away for more than a week, it's probably advisable to turn off the hot water tank, too. There's a separate switch for this at the fuse box.

VAPOR BARRIERS

ADDING A VAPOR BARRIER

I live in a 2½-storey, double brick house about 50 years old, and am always looking for ways to save energy and cut my heating bills. I would like to put a vapor barrier on the walls, and have thought of covering them with aluminum foil, then gypsumboard. Or would a heavy vinyl wallpaper do the same job?

What job? A vapor barrier on the walls won't save energy or reduce your heating costs. All it is supposed to do is prevent humid household air from penetrating the wall, where it could condense within the bricks and cause them to spall or flake. But if you don't have this problem—and very few brick houses do—then I see no point in applying a vapor barrier.

If you want to save heat, then you should *insulate* the walls. Aluminum foil applied like this is not an effective insulation. And the tiny cavity inside the double brick wall is of little value for this purpose, so the most practical thing to do is apply 2" foamboard on the inside and cover this with gypsumboard, which will

give you a new wall surface for painting or papering. The only other way to do it is to apply foamboard on the *outside* and cover it with siding, but this is a drastic treatment for a brick house.

VAPOR BARRIER IN ATTIC

In the course of insulating our attic to make additional rooms, I called in an electrician to install some wall outlets and switches. While talking to him I mentioned that I was going to staple a polyethylene vapor barrier over the insulation, to which he replied that he knew of several cases where this had caused water to be trapped in the insulation, ruining the ceiling below. I would appreciate your views on this.

It all depends on where the insulation is going. If it is in the floor of the attic, then your electrician is right. The vapor barrier should go underneath the insulation, not on top of it. But if the insulation is being placed in the walls of the new rooms, the vapor barrier should be placed as you plan to do it. The point to remember is that the vapor barrier always goes on the warm side of the insulation.

CEILING VAPOR BARRIER

I have been putting more insulation in our ceiling, but have run into a problem for which I get different answers. The original insulation (about 3") has a vapor barrier on the bottom, facing the ceiling. The new insulation batts also have a vapor barrier on one side. Should I lay them with the vapor barrier up or down?

If there's already a vapor barrier under the insulation, you don't need another one, so you should slash through the vapor barrier face of the new insulation with a razor knife before it is used.

CEILING INSULATION PROBLEM

We had 1½" of insulation in our ceiling, and I recently increased this by stapling 2½" batts to the joists in the attic. Then I covered them with polyethylene sheet vapor barrier. I've been told that this is not the right way to do this. If so, how can I correct it?

You shouldn't have a vapor barrier *on top* of the insulation, and you have two of them—the built-in vapor barrier in the batts, plus the polyethylene sheet. The only vapor barrier you need is the one *under* the original insulation.

First take off the polyethylene vapor barrier completely, then use a sharp razor knife to slash through the vapor barrier face of the new insulation. I would make a diagonal cut about every foot.

Make sure you have plenty of ventilation in the attic. One square foot of screened vent for every 300 square feet of ceiling is recommended. Half of this should be along the lower edge of the roof (under the soffits, for instance) and the other half near the ridge, such as high in the gables.

VAPOR BARRIER ON BASEMENT CEILING

You've answered a lot of questions about vapor barriers, but not this one. We have a holiday home with a walk-out basement. The main floor level is fully insulated, and so are the walls and ceiling in the basement, which is not finished yet. When the basement is completed we plan to use it for living accommodation during winter visits, leaving the upstairs unheated, although occasionally we might use both areas. The question is, where should the vapor barrier go in the basement ceiling, above or below the insulation?

If the basement is heated and being lived in, and the upstairs is not, then a vapor barrier is required on the basement ceiling, immediately under the ceiling tiles or panelling. This follows the simple rule that the vapor barrier always goes on the warm side of the insulation. The humidity in the basement living quarters will rise with cooking, bathing, washing, etc., and a vapor barrier is needed to prevent this humid air from passing through the insulation and condensing on the underside of the cold floor above. Conversely, if you planned to heat the upstairs but not the basement, then the vapor barrier would have to go on top of the insulation, just under the upstairs floor.

DOUBLE VAPOR BARRIER

We had an addition put on our house this summer and hired some handymen to do the work. The wood frame structure was covered with gypsumboard sheathing and building paper on the outside, then someone offered us large sheets of plastic which they said would make the walls completely waterproof. After this was put on the walls were faced with asbestos-cement board siding. Inside the walls were insulated with 3½" kraft-faced batts. They haven't been panelled yet. Now that the cold weather has come I've

noticed that the insulation is soaking wet and water is running down the inside of the wall, behind the insulation. Did we make a mistake in putting that plastic sheet on the outside of the walls?

I'm afraid so. The outside walls are required to be porous to permit any water vapor that gets inside the walls to escape. Theoretically the vapor barrier on the insulation will keep the moisture out of the walls, but some will always leak through, and since it can't get out it will condense at the back of the insulation, inside the wall.

If you will apply a polyethylene vapor barrier on top of the present insulation, then cover this with drywall panelling and two coats of paint, the problem may be considerably reduced. But that impervious outside membrane can still cause serious trouble, including eventual rotting of the wood frame. If I were you I would have the siding removed, take the plastic film off the outside of the wall, and then replace the siding.

TWO VAPOR BARRIERS

My husband and I have recently finished putting a layer of 4" fibreglass batts on top of the 2" batts that were already in our attic. The first layer of batts has a vapor barrier on the bottom, and we put down the second layer with the vapor barrier on top, stapled to the joists. I have been told that this is wrong. If so, what can we do about it?

If insulation is placed between two vapor barriers, as you have done, there is a good chance that condensation will collect between them, reducing the value of the insulation and perhaps wetting the ceiling below.

The remedy is simple. Just slash the vapor barrier face of the top batts with a razor knife to permit air or moisture vapor to pass through them. You should also make sure you have plenty of ventilation in the attic—at least one square foot of screened vent for every 300 square feet of ceiling.

TWO VAPOR BARRIERS?

After reading a recent answer in your column, I think I made a mistake when I finished my basement. I put building paper against the concrete wall, then built a stud frame wall with insulation batts, polyethylene vapor barrier and panelling. I believe this gives me two vapor barriers, one on each side of the insulation, and I'm afraid this will cause condensation problems within the wall. Is there any way I can correct this without tearing the wall down?

Don't worry about it; you haven't done anything wrong. Building paper is reasonably permeable to moisture vapor, and is often recommended in this situation to keep the wood frame wall from coming into direct contact with the concrete. As long as you have a good vapor barrier on the warm side of the insulation you should have no trouble.

NEED FOR VAPOR BARRIER

We have an old wood frame house with no insulation in the walls. A local firm will blow insulation into the walls, but they say there's no way then can add a vapor barrier, which I understand is necessary to prevent condensation inside the walls. What do you recommend?

When a house is built today, building codes require that a vapor barrier be installed on the warm side of the insulation to keep moist household air from penetrating the wall and condensing somewhere inside the insulation. It is impossible to add a vapor barrier to an old house, however, when insulation is put in the walls. And experience has shown that it isn't really necessary as long as care is taken to seal cracks and other openings in the wall.

Window frames and baseboard molding should be removed and caulking placed around the window openings and along the bottom of the wall—places where air leakage commonly occurs.

A reasonably good vapor barrier can be achieved by applying a coat of aluminum paint, then two coats of alkyd or other oil-based paint. But this is rarely necessary, since most vapor penetration is caused by leakage, not permeation.

CEILING INSULATION

I'm going to add more insulation in my ceiling. There is no vapor barrier under the 2" or 3" or loose insulation that is there now. Do I have to remove this and put down a vapor barrier or can I simply lay the vapor barrier on top of the insulation before I put in some batts?

The proper way to do this is to move the loose insulation over and lay strips of 4-mil polyethylene film on top of the ceiling between the joists. Cut the strips 4" wider than the space between the joists and let the plastic film ex-

tend 2" up the sides. Replace the loose insulation and lay friction-fit batts (with no vapor barrier) on top of it, or use loose fill insulation such as cellulose fibre or fibreglass pouring wool.

That's the proper way to do it, but it is common practice today, I'm afraid, to pile on more insulation without bothering about a vapor barrier underneath. If the attic is well ventilated—at least one square foot of screened vent for every 150 square feet of ceiling—and the humidity in your house is not high enough to cause condensation on your windows during cold weather, this is unlikely to cause any trouble. But without a vapor barrier in the ceiling there is always the possibility of frost forming under the roof and dripping on the insulation in the attic.

If you do put in a vapor barrier, remember that it always goes on the warm side of the insulation—on the bottom, in this case, not on the top or in the middle.

WET REC ROOM WALLS

I finished the walls of my basement by putting up 2 × 4 studding, placing insulation between the studs, and then covering the wall with panels. During very cold weather this past winter I noticed water on the floor at the bottom of the outside wall. Upon removing a panel, I discovered that the wall was wet be-

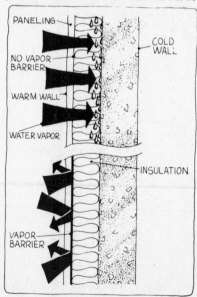

PANELING

COLD WALL

NO VAPOR BARRIER

WARM WALL

WATER VAPOR

INSULATION

VAPOR BARRIER

hind the insulation, and the moisture was running down the wall onto the floor. The wall never leaked before, and still seems to be in good condition. Can you tell me what caused this and what I can do about it?

I don't think the wall is leaking. The problem is almost certainly caused by condensation due to the lack of a vapor barrier on the warm side of the insulation . . . or air leakage through whatever vapor barrier you do have. After the insulation is placed between the studs, the wall should be covered with an unbroken sheet of polyethylene film, lapped over the ceiling and the floor for a tight seal. The panelling is applied on top of this.

This will keep the warm, humid household air from reaching the cold wall and condensing there . . . which is the cause of your trouble. Reducing the humidity in your house will also help. (See CONDENSATION.)

VAPOR BARRIER ON BASEMENT WALL

We recently had our basement finished by a carpenter. He fastened black plastic film to the wall with 2 × 2 strapping, put fibreglass batts between the strapping, stapled clear plastic film to the wall, then applied ½" gypsumboard, which was taped, filled and painted. Now we've been told that it was wrong to use the plastic film against the concrete, that this will trap moisture inside the wall. Is this true?

Probably not. The only place this could happen is where the basement wall is above ground level. And if the inside plastic vapor barrier is effective, even that is unlikely. I wouldn't worry about it.

I think it was a mistake, however, to put up a wall that would only take 1½" batts. These have an insulation value of only R5. You would have been much better off with a 2 × 4 frame wall and 3½", R12 batts . . . more than twice the insulation value.

POLYETHYLENE VAPOR BARRIER

I have a roll of 6-mil plastic sheet to use as a moisture barrier over basement insulation, but my father-in-law says it will rot and the only thing to use is aluminum foil. Is this right?

Six-mil polyethylene sheet is as good a vapor barrier as you can get, and a lot better than aluminum foil, which comes in narrower widths and therefore has too many gaps where the sheets overlap. It also tears very easily.

And polyethylene doesn't rot . . . unfortunately; if it did there wouldn't be such a problem getting rid of the hundreds of tons of containers that are made out of it each year.

VAPOR BARRIER UNDER FLOOR

Our cottage has a linoleum floor on plywood above a crawlspace. I plan to fasten insulation batts across the joists from underneath, and then cover this with a sheet plastic vapor barrier. Do you have any other suggestions?

Yes, don't do it that way! A vapor barrier must always be on the *warm* side of the insulation . . . immediately under the floor, in this case. If you put the vapor barrier *under* the joists, you'll just trap the moisture inside the insulation where it will condense and promote rotting of the wood.

APPLYING FLOOR INSULATION

When applying insulation under the floor of our cottage from the crawlspace underneath, should the vapor barrier face of the batts be turned upwards or downwards?

The vapor barrier always goes on the warm side of the insulation, the top side, in this case.

END Vapor Barriers

VARNISHED VERANDAH

The pine floor of our large verandah was finished with urethane varnish a few years ago. Most of it still looks fine, but there are a few areas where the varnish is becoming discolored and is even peeling off. Is there any way I can patch the bad areas? Is there a better finish I should use?

There is no clear, varnish finish for wood that will stand up to more than a few years' outdoor exposure. When it begins to go, as yours is doing, the only solution is to sand the floor down to bare wood and then paint it. Patched areas are usually apparent, and often don't adhere properly around the edges.

EXHAUST FANS

You recently advised that kitchens and

Vents

bathrooms are the main source of humidity that causes condensation on windows and walls during cold weather. We have this problem and would like to install exhaust fans in our kitchen and bathroom to remedy it. What size of vent fans do we need to do the job properly? Our bathroom is small, but we have a fairly large (12' × 12') kitchen.

A kitchen fan should be powerful enough to change the air once every 4 minutes. A bathroom fan need only change the air every 8 minutes, Fans are rated according to the number of cubic feet of air they will move in one minute (CFM), so it's a fairly simple matter to calculate the size of fan you need.

Your kitchen contains about 1,150 cubic feet. Divided by 4, this gives you 288 cubic feet per minute. Allowing for some loss of power in the ductwork, you should probably buy an exhaust fan with a 300 CFM rating.

Your bathroom probably contains about 360 cubic feet, which means the fan should move about 45 cubic feet per minute. A 50 CFM fan would probably be about right.

A direct, through-the-wall exhaust fan is most efficient. If the ductwork is more than a few feet long and contains one or more right-angle bends, you will need a fan with a greater capacity.

VENT HOOD FOR GAS STOVE

I want to put a vent hood over our kitchen stove to remove cooking odors and grease, but was told that this can't be done with a gas stove because the suction will draw the flames. Is this true?

No. There's no reason whatever why you shouldn't use a vent hood over a gas stove. It's done all the time.

VENTING PROBLEM

When the vent hood over our kitchen stove was installed five years ago the electrician recommended venting it directly through the wall. During the winter, however, cold air would come in and we had to stuff it with insulation. Last fall we decided to vent it into the attic instead, but we are still getting cold air. What's wrong? Other houses don't seem to have this problem. Should we vent it up through the roof, instead of into the attic?

The range hood should not be vented into the attic because of the problem of condensation and grease build-up under the roof. I think the best place for the vent, is through the outside

wall, where it was. There should be a flap or damper on the outside of the vent duct to prevent air from blowing in. Perhaps the original flap didn't fit properly.

The fact that air is being sucked into your house through such openings suggests that it is too tightly sealed, and that not enough outside air is getting in to replace the air that is being drawn in your furnace and up the chimney. Opening a basement window a bit may overcome this problem.

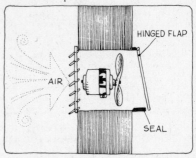

VERANDAH FLOOR

We have a wooden verandah at the back of our house, with no roof protection. We covered the floor with hardboard panels and saturate it every spring with linseed oil, but it is not in very good condition. Can we cover the wood floor with something permanent?

If you try to seal over the wood floor you will only encourage it to rot. Better to rebuild it with open gaps that the water can run through, such as 2 x 4s on the flat, about ¼" apart.

CRACKED VINYL UPHOLSTERY

We have a comfortable lounge chair several years old that is covered with vinyl upholstery. It's in good shape except that the vinyl has got hard in places and is beginning to crack. Is there something I should have been doing to prevent this, and is there anything I can do now to make the vinyl soft again?

The answer to both your questions is No, I'm afraid. The plasticisers used to make these vinyl materials soft and flexible evaporate in time, and there's no way to prevent this, or to reverse it. These materials are getting a lot better, however. The first vinyls used to dry out in a matter of months; the best ones today will stay flexible for many years. All you can do now is have the chair re-covered.

WALL ANCHORS

The walls in our apartment are plastered over a soft, crumbly concrete. We are allowed to hang things on the walls, but I can't find anything that will support any weight. Those plastic screw anchors won't hold in the crumbly wall. Is there any other way we can do it?

Get a package of epoxy putty, the kind that comes in two foil-wrapped sticks—you cut off equal pieces of both and mix them together just before using. Drill the hole in the wall a little larger than required for the plastic anchor. Blow out all the dust. Now put a small ball of the epoxy putty in the hole and push in the plastic anchor until it is flush with the wall. Some of the soft putty should squeeze out around the edge of the hole; scrape it off flush. If you leave this overnight you will find that the anchor is firm enough to hold just about anything.

WALLPAPER

WALLPAPER—BATHROOM

Is it wise to paper walls above the tile over the bathtub?

The best wallcovering to use in a bathroom is vinyl-coated fabric, but good quality, higher-priced vinyl-coated papers stand up reasonably well, too.

PAPERING A BATHROOM

We recently papered a plaster wall in our bathroom, and now the paper is peeling off and the plaster is moldy. The plaster has never been painted, and was given a coat of wall size before the paper went on. We would like to paper it again, but don't know how to treat the moldy wall or how to apply the paper to prevent this trouble from recurring.

The mold was probably caused by using a non-waterproof paper and an adhesive that did not contain a fungicide. The mold can be removed by washing the wall down (after the paper has been removed) with a strong solution of liquid chlorine laundry bleach; about one cup to a quart of water. When the wall is dry, apply a coat of enamel primer. Then apply a waterproof, vinyl-coated paper or fabric wallcovering with one of the special adhesives sold for use with these materials.

MOLD ON BATHROOM WALLPAPER

The top part of our bathroom walls is papered, and a black mold has been forming there. I clean it off and it keeps coming back. Is there any solution I can use to get rid of it?

No. You can kill it with a strong solution of chlorine laundry bleach, but it will keep coming back as long as the paper is kept moist by steam condensing on the cold walls. A bathroom vent fan is the best answer.

HAIR OIL STAIN ON WALLPAPER

Oily hair dressing made a spot on our wallpaper, which we covered with another layer of wallpaper. Now the oily patch is coming through again. What can I do about it?

Apply one of the spray-on, powder type spot removers, such as K2r.

REMOVING PAINTED WALLPAPER

We recently bought a house in which most of the rooms have been wallpapered (including the ceilings) and then painted over. Is there an easy way to remove this?

If you're lucky, it will be dry-strippable paper, which can just be peeled off, paint and all. Find a seam, then use a razor knife to cut through the paint and see if you can lift up the edge of the paper. Use a putty knife to loosen more of the paper, then just peel away.

But if you find that the wallpaper is firmly stuck to the wall, buy or rent a scraping tool from a wallpaper store. This scores the surface of the paper through the paint so that water can penetrate. You can buy chemicals that you mix with water to speed up the penetration. A wallpaper steamer (which you can also rent) will do a much better job. But no matter how you do it, this won't be an easy job.

REMOVING WALLPAPER

Some of our rooms have been papered over latex paint on gypsumboard drywall. Can we remove the wallpaper without damaging the cardboard face of the gypsumboard panels?

It depends on how the wall was treated and what kind of adhesive was used. Most wallpapers are now pre-pasted with a dry-strippable adhesive that just peels off when you want to remove the paper. But it doesn't work over latex paint; this must be covered with an alkyd or oil-base primer before the wallpaper is applied. If your walls weren't treated this way, you will have to soak the paper to remove it. You will also have to do this if the paper was applied with a regular wallpaper paste. If you use warm water and detergent, or one of the special wallpaper removing preparations, there is no reason why you should damage the gypsumboard, however. Use a broad-bladed scraper to start, then peel by hand.

REMOVING WALLPAPER FROM MIRROR

Six, mirrored, sliding glass doors in our house were covered with a self-adhesive, woodgrain wallpaper by a previous occupant. How can I take this off without damaging the mirrors?

This kind of adhesive dries very hard and isn't usually affected by wallpaper remover solutions. I think you'll have to scrape and peel it off. You can get a 3'' wallpaper scraper from a paint and wallpaper store, or use a razor-blade scraper, the kind used to remove paint off windows. These should not damage the glass face of the mirrors.

When the paper starts to peel off, you may find it helps to use an electric hair-dryer to soften the adhesive. With luck you may even be able to peel long strips off by hand.

WALLPAPER SEAMS

How can I keep wallpaper seams from showing through when I paint over them?

You can fill the seams with patching plaster, but they usually aren't very noticeable, anyway. However, there are other problems with painting over wallpaper that may give you more trouble. Paint sometimes loosens the adhesive behind the wallpaper, causing it to lift under the paint. Some dark colors may bleed through light-colored paints unless they are sealed with a coat of shellac first. And paint will not stick to certain metallic wallpapers. Better check before you proceed.

SHRINKING WALLPAPER

I papered our living room with quite expensive heavyweight paper. I followed the instructions carefully and tried very hard not to stretch the paper, but still the seams split open after the paper dried. What did I do wrong?

Heavy papers have a tendency to shrink more than normal weight ones, simply because they absorb more water. Even professional paperhangers run into this problem occasionally, but they know when to expect it and can generally counteract it by not letting the paper get too wet. Some papers are worse than others, however, and it would seem that you picked a bad one.

STRIPPABLE WALLPAPERS

I have moved into an apartment for the first time and would like to brighten some of the rooms with wallpaper. However, my lease stipulates that wallpaper will have to be removed and the walls returned to their present painted condition when I leave. What kind of paper can be taken off later without marking or damaging the paint? My landlord wants $50 to paint just one wall!

You could paint it for much less than that yourself, of course, but the answer to your question is that there is no such paper. There are a lot of "dry strippable" wallpapers on the market, but the term is somewhat misleading. Many people expect such papers to peel off completely, leaving the wall in its original condition—clean and unmarked. Unfortunately, this is not the case.

Walls painted with latex require the application of an oil-based primer-sealer before dry strippable papers are applied, and this will still be visible when the wallpaper is removed. Such a primer may not be required if the wall is painted with a high-quality, oil-based paint, but a residue of adhesive may still be left behind when the wallpaper is removed, and this will require vigorous scrubbing that is very likely to mar the finish.

Dry strippable papers work well if you plan to apply another wallpaper, but they don't restore the original paint finish.

(Just to add to the confusion, there are also "peelable" papers that separate into two layers when they are removed. The layer that stays on the wall provides an acceptable base for another paper, but it's not recommended for painting.)

MILDEW ON VINYL WALLPAPER

Several months ago I papered a small bathroom with a fabric-backed vinyl paper. It was applied over a gloss enamel paint with a pre-mixed wallpaper paste. Almost immediately mildew began to appear along the seams and in spots on the wall. I peeled the paper back in one place and found a heavy growth of mildew under the stain on the paper.

I went back to the store where I bought the paper and was told to remove the paper and wash the mildew spots with TSP, then use a wall sizing material and reapply the paper. Now the mildew is spreading as badly as before. The paper is expensive and I hate to waste it. Can you tell me what is wrong and what, if anything, I can do about it?

The problem is almost certainly caused by using incorrect adhesive. Ordinary wallpaper paste is not suitable; you need a special, mildew-proof adhesive made for use with these impervious, vinyl wallcoverings.

You will have to remove the material again and then scrub all the adhesive off the wall and the back of the vinyl. To kill any remaining mildew and get rid of the stains, use the following solution: ½ cup of trisodium phosphate (TSP) and 2 cups of liquid chlorine laundry bleach to 3 quarts of warm water. If the wall is still shiny, rub it down with medium grade sandpaper to remove the gloss and provide a "tooth" for the new adhesive. If you now reapply the wallcovering with an adhesive recommended for this material, you shouldn't have any more trouble with mildew. As an added protection, however, I suggest you put in a bathroom vent fan to reduce the humidity.

WALLPAPER PROBLEM

The previous owner of our house applied vinyl wallpaper directly to the drywall panelling without any preparation. We wanted to change the paper, but when we stripped it off, only the vinyl surface came away. The backing remained on the wall, and I don't know how to get it off. I'm afraid to use steam or water in case it damages the drywall. What should I do?

That's the way most vinyl papers are supposed to peel off. They strip away from a thin paper backing, which is normally left on the wall to be painted or papered over. If the wall has been properly sized or primed, the paper backing can be removed quite easily with a wet sponge, but in your case I would just leave it there and apply the new paper over it.

END Wallpaper

REMOVING WALL PLUGS

I attached some shelves to my plaster wall with those folding metal wall anchors, the kind you insert in a hole and then screw up until they tighten from the back. Now I've taken the shelves down and want to fill the holes, but the ends of the plugs themselves protrude slightly, and I don't know how to remove them.

You do it by straightening out the metal plug again. Unscrew the bolt part way and then tap it back again. Keep on doing this until the metal plug is straightened out behind the hole and can simply be pulled out.

COLD WATER WASHING

I have heard a lot about the use of cold water instead of hot water for doing the laundry. It is supposed to be better for the clothes and also save electricity. But does it really work?

Any soap or detergent works best in hot water, and cleaning ability decreases with the temperature. The key question is: How low can you go? According to a recent technical bulletin issued by the Maytag Company, laundry detergents are not effective at water temperatures below 16° Celsius (60° F.), and in many cities the domestic water supply is below this temperature throughout the entire year. Manufacturers of "cold water detergents" claim that their products will still work at this temperature, though not as efficiently as at higher temperatures, they admit.

So it would seem inadvisable to attempt to do your laundry with cold water right out of the tap. It does make sense, however, to reduce the temperature of the wash water for much of your laundry, using very hot water for heavily soiled items. In any case, warm water is best for bright colors and synthetic fibres.

The most logical way to save hot water is to use cold water for all your rinsing. It is just as effective as warm or hot water.

SLUDGE IN WASHING MACHINE

A grey sludge has collected under the revolving drum of our automatic machine, and it comes through the holes to leave grey spots on the laundry. I can't take the tub out to clean underneath it, what can I do?

This is a fairly common problem, and it's caused by not using enough detergent to break up the natural body oils in the laundry. Check this the next time you do a wash by stopping the washing cycle after two or three minutes and looking to see if there is a continuous blanket of fine-textured suds about 1½" thick on top of the water. If you can see patches of water, or the bubbles are large and break up as you watch them, then you're not using enough detergent. Add about a quarter of a cup and run the washing machine for another two or three minutes, then check again. Repeat until you have an unbroken blanket of fine foam on the surface. The total amount of detergent you have used is the correct amount for you to use regularly.

The sludge can be removed by emptying a one-pound box of washing soda into the detergent dispenser and then putting the washer through a complete cycle without any laundry in it.

WINTERIZING A WASHING MACHINE

We have an automatic washing machine at our summer home, which we will soon be closing up for the winter. How do I remove all the water from it to prevent frost damage?

Shut off the water supply, then disconnect and drain the inlet hoses. Set the timer to a fill cycle and operate the washer for a few seconds to clear the water valve. Empty the drain hose and remove the electrical plug from the wall outlet.

BLACK WATER

Ever since we had a new electric hot water tank put in some months ago the hot water has been coming out distinctly black, as if ink had been mixed with it. If allowed to stand, it leaves a black deposit on the bottom of the glass. The plumber says there's nothing wrong with the tank and suggests that the trouble is due to our old galvanized piping, but we never had this problem with our old tank. What is your advice?

Black water is caused by the action of certain bacteria that thrive in the warm, oxygen-free environment at the bottom of an electric hot water tank. These bacteria convert the sulphates found in some water supplies into finely powdered black sulphides of copper or iron. Sometimes the hot water will have a rotten egg odor, as well.

One remedy is to remove the magnesium anode that hangs inside the tank. This is put there to reduce corrosion, but it also removes oxygen from the water and that promotes the growth of the bacteria. Removing the anode may solve the problem, but it also voids the warranty on the tank. Some manufacturers will substitute an aluminum anode that doesn't seem to cause this problem.

Another remedy is to kill the bacteria by adding a 3% solution of hydrogen peroxide to the water in the tank—16 ounces for a 40-gallon tank, 24 ounces for a 60-gallon tank. This can be done by siphoning it through a hot water tap on the floor above the tank. The mixing faucet in the kitchen is most convenient.

Close the cold water supply valve on the tank. Put a bucket under the drain valve at the bottom of the tank and open it so that just a trickle of water comes out. Then go upstairs and place the spout of the kitchen faucet in a shallow pan filled with the peroxide solution. If you now open the hot water tap very slowly it will suck the solution out of the pan. Close the tap as soon as the pan is emptied, then fill it again with plain water and open the tap again to suck this into the tank.

Finally, close the kitchen tap and the drain valve on the tank and open the cold water supply valve. Don't draw any hot water from the tank for one hour to give the peroxide a chance to work. It's perfectly harmless and does not affect the taste or appearance of the water. As the tank is used the black sulphides will be removed and the water will become clear again.

CLOUDY WATER

When I run hot water in my sink it is very cloudy, as if there was something like chalk in it. Eventually it clears; I guess it settles to the bottom of the sink, although I can never find any powder there. About 6 months ago we were told that it was because our hot-water tank was corroded, so we had a new one put in, but it hasn't made any difference. The house is only 12 years old and all of the pipes are copper. I would like to know what is in the water and what we should do about it.

It sounds to me as if you just have microscopic air bubbles in the water. When water is heated, the air dissolved in it tries to escape, and it does this when the pressure is released at the tap. The resulting cloudiness looks like a white powder in the water, but it's just air. To prove this for yourself, just fill a glass with hot water from the sink tap. I think you'll see the cloudiness rise to the top and disappear. It is quite harmless, of course. Lowering the temperature of the water should help.

LIME DEPOSIT IN TOILET BOWL

We have hard water in our area. Would you please tell me how to remove the lime deposit

that has built up inside our toilet bowls. I have tried everything from vinegar to kettle scale remover, but the lime is still there.

Vinegar or any other mild acid will dissolve the lime if it's given enough time. You should be able to see the lime bubbling or foaming as it dissolves. Pour about a pint of vinegar or four ounces of muriatic acid (available at any hardware store) in the toilet bowl and leave it there until the deposit stops foaming.

VINEGAR

SWEATING WATER PIPES

What can be done to prevent the water pipes in our basement ceiling from sweating and dripping on the ceiling tiles?

Most hardware stores sell rolls of fibreglass or foam insulation about three inches wide backed with aluminum foil or vapor barrier paper, made for this purpose. It is simply wrapped around the cold water pipes and tied in place.

WATER TEMPERATURE

I have a 40-gallon electric hot water tank with two 3,000-watt heating elements, each with its own temperature control. Should these both be set at the same temperature, or one higher than the other? And what is the correct temperature?

Both elements should be set for the same temperature—between 140° and 150°, depending on personal preference.

WATERPROOFING SOLUTION

A while back I read of a silicone compound that you could paint on leaky basement walls to

waterproof them. The same material could also be used to waterproof a roof, but I believe you had to spray it with plastic foam first. I can't seem to find where to buy this material.

I think you've got your information a little mixed up. Silicones are only water *repellents*, and they're applied to the outside of brick and other masonry walls to help them shed rainwater. They are no use on the inside of a basement wall below ground level, and we've never heard of them being used on a shingle roof. There are tar-like compounds that can be used to patch up small holes in asphalt shingles, but more serious leaks require re-roofing.

USING AN OLD WATER SOFTENER

I have an automatic water softener that has been in storage for about five years. The mechanism seems to be in good working order but I am wondering if the resin granules in the tank will have deteriorated with age.

The resin granules shrink when they dry out, and some of them will crumble when they are wet again. Try regenerating them with a salt solution to see if there is much resin loss when you backwash. A moderate amount can be made up by adding more resin granules to the level indicated in the instruction manual. If there is much resin loss, however, it would be better to have the granules replaced entirely. Call the manufacturer's service representative for this.

SEDIMENT FROM WATER SOFTENER

I have a fully automatic water softener that's giving me trouble. As soon as the softening cycle is finished, a sediment of tiny red granules comes out of the cold water taps, and I have to keep running the water to flush this out. It also gets into the toilet flush tank. Can you tell me what's causing this?

The sediment sounds like resin beads from the water softener. There are three ways these could get into the water line. There could be too much resin in the tank. The inlet or outlet manifold of the softener tank could be cracked. Or the backwash pressure may be too strong. The company that supplied the equipment should be called to service it.

CLEANING WATER SOFTENER

Our water softener has worked very well for

many years, but it seems to be getting weaker, and must be regenerated more often. I suspect that the crystals need to be cleaned, and would like to know if I can do this myself.

The polystyrene resin beads play an active part in the ion exchange reaction that substitutes sodium (from the brine) for the calcium and magnesium in the hard water salts. Theoretically, this reversible process can go on indefinitely, but like the storage battery in your car, the materials deteriorate in time.

The resin bed in a water softener usually outlasts the tank, but sometimes it fails much sooner due to the buildup of iron and other impurities. When this happens there are three things you can do:

You can buy a chemical "reactivator" that removes iron and sulphur deposits. This is available from any water softener dealer; it's easy to use and the instructions are on the bottle.

You can have the tank cleaned and reactivated at the factory, using much stronger chemicals than the do-it-yourself preparation.

If the resin bed is in extremely bad condition, you may have to have it replaced entirely.

WATER IN SALT TANK

We have a 2-tank water softener, and the salt tank holds 200 pounds. How much water, if any, should be left in the salt tank after the regeneration cycle?

Anywhere from 6" to 12". This is controlled by a float that is set at the time the water softener is installed. The residual water provides a brine solution for the next regeneration cycle.

SWEATING WATER TANKS

I have a deep well pump, with a 30-gallon cold water tank and water softener tank. Both of them sweat a lot in the summer, and create puddles of water. I've tried wrapping them with 3" batts of fibreglass insulation, but it doesn't seem to do much good. What do you suggest?

Insulation is the answer, but you forgot to wrap the insulation with a polyethylene sheet vapor barrier. This is necessary to keep the moist warm air from passing through the insulation and reaching the cold walls of the tank. Make sure the vapor barrier is well sealed with tape, with no gaps through which the moist air can enter.

LOWER WATER TEMPERATURE TO SAVE ENERGY

I have a 40-gallon hot water tank, and recently reduced the water temperature from 150°F to 130°F to save electricity. Friends tell me that this won't work because I'll just use more hot water when I have a bath, for instance, since I won't be mixing it with as much cold water. I say that it costs less to keep water at 130° than at 150°, regardless of how much is used. Am I right?

You certainly are. The hotter the tank, the more heat it will give off. But the heat that escapes isn't necessarily lost. In the winter it helps to heat the house, although electric heat costs more than oil or gas. The heat is certainly wasted in the summer, however, and less will be wasted if the water is kept at a lower temperature. Another way to do this, of course, is to wrap the tank with additional insulation. If you do both, you'll really reduce your energy consumption. This isn't a frivolous idea, either; in the average home, hot water accounts for 20% of total annual energy consumption, including the winter fuel bill.

WEATHERSTRIPPING

We have added insulation in the attic for a total of R30, and have also insulated our basement walls. Do you think it would pay us to have all the doors and windows weatherstripped to prevent air leakage, too?

This depends on how much air leakage you have. The air in your house must be changed completely about once every two hours in order to remove household odors, supply fresh air for the furnace and the occupants, and, most important, to control humidity. If you don't have enough ventilation, the humidity will soon build up to the point where condensation begins to form on cold windows and walls.

If the air in your house is very dry, and you never get any condensation on the windows, then it might pay you to do some weatherstripping—a little at a time until you reach the point where the windows steam up occasionally. But if you are already at that stage, weatherstripping will only bring condensation problems.

WEATHERVANE AND LIGHTNING

I have put a wrought-iron weathervane on the roof of my bungalow. Will this attract lightning, and should it be grounded?

A weathervane doesn't attract lightning any more than any other part of the house that is at that height. If there are other objects nearby that are higher—telephone poles, chimneys, trees, or houses—they would be hit first. You really have no more chance of being hit *with* it, than *without* it. A grounded lightning rod is only useful if your house is in an open, exposed area, or on the top of a hill.

BEACH WEEDS

How can we safely kill the grass that grows in the sandy beach at our lakeside cottage?

Common salt is a safe and effective weed-killer. Sprinkle it on generously and then water it in. Stubborn weeds may require two or three applications, a few days apart, but no plant can survive the salt treatment.

WELL WATER CONTAMINATED?

I'm afraid that the water from our septic tank disposal field may be getting into our well water. I've heard there's a dye you can put into the toilet which will be quickly spotted in the well water. Can you tell me what this is?

There are several fluorescent dyes that show up clearly, even in concentrations as low as 25 parts per billion. They're available only in commercial quantities from dye houses and chemical supply companies, however. See your local health officer, he may be able to conduct the test for you.

OILY WATER

The water from our well is not polluted, but it contains an oily substance that floats on tea or coffee. How can we find out what this is?

Most likely this is oil from the pump, but it could also be a natural oil that is formed by decomposing vegetable matter in swampy areas. Write to your government water resources department and ask for a well-water sample bottle and test application form, both of which you fill and return to the laboratory.

OIL IN WELL WATER

We're having trouble with fuel oil contamination in our well water. Is there any kind of a filter that will remove this?

A combination charcoal and diatomaceous earth filter *sometimes* works, but not always, unfortunately. Manufacturers of water purification equipment (see the Yellow Pages) will be glad to test a sample of your well water and recommend a suitable filter.

SULPHATES IN WELL WATER

We dug a well and were lucky enough to find water quickly, but now we discover that it contains a lot of Glauber's salt. Is this harmful, and how can we get rid of it?

Glauber's salt (sodium sulphate) is a mild laxative, and is generally considered undesirable in drinking water. Sodium salts cannot be removed by the usual water-softening equipment, but they can be taken out by what is called "reverse osmosis," using a membrane that holds back some 90% of all dissolved salts. Small, home-sized units are available. Look in the Yellow Pages under "Water Purification Equipment".

SULPHUR WATER

The water from our well has a rotten egg smell. It also tastes funny. Is there any way we can reduce or eliminate this?

This is generally caused by bacteria that break down dissolved sulphates and protein matter and produce hydrogen sulphide, the rotten egg gas. Not only does this give a taste and smell of sulphur in the water, it also promotes corrosion of metal parts and turns silverware black.

The cure is to chlorinate the water to oxidize the hydrogen sulphide and release the sulphur, which is then trapped in a microfilter. A charcoal filter removes the chlorine, leaving pure, tasteless water.

A special filter system that will do all this automatically is available from companies that sell water softening units. The system will also remove dissolved iron.

WATERLOGGED WELL SYSTEM

Our country home has its own well and pump system. We are having trouble with the tank becoming waterlogged, causing the pump motor to work too much and become overheated. We were told that our automatic washer was the cause.

An automatic washer wouldn't cause this trouble. It sounds as if something is wrong with the air control on the water tank. The latest device to prevent this trouble is a simple plastic "air separator" that costs about $10. This is installed inside the tank and replaces the outside air control.

CLEANING WICKER

I recently purchased a small, ornate wicker chair. It's not very dirty but I would still like to clean it up a bit. Will water make the wicker brittle? Would you suggest a finish of some kind?

It does no harm to wet wicker furniture—in fact some authorities say that it should be soaked once a year to *prevent* it from getting brittle. Wicker can be cleaned by scrubbing it with a soapy ammonia solution.

A finish isn't necessary, but it will be somewhat easier to clean next time if you brush the wicker with shellac or a penetrating oil-resin finish such as Danish oil and let it dry thoroughly before using it. Or you could use a satin urethane varnish. Any of these will darken the color slightly, however.

WINDOWS

BIRDS vs WINDOWS

Birds keep hitting the glass of our large living room window. What can we do to prevent this?

Unless you want to keep the drapes drawn, the best thing to do is hang a few brightly colored, weighted ribbons down from the eaves in front of the window.

CLEANING WINDOWS

When I clean the outside of my windows I can't seem to remove a pattern of dots on the glass behind the screens. This is mostly on the lower half of the windows. None of the cleaners I have tried do any good. Do you know of a solution I can use?

The spots consist of aluminum salts produced on the screen by air pollution, then deposited on the glass by rain. They can be removed with any of the aluminum cleaners sold at hardware stores for use on garden furniture, door frames and similar items.

CONDENSATION ON STORM WINDOWS

We went to a lot of expense to have aluminum storm windows installed on our house, in order to eliminate condensation problems. Now we are having trouble with condensation on the *storm* windows. Is there anything more we can do about this?

Condensation forms on the inside of the outer window when warm, moist air from the house leaks into the space between the two windows. There are two things you can do. First, seal all the cracks around the inside window with some form of weatherstripping . . . felt, tape, putty, sponge strips . . . to keep the household air from reaching the outer window.

If this doesn't stop the condensation, the next thing to do is ventilate the space between the two windows. Ideally, a storm window should fit loose enough to allow some ventilation behind it. If it fits too tight, try putting some small wedges in the top and bottom corners to let the air get in. You can also drill holes in the top and bottom of the frame to provide ventilation for the storm window.

FROST ON WINDOW FRAME

We had an expensive new aluminum window frame installed in our living room, 12 feet wide and 6 feet high, with 4 sealed double-glazed, insulated glass panels. During the cold weather frost forms on the inside of the metal frame up to a quarter of an inch thick, and when this melts we end up with a mess on the floor. We even had a new forced air furnace installed to overcome the problem, but it hasn't helped. The firm that installed the window say it doesn't know what's wrong. Can you help us?

I know what's wrong, and so does the firm that put in the window! This common problem is caused because we use uninsulated metal window frames in houses. Commercial buildings use more expensive insulated window frames, with a thermal break between the outside and the inside of the metal frame.

It makes little sense to put storm windows or expensive insulated glass in a solid metal frame like this. I know of no way to insulate the metal frame and prevent it from frosting up. The only other thing you can do is lower the humidity in the house to the point where there is no condensation on the cold frame, and that's going to mean very dry air.

Increasing the ventilation to bring in more dry, outside air is the best way to do this.

WINDOW CLEANER

Can you give me the name of the chemical to use to make my own window cleaner?

There are a number of inexpensive chemicals you can use. Two or three ounces of vinegar in a quart of water works very well. So does liquid household ammonia—or methyl hydrate (any paint or hardware store). Add a few drops of detergent to any of these solutions and you have a cheap and very effective window cleaner. And old newspapers make the best wiping cloths.

DOUBLE WINDOW

I have a window in the kitchen that has two panes of glass separated by a ¾" strip of wood. The outside pane is puttied, but the inside pane is just held in place with wood molding. During the winter this window was nearly always steamed up between the two panes of glass. Can you tell me how to overcome this problem?

This window is the wrong way around. The *inside* pane should be sealed to prevent humid household air from reaching the cold outside pane. And the outside pane should be loose, so a little air can circulate behind it. Remove both panes, clean them, then replace as I have suggested; putty the inside pane and use the wood molding to hold the outside pane in place.

HEAT LOSS THROUGH WINDOWS

Our electrically-heated home has two 24' window walls, one facing north, the other south. They both have sealed, double-glazed panes with a ½" air space, but I think there's still a lot of heat loss through them. We have considered bricking up part of the windows, but hate to lose the view. Adding a third window-pane seems another possibility, and we have thought of using insulated shutters during the winter months. We would very much appreciate your suggestions.

Recent studies by the National Research Council have shown that double-glazed windows facing south actually provide a net heat *gain* during the winter, rather than the heat loss that had been expected. This is due, of course, to the solar heat that is brought in. The addition of a third pane will save even more heat, so add it if you can, either inside or outside. The use of heavy drapes at night will also help.

The large north window, however, represents a major heat loss even if you add a third pane. If it's possible, I would recommend covering all or most of this window during the winter with plywood panels backed with 2 inches of foamboard.

WINDOWS NEED PUTTY JOB

We had our house painted a few years ago by a man who did a good job except that he just painted over the crumbling putty around the windows. Now all our windows need redoing and I would like to have this done before we have the house painted again. Should we get a glass company to do this job?

That should really be done by the painter as part of the preparation work, like scraping off loose paint and filling cracks in the wood. Never agree to a painting job without a signed statement of exactly what is to be done, and in your case this should include renewing the glazing compound in the windows. This is a tedious job, however, and a lot of painters don't like to do it. If yours is one of them, I suggest you find another painter. But be prepared to pay for the extra time this work will involve.

WINDOW PUTTY

The big window at the front of our house is in bad condition. The paint is peeling and the putty around the glass is cracked and is falling out. What is the best way to repair this?

First remove the old paint with an electric or infrared propane paint stripper. This can also be used to soften the putty so that it can be scraped out easily with a putty knife. Replace the putty with glazing compound. Old-fashioned linseed oil putty is rarely used for this purpose today because it dries out and crumbles in a few years. Special glazing compounds, available at all hardware and building supply stores, are easier to work with and remain flexible for many years. Use a putty knife to spread it on the window frame, then draw the knife along at a 45° angle to press the compound into the groove and remove any surplus. The window can be painted after 24 hours, or when the glazing compound is dry to the touch.

REFLECTIVE FILM ON WINDOWS

I was thinking of applying reflective film to

the inside of the windows on the south side of our house to reduce the solar heat that comes in during the summer. But the area we live in is very cold in winter, and I wonder if this wouldn't keep out solar heat then, too.

It will indeed. Although it might also reflect some of the room heat back into the house, you will still lose much of the benefit of solar heat during the winter.

There's another problem, too. In your area you may be using sealed, double-glazed insulating windows. If you apply reflective film to these the buildup of heat inside them can break the seal or crack the glass. The use of such film on thermal glazing voids the warranty, in any case.

SLIDING WINDOWS

We have double pane sliding glass windows in our house, and they sweat continually inside the outer panes when the weather gets cold. They have a clamping mechanism that is supposed to hold the sliding panes together, and I have tried adding weatherstripping tape, but they still sweat. I'd like to be able to see outside during cold weather.

This has always been the weakness of the sashless sliding window. Various sealing and clamping systems have been devised, but manufacturers admit that they still haven't found the answer. All you can do is reduce the humidity in the house by increasing the ventilation.

REPAIRING LEADED GLASS WINDOWS

I have two leaded glass windows with diamond-shaped panes in my living room. Over the years the putty that holds the glass in the metal channels has crumbled away or been washed out, and now the windows leak. How can I fix them?

Repairing leaded glass, like making it, is a slow and tedious job, which is why you don't see much of it done any more. Use a dull knife to open the lead channel slightly and scrape out the loose putty. Then fill the space with any soft glazing compound, working it in with a thin piece of wood, a popsicle stick, or even your fingers. Tubes of glazing compound are available at any hardware store, or you can use ordinary linseed oil putty thinned with a few drops of turpentine.

The lead should then be tapped down gently against the glass with a block of wood. Have someone hold another block of wood against the other side of the glass. Wipe off any surplus glazing compound.

STICKING WINDOW LATCHES

The latches on my windows are not functioning properly due to careless painting. How can I remedy this?

You can overcome this problem quite easily by removing the latches and dropping them into a jar of paint remover for approximately an hour. Clean them off with steel wool or an old toothbrush. To ensure they will work easily in the future, apply a few drops of lubricant, and wipe away the excess. You will find that they will work like new—until the next careless paint job.

STUCK WINDOWS

We have taken over a bungalow that was neglected for about two years, and one of the problems is that the double-hung, wood frame windows are all stuck. I can't even pry them up with a chisel. What can I do?

If the window sash (the part that slides up and down) and the frame have been painted together, you can free them by running a sharp knife along the joint. Inserting a broad chisel between the sash and the inside stop at several points, then rocking it gently, often helps to break the paint bond and loosen a window.

Sometimes the trouble is caused because the frame has shrunk and jammed the sides of the sash. One remedy is to take a block of wood slightly thinner than the groove the window slides in, put it in the groove above the window, and tap it gently with a hammer. This may move the frame enough to let the window slide freely.

If these tricks fail, your best bet is to use a broad chisel to remove the inside wood stop strip from one side of the frame. This will allow you to remove the sash from the frame. Disconnect the sash cord and plane the window sash enough to give it a smooth fit. A little candle wax rubbed on the side of the sash makes a good lubricant.

THERMAL WINDOWS

We have three insulating glass windows side-by-side in the living room. Condensation forms inside one of them. Is there any way this can be repaired?

No. Insulating windows made of two sealed panes cannot be repaired once the seal is broken. They must be replaced with new units. These are usually guaranteed for 10 years, however. If they haven't been in that long, and you know who supplied them, you may be able to get a warranty replacement.

DRIPPING WINDOWSILL

The rain drips off our windowsills and runs down the stucco wall of our house, staining it and causing cracks. How can we stop this?

The windowsill is supposed to slope down at the outside to prevent the rain-water from running back and down the wall. Also, there's usually a sawcut along the underside of the sill, forming a drip trap. Perhaps yours needs to be cleaned out.

If this doesn't work, attach a strip of ¾" cove molding, or a similar piece of wood, underneath the front edge of the windowsill to form a drip edge that will keep the water runoff away from the wall.

You can patch the stucco with any of the latex-cement concrete patching materials. And you can cover the stains by painting the stucco with any exterior latex paint.

WINDOW WELL DRAINAGE

Water builds up in the concrete window wells around our basement windows, and leaks in at the bottom of the frame. There is gravel about 8" below the sill, but underneath this is just earth. Should I dig this out and put in gravel?

That would certainly help, but I think you should also put in drainage tile from the bottom of the well down to the tile system at the base of your foundation wall.

TEST FOR ALUMINUM WIRING

I have aluminum wiring in my house and am worried about the possibility of the duplex outlets and switches overheating. Should I remove them from the outlet boxes periodically and tighten the terminal screws? Is there any way I can tell if they are overheating?

Removing and replacing the outlets or switches could be hazardous if you're not very careful, and would also subject the aluminum wires to stresses that could damage them. It's better to leave them alone and be on the alert for signs of overheating. One simple test is to attach a small piece of plastic label tape—the kind you use in Dymo and similar lettering devices—to the face plate near one of the screws. The tape should bear the word "SAFE" or the letter "S". If the electrical outlet overheats, the lettering will disappear. Call your electrical inspection authority immediately, and don't use the offending outlet or switch until it has been checked.

DOING YOUR OWN WIRING

I am building some rooms in my basement, and want to do as much of the work as I can myself to save money. A friend tells me that I am not allowed to do my own wiring, however. Is this true?

No. You are allowed to do any work you want to on your own house, but you will, of course, have to take out the necessary permits and pass the required inspections. Electrical inspectors are quite rightly concerned about home handyman wiring done without permits or inspections, and often without any knowledge at all of even the most elementary rules of electrical safety. Your local inspector will welcome your interest in doing the job properly and will be glad to answer your questions.

DUPLEX OUTLET BLOWS FUSE

One of the duplex outlets in our kitchen was arcing when we pulled out the electric kettle cord, so I bought a new outlet and wired it in exactly as the old one was. When I turned the power back on it blew a fuse immediately. It blew a second fuse, too, so I replaced the old outlet and it works the way it did before. What did I do wrong?

Homes that have been built in the last 20 years generally have one or more duplex outlets in the kitchen that are each wired to two separate circuits, allowing you to plug in two high wattage appliances, such as a toaster and a kettle, at the same time without blowing a fuse. These are easy to identify because they have a white wire on one side and a black and a red wire on the other.

To separate the two circuits in the receptacle it's necessary to remove the break-off strip between the two brass terminal screws where the black and red wires are connected. This can be done very easily with pliers or a screwdriver.

The arcing may not mean that there's anything wrong with the present receptacle, however. An electric kettle takes a lot of current—as much as 1200 watts, or 10 amps—and this will normally produce a spark when the plug is withdrawn. But if the arcing seems excessive, the spring contacts in the receptacle may be loose and it would indeed be a good idea to replace it, after removing the break-off strip as described above.

EXTENSION CORDS

I used an extension cord to connect my window air conditioner to the wall outlet, and when I touched it the other day I found that it was hot. Is there something wrong with my air conditioner?

No, but you are using the wrong kind of extension cord, a mistake that can be dangerous. Most people are unaware of the fact that extension cords come in different gauges to handle different electrical loads. Lightweight cords suitable for lamps, radios and other low-wattage appliances cannot carry the amount of current used by an air conditioner without becoming dangerously hot.

An extension cord for an air conditioner must have a current capacity of at least 13 amps. This is marked on a paper tab or a plastic disc, but neither of these is likely to survive very long in normal household use. An air conditioner should also be grounded to prevent the possibility of shock, so you will need a 3-wire extension cord with a 3-prong, grounded plug and socket.

FUSE KEEPS BLOWING

A fuse blew when we used the toaster in our dining room the other day, and it keeps blowing every time we replace it. What could be wrong?

Most likely there's a short circuit in the toaster itself. Replace the toaster with a portable lamp and then see if a new fuse restores power to the circuit. If it does, look for a short circuit in the toaster or take it to a service depot.

If the fuse still blows, the short circuit must be in your house wiring. Call an electrician.

GROUNDING ELECTRICAL OUTLETS

Our house isn't exactly old, but it was built before all the electrical outlets were required to be grounded for safety. Only one outlet in the kitchen and one in the laundry room are grounded. We have an electric lawnmower and a lot of workshop power tools and other appliances with 3-prong plugs, and we've been using special adapters to plug them into the existing outlets. Is it possible for me to ground some of these outlets myself, or would we have to have the whole house re-wired?

That's a very sensible suggestion. It's probably impractical to ground every outlet unless you had the house re-wired, but it isn't too difficult to ground the outlets where hand-held power tools are commonly used...basement, garage, outdoors.

First turn off the power to the outlet either by opening the main switch at the service panel or by disconnecting the fuse or circuit breaker that serves that particular outlet. Remove the face plate and the outlet, unscrew the wires and connect them to a new, 3-prong, grounded duplex outlet (the only kind you can buy today, as a matter of fact).

You'll notice a green screw connection on the end of the duplex outlet; this is for the ground wire. Fasten one end of a length of #14 copper wire to this and the other end to the nearest water pipe. The wire doesn't have to be insulated, but that's probably the only way you can buy it at the hardware store. You can also buy copper strap connections for the pipe.

If the wall is not finished and the outlet box is exposed, you can run the wire out to the water pipe through one of the holes in the side of the box. If the wall is finished, you may be able to fish the wire down through the wall to the nearest water pipe, but you can run it outside the wall if you have to, because it's not carrying any current and can't give you a shock.

60-AMP vs 100-AMP WIRING SERVICE

I hear a lot of talk these days about the need for a 100-amp wiring service in a home, instead of the once common 60-amp service. Is this really necessary? I know of many homes with 60-amp service that seem to have all the large appliances anyone would need. Or are these large appliances, such as a clothes dryer, on an additional circuit? How can one tell the amperage of the service from examing the main panel?

If you were building a new house, for the small additional cost it would certainly pay you to have 100-amp electric service. There is less chance of overloading the main fuses, and enough spare capacity to accommodate unforeseen appliances or additional circuits. On the other hand, 60-amp service is quite capable of handling an electric stove, dryer, and washing machine and still have enough capacity for 12 additional lighting and outlet circuits. Trouble will only come if too many of these are in use at the same time. In my house, for instance, the main, 60-amp fuse was blowing or overheating when both the clothes dryer and the oven were on at the same time, so we had 100-amp service put in and have had no trouble since. You can tell the amperage of your service by looking at the large fuses in the main switch panel. These will be marked 60-amp or 100-amp.

UNGROUNDED WIRING

Our new dishwasher has a 3-pronged, grounded plug that won't fit in the 2-pronged wall outlets we have in our kitchen—and in the rest of the house, which was built about 30 years ago. When I went to replace an outlet with one that takes the 3-pronged plug I discovered that there are only two wires to connect; there is no bare ground wire in the outlet box. Does that mean that our house wiring is not safe? Is there any way we can provide grounding for the dishwasher, at least?

If you don't have 3-hole receptacles (or "outlets") in your house, then you don't have grounded wiring. Grounded wiring is safer and has been required for many years in new home construction. But probably more than half the houses in the country don't have it, and there are no regulations requiring it in older homes— unless they are being rewired for other reasons, such as major remodelling.

The proper way to provide a grounded receptacle for the dishwasher is to have the circuit rewired back to the main service panel. You can ground the one new receptacle, however, by running a length of #14 copper wire from the green terminal on the bottom of the receptacle to a metal grounding strap fastened to one of the water pipes under the kitchen sink. Before touching the wiring be sure to turn off the power to the outlet by removing the fuse that controls this circuit.

EXTERIOR WOOD STAIN

Can you give me a formula for making my own exterior wood stain?

Exterior wood stains consist essentially of linseed oil, thinner, and pigments. Water repellent and wood preservative are sometimes added.

You can make a good stain with: 1 gallon of boiled linseed oil, 2 quarts of petroleum solvent (mineral spirits) and ½ pint of pigment-in-oil. Half burnt sienna and half raw umber gives a good cedar color.

For a better stain, substitute 1 quart of 5% pentachlorophenol wood preservative for one of the quarts of petroleum solvent, and also add 6 ounces of paraffin wax. The latter should be melted and mixed with the penta preservative and the petroleum solvent before adding the linseed oil and the pigment. This makes about 1½ gallons of stain.

WOOD STOVES

BASEMENT FIREPLACE

We would like to install a Franklin fireplace in our basement family room, but don't have a spare chimney to connect it to. Is there any way we can use a metal chimney without having to go up through the floor to the roof?

Such installations are commonly made by knocking a hole through the top of the concrete wall, then running insulated metal flue pipe out through the wall and up the outside of the house. Check to see if this is permissable in your area.

BURNING COAL IN A STOVE

I have an airtight, cast iron wood stove. Is it safe to burn coal in it?

Few wood stoves are designed for use with coal, which burns at a much higher temperature than wood. To burn coal safely, a stove requires a firebrick lining or special, double-walled, heat-resistant construction. A grate is also necessary.

The best advice is to check the manufacturer's literature. If this doesn't say specifically that the stove is designed to be used with coal, don't try it. It could be dangerous.

CONNECTING STOVE TO FIREPLACE CHIMNEY

We have a fireplace in our living room. The family room is right beside it but a few steps lower, and we would like to install a wood stove there. Can we connect the stovepipe to

the fireplace chimney? The stove can be shut off with a damper.

No. It is against building regulations to connect any other fuel-burning unit to a fireplace chimney.

FIREWALL FOR WOOD STOVE

I'm planning to put a wood stove in my cottage. In order to conserve space I want to place it no more than 4" from the gypsumboard wall. Will this be safe enough if I cover the wall with ceramic tiles?

No. Ceramic tiles are not flammable, certainly, but like brick, asbestos-cement board and sheet metal, they conduct heat well enough to burn combustible materials behind them. The firewall material must be held at least 1" away from the wall on metal spacers, and left open at the top and bottom for the free circulation of air behind the fireshield. Sheet metal will do, but asbestos-cement board makes a good base for ceramic tiles.

Even with this construction, however, the stove should be no closer than 12" to the wall.

LENGTH OF STOVEPIPE

I am installing a wood stove in my house and would like to know if there is any limit to the length of the stovepipe. I figure the longer this is the more heat will be radiated into the room.

That was true before the days of airtight wood stoves. Now we know the pipe should be as short as possible to reduce creosote buildup, caused mainly by low flue temperatures.

A long stovepipe can also be a fire hazard. It should be supported at every joint, have a slope of at least ¼" to the foot, and be not closer than 18" to any combustible material, including the wall and ceiling. But even then, if creosote deposits build up inside the pipe and catch fire, it would quickly become hot enough to set the ceiling on fire.

All things considered, I don't think this is a very good way to conserve heat. It would be better to locate the stove close to the chimney and control the draft for the most efficient use of your fuel.

WOOD STOVE SMOKING

We have used a Franklin wood stove in our living room for several years. The stove was about 2' from the wall, and last year we had the

wall faced with brick and moved the stove about 12" closer. That was the only change, but now the stove doesn't draw properly and smokes a lot until it gets going. We can't understand what's causing it. Can you help?

It sounds as if the pipe was pushed too far into the chimney when the stove was moved back. This would reduce the draft considerably, of course. The stove pipe should project into the chimney beyond the bricks and just slightly into the flue—but no further.

I must point out, however, that a layer of brick does not do much to protect combustible materials behind it, because it conducts heat very well. The stove should still be 36" away from the wall.

WOOL SHRINKAGE

I have a hand-knitted baby shawl that was accidentally put through the automatic washer with very hot water. It shrank badly, and I'd like to know if there's any way I can get it back in shape.

The Wool Bureau says there's nothing you can do to un-shrink wool if it has become severely felted and matted. If there's only a slight amount of shrinkage, however, the Bureau suggests you soak the shawl in a lukewarm solution (100°F) of fairly strong salt water to loosen the fibres. Rinse it out, roll it in a towel to remove excess water, then stretch it out to dry.

Another trick that sometimes works is to put the garment in a tepid solution of fabric softener, about three times normal strength. Let it soak for a few minutes, and then work it gently with your hands to loosen the fibres and stretch the garment back to size.

Shrinkage is influenced by agitation, as well as by temperature. Use only lukewarm water, and keep the movement or manipulation of wool to a minimum during washing to reduce shrinkage.

HANGING A ZEBRA SKIN

We purchased a large zebra skin in Spain this year, and now I can't figure out how to hang it on the plaster wall in our living room.

I finally found an expert on this subject, a man who imports zebra skins. It turns out that the answer is ridiculously simple. Use a staple gun. This makes pinholes in the plaster, but they are easily filled.

Index

Index

Index

Index

Index

Index